STRATEGIC MARKETING FOR SUCCESS IN RETAILING

STRATEGIC MARKETING FOR SUCCESS IN RETAILING

A. Coskun Samli

QUORUM BOOKS
Westport, Connecticut • London

Library of Congress Cataloging-in-Publication Data

Samli, A. Coskun.
    Strategic marketing for success in retailing / A. Coskun Samli.
        p.   cm.
    Includes bibliographical references and index.
    ISBN 1–56720–186–5 (alk. paper)
    1. Marketing—United States.   2. Retail trade—United States.
    I. Title.
    HF5415.1.S24   1998
    658.8'7'00973—dc21   98–10661

British Library Cataloguing in Publication Data is available.

Library of Congress Catalog Card Number: 98–10661
ISBN: 1–56720–186–5

First published in 1998

Quorum Books, 88 Post Road West, Westport, CT 06881
An imprint of Greenwood Publishing Group, Inc.

Printed in the United States of America

(∞)™

The paper used in this book complies with the
Permanent Paper Standard issued by the National
Information Standards Organization (Z39.48–1984).

10   9   8   7   6   5   4   3   2   1

This book is dedicated, first and foremost, to Stanley C. Hollander for giving me my start, and to hundreds of retailers who worked with me and taught me most of what I know about retailing. I hope this is a good payback.

Contents

Exhibits

Preface

This book is for those retailers (or retailers to be) who can analyze and logically explain the factors in the market as they influence the store. Thus, it is not a cookbook. It does not provide just simplistic recipes. Rather, it emphasizes proactive retail marketing strategies for success. This is based on knowledge, reasoning, and the joining of theory and practice.

There are almost three million retailers in the United States employing more than 20 percent of all working Americans. There are almost eleven retail stores per thousand of population. Each of these, on the average, sells over $733 thousand per year. All together, American retailing has a sales volume of $2 trillion. Thus, retailing is a very important aspect of the total business world. As consumers, we collect the fruits of economic advancement and industrial progress at the retail level by being able to buy more, better, and highly sophisticated products. Even though it may not be commonly realized, much of the manufacturer's marketing efforts either pay off or are wasted at the retail level. Thus, retailing is the firing line for most marketing plans and managerial decisions.

Despite its important role in society and in the distribution system, retailing has been somewhat neglected in the marketing-related literature. If, for instance, one considers the elaborate models, research, and body of sophisticated knowledge accumulated in such areas as consumer behavior or marketing research, it becomes clear that retailing has been lagging behind. It simply does not have the theoretical and research bases that are necessary for any mature discipline of study and knowledge. Furthermore, retailing is not placed carefully in the business administration curricula. Despite the fact that a large proportion of business administration graduates work in the retailing sector, they are not prepared for these jobs because they have not even taken a course in retailing. The mainstream business curricula usually share a course with colleges of home economics (or colleges of human resource development). In essence, both marketing students and home economics students have access to a retailing course. Though this practice is not necessarily bad, retailing should be more carefully interwoven with standard marketing curriculum, just as are consumer behavior and marketing research courses. What colleges of home economics perform is very laudable, but colleges of business must do more in this area.

Though the research methodology is not absent and, in fact, good research information is available in nonretailing literature on many aspects of retailing, previous retailing books have failed to assimilate such information. Thus, most retailing books have not focused on this wealth of knowledge. At least part of the reason is that almost all retailing courses are taught at junior colleges and/or undergraduate levels. At these academic levels, the emphasis is on "how-to" approaches. Much sophisticated research, therefore, has been unnoticed, if not completely ignored.

It is necessary to take the position that practice is strengthened if the theory behind it is understood. It is indeed necessary to bring the theory and practice together if we are to expect better results from the retailing sector in our society or, indeed, anywhere in the world. This is the overall goal of this book. It makes a very deliberate effort to combine retailing theory and practice. Since the theory is based on continuing research, a special effort is made here to cite some of the early retailing classics as well as other key research works so that the readers will appreciate just how we got here. This author firmly believes that if we do not know where we are and how we got here, we cannot go anywhere. Under such circumstances, there cannot be any progress.

One additional point of emphasis here is small- and medium-size retail establishments. Most retailing books emphasize large national retail establishments and retail chains. This book, without necessarily ignoring large-scale retailing, emphasizes small and medium-size retailers and their retail marketing strategies. This author believes that the future is in small-scale retailing establishments. If managed properly, they are flexible, close to consumers, and more adaptable to environmental changes and consumer behavior patterns.

This book is far from being a retailing cookbook. It makes a very concerted effort to combine theory and practice in such a way that the individual retailing decision maker can think for himself or herself and can make strategic decisions that are mutually beneficial to the store and the consumer.

THE EXPECTED RETAIL REVOLUTION

It is assumed that in the near future retailing will take its rightful place in the academic arena. There will be more retailing courses at the graduate level as well as greater use of research findings and theory at the undergraduate level. Many retailers will hire young people with master's degrees in business, and many consulting firms will find themselves more involved in retailing research. But, above all, there will be more small retail establishments owned and operated by educated people who have a vast understanding of the theory and how to apply it to their own practice. This is so because owner-operated retailing is one of the last bastions of opportunity for independence and riches. As the society becomes more sophisticated and complex, these opportunities disappear.

Though this book is aimed at graduate-level courses in retailing as well as some of the more advanced graduate courses in marketing and some key undergraduate courses, it will appeal primarily to the young and ambitious retail decision makers who would like to do just a bit better than their competitors. They understand the importance of research-based decision making. They realize the value of strategic decisions and strategy development as opposed to making only simple routine decisions to take care of daily operations. This book will also appeal to professional researchers and consultants, not because it is primarily a research-oriented book, but because it raises many research-related issues that are pertinent to a proactive decision-making orientation in retailing.

By combining research findings and retail marketing strategy implementation, we not only can bring theory and practice together, we can also achieve an important balance. This balance will address the often neglected finer points of marketing strategy development for retailers. In this sense, this book makes a real contribution. It raises many issues that will need further research. Hence, those who are pursuing research in the retailing area as well as those who are managing retail establishments will find this book quite useful.

Most books on retailing have approached the subject matter as a craft, using a "how-to-do-it" method that has led them away from creative thinking and effective planning in the marketing strategy area. Similarly, the existing approach has directed retail decision makers in the direction of very heavy emphasis on accounting, retail financing, and retail operations of retailing giants. In essence, the direction has not been one of proactive decision-making behavior. However, as retail competition gets keener, as the retailing environment becomes more and more adverse, and as there are more small retailers in the marketplace, success in retailing will be equated with the ability to develop effective retail marketing strategy rather than simply day-to-day housekeeping operations. In other words, in the near future those retailers who do not have a game plan and are not proactive are likely to fail.

In developing a retail marketing strategy, this book proposes the concept of *differential congruence* as the basic philosophy of success as well as the keystone for retail marketing strategy development. This concept is applicable to large retailing giants as well as to small retailing establishments. The concept, in essence, advocates the retail store to be just different enough to delight its customers and hence develop a mutually satisfactory bonding. Throughout this book, examples relating to differential congruence for small retailers are presented. Small-retailer orientation is another feature of this book that is rather neglected in many other retailing books. It must be emphasized at the outset that good understanding and implementation of retail marketing strategies are important to all retailers and not just to retailing giants. In fact, in order to cope with the giants and take advantage of the existing market opportunities, small retailers need to develop effective marketing strategies.

This book is based on the conceptual framework of developing an effective retail marketing strategy. This framework is composed of three key components: planning the strategy, implementing the strategy, and evaluating the performance (Exhibit P.1). However, without a theoretical construct and reasonable understanding of the current position of the store in the marketplace, the strategy cannot be planned or implemented effectively. As seen in Exhibit P.1, retailing research is a necessary component of this paradigm.

Whereas standard books on retailing usually contain a separate chapter on retailing research, retailing research topics and concepts are spread throughout this book. Thus, important research topics supporting the theory and facilitating strategic decision making are related to important topical areas in separate chapters.

One of the important features of this book is that every chapter represents a bird's eye view of international retailing. It presents a contrast between the American scene and some of the key retailing patterns around the world. Contrasting the American experience with a world view can provide the reader with a better understanding of what is happening in the wonderful world of retailing.

The book comprises seventeen chapters. The introductory chapter presents an overview of retail marketing strategy development, and the first few chapters explore the externalities of retail marketing strategy development, namely, a theory of retail competition (Chapter 2) and major trends in retailing (Chapters 3 and 4). Chapter 5 delves into a more specific topical area: the downtown versus shopping center conflict as it relates to individual retailers. In recent years, there have emerged certain other viable alternatives. These also are discussed here.

Chapters 6, 7, and 8 bring external factors closer to the individual retail store. Whereas Chapter 6 explores market potentials and feasibility, Chapter 7 examines specific aspects of consumer behavior pertaining particularly to retail purchase behavior. Chapter 8 expands on the foundation established in Chapters 6 and 7, and it explores segmentation not only as a strategic alternative but as a fact of life in modern-day retailing. Without segmentation, there could not be differential congruence and a corresponding competitive edge. But in recent years, marketing literature has gone beyond this. "Niching" is more specified segmentation that is also discussed.

Alternative retail marketing strategies are discussed in Chapter 9. Since effective retail management involves the development and manipulation of a store image, Chapter 10 provides a paradigm for managing the retail-store image. Perhaps most important aspect of retail marketing is simply constructing and maintaining the desired image.

The market's perception of the retail-store image often differs from the one that is perceived by the management itself. Chapter 11 explores this dichotomy as a diagnostic tool. Store image is perceived differently by different constituencies, such as customers of the store and the store's own management. This difference can be used quite effectively to direct management to strengthen its strategic planning and prioritization of the areas of important decision making. One of the key factors in building and manipulating the store image is personnel. Chapter 12 explores the human resource development area as a key tool of proactive behavior in retailing. Here the disappearing-people aspect of retailing is carefully analyzed. If the perceived store image is in congruence with the self-image of its customers, then the store is successful in creating strong degrees of customer satisfaction that will lead to customer loyalty. This is the key theme of the book: differential congruence leading to a competitive edge. This chapter also discusses the measurement of store loyalty.

Retailing mixes are retail management's tools for implementing the overall strategy and for fulfilling the store's objectives. Chapters 13, 14, and 15 discuss these mix components: (1) promotion, (2) merchandise mix (or service mix), and (3) price mix. These chapters are very critical in understanding the implementation of the planned strategy.

Three of the last four chapters explore the ways that effectiveness of the implemented strategy can be determined. After all, it is necessary to determine the effectiveness of the retail establishment as quickly and as accurately as possible.

The chapter on Retail Information Management Systems (RIMS), Chapter 16, delves into establishing a general system in order to ascertain the degrees of success or failure in implementing retail marketing strategies. Also in this chapter, a special attempt is made to examine computer applications in relation to retailing decisions and the emerging information technologies. Unless the modern retailer can use these effectively, there cannot be the differential congruence that provides the retail establishment the competitive edge.

Chapter 17 explores a most important topic—control—describing retail control functions for specific and general uses. Since the existing literature puts undue emphasis on financial controls, this chapter attempts to balance the picture by examining nonfinancial control mechanisms. Again, a special attempt is made to introduce some of the most recent computer-related developments to the readers. These computer software systems are applicable to both financial and nonfinancial feedback and control areas.

Throughout the book, reference is made to numerous retailing cases. These reflect more than thirty years of consulting and research. These are all real cases accentuating some of the key points made in numerous chapters. Each case is a separate real experience without which the contents of this book will have little relevance. The reader must relate the book's contents to the real world through these cases and, of course, his or her own personal experiences.

In addition, many of the reference lists at the ends of the chapters contain items not specifically cited in the text that should be very valuable to a student of retailing.

Exhibit

Exhibit P.1
The Key Phases of Retail Marketing Strategy Development

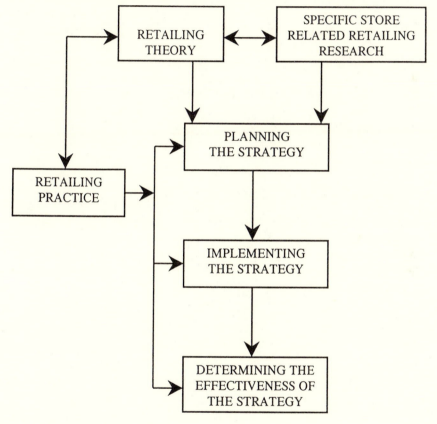

Acknowledgments

This book reflects my efforts of many years as a teacher, researcher, and consultant. It combines my field research and my experiences as a consultant. During the many years of my teaching, I learned to get my graduate students involved in thinking, reasoning, and, above all, researching and generating information.

Many people have been extremely helpful in the development of this book. It all started at Michigan State University, where Stan Hollander not only made a profound impression on me personally, but convinced me of the importance of retailing. I started teaching and doing research in retailing in 1961 at California State University, Sacramento. I taught retailing at the graduate level at Virginia Tech, where my ideas and my knowledge of retailing particularly flourished. A number of graduate students under my direction developed significant projects and theses. Two of my doctoral students, Robert Zimmer of California State, Fullerton, and Douglas Lincoln of Boise State University, worked with me closely during these years of exploration and development. Dr. Lincoln wrote a dissertation under my direction which influenced my thinking.

My students at the University of Hawaii, where I taught many summers, alerted me to international and multicultural aspects of retailing. They undertook many valuable projects that expanded my knowledge base.

Professor Laurence Jacobs of the University of Hawaii interacted with me and collaborated on a number of projects. We spent many hours exchanging ideas on our favorite topic, retailing. Professor Roger

Dickinson of the University of Texas at Arlington always managed to give me a good discussion. His immense background in retailing certainly gave me new ideas and numerous new concepts to explore.

Dr. Ronald Adams of the University of North Florida never hesitated to tell me when he believed that I was wrong. My friend and coauthor of many years, Professor Joseph Sirgy of Virginia Tech, was always available to answer my questions and argue with me on topics relating to specific issues in retailing. He inspired me with his scholarship and research efforts. My co-chair of numerous major retailing conferences, Jay Lindquist, and Robert L. King, were instrumental in my development regarding retailing theory and practice.

Professor Adel El-Ansary of the University of North Florida has always been an inspiration and a solid source of ideas. I spent quality time with him.

Two friends from Florida Atlantic University, Dr. David Georgoff and Dr. Eric Shaw, were always there to share my enthusiasm about retailing. My dear friend, Ed Mazze of the University of North Carolina–Charlotte, has always been available to exchange ideas.

My dean, Earle Traynham, has been particularly helpful by providing me with the necessary support to write this book. My department head, Dr. Robert Pickhardt, also has been available for encouragement and moral support, which at times I need desperately.

This book could not have been written without the research help received from my graduate assistants. First, N. Mehmet Ongan, now of Eastman Kodak Company, helped me to start the project and contributed extensively to the development of Chapter 12. Tracy Brownlee, my previous assistant, stayed with me throughout the duration of this project. She, with her refined research skills and enthusiasm, gave me the ideas, research support, and sometimes much-needed direction throughout the project. My current assistant, Tomas Jedlik, filled in the gaps and did some of the much-needed last-moment research.

Our secretaries, Gwen Bennett and Barbara Woods, were always there when I needed a helping hand. Just as with my previous books, this book could not have been completed without the outstanding skills of my previous secretary, Leanna Payne. Karren Duffy was available and filled in the gap and responded to my at times unreasonable demands.

Hundreds of my graduate and undergraduate students listened, argued, agreed, or disagreed with me about the points that are made in this book. They were patient, attentive, and genuinely interested to listen to my at times quite out-of-the-ordinary ideas. I owe them much. Finally, Bea Goldsmith read parts of the book, argued, and advised me to come down to the realities of the wonderful world of retailing. Her contributions are quite visible in this book, as they were in some of my previous books.

To hundreds of retailers with whom I worked, interacted, and exchanged ideas, I certainly hope that I made a contribution to their professional well-being. I thank them. Dozens of retailers for whom I have done consulting work may see themselves or may find their problems in my pages and paragraphs. Believe me, I have learned a lot from you, and I am grateful.

To these and many other people who over the years made a contribution to my thinking or knowledge base, I extend my heartfelt gratitude. I hope that this book, by making a modest but noticeable contribution, will be a payoff for their trouble. Many, many years of hard work, consulting, and research activity emerge within the pages of this book. My most important wish is that it makes a difference. As retailers read this book and benefit from it, I will consider myself very fortunate and highly rewarded.

Chapter 1

Introduction: Retail Marketing Strategy—An Overview of Differential Congruence

Dayton Hudson, one of the largest general merchandise retailers in the United States during the early 1980s, has been following a growth strategy based on carrying merchandise that largely represented quality, fashion, and value. It had grown from 100 stores to 1,000 stores in fourteen years. Their growth rate during this time was over 20 percent a year. But during the early 1980s the profile of the American economy changed. Department stores started losing ground. For fashion and high value, Americans started frequenting smaller specialty stores and upscale boutiques. At the same time they started frequenting discount stores for general household needs and low prices. Hence, Dayton Hudson had to scale down, regroup, and change focus. While they deemphasized the growth of their department stores (from 36 to only 63 between 1984 and 1994), the number of their Target Stores (a relatively upscale discount department store chain) increased from 216 in 1984 to 554 in 1994. They sold B. Dalton Bookseller stores and expanded somewhat the Mervyn's stores chain (a middle-class apparel, soft goods, and gifts store chain) from 126 in 1984 to 276 in 1994. The company's sales in the 1990s increased around 10 percent per year and reached $21 billion with much more modest increases in their profit picture (Macke 1983; Dayton Hudson Corp. 1995).

Domino's Pizza, on the other hand, had scaled down its offering from a full-fledged Italian restaurant to just take-out pizza. As a restaurant it was not doing well, as a take-out pizza operation, it did very well. In 1984 it had nearly 2,000 units scattered throughout the country. Their annual sales volume was more than $625 million (Whalen 1984; Samli 1989). During that period, the company's growth rate exceeded 40 percent. They were expanding fast into the residential markets. But during the late 1980s and early 1990s their competition increased. Competitors cut into Domino's markets in such a way that their sales volume declined in the early 1990s. In 1994 Domino's made another upsurge by expanding its menu (salads, sandwiches, and chicken wings) and by following a very aggressive marketing strategy reinforcing its new product innovations and its commitment to excellence. Its growth rate was approximately 5 percent ("Domino's Pizza Continues Turn-Around" 1995).

Publix Supermarkets, Inc., an upscale supermarket chain with special emphasis on baked goods and deli departments, has been following a relatively slow but deliberate growth strategy. While it operated 351 stores in 1988, this number has grown up to 470 stores. Its sales have been increasing around 10 percent a year (Backman 1995). The company has always emphasized good service and clean stores by stating that shopping in Publix stores is a pleasure.

These are just three strategies. Whereas Dayton Hudson changed its focus, Domino's expanded its offering. Both managed to counteract the adverse market conditions. Publix continued focusing on a specific market segment and reinforcing its strategic orientation. From these three examples it can be seen that there are countless strategic options that are open to retailers. However, it is clear that unless the retailer thinks in terms of strategic planning and acts accordingly, its chances of survival, growth, and prosperity are rather limited in view of steadily increasing retail competition. Retail organizations, as a result of increasing competition, have been moving in the direction of planning their marketing strategies more succinctly and deliberately.

When retail organizations make the major shift from an old-fashioned merchandise management orientation to a strategic marketing orientation, the development of a functional marketing plan for the implementation of the strategic plan gains in importance (Mason, Mayer, and Ezell 1994; Samli 1989). Successful, well-managed retailers, by definition, find properly implemented strategic marketing plans to be a necessity. This book is about this vital concept: strategy formulation, development, and implementation. May et al. (1986, 32) posits, "Retailing is facing a period of intensifying competition, a period in which it will become even more difficult to obtain and maintain a competitive advantage. . . . The pursuit of a competitive advantage requires what is now skill not typically found in retail marketing."

This skill is the focus of this book. It dwells upon the special know-how of retail marketing. Retail marketing is conceptualized here as going beyond day-to-day activities, how-to approaches, or fail-safe recipes that do not even work. Instead, retail marketing emphasizes strategic planning and the decision-making aspects of retailing. Consider, for instance, the May Department Store's company mission:

The May Company stands for excellence in retailing achieved through a premier organization, by leading our markets in innovative execution of superior merchandising skills and delivering a quality level of service to the customer. (Quoted from a mission statement presented before the American Marketing Association [AMA] Consortium on Retailing, University of Alabama, July 1987.)

Here, the company is emphasizing excellence (long before total quality management [TQM] became a buzzword; see Chapter 12) by developing and implementing superior merchandising skills and providing high-quality service to the markets it is catering. The May Company statement displays the retail marketing concept as long as the company can deliver its mission goals. Such implementation of the retail marketing concept can provide a competitive edge in retail markets.

A series of logical and research-based steps and major tasks must be performed if a retail establishment is to be viable and prosperous (Miller 1981; Kerin and Miller 1981; Samli 1989; Mason, Mayer, and Ezell 1994; Berman and Evans 1995). By providing an overview of the sequential steps and tasks to be performed, this chapter aims at establishing general guidelines for developing successful retail marketing strategies. There are four key components in a successful retail marketing strategy: establishing the goals, planning the strategy, implementation through a marketing plan, and evaluation. This chapter highlights the development of retail marketing strategy by elaborating on these four components briefly. As such, the chapter elaborates on the focal point of this book and provides a basic summary of it.

GOALS

The first component of successful retail marketing strategy is establishing the goals for the establishment. In order to develop the retail establishment's goals, the organization must carefully articulate the retail objectives and positioning. According to Samli (1989), articulating retail objectives and positioning implies the unique ability to match external uncontrollable variables with internal controllable tools of management in such a way that the retail establishment achieves a noticeable and definable competitive advantage. Certainly, Cartier's, Neiman-Marcus, Bloomingdale's, and Wal-Mart have been quite successful in positioning themselves effectively and achieving competitive advantage. However, considering the turbulent market conditions in retailing, it may be safe to say that for each successful establishment that manages to establish clearly defined and realistic goals, achieve effective positioning, and develop significant competitive advantage and differential congruence, many establishments fail to achieve these. As a result, they fail because of the lack of effective planning for a successful marketing strategy development, implementation, and control.

In order to establish realistic goals, the retail establishment must have adequate knowledge of uncontrollable externalities. This knowledge would, indeed must, lead to establishing market opportunities. Market opportunities are based on total market potentials that are scaled down by the nature and intensity of threats—or competition. The retailer needs to be familiar with local, regional, national, or even international trends that are influencing the establishment's markets. Similarly, the retailer must evaluate the actual and potential competition. Sears did not quite assess its market opportunities and potential competition in the retailing sector, and after so many years of being the number-one merchandiser in the world, lost its position to Wal-Mart.

Once the retailer assesses the external conditions and the resultant net market opportunities, the retailer needs to take a good hard look at the retail establishment (Exhibit 1.1). This implies a critical evaluation of the firm's strengths and weaknesses. The firm's strengths can be its existing image, personnel, financial resources, merchandise mix, administrative know-how, location, private brands, existing inventory, delivery system, and other physical facilities such as warehousing equipment, and so on. However, any and all of these factors can also reflect a weakness. Thus, objective evaluation of these features is a must to proceed in the direction of developing and implementing the most adequate marketing strategy for this particular retail establishment.

Upon the assessment of external conditions and internal evaluation of the retail establishment's resources, it is possible to establish goals. For existing firms, instead of establishing goals, the revision of these goals, if necessary, would be the next step. Whether the original goals are established or revised, at this point the retail establishment is quite cognizant of its direction and where it wants to go. On this basis it can begin to formulate its marketing strategy. McDonald's, for instance, has opted to cater to young families with little children. On the basis of this premise, every new McDonald's unit is adding a nice children's playground attachment.

Clearly defined retail targets and particular positioning goals are necessary prerequisites for effective planning. One retail establishment might consider itself a mass-merchandiser and might wish to position itself between Sears and Wal-Mart. Another retailer might aim at differentiating and positioning itself as an upper-middle-class apparel store such as Gap. However, here Gap must successfully differentiate itself from, say, The Limited and Mervyn's. Yet a third retail store might be a segmenter keying its imported gifts to primarily "cosmopolitans" in the community and positioning itself above Pier 1 Imports.

Ability to spell out the objectives and position the retail establishment realistically provides the foundation for the retail establishment to develop a strategic plan that will lead the business to success. Exhibit 1.2 illustrates the components and sequential ordering of the overall retail strategic marketing planning process. Exhibit 1.2 illustrates the four components of a successful retail marketing strategy: establishing the goals, planning the strategy, implementation of the marketing plan, and evaluation.

Analyses of available information and evaluation of market trends and relationships among various factors and indicators enable the decision makers to assess market opportunities. It is not only existing market opportunities but prediction of their status in the future that are the driving factors of retail marketing strategy.

In developing the strategy, the retailer must determine and prioritize retail segments. The retailer must obtain as much information on the specifics of these segments as possible. Woodward and Lothrop of Washington, D.C., for instance, on the basis of analyses and predictions in the late 1970s and 1980s, expected the African-American segment of the apparel market to grow substantially. Hence, it has made plans to enter this particular market segment. Once this decision was made, the company was able to program the retail effort effectively.

Two critical factors in Exhibit 1.2 deserve special attention. First, the value of feedback is in its becoming *feedforward*. The faster feedback becomes feedforward, the more effective is the retailer's control mechanism. Because of feedback, the retailer determines how successful its marketing plans are. Feedforward implies corrective action is taking place rapidly and hence the control mechanism is activated fully.

But, behind the feedback, feedforward, and controls is organizational learning. In order for the retailer to improve the overall performance, there must be learning. Retail establishments that exercise organizational learning, which means gaining new insights that potentially alter behavior, and learning from practices, developments, or outcomes, are most likely to be successful.

Perhaps the most important lesson to be learned by the retailer is efficient consumer response (ECR). Growing consumer focus in retailing (a reality for survival) has been facilitated by modern computer-planned distribution efficiencies that provides a quick response system. By using modern computer information technologies such as electronic data interchange (EDI) and bar-coding, retailers such as Kroger, Shaw's, Giant Food, and Dominick's have developed rapid flows of information between and within their organizations. Such rapid information flows, among others, are showing their impact in continuous replenishment of inventories and other inventory-level management and service levels for customers (Margolies 1995).

Just what kind of game plan is needed to reach and satisfy retail targets is the question that provides the details of the marketing plan. In this plan, the details of retail mixes need to be carefully planned. The components of these mixes and their relative weights (or importance) must be carefully spelled out.

The implementation of the strategic plan is performed by using four different retail mixes. All of these mixes must be consistent and work in the same direction for the retail establishment. As seen in Exhibit 1.3, the retailing mix has four major components: goods and services, communications, pricing, and human resources.

Goods and Services Mix

The goods and services mix is the reason for existence in retailing. Without the proper merchandise and service combination most appropriate for its target, the retail establishment does not have a chance to cater to the needs of this target or to fulfill the goals to which it aspires. The effectiveness of the goals and services mix depends on numerous conditions. Samli (1989) expressed these conditions in the form of seven questions to which is added an eighth:

1. How does the product and service mix fit the communication mix?
2. How does the product and service mix fit the physical distribution mix?
3. Is the product and service mix appropriate for the market segment at which the firm is aiming?
4. Do we have appropriate controls and feedback to update the product and service mix?
5. Are the goods and services that are offered in the total mix compatible?
6. Is the product and service mix different from that of the competitors so that the firm will have comparative advantage?
7. Is the product and service mix compatible with the image the retail establishment is projecting?
8. How does the product and service mix fit the human resource mix?

Communications Mix

It must be understood that in a market system each retailer is part of an information network receiving and transmitting information. The retailer is separated from the consumer in terms of time and space and must overcome these barriers. This task is performed by the communications mix (Lazer and Kelly 1961; Samli 1989). The retailer participates in the overall communications network, first by obtaining information about the market, second by communicating with its market segments, and third by providing information to both its customers and noncustomers in the market. The communication mix has many components. They all function in the direction of making the retail establishment better recognized and differentiating it from its competitors. Exhibit 1.3 illustrates various key components of this mix. Though this is not an exhaustive list, it points out the many ways a retail establishment can communicate with the market. Perhaps the worst thing a retailer can do is to be a "best kept secret."

Pricing Mix

The pricing mix has three critical components: efficiency, competition, and image. The efficiency component implies the firm's efficiencies in running the retail establishments that are passed into the store's customers through lower prices. The competitive component indicates the retail establishment's use of the pricing mix as a major competitive tool. Discount stores, bargain basements, outlet stores, and other similar retail operations use prices for that purpose. Many of these have the policy of "if you find a cheaper price than ours, we will match it." Finally, the image component means the store is using its prices in order to enhance a specific image. The store may wish to promote an image of being a reasonable place with some exceptional buys. However, such a strategy cannot be implemented without carefully planned pricing practices by the store and without articulating its competitive edge in comparison with its major competitors.

Human Resource Mix

Retailing is as much a people business as a business can get. Though its human resources aspects has many other dimensions relating to management, personnel, training, and so on, it must be reiterated that a retail establishment without a friendly, talkative, knowledgeable, and understanding group of employees cannot possibly succeed. As depicted in Exhibit 1.3, personal selling aspects of a retail establishment is the final contact with the customer, and unless the customer is happy with this contact, there will be no repeat business. Thus, the retailing people must have information and pass it on to customers, interact with them, make them satisfied, and keep them in this state of mind. But other nonselling personnel in the retail store must be equally customer oriented. They must go out of their way to help the customers so that they will come back again and again.

Putting All the Mixes Together

In many ways, retailing is developing an image and manipulating it as needed. This manipulation can be accomplished only by proper uses of the four components of the retail mix. As seen in Exhibit 1.3, all four of the mixes have a store image component. Indeed, all of the activities in each and every mix have direct and indirect impact on the overall store image. They are all either in the process of developing an image, maintaining the existing image, or modifying the existing image. In all of these cases the components of the mixes may not work in the same direction and hence some of them may nullify each other's impact. Certainly, such a series of interactions is likely to block the optimization of the image of the retail establishment. Thus, the integrated retailing mix must be completely congruent with the image the retail store is attempting to project. Lack of congruence in this case means that even though the four mixes are integrated they are not aiming at the intended market segment and hence they are not capitalizing on the possible differential congruence the retail store could enjoy.

STORE IMAGE MANAGEMENT

From our discussion thus far, it is clear that managing the store image can be easily equated with the overall retail marketing management. A consumer who goes to Cartier's, Neiman-Marcus, or Wal-Mart knows what to expect and is making a deliberate choice.

This choice, to a substantial extent, is generated by the store image that is being conveyed to this particular consumer and perhaps a consumer-to-be. We also emphasized the fact that in managing the store's image, the mixes must first be consistent among themselves and then the projected image should be consistent with the market to which the store is aiming.

The store image is obviously very important. It represents all the aspects of communication that the store performs which are geared to a specific marketplace or market segment. It is also the most significant retail marketing management feedback that provides decision makers with specific strategic alternatives, and it guides management in making the adjustments needed to fulfill specific goals.

Thus, retail marketing management revolves around store image management. Total marketing strategy is formulated, implemented, tested for effectiveness, and adjusted for better congruity between the image and the market segment, all within the context of the existing and aspired store image. As Samli states (1989, 7), "Image as a whole is synergistic. Although it has numerous components such as appearance of the store, attitude of the salespeople, quality of the merchandise, internal layout, and many others, the image involves more than the sum total of all of these elements. It is the unity and congruence among these elements that determine the nature of image."

Regardless whether it is existing or aspired, image is a major help in formulating and implementing strategy. If, for instance, the store is aiming at the older, well-to-do segment, a dynamic youthful image is not likely to be successful. The following example illustrates this point.

The Glo-wood Restaurant was located adjacent to a major metropolitan university. It was open twenty-four hours a day, seven days a week, and catered primarily to students and unskilled blue-collar workers employed in that particular area. A good atmosphere of communication and relaxation prevailed in the restaurant. Food was cheap and waitresses were friendly. The establishment was always crowded and hence very successful. When the owners (a husband and wife) were ready to retire, they sold the restaurant. The new owner wanted to make the restaurant an elegant, high-class place. He changed the interior, the menu, and the appearance of the establishment. In less than six months he was out of business. The elegant image he created was not acceptable to the existing market segment. The regular customers did not feel comfortable in the new environment. The new owner failed to keep the existing clientele and to attract other people from other market segments because of competition and the socioeconomic makeup of the immediate community.

As seen in this case, developing a retail marketing strategy without paying attention to image is most likely to end in failure. Once the firm decides upon its goals in terms of positioning and its market segment, then it must decide just what kind of image can fulfill these goals. It must be carefully underlined, however, that there are two kinds of image: the intended image and the perceived image. These two must be the same if the retail establishment expects a successful performance. Consider the following example.

A bank in the Midwest considered itself to be the elite or upscale bank in the community catering to the upper middle class. It has been promoting an image accordingly. The services it offers are more expensive and somewhat more unique and the layout is rather plush. However, research undertaken by the nearby university indicated that the bank, in actuality, was catering primarily to the lower middle class. Its customers did not really care for all the frills that the bank offered.

The discrepancy between the intended and the actual image is rather obvious in this case. If the intended image is not the same as the received image, this bank or any retail establishment that is experiencing a similar situation is likely to be wasting a lot of resources in claiming to be something that it is not. Since customer satisfaction depends heavily on the completeness of the overlap between the intended and the actually perceived image, this situation is likely to create a certain amount of customer dissatisfaction. Hence, the expected customer-satisfaction-driven customer loyalty is not likely to be achieved.

This point is further elaborated in Exhibit 1.4. Three situations are depicted in the exhibit. Situation A illustrates a great failure. There is no similarity between the intended image and the perceived image. The store clearly is claiming to be something that it is not. Situation B depicts partial success. Even though in some areas the store's claims are realistic, in most areas they are not. Hence, there is a significant difference between what the store claims it is and what outsiders perceive it to be. Finally, situation C is a success story. Though not 100 percent, the intended image is very similar to the perceived image. These two may never be exactly the same, but they could be extremely close to being the same.

CONSUMER SELF-PERCEPTION

In Exhibit 1.2, the opposite to store image management is consumer self-perception. This particular concept must be entered into the equation if the retail establishment expects to be successful. Every individual has a perceived self-concept that reflects itself in the form of a self-image. The self-image is likely to be formed by the individual's psyche, through the influences from various sources in the total environment. The environment includes membership in large groups, for example, socioeconomic class, subculture, or ethnic group, as well as small groups, such as the family, reference group, or peer group. It also includes educational institutions and many other direct and indirect variables. All of these environmental factors make an impact on the individual's psyche which forms the self-image through certain specific influences. Among these influences are cognitive and affective influences as well as personal and interpersonal influences. While cognitive implies learning, affective, in general terms, means evaluation. Personal influences come from individuals' own initiative and the store image can be measured and evaluated realistically only within the constraints of the individual's own perceived self-image. For instance, the individual may perceive himself or herself as youthful, dynamic, and open to new ideas and new products. But the same person may perceive the store to be static, stuffy, and not modern enough, will feel very uncomfortable during a few visits to the store, and subsequently will stop going there. However, if the individual perceives the projected store image as dynamic, youthful, and open to new ideas and new products, there will be a congruence between the store image and the consumer's self-image. This situation leads to a high level of customer satisfaction.

The planned retail marketing strategy therefore aims at a project congruence between self-image and store image. In reality, even though this relationship may not be perfect, by bringing the two closer together and, hence, by increasing the degree of congruence between the two, the retail establishment can increase its probabilities for success.

CONSUMER SATISFACTION

As seen in Exhibit 1.2, the bottom line for all retail management activity is customer satisfaction. If the store can satisfy customers' needs, it will be able to survive and prosper. Prosperity is generated by the positive profit picture which is the market's reward to the store for a job that is being done well. It is obvious, therefore, that the retail establishment must provide satisfaction to its customers. The degrees of customer satisfaction (or dissatisfaction) must be determined periodically to avoid a negative profit picture. In addition to periodically asking the store customers for their degree of satisfaction, the retail store aims to determine the degree of congruence between customer self-image and store image. If the image and self-perception of the market segment (self-image) are not congruent, then major decisions need to be made. Obviously, one of the firm's key options is to revise its goals, segmentation, and positioning. In addition, there may be other alternatives based on the components of the four retailing mixes. There may be major or minor changes in one or more of the components of these mixes.

The final component of the retail marketing strategy development, as seen in Exhibit 1.2, is the feedback. Of course, feedback goes hand-in-hand with the control mechanism. Though there should be feedback at every step of the way in retail store management, a general overall feedback regarding the store's general performance must be obtained at the end of all retail marketing efforts. Throughout this book, customer satisfaction is considered to be a function of differential congruence.

FEEDBACK AND CORRECTIVE ACTION

Examining the degree of customer satisfaction is a necessity and must be done periodically and regularly. Regular research in this area provides direction for retail marketing, planning, and control. If there is no effective feedback, the retail establishment cannot make reasonable adjustments in its business procedures and cannot exercise an effective control activity. It is, therefore, very easy to make a case for periodic retail market research studies that provide the basis for feedback and control (Gentile and Gentile 1978).

Feedback and control work almost simultaneously and both facilitate effective planning. As part of the planning process, certain feedback and control criteria must be established. The adequacy or inadequacy of the overall performance indicated by feedback should automatically trigger the control mechanism and make immediate adjustments in the management's plans. The adjustments through the control mechanism may result on financial parameters, market share, percentage increase or decrease in sales and expenditures, customer turnover, and many other effects. Thus, as feedback facilitates planning by providing direction, controls keep the implementation effective.

THE THEORY OF DIFFERENTIAL CONGRUENCE

It must be understood that the retail establishment has numerous strategic alternatives. As it uses the retailing mix it planned, it will invariably appeal to a specific segment in the market. In implementing its strategic plans by using its retailing mix, the retail establishment is managing and manipulating a store image. This is reinforced or reduced by the separate images of the products that the retail store uses.

These two images combined make an impact on the particular market segment to which the store has been appealing. The individuals in that segment have a self-image which they nurture. If this self-image and store image overlap and show a positive congruence, consumer satisfaction is achieved. As the store manages to satisfy its customers and keeps them satisfied, these customers become loyal to the store. Thus, the store develops a loyal following. This situation was termed by Wroe Alderson (1957) as "differential advantage." This book modifies this concept slightly and coins it differential congruence. The retail store not only is successful in creating congruence between its image and its customers' self-perceived image, but also successful in differentiating itself from its competitors. As seen in Exhibit 1.5, differential congruence creates store loyalty, which means successful retail management with resultant financial rewards.

INTERNATIONAL CORNER

With the expansion of world trade, there have been some significant changes in retailing all over the world. First, inside the United States, many foreign-made products appeared, among these home electronics coming from Pacific Rim countries and textiles coming from Southeast Asia. Many of these are labor-intensive products or ultramodern high-tech products. In either case, there are significant cost savings. Hence, these products are readily available in American retail stores and save substantial sums for American consumers.

The second impact has been in the direction of having foreign retailers coming to the United States or becoming partners with U.S. retailers. Examples of foreign retailers coming to the United States are Benetton or IKEA. These retailers have been successful either by uniqueness of their merchandise and atmosphere or by their efficient management.

The third impact is related to the American influence on foreign retailing. Some American retailers have gone overseas: K-Mart in the Slovakian Republic, Wal-Mart in Mexico, and Toys 'R Us in Japan are examples. These retailers have been successful because of their uniqueness or their reputation.

Finally, the fourth impact has been retailing that is related to tourism. In many major cities of the world, retailing complexes are emerging that are geared to tourists rather than local people. In Hong Kong, Singapore, Istanbul, or Malaysia, many such ultramodern complexes have come into being because of the expansion of world trade and world travel. International retailing is quite different than domestic U.S. retailing. In every chapter of this book is a section dealing with these issues.

SUMMARY

In a way, Exhibit 1.5 summarizes this chapter. It depicts the chief aspects of the total retail marketing strategy. The chapter points out that all retail establishments have some special attributes; however, whether these are desirable ones and how they should be manipulated will determine the direction and the effectiveness of retail marketing strategy. Store attributes are reflected on the store image that is projected in the market. If this image and the target market characteristics are in harmony, the retail store is likely to enjoy a high degree of differential congruence that means its customers think that it is different. The difference of the store is what the customers find very acceptable. Differential congruence creates customer loyalty, which in essence means the customers are satisfied. Feedback provides information about the presence or absence of differential congruence and the control mechanism enables the retail establishment to readjust so that it can achieve desirable results.

It must be reiterated that this chapter presents the general plan of this book. Retail marketing management commences with the establishment of retail objectives and positioning. Development of strategic plans follows analyses of the opportunities and threats, evaluations of strengths and weaknesses, and predictions and future assessments. At the stage of the development of the strategic plan, retail market segments are determined, a detailed marketing plan is prepared, and components of the marketing mix (and four submixes) are decided upon. The four marketing submixes create the store image. This is a very critical concept. Managing the store is basically manipulation of the store image, which must be congruent with the self-perception of store customers. Only then is it possible for the store to successfully satisfy its customers' needs and be profitable. Finally, determining the degree of differential congruence through research and feedback will enable the store to generate a powerful control mechanism.

Exhibits

Exhibit 1.1
Establishing Retail Objectives

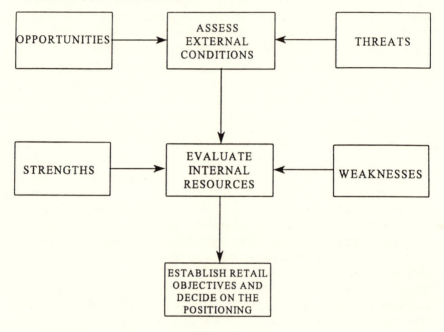

Exhibit 1.2
The Planning Process in Retail Management

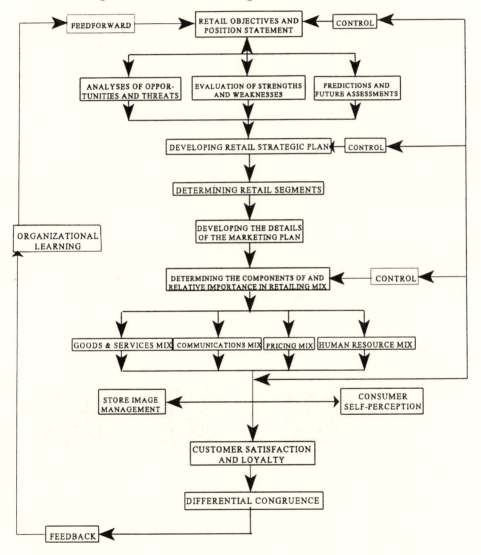

Exhibit 1.3
Components of Retail Mixes

Goods and Service Mix	Communication Mix	Pricing Mix	Human Resource Mix
Merchandise	Advertising	Price Level	Personal Selling
Variety and Assortment	Catalogs	Price Lines	Customer Services
Guarantee and Exchange	Store Layout	Markdowns	Interaction with Customers
Customer Services	Public Relations	Markups	Merchandise Information
Credit	Internal Displays	Price Perceived Quality	Salespeople's Advice
Alterations and	Window Displays	Efficiency	Support People:
Adjustments	Telephone Sales	Components Affecting Prices:	Maintenance
Delivery	Sales Promotion	Warehousing	Cleaning
Parking	Special Sales	Handling goods	Security
STORE IMAGE		Computerized controls	Delivery
	STORE IMAGE	STORE IMAGE	STORE IMAGE

Exhibit 1.4
Degrees of Success in Retail Image Management

A

Intended
Image

Perceived
Image

FAILURE

B

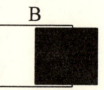

Intended Perceived
Image   Image

PARTIAL SUCCESS

C

Intended and
Perceived Images

SUCCESS

Exhibit 1.5
The Continuity of Retail Marketing Strategic Development

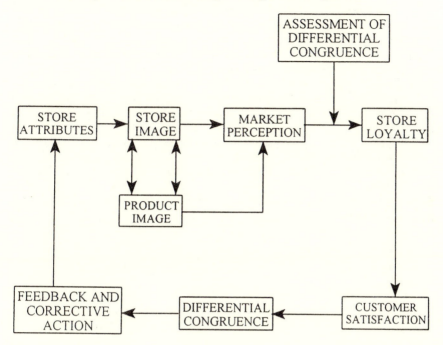

References

Alderson, Wroe. 1957. *Marketing Behavior and Executive Action*. Homewood, Ill.: Richard D. Irwin.

Backman, Lisa. 1995. "Publix Profits Expand with Stores." *Tampa Tribune*, 6 April.

Berman, Barry, and Joel R. Evans. 1995. *Retail Management*. Englewood Cliffs, N.J.: Prentice Hall.

Dayton Hudson Corp. 1995. *Company Report*. C. J. Lawrence/Deutsche Bank Securities Corporation.

"Domino's Pizza Continues Turn-Around." 1995. *Business Wire* (Ann Arbor, Michigan), 6 February.

Gentile, Richard J., and Anne Gentile. 1978. *Retailing Strategy*. New York: Labhas-Friedman Books.

Kerin, Roger, and Richard Miller. 1981. "Diversity of Retail Operations and Financial Performance." In *The Changing Marketing Environment*, ed. Kenneth Bernhardt et al. Chicago: American Marketing Association.

Lazer, William, and Eugene J. Kelly. 1961. "The Retailing Mix: Planning and Management." *Journal of Retailing 37* (Spring): 32–44.

Macke, Kenneth A. 1983. "Managing Change: How Dayton Hudson Meets the Challenge." *Journal of Business Strategy* (Summer): 78–81.

Macke, Kenneth A., Morris L. Mayer, and Anthony Koh. 1985. "Functional Marketing Plan Development in Department Store Retailing." *Journal of the Academy of Marketing Science* (Summer): 161–182.

Margolies, Jeffrey M. 1995. "The Grocery Industry and ECR." *Chain Store Age* (November): 92–94.

Mason, J. Barry, Morris L. Mayer, and Hazel F. Ezell. 1994. *Retailing*. Burr Ridge, Ill.: Richard D. Irwin.

May, Eleanor G. et al. 1986. "Marketing—in Concept and in Practice." In *Retailing: Theory and Practice for the 21st Century*, ed. R. L. King. Miami: Academy of Marketing Science and the American Collegiate Retailing Association.

Miller, Richard. 1981. "Pathways to Growth in Retailing." *Journal of Business Strategy* 3: 25–35.

Samli, A. Coskun. 1989. *Retail Marketing Strategy*. Westport, Conn.: Quorum Books.

Whalen, Bernie. 1984. "People Oriented Marketing Delivers Lots of Dough for Domino's." *Marketing News*, 16 March, sec. 2, pp. 4–5.

Chapter 2

Multiple Layers
of Retail Competition

Exhibit 2.1 illustrates the multidimensionality of retailing competition. Five levels of competition are identified in the diagram. While Level 1 deals with the most specific aspects of retailing and identifies how retailers actually compete, other levels indicate additional dimensions that profoundly influence and modify this competition. Level 5 is the broadest level that identifies the economic dimensions of retail competition. A successful retailer must understand the varying nature of retail competition at each level, and must be able to cope with the prevailing competition according to that level's competitive patterns.

COMPETITION THROUGH RETAILING MIX

In Chapter 1, Exhibit 1.3 illustrates four types of mixes: goods and services, communications, pricing, and human resources. The same exhibit also illustrates some of the key elements of each of these four mixes. Any and all of these mixes are competitive weapons of individual retailers. Through these mix components, the retailers manage to appeal to their intended markets, to project the intended image, and to cope with all layers of competition.

If the retailer is successful, it is then creating a differential advantage over its competition which, in time, will become differential congruence. The Limited Express has a certain layout and certain fashionable merchandise to appeal to teenagers and young adults. It advertises accordingly and its personnel reflect the same behavior and values as the intended target market. Gap, on the other hand, a more upscale apparel outlet, caters to an older and somewhat economically better-off group with more casual and classical attire. These two are competing peripherally and using their respective marketing mixes to do well. This is Level-1 competition which is the grassroots level.

In dealing with Level-1 competition, Samli (1989) identified two structural theories that systematically explain retail competition at this level. These are structural theories in the sense that, given the nature of retailing structure, they are basic and consistent under all circumstances. The two structural theories dealing with first-level retail competition are margin–turnover classification and natural dominance theory.

The Turnover Classification Theory

Ronald Gist (1968) introduced a general framework to examine the retail structure in order to facilitate a better understanding of the competitive patterns of retail establishments. Such an understanding can easily be incorporated into the retail strategy formulation. This framework is based on the intricate relationship between retail margins and retail turnovers. Margin is a percentage markup at which the inventory in a store is sold, and turnover is the number of times the average inventory is sold in a given year. On the basis of the margin–turnover relationship, retail establishments can be divided into four distinct categories: high margin–high turnover stores, high margin–low turnover stores, low margin–high turnover stores, and low margin–low turnover stores.

All retail stores fall into one of these four categories. Certainly within the same category there may be variations, but these are not wide variations. It is important for a retailer to evaluate its immediate competitors' position within this basic classification. For instance, if Mr. Smith realizes that his immediate competitors at this level of competition are lower than others, and he has to position his business vis-à-vis these competitors, he has some options. Within the parameters established by his competitors, he has the option to position his business as slightly higher priced or somewhat lower priced, but only within this group.

As a retail store is placed in its proper quadrant in Exhibit 2.2, the general parameters of its retail marketing strategy are established. These strategies, at the store level, must be carefully implemented in catering to the store's particular target market. As seen in Exhibit 2.2, the retail marketing strategy depends on the particular location of the store in the exhibit. For instance, if Cartier's were to move in the direction of becoming a high turnover–low margin store, it certainly cannot maintain its current status, its current image, and its current clientele. Perhaps the most important point in Exhibit 2.2 is the two extremes of a retail marketing strategy spectrum. On the one end, there is a low margin–high turnover strategy, which is depicted by any discount store (K-Mart, Wal-Mart, etc.), and at the other end is the high margin–low turnover strategy. The exclusive jewelry chain, Bulgari, is in the latter category. Connoisseurs of jewelry can easily identify Bulgari pieces. The details of these strategies are depicted in Exhibit 2.3.

It is clear from Exhibit 2.3 that retail marketing strategies at the store level are based on merchandise mix sold, varieties of assortment carried, services offered, location of the store, human resources of the retail establishment, prices, overall promotional activity, and, last but perhaps the most important of all, quality (Samli 1989).

Perhaps one of the most important considerations is that there must be consistency on the part of the store regarding these features. For instance, if the company is positioning itself in the low margin–high turnover area, it should not have an expensive jewelry or fur department that does not belong in the merchandise mix of such a store. Nor should the store consider advertising on the basis of services and quality it offers.

The high margin–low turnover retail establishments basically emphasize customers coming to the store because they know it well or they know it by reputation and then buying in the store. The store ambience, the salespeople, and all the other features (Exhibit 2.3) would help sell the unique and good merchandise to customers. They will stimulate the customers' buying more in the store.

On the other end of the spectrum, low margin–high turnover stores imply that most merchandise is pre-sold and, of course, almost all sales are based on self-help. Personnel, ambience, and other store features are not likely to contribute more to the store. Thus, in these stores, low prices, brand awareness, and price-based advertising are extremely critical (Mason, Mayer, and Wilkinson 1993; Samli 1989; Gist 1968).

Natural Dominance Theory

Natural dominance theory (Hirschman 1979) provides critical insight into retail competition at both Layers 1 and Layer 2 depicted in Exhibit 2.1. This theory is based on the premise that general merchandise retailers can be grouped into three different categories: (1) traditional, well-respected, upscale department stores such as Bloomingdale's or Marshall Fields; (2) national chain department stores such as Sears or Montgomery Ward; and (3) full-line discount department stores such as Wal-Mart or K-Mart. These stores are present in their respective groups. As seen in Exhibit 2.2, there are three layers depicting three different groups (or markets). Whereas the highest quality and highest prices are represented by the first group, the second group are medium price and medium-quality retailers. Finally, the third group represents the lowest prices followed by the lowest quality.

Traditionally, the stores in the first group cater to local markets. They are typically independent (local or regional) and, hence, they are quite flexible and respond quickly to changing conditions in the retail environment. They thrive on extensive customer service, store credit, and quality brand merchandise.

The stores in the second group are mostly centrally controlled. This means they are part of a chain where the key marketing decisions are not made at the local level. Their marketing programs are developed and administered on a national basis and, as a result, these stores are not completely responsive to local changes and local needs. They emphasize store brands (their own brands) heavily, and their promotional activity is based primarily on the use of national themes and national media.

The third group of stores emerged to cater to customers' need to not be pressured and to shop at their own pace through self-service. These stores are discount department stores. They are built and laid out inexpensively, they carry relatively lower priced merchandise, and they provide additional convenience by providing ample parking. During the 1980s they were, more often, freestanding institutions. They were built in lower-priced land areas and did not have many stores around them. Their low-priced merchandise typically is the second category in national brands. Thus, they have cheaper versions of national brands. These stores minimize customer services. Today, these stores are not nearly as freestanding as they were in the 1980s. Instead, they are becoming anchor stores in the malls and shopping centers.

The essence of natural dominance theory is that these three types of department stores can be positioned on a price–quality continuum (Exhibit 2.4), and they attract a certain type of retail establishment to create their own clusters. In the eyes of consumers, these department store offerings are already distinguished in terms of different levels of quality, price, and (though it is not shown in Exhibit 2.4) service. Stores in each group offer a *concentrated variety* in the unique, multiple merchandise lines they carry. This concentrated variety is seen as the primary advantage of each department store and its satellite group of specialty stores.

In the early 1990s, total quality management emerged as a major managerial tool to enhance a firm's competitive advantage. A six-step activity has been suggested for TQM: (1) what the customer wants, (2) what the customer is not getting, (3) cause of problems, (4) corrective action alternatives, (5) corrective action and implementation, and (6) monitored results (Samli 1996). Major retailers have been taking TQM into consideration and, in many cases, this has enhanced their service component.

Each department store that is located on the price–quality continuum attracts certain specialty stores and, as a group, each layer offers different goods and services. Hence, each group has its own product classification dominance. The chances are, for example, that the fashion lines and brands in the traditional department store's satellite specialty group cannot be matched by the group clustered around the discount department store. Exhibit 2.5 illustrates how this grouping process takes place at each level.

These three separate groupings reflect a stable retail structural mix system. Each mix of stores is consistent within itself and appeals to certain socioeconomic consumer groups. If Cartier's, Charles Jordan, or Tiffany's were to be located adjacent to Wal-Mart, or if K-Mart, in addition to its regular merchandise lines, were to carry the lines that are typically carried by these three stores, there would be a structural inconsistency and, therefore, instability.

On the basis of natural dominance theory, it is expected that not only each group of stores will offer a concentrated variety such as fashion merchandise, gift items, staple foods, and so on across a number of merchandise lines, but also each group achieves a *unique classification dominance*. Through its concentrated variety, each group establishes its uniqueness. This implies that each department store shown in Exhibit 2.4 establishes itself on the price–quality continuum and attracts certain specialty stores to group together, thereby presenting a concentrated variety of merchandise in which each group achieves its own unique classification dominance. Thus, these three types of department stores form their own locus of merchandise control within the group of stores they have attracted to form a cluster. In any community, there exists a price–quality continuum, and each cluster of stores on the continuum presents all, a concentrated variety, a classification dominance, and a resultant locus of merchandise control.

The classification dominance that is initiated by each department store in Exhibit 2.4 is based primarily on consumer perception. Consumers would perceive, for instance, the traditional department store group's classification dominance as an economic and social risk. They know that if they need upscale fashion apparel or china and crystal gifts they have to go to the traditional department store group. The perception that is (or must be) created by the group is that good quality and good value in the particular product classification offered by the group presents a "sure thing" in terms of a good purchase decision, and that such a decision would meet the approval of other people in the consumer's immediate social circle. Thus, the merchandise line control based on merchandise classification by each group is the crux of natural dominance theory. The merchandise groupings are presented in Exhibit 2.6.

Dominance theory brings in the perceived risk of price, quality, and service-conscious consumers into manageably structural consistency and stability. It creates an intensive competition concentrated within the three levels of the price–quality continuum. The degree of competition will be substantially less intense along the continuum or between the levels of groups. However, it intensifies intralevel competition, giving each type of department store and its satellites a certain type of demand-generated monopoly which is based on successful management of supply. Given price points, quality levels, service variety, and merchandise mixes comprise the management of supply. To the extent that this supply management satisfies customers' needs and reduces the perceived risk of shopping around and buying products that are needed and wanted, there is a power base developed by each group. This power base which is designed to attract customers and diminish their perceived risks is the essence of natural dominance theory. According to this theory, "Each of the three types of department stores is more supportive of and complementary with other types than competitive, inasmuch as their sphere of dominance is in noncompeting merchandise lines, and they are differentiated on the basis of price" (Samli 1989, 26), quality, and service.

Thus, natural dominance theory posits that Wal-Mart is competing with K-Mart but is not directly competing with Bloomingdale's or Neiman-Marcus. The competition that exists at each level is accentuated by the type of stores each of these three department stores attracts (Exhibits 2.4 and 2.5) and, hence, based on merchandise classification dominance and concentrated variety, each shopping complex establishes its power base. However, if Cartier's, Charles Jordan, or Tiffany's were located adjacent to Wal-Mart, the natural dominance would be eliminated by the diminished classification dominance and questionable concentrated variety. Hence, a key provision of natural dominance theory is the proper grouping of retail stores. If the natural dominance cannot be established or classification dominance cannot be enhanced, then the specialty store should not locate in the proposed site next to the department store in question. Natural dominance theory, therefore, provides special insights into retail competition. It also enhances the understanding of retail location and total merchandise mixes.

COMPETING WITH OTHER RETAIL INSTITUTIONS

Our discussion thus far has been related to Levels 1 and 2 in Exhibit 2.1. Level 2 is related to competition among retail institutions at the same level. At any given time, in population centers such as cities or towns, many retail establishments that are quite similar are competing with each other: Sears and Montgomery Ward, Wal-Mart and K-Mart, Kroger and Winn Dixie.

All these stores are, first and foremost, involved in competing with each other and trying to develop a competitive advantage. There are many generic ways of competing. Samli (1989) identifies four specific types of retail competition at this level. All of these are intrainstitutional ways of developing a competitive advantage. Four distinctly different patterns are identified: imitation, deviation, complementation, and innovation.

Imitation

As seen in Exhibit 2.6, all retailers have certain traditional lines of merchandise that they are expected to carry. Thus, almost all retail establishments consider carrying such basic inventories. Of course, all competitors have these basic lines. If one were to analyze the depth and breadth of inventories carried by Wal-Mart and K-Mart, there may not be any significant difference. As Samli (1989, 121) states, "In retailing competition, a 'basic' inventory that will appeal to the 'core' market is essential. Naturally, especially for larger retailers, these core markets are similar; hence, the overlap in merchandise and service mixes becomes logical."

Many small retailers also use imitation as a method of competition. In this case, small retailers who lack a clear-cut mission or a well-defined target may imitate the large retailer to stay in business. There have been shirt and tie specialists who are located next to, for example, Sears. They hope that by having a little more detailed inventory they will pick up part of the traffic that the large retailer is attracting.

Deviation

Though at the core many retailers may imitate each other, at the fringe of their activities they may deviate from each other's practices, merchandise, and service mixes. This way they also deviate in their image-building efforts. Thus, even though Wal-Mart and K-Mart overlap in 80 percent of their activities, media mixes, product–service price, and human resource mixes, at least 20 percent of difference distinguishes the two. In fact, that 20 percent is the key to their way of managing their own clientele.

Complementation

Certain consumer products are sold most readily when the choice that is offered is greater. This particular principle is primarily applicable to shopping goods. When consumers shop around for better prices and better bargains, they will shop more readily when they have larger numbers of alternatives to choose from. Thus, it is quite common to see a number of fast-food restaurants, a number of jewelers, or a number of apparel outlets located together.

Innovation

Retail establishments compete with their immediate competitors by being innovative and generating a differential advantage. In addition to carrying unique merchandise, handling the merchandise differently, or serving their customers in more unconventional ways, retail establishments can also manage their image more uniquely than their competitors. Pizza Hut's eating the pizza the wrong way campaign, McDonald's joint promotion with Batman merchandise lines, and the like are examples of innovative competition. Though in innovative competition there are higher cost and risk factors, there is also a greater opportunity to establish a competitive advantage.

INTERINSTITUTIONAL COMPETITION

The third layer of retail economic competition, as displayed in Exhibit 2.1, is interinstitutional competition. Different types of retail institutions have emerged in the American scene during the past thirty years or so. Each of these compete for the same consumer dollar in different ways. Exhibit 2.7 illustrates how different types of retailers create interinstitutional competition. Of these, four need a little explanation. Combination stores combine supermarket and general merchandise sales under the same roof. Superstores are also primarily food based. They are larger and more diversified than conventional supermarkets, but not so sizeable and diversified as combination stores (McCune 1994). Box stores are also food-based discounters. They offer a small selection, limited hours, few services, and only a few national brands. Finally, warehouse stores are primarily discounters, though they also offer limited selection in food lines. They have a strictly no-frills setting.

In recent years, a new concept has been emerging. This is called *supercenters*. These are very conveniently located, low-price, high-variety merchandise retail facilities. They thrive on the one-stop shopping concept and attract consumers from distances as far as 100 miles (Leah 1995; Flickinger 1995).

Exhibit 2.7 indicates, for instance, that convenience stores such as 7-11s, regional groups such as Gate (in Florida), and the like emphasize convenient location as their key competitive weapon. Supermarkets emphasize not only location but also product mix, promotion, and price as competitive tools. Specialty stores, on the other hand, must emphasize all retail mix areas, but above all the service-personnel category.

GEOGRAPHIC DIMENSION OF RETAIL COMPETITION

The fourth level of retail competition is the geographic dimension, as shown in Exhibit 2.1. Space that is used to locate in is identified as the market to evaluate the changes in competition. This is a very critical dimension in developing an effective overall retailing mix. In retail competition, the spatial dimension is easily construed as a key factor. Its impact reaches three distinct levels: location of town where the store is, location of the shopping complex of which the retail store is a part, and the actual location of the store.

Location of Town

Outshopping or intermarket flow of consumers is a critical consideration in retailing and, hence, will be discussed in greater detail elsewhere in this book. However, it must be stated at the outset that the town in which a retail establishment is located makes a difference. Some towns and some cities are more dynamic than others. Retailing in such locations may thrive. Citizens and consumers may be quite satisfied with the existing retail facilities. They may be quite loyal. Similarly, of course, people may be quite unhappy with the retailing facilities of the town. Their overall offering, the services, the prices, and so on may be unacceptable.

Location of the Shopping Complex

The spatial dimension becomes more critical and also more pronounced when clear-cut patronage preferences are exhibited or expressed toward a given shopping complex where the retail store is located or is considering to locate. This is true regardless of the specific nature of the retail complex. It could be a major shopping center, a local cluster, a regional mall, or downtown. Each of these complexes may have its own strengths and weaknesses that a retail establishment must consider very carefully before locating there and must assess periodically afterward.

If people, for a certain reason, prefer to go to a particular shopping complex and are loyal to that complex, this loyalty spills over to all of the stores in this complex. Thus, if the retail establishment manages to locate in this complex and fits into the total offering of this complex, it will enjoy a built-in advantage. Thus, location itself could provide a substantial degree of market superiority, leading to differential congruence for the particular retail store under consideration.

The retail location options are abundant and quite variable. First and foremost there is a spectrum of general location alternatives, such as the remainder of the country or the central city. Over and beyond this general selection, there are multiple options. Exhibit 2.8 illustrates some of these key options. The reader must realize that, in practice, for each one of the standard location options there are actually dozens of sites. In other words, there is more than one retail center and, if this is the option, any one of the existing or developing retailing centers can be a location choice.

A systematic analysis of retail options is displayed in Exhibit 2.8. These are self-explanatory options. There will be some references made throughout the book, and some of these options will be discussed later on, accordingly. It must be emphatically stated that there is no ideal location option. However, some options are better than others. The degree of differential advantage that is obtained by the retail store based on its location would depend on how adequate the location decision was regarding the capabilities, basic functions, and intended image of the store vis-à-vis the general offering and the image that the complex is projecting and, above all, the customers and their particular needs. The strengths and weaknesses of each alternative in Exhibit 2.8 are found in a typical retailing book that deals with the basics; for example, Mason, Mayer, and Wilkinson (1993); Berman and Evans (1995).

It must be realized that the retailer at any given time has multiple location options. It is critical to think that these options exist any time and not only at the beginning. The retailer may find it extremely important to move away from a location if the retailing complex with which it is originally associated is not doing well. It is always important to think that relocation, at times, may be necessary. Thus, location is a variable, not a fixed factor to reckon with, which was the case in the past. It is quite possible that a specific type of location may be appropriate at the beginning, but the store may need a different location as it matures and projects a different image.

Specific Site of the Store

In addition to the first two location dimensions, the town and the shopping complex, the specific site that the retail store occupies can be a powerful tool in enhancing the competitive advantage. A neighborhood fast-food store or an ice cream parlor are typical examples. Even though they may not have other distinguishing characteristics because of their very favorable locations, these stores may generate substantial profits. Almost by definition, if a retail store can fulfill its target market needs, it is bound to develop a competitive advantage.

As seen from our discussion thus far, the spatial dimension of retailing could yield competitive advantage leading to the development of differential congruence. Our discussion indicates that these three dimensions of location must be considered from the general (the location of the store in the city), to the specific (the exact site the store will occupy). Each of the three dimensions must be considered separately and thoroughly. Thus, as can be seen, retail location is a key consideration in analyzing retail competition.

Ability to locate wisely is a critical factor for multiunit retail-service chains. Major retailers, such as Kroger, Wal-Mart, International House of Pancakes, or Holiday Inn all have developed specific location criteria. Holiday Inn in the 1970s and 1980s was so good in selecting sites that Econo-Travel or Econo Lodge used to follow Holiday Inn without undertaking their specific location analysis. By locating next to Holiday Inn, they expected a major trickle-down clientele.

THE NATURE OF MARKET COMPETITION

Level 5 in Exhibit 2.1 is the broadest way of describing retail competition. The retailing sector can easily be described as the typical example of monopolistic competition. In this type of competition, all establishments are unique in their way, and no two establishments are considered exactly alike. Because of its merchandise mix, promotion mix, price mix, human resource mix, location, layout, and other unique features, each establishment has a certain power of monopoly. This monopoly power shifts the demand curve to the right and makes it less elastic. Shifting the demand curve to the right means that there will be more demand for the store's merchandise at different price levels than it would be under perfect competition. That monopoly power makes the demand curve less elastic implies that there will be more customer loyalty. This situation is displayed in Exhibit 2.9. As seen in Part A of the exhibit, demand is relatively elastic, depicted by the price change from Pm_1 to Pm_2. The increase from Pm_1 to Pm_2 brings about a more than proportionate decrease in the quantity sold (from q_1 to q_2).

As can be seen, the lost revenue area is much larger than the gained revenue area depicted by Pm_1, Pm_2, and L. In the B side of the exhibit, the same price increase from Pm_1 to Pm_2 creates a small decrease from q_1 to q_2 in quantity sold. The area depicting lost revenue is substantially smaller than the area indicating an increase in the revenue (Pm_1, Pm_2, and L). Thus, whereas an increase in price generated a net loss in the elastic demand situation, it generated a net increase in the revenues in the inelastic demand situation.

The customers of Gucci are more likely to be loyal than the customers of The Limited or 7-11. This means while Gucci is facing a relatively inelastic demand, The Limited or 7-11 is facing a relatively elastic demand. Though it should not be taken advantage of, Gucci can raise its prices a little and get away with it. On the other hand, The Limited and 7-11 will have a negative experience when they increase their prices.

Less than perfect competition is the realistic way of describing the milieu of retailing. No retailer would have perfectly elastic demand and, as each retailer succeeds in developing certain specific features that will create competitive advantage leading to differential congruence, each retailer would face varying degrees of demand inelasticities. The more inelastic the demand, the more the customers of the store think that the store has no substitutes, and the more they are loyal to it. This means the retailer has managed to establish some monopoly power. The ability to create this monopoly power indicates the retailer's ability to use the four layers of retail competition to its advantage to create differential congruence. The monopolistic competition setting provides an opportunity for retailers to use competitive managerial skills and imagination.

The conditions of monopolistic competition, discussed in any standard economics textbook, must be understood by the retailer who is functioning in such a setting. These conditions are (1) relative ease of entry, (2) relative ease of exit, (3) less than perfectly elastic demand function, (4) less than perfect information for the individual retailer, (5) the possibility of acquiring additional information, and (6) less than rational consumers with varying degrees of being informed (Samli 1989). Under these circumstances, the retailer must be able to establish its differential congruence for survival and prosperity.

The conditions of differential congruence, in less than perfect competition, do not have to be purely factual. For instance, Sears claims that it has the best car battery values for the price charged. This claim may not be totally factual in that there may be other buys that are equally reasonable or even better. However, through its special skills in advertising and promotion, if Sears can persuade the consumers to believe that its claim is factual, then the company can establish advantage over its competitors. Similarly, Wal-Mart may promote its selling of only American-made products. Again, if it can convince the consumers about this, then it will achieve advantage over its competitors.

Thus, in monopolistic competition of the retailing world, competitive advantage leading to differential congruence may be based on real or make-believe features that the retailers either have in reality or simply claim to have. Even if the retailer is bolstering make-believe features, if the retail establishment can do a convincing job and appeal to its target markets, it can be quite successful. However, if the claims are outrageously out of line, then the whole process could backfire. The skills to achieve competitive advantage, to know just how far to go and when to stop, are not equally available among all retailers. Such skills require know-how, information, and experience. Some retailers have such skills instinctively; others may never possess them. Successful retailing strategy is the outcome of these skills leading to differential congruence. There is no one best strategy. A small women's clothing chain may position itself as an upscale specialty store, may emphasize high fashions, and may charge high prices. On the other hand, a discount chain such as Wal-Mart can prosper by locating in small rural communities which major chains or other well-known merchants may avoid. Of course, this is how Wal-Mart started its spectacularly successful journey toward the number-one retailer's position (Berman and Evans 1995). These are different strategies and both of them work well.

DIFFERENTIAL CONGRUENCE: EVERY RETAILER'S CONCERN

As retailers understand that they are all different and that, if deliberately created, such differences can be extremely appealing to their intended markets, they are relying on their different ways of doing business to create customer loyalty. This is differential congruence. The term "congruence" here implies that what the customers think of themselves and of the retail store are congruent. As early as 1957, Alderson suggested that all marketers strive for differentiation, which implies that the retail establishment can manage its uniqueness through the strategic posture it maps out for itself. If the uniqueness that is claimed is understood and appreciated by the market, differential congruence sets in and success follows. Thus, the store's perceived image and the customer's self-image are congruent. The extent of this congruence is the critical factor. The stronger the congruence, the more unique the customers think of a retail establishment. Customers of Neiman-Marcus or Gucci are considered quite loyal. They come back again and again because they appreciate the uniqueness of these stores, they identify themselves with these stores, and their needs are satisfied in these retail establishments. It must be understood, however, that a neighborhood convenience store or a small specialty store can also command a high degree of loyalty because they plan and implement good marketing strategies that will please their customers.

The search for differential congruence in retailing is never ending. It is necessitated by the very nature of the milieu within which the retail firm has to function. The milieu is the particular corner of the market in which the retailer attempts to establish a niche. The retailer must be successful in providing unique goods and services for its target markets so that customer loyalty can be achieved.

INTERNATIONAL CORNER

It is reasonable to add one more layer to the five-layer analysis of retail competition presented in Exhibit 2.1: international competition. As millions of tons of raw materials, parts, and finished products flow internationally every day, retailing is facing a new type of competition and, of course, a new type of competitive advantage. Many products are produced in different parts of the world. Different varieties, different qualities, and above all, different price options are available to the retailer. In fact, some people predict that by the year 2010 retailing will truly be a global industry. Many retailers who entered the developing markets of the world in the 1990s are likely to be rewarded handsomely ("Performing a Reality Check" 1993). Countries other than the United States that happen to be substantially consumer oriented are experiencing rapid economic growth, causing a noticeable improvement in their living standards. They are becoming more consumer oriented. They also are experiencing similar trends as in the United States. Retailing is moving in the direction of more specialized stores, such as Home Depot, The Limited, and Toys 'R Us. As retailing is developing in these countries, retailers are making enough progress to become international. In 1991, the top 100 retailers in the world represented over $1 trillion in sales. A large majority of them expanded their operations outside their base country. European retailers have been more aggressive in this direction (Howard 1994).

Competition may come in different dimensions; foreign countries may compete with the retailers at home. They may buy into existing American retailers. They may compete by using their brand names and their store names. Competition may also be accelerated by those who are globally outsourcing.

SUMMARY

This chapter explores different dimensions of retail competition. All retailers, knowingly or unknowingly, search for differential congruence which would materialize only when the retail establishment is competing successfully. Retail competition is explored in this chapter within the constraints of five specific layers with multiple dimensions in some of the layers.

Retailers, first and foremost, must compete by using their respective retail mixes. Two key theories relating to retail mixes are discussed in the chapter. Retailers must understand the margin–turnover classification and the impact of this classification on retail competition. The second theory considered at this level of retail competition is natural dominance. This theory posits that there is an order in retail establishments' coming together and combining their efforts. This is the way they compete at certain levels and under different conditions.

Level 2 is related to competition with other retailers at the same level. Retailers compete with other retailers somewhat similar to them, by imitation, deviation, complementation, and innovation.

The third level of competition is competing with other retail stores that are quite different from the retail establishment in question. Intrainstitutional competition of this sort requires special attention because new retail institutions are emerging and the way they compete must be understood and coped with.

The fourth layer of retail competition deals with geographic dimension. Here the city, county, or the like where the retail establishment is located is critical. The retailer's association with other retailers by being part of a shopping complex is also critical. Finally, the specific site where the retail establishment is located is an extremely important consideration in retail competition.

Finally, the fifth layer deals with the economy within which the retailer functions. Monopolistic competition provides an opportunity to every retailer to establish a differential congruence by developing and implementing a successful retail strategy.

Exhibits

Exhibit 2.1
Multidimensional Retail Competition

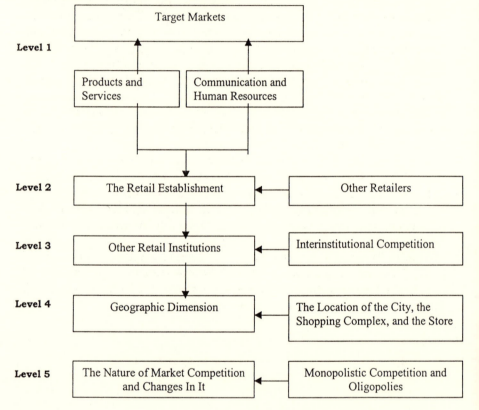

Exhibit 2.2
Margin–Turnover Classification

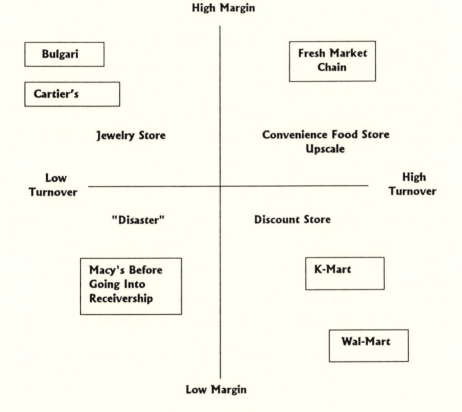

High Margin

Bulgari

Fresh Market Chain

Cartier's

Jewelry Store   **Convenience Food Store**
                          Upscale

Low   **High**
Turnover   **Turnover**

"Disaster"   **Discount Store**

Macy's Before Going Into Receivership   **K-Mart**

Wal-Mart

Low Margin

Source: Adapted and revised from Samli (1989).

Exhibit 2.3
**The Implications of Margin–Turnover Classification on a Store's
Marketing Strategy**

Store Level Strategy Factor	Low Margin High Turnover Stores	High Margin Low Turnover Stores
Merchandise Mix	Mostly pre- or self-sold	Sold in store
Assortment	Shallow and wide	Deep and narrow
Services Offered	Few or "optional with charge"	Many services
Location	Isolated or anchor in malls	Cluster or mall
Human Resources	Few people to help out	Many salespeople who are knowledgeable
Prices	Below the market	Above the market
Promotion	Emphasizing price	Institutional, image enhancing
Quality	Acceptable	Superior

Source: Adapted and revised from Mason, Mayer, and Wilkinson (1993).

Exhibit 2.4
The Price–Quality Continuum

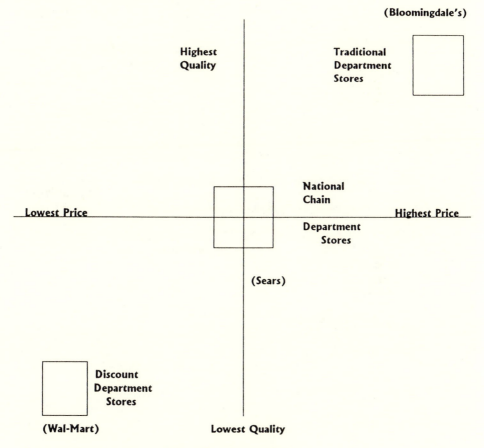

(Bloomingdale's)

Highest
Quality

Traditional
Department
Stores

Lowest Price

National
Chain

Highest Price

Department
Stores

(Sears)

Discount
Department
Stores

(Wal-Mart)

Lowest Quality

Source: Adapted and revised from Hirschman (1979).

Exhibit 2.5
Retail Market Structure

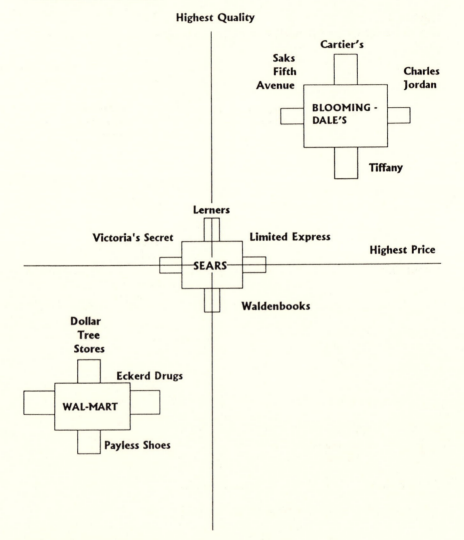

Highest Quality

Cartier's

Saks
Fifth
Avenue

Charles
Jordan

BLOOMING -
DALE'S

Tiffany

Lerners

Victoria's Secret

Limited Express

Highest Price

SEARS

Waldenbooks

Dollar
Tree
Stores

Eckerd Drugs

WAL-MART

Payless Shoes

Source: Adapted and revised from Hirschman (1979).

Exhibit 2.6
Merchandise Line Classification

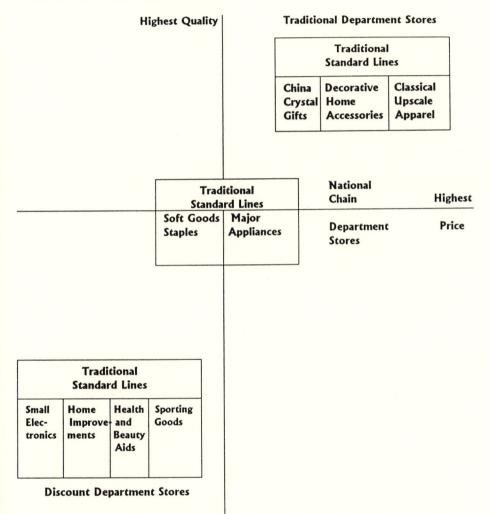

Highest Quality

Traditional Department Stores

Traditional Standard Lines		
China Crystal Gifts	Decorative Home Accessories	Classical Upscale Apparel

Traditional Standard Lines	
Soft Goods Staples	Major Appliances

National Chain

Department Stores

Highest

Price

Traditional Standard Lines			
Small Electronics	Home Improvements	Health and Beauty Aids	Sporting Goods

Discount Department Stores

Exhibit 2.7
Retail Mixes as Strategic Tools

Type of Retailer	Location	Product Mix	Service Personnel	Promotion	Price
Convenience Stores (7-11s, Gate, etc.)	+	-	-	-	-
Supermarket (Kroger, Publix, etc.)	+	+	-	+	+
Combination Stores (K-Mart)	-	+	-	+	+
Superstore (Albertsons)	-	+	-	+	+
Box (Limited Line) Store (Jewel T)	+	-	-	-	++
Warehouse Stores (Sam's)	-	-	-	-	++
Specialty Stores (The Limited, Gap, etc.)	+	+	++	+	+
Supercenter (Safeway, Fred Meyer)	+	+	-	-	++

Key: (–) no emphasis, (+) emphasis, (++) super emphasis.

Exhibit 2.8
Key Location Alternatives

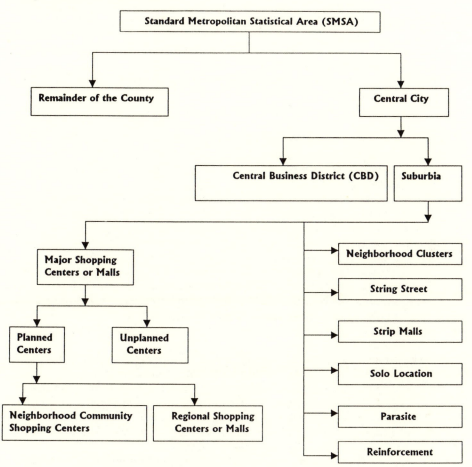

Source: Adapted and revised from Mason, Mayer, and Wilkinson (1993).

Exhibit 2.9
The Demand Function in Competitive Advantage

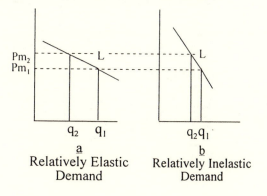

References

Alderson, Wroe. 1957. *Marketing Behavior and Executive Action*. Homewood, Ill.: Richard D. Irwin.

Berman, Barry, and Joel R. Evans. 1995. *Retail Management*. Englewood Cliffs, N.J.: Prentice Hall.

Flickinger, Burt P. III. 1995. "Wal-Mart vs. the World: Who Wins?" *Progressive Grocer* (April): 19.

Gentile, Richard J., and Anne Gentile. 1978. *Retailing Strategy*. New York: Labhas-Friedman Books.

Gist, Ronald R. 1968. *Retailing: Concepts and Decisions Making*. New York: John Wiley and Sons.

Hirschman, Elizabeth C. 1979. "Retail Competitive Structure: Present and Potential." In *Educators Conference Proceedings*, ed. Neil Beckwith et. al. Chicago: American Marketing Association.

Howard, Kim. 1994. "Global Retailing 2000." *Business Credit* (February): 22–25.

Kerin, Roger, and Richard Miller. 1981. "Diversity of Retail Operations and Financial Performance." In *The Changing Marketing Environment*, ed. Kenneth Bernhardt et al. Chicago: American Marketing Association.

Lazer, William, and Eugene J. Kelly. 1961. "The Retailing Mix: Planning and Management." *Journal of Retailing* 37 (Spring): 32–44.

Leah, Rickard. 1995. "Supercenters Entice Shoppers." *Advertising Age*, 20 March, 1–10.

Macke, Kenneth A. 1983. "Managing Change: How Dayton Hudson Meets the Challenge." *Journal of Business Strategy* (Summer): 78–81.

Mason, J. Barry, Morris L. Mayer, and Anthony Koh. 1985. "Functional Marketing Plan Development in Department Store Retailing." *Journal of the Academy of Marketing Science* (Summer): 161–182.

Mason, J. Barry, Morris L. Mayer, and Judy Wilkinson. 1993. *Modern Retailing*. 3d ed. Plano, Tex.: Business Publications.

May, Eleanor G. et al. 1986. "Marketing—in Concept and in Practice." In *Retailing: Theory and Practice for the 21st Century*, ed. R. L. King. Miami: Academy of Marketing Science and the American Collegiate Retailing Association.

McCune, Jenny C. 1994. "In the Shadow of Wal-Mart." *Management Review* (December): 10–16.

Miller, Richard. 1981. "Pathways to Growth in Retailing." *Journal of Business Strategy* 3: 25–35.

"Performing a Reality Check." 1993. *Chain Store Age Executive*, 15 December, 33.

Samli, A. Coskun. 1989. *Retail Marketing Strategies*. Westport, Conn.: Quorum Books.

———. 1996. *Information Driven Marketing Decisions*. Westport, Conn.: Quorum Books.

Whalen, Bernie. 1984. "People Oriented Marketing Delivers Lots of Dough for Domino's." *Marketing News*, 16 March, sec. 2, pp. 4–5.

Chapter 3

The Changing Retail Population and Managerial Implications

As we analyze retail population, its trends, and its composition, we learn much about this very dynamic sector. There are visible and critical changes, not only in the institutional makeup of retail establishments, but also in important characteristics as to their size, their numbers, their efficiency factors, their entries, as well as their exits. This chapter first discusses the trends in the retailing sector in terms of the numbers, sizes, and efficiency factors. Second, an attempt is made to identify and examine the factors that influence and perhaps cause these trends.

One of the most important considerations in the retailing sector is the number of retail establishments vis-à-vis the total population. As Exhibit 3.1 illustrates, the number of retail establishments per thousand population declined until 1982. Since that time, the number has been going up. As indicated in the exhibit, in 1992 it had come up to 10.45. This situation can partially be explained by at least three propositions:

Proposition 1: According to Samli (1993), the American economy has not been growing adequately. This fact, combined with much downsizing that went on between the early 1980s and mid-1990s, created almost a necessity for many people to go into business for themselves.

Proposition 2: As retailing becomes more cost conscious and primarily dominated by chains, stores become too cost conscious and somewhat removed from the consumer. This void is filled with small entrepreneurial retailers.

Proposition 3: Retailing activity in terms of total volume reached certain levels that support small independent retailers reasonably well.

Regardless of which of the three propositions is correct or whether all three contribute to the total number of retailers in existence, the bottom line is that the volume of retail business per store has been increasing steadily and proportionately. Exhibit 3.2 illustrates this point. As seen in the exhibit, sales volume per retail establishment became quite respectable around 1977 and kept on increasing in large proportions ever since. It must be realized that an average sales volume of $733 thousand (for the year 1992) is likely to yield a very good return on investment. This is discussed later on in this book.

The steadiness in the retail sales vis-à-vis per capita income illustrates the steadiness of the increase in the retail sales volume. Exhibit 3.3 indicates that since 1967 retail sales volume per person in America has been approximately one-third of the individual income. The chances are that this proportion is likely to remain approximately the same. Hence, major increases in overall retail sales would depend upon whether the economy is robust and growing steadily or whether it is slow and recessionary. As will be seen later on in this book, such analyses could provide estimates for national retail chains which could be used in their strategic plans.

Again, during the past twenty-five years (1967 to 1992), the portion of retailing that is attributed to the efforts of corporate entities has grown substantially. This may indicate that, with modern bankruptcy laws, it is safer for all businesses to incorporate. Simultaneously, it may indicate that even the very small entrepreneurial retailers are sophisticated enough to incorporate. Exhibit 3.4 illustrates, however, that around 1987 the dominance of corporate entities slowed down. By 1992, the percentage of businesses that were incorporated in retailing went down from 42.7 percent to 39.1 percent, and the total retail sales volume that is controlled by these corporate entities also went down, from 88.9 percent to 86.9 percent of the total (Exhibit 3.4). Obviously, the corporate entity in retailing controls a very large proportion of the total retailing volume. The question is if there are too many small incorporated retail establishments emerging and if these are not extremely vulnerable. Samli (1993) maintains that there are many such establishments. In the current turbulent American markets, these small businesses, unless managed properly, are extremely vulnerable, and many of them cease to exist in the short run. Thus, small-scale retail management must be taken very seriously and much needs to be done in this area.

One of the most important trends in the retailing sector is the number of multi-units and their relative share of the total retail sales volume. The topic is particularly important in terms of determining opportunities for individual independent retail establishments. Multi-units or retail chains provide opportunity for individuals to be managers of their specific business and still be exposed to successful business practices under the names of many chains. Many retail chains succeed this way.

Between 1967 and 1982, the number of multi-unit business establishments grew from 12.5 percent of all retail establishments to 21.6 percent of all retail establishments. Their number did not go up proportionately to the total number of retail establishments. Since 1987, the number of retail chains as a percentage of total retail establishments has declined (Exhibit 3.5). However, their share of the total retail sales volume kept going up. As seen in Exhibit 3.5, the relative share of retail chains of total retail sales has gone up from 39.7 percent in 1987 to 58 percent in 1992. It is clear that retail chains have been performing well. This point is also reinforced by the steady increase in sales per establishment. Perhaps, however, they may have reached a plateau in numbers. Does it mean that the total market is reaching a point of saturation? This remains to be seen. In the meantime, in general terms, the performance of retail chains must be analyzed further to determine if additional knowledge could be gained to make retailing performance more successful.

When compared with retail chains, independent retailers have not been performing nearly as well. Exhibit 3.6 illustrates this point. The share of independent retailers of total national retail sales has gone down from 60.4 percent in 1967 to 42 percent in 1992. In terms of dollars, their sales volume is still growing but only at a decreasing rate as it is compared to total retail sales volume and the sales volume of retail chains. Sales per establishment has slightly more than tripled between 1967 and 1992. However, if this is compared to the quadrupled sales volume of chains during the same period, it appears that retail chain stores are performing substantially better.

American retailing department stores have always been a critical institution to reckon with. Chapter 2 discusses that different department stores set the tone for natural dominance theory. In exploring the performance of department stores in the United States, one finds out that they have been holding their own. As seen in Exhibit 3.7, department store sales have captured about 10 percent of total retail sales in the country. The relative share of department stores of the total retail sales reached its highest point in the mid-1970s. In 1976, this share was over 11 percent. In recent years, this share is slightly under 10 percent. On the other end of the spectrum, discount stores have been challenging department stores. Unlike department stores, discount stores emphasize high volume, low cost, and fast turnover in selling a broad merchandise assortment at lower than typical market prices. They do not provide customer services. Their soft goods typically carry private brands (about 40 percent of their total sales), whereas their hard goods have well-known manufacturer brands (about 60 percent of their total sales) (Berman and Evans 1995). However, it also appears that discount stores are maintaining their relative share of the total retail sales volume, which is still smaller than that of department stores. But they have not taken over. They appear to have 6 percent of total retail sales volume.

Though they have gone through a somewhat dangerous period, and indeed some have called them an endangered species, department stores have managed to maintain their market share. They owe this outcome to their rather aggressive marketing strategies starting in the early 1990s. They have, in general, focused on their most dependable niches: upscale apparel and home furnishings. Within these niches, they manage to differentiate their merchandise and cut prices by developing private-label apparel offerings. They are also cutting costs by demanding more from suppliers (Chandler 1995).

If department store sales and particularly the growth rate in these sales were to be compared with that of discount stores, a somewhat different picture emerges. Exhibit 3.7 illustrates the overall growth rate displayed by the discount store's performance, indicating that this particular retail institution is faster on the move and really pushing department stores to the limit in terms of improving their differential congruence. Perhaps the net outcome of this competition is consumer benefit. It is certainly hoped that the competition will continue to benefit all parties concerned.

Department stores still have an important additional feature. They absorb a large proportion of total retail employment. Exhibit 3.8 indicates, however, that this share has gone down from 13.1 percent of the total in 1967 to 9.3 percent of the total in 1992. An important observation here is that in the 1960s and 1970s department stores had a sales force which represented a larger proportion to the total than their sales volume, whereas they have been pressured by discount stores and have settled at a total employment share which is slightly lower than their share of total sales. This indicates that they are reducing the services that they offer through people. This, in the long run, may not be in their best interest, since their regular customers expect knowledgeable, helpful, courteous, and informed sales and service people.

Many retail establishments deal with a variety of retailing services. Among these are travel agencies, retail banking, and eating and drinking establishments. Of all these establishments, perhaps eating and drinking establishments are the most important. Thus, some information is presented on the performance of this sector.

Exhibit 3.9 provides some important facts. Overall sales of eating and drinking places per establishment have always been slightly below the sales volume per establishment in retailing. This may indicate that they have to carry higher markups to survive. Another fact reported in Exhibit 3.9 is that the number of these establishments has been volatile. From a very large jump between 1967 and 1977, a significant decline between 1977 and 1982 is observed. Another significant jump is nullified again by a substantial decline during the two census periods.

On the average, however, their number and their total sales volume has increased substantially. This may indicate the societal need for having more eating and drinking places. With the steadily increasing number of two-paycheck families in our society, this segment of the economy makes this overall upsurge a necessity. There may be many new opportunities for entrepreneurs in this area. Assuming the presence of imagination, understanding of the market, compassion for consumer needs, and, above all, efficiency, this sector may prove to be an area of opportunity, not only in the United States but in many parts of the industrialized world. Chances are that, just as with the retailing sector, this sector will continue growing despite noticeable fluctuations.

RECENT TRENDS IN DIRECT MARKETING

In recent years, direct marketing has been a major development in American retailing. Direct marketing is a type of retailing in which consumers are exposed to goods and services through a nonpersonal medium. They order these services and products by mail, telephone (Berman and Evans 1995), or even by computer. Thus, any catalog, mail, television, radio, magazine, newspaper, or telephone directory exposure that stimulates customer action and triggers ordering certain products by telephone is direct marketing. The recent upsurge in this activity is due to cable TV channels in most communities, narrowly known as "telemarketing." The total volume in direct marketing is estimated to be over $140 billion. Almost ninety million people a year are ordering one or more items a year by phone. These numbers are growing, indicating that this form of marketing could be a threat or a boon for retailing. It certainly is a force to reckon with. What are the trends in society stimulating direct sales? What is it that direct marketing can do that may be considered a competitive edge?

A number of societal trends can be cited that support direct marketing. Among these are changing lifestyles, consumer demographics, increasing retail competition, technological developments, and new types of catalogs.

Changing Lifestyles

The lifestyles of consumers have been changing. First, the number of dual career or dual paycheck families is increasing. Second, longer commuting time to and from work for suburban dwellers and traffic congestion for urban dwellers limits available time for shopping. Third, at work place in recent years, work has become more and more demanding. The resultant longer work hours are changing lifestyles of consumers. Fourth, there are more single parent families than ever before. Consumers, as a result of their improving experiences with direct marketing and the increasing time pressures of their daily lives, are opting for the convenience of direct marketing.

Consumer Demographics

Today, more than ever before, there is a large group of senior citizens. These people may be more interested in direct marketing than fighting traffic and coping with crowds in order to shop. Also, there are more "latch-key kids" than ever before. The older groups such as early- and mid-teen youngsters have quite a bit of time and money. They are also likely to participate in some phase of direct marketing.

Increasing Retail Competition

Retail competition is increasing. In fact, there is a general tendency to believe that the field is somewhat overcrowded. As a result, some retailers have been exploring direct marketing so that they can tap relatively less tapped retailing markets. It has been estimated that in the early 1990s more than five thousand companies sent about ten thousand different catalogs through the mail (Berman and Evans 1995; Silverman 1989).

Technological Developments

Because of the computer-related technological revolution, it has become economical for retailers to handle direct marketing. They can process customer orders and shipments, manage inventories, and develop databases of prospective customers. Customers use videodisk kiosks, videocassette catalogs, and personal computers to interface with the seller and order products easily (Berman and Evans 1995).

New Types of Catalogs

Catalogs have been in retailing for decades. However, recently they are being changed in a dramatic manner. They are becoming "specialogs." Instead of one big catalog, companies are sending dozens of catalogs geared to specific target markets. For instance, there are specialogs for gifts, shoes, sports, intimate apparel, and the like. These new catalogs have been rather effective in communicating with the specific target markets and motivating them to purchase.

FACTORS INFLUENCING RETAIL TRENDS

As seen from the data presented in the first part of this chapter, the retailing sector presents various trends and patterns. There are many factors behind these trends that are responsible for their formation. In Exhibit 3.10 many of these factors are listed. They are categorized in two key categories, external and internal. The third portion of the exhibit deals with the key theories of retail institutional changes.

External Factors

Five key factors are identified in this category. They are perhaps the most important forces behind the formation of the key retailing patterns and changing practices: (1) economic conditions, (2) changing consumer needs, (3) sociological factors, (4) changing competition, and (5) political changes.

Economic Conditions

Economic conditions affect the retail population in two distinct ways. The first is through business cycles, and the second is through the cost of doing business under certain economic premises.

Business cycle development has profound impact on the business population (Samli 1964, 1993). Most of the businesses that fail or discontinue during the height of business cycles are retailers. Since our market system is somewhat less than perfectly competitive, we cannot, with any degree of certainty, know that the businesses that fail are weaklings. They are inefficient and, hence, their failure or discontinuance is a good thing. However, regardless of their efficiency or inefficiency, the critical consideration here is that many retailers disappear as the economy experiences recessions.

The cost of doing business in retailing has been going up steadily and sharply. A number of economic factors are responsible for much of this increase. Among these are the costs of developing and maintaining a modern store, labor costs, rental costs, and costs of carrying larger inventories that are important for retailers to maintain a competitive edge. Modern retailers are pressured to run stores with modern features in good locations. Most retailers, particularly small retailers, have problems with the physical facilities. Because modern retailers are forced to offer more new services, such as a liberal return policy, free delivery, packaging, free information, and the like, running modern stores is becoming more expensive. One of the additional issues for the modern retailer is to make sure that customers can find what they are looking for on the premises. In addition to air conditioning, background music, and modern displays, they have to develop elaborate internal layouts. All of these are costly propositions; however, they are also part of the overall image that the retail establishment is projecting.

Many retailers do not own their buildings and cannot make the necessary improvements while controlling costs. The land and buildings are mostly owned by absentee owners who are not in tune with the retailers' well-being.

Increasing need for sophistication on the part of the modern retailer has been forcing the improvement of human resources used in this sector. The labor costs, as a result, are also on the rise. Though not too widespread, unionization of retail personnel also shows adverse effects.

Despite all the knowledge in logistics and inventory control, the modern retailer has not been too successful in reducing inventories. Indeed, because of the competitive advantage they can produce, inventories have been increasing in size and in variety. Even though they have fewer units of the same kind, because, on the average, they carry greater variety, their total inventories are larger than ever before.

Changing Consumer Needs

A minor portion of this topic was discussed earlier in conjunction with direct marketing; however, there is much more to be said. During the past two decades, economic conditions deteriorated. Though inflation has not been too bad, the performance of the American economy has been rather discouraging. Incomes increased only for the upper 5-percent and upper 20-percent categories (Samli 1993). In real terms, the income of blue-collar workers has been declining. As a result, consumption patterns are changing. Some necessities are emphasized in purchases, such as food, medicine, and apparel. The growth has been rather unsteady for gift items, entertainment, eating and drinking places, and some other selected services.

The average education in the United States has been increasing. By definition, changing educational background brings about changes in consumption patterns and perceived needs. Studies have shown that higher levels of education enhance emphasis on housing, leisure time activities, other cultural undertakings, education, more sophisticated unique foods, and other selected services. Higher education does not seem to stimulate automobile and apparel purchases (Samli 1989). Thus, as education increases, the impact on retailing is not evenly distributed. Simultaneously, high school dropouts and certain ethnic groups have shown a decrease in their level of literacy. Such patterns also have direct and indirect impact on retailing.

American society is changing in terms of activities, interests, and opinions. Such changes have a direct impact on lifestyles. This impact, in turn, has direct and indirect influences on retailing. People who are loosely classified as cosmopolitan, jet-setters, Yuppies or Generation Xers have reasonably identifiable lifestyles and consumption patterns.

As mentioned, Americans have more leisure than ever before. With increasing leisure time and activities, demand for certain types of leisure-related products also increase. In the mid-1990s, for instance, the Jacksonville Jaguars and the Carolina Panthers entered the professional football scene. These two teams brought about a tremendous amount of retail sales of sports paraphernalia related to these two clubs. In addition to sports, there are other leisure and hobby-related products and recreational activities that have made significant changes in consumption patterns and resultant retail activity.

Perhaps the most significant changes in lifestyles have been in the area of values. These are health related: being more informal, being more efficiency conscious, and being engaged in do-it-yourself products and activities. Americans have become more cognizant of health-related products, food value, and exercise. Casual apparel and informal behavior have become mainstream rather than exceptional. However, buying power-driven tools saves time by being efficient. Thus, consumers can pursue other activities of higher priority. This total pattern has become a part of American life. Finally, almost all Americans have been involved in some aspect of do-it-yourself activity. Hence, home improvement centers in major discount or department stores as well as other similar businesses have been emerging.

It is extremely important that the modern retailer understand these trends and adjust business accordingly. All changes in the marketplace can and should be interpreted as opportunities.

Sociological Factors

The movement of the people in a society and their characteristics are particularly critical for the retailing sector. During the 1960s and 1970s, major population movements to suburbia gave rise to suburban shopping centers. Since then, population movements have been more in the direction from "rust belt to sun belt." In other words, people moved from the Northeast to the Southeast and Southwest. It is of the utmost importance that retailing follow the population movement. Without population, retailing cannot succeed. There is typically a high correlation between high density population centers and number of retailing establishments.

During the 1980s and 1990s, ethnicity emerged. Particularly in the Southeast and Southwest, Hispanic Americans, Asian Americans, and

African Americans have been influential in creating ethnic eating and shopping places. Retailers and managers of eating and drinking places need to satisfy such unique demands in order to survive and succeed.

The Nature of Competition

Retail competition has been changing. Three specific dimensions of change can be identified: institutional, spatial, and functional. Institutional changes in retail competition were primarily discussed in the first section of this chapter. Our discussion in this area indicated that large chains include small, individual retailers that must find new ways of catering to the consumer or cease to exist. Corporate entities appear to be stronger in terms of ability to survive as well as market share captured. Department stores are barely maintaining their relative share of the retailing market, and discounters are gaining ground. Simultaneously, direct marketing has been gaining momentum.

Spatial competition relates to the movement of retailing in pursuit of population. As discussed in Chapter 2, there are many location options for a retailer. However, the most dramatic spatial development in retailing has been the movement from downtowns to suburban shopping centers. This critical topic is discussed in detail in Chapter 4.

Finally, the third dimension of retail competition is the functional dimension. This, in essence, has two distinct paths, price competition and nonprice competition. Focus on price in retailing is perhaps as old as retailing itself. Small retailers with very few distinguishing features are particularly likely to take this route. Price competition also has been the key theme of discount stores, which claim to have the lowest prices.

Emphasizing nonprice competition, on the other hand, has led retailers to develop a large variety of practices that make shopping at their establishments easier and more pleasant. Among these are a large variety of customer services, different forms of store layout, special signs for customers to find what they are looking for, background music, a large variety of merchandise, special emphasis on displays, development of in-house brands, and specific concentration on certain well-known brands. All these are used to establish a particular store image and, hence, differential congruence.

Political Environment

The prevailing political climate is critical to retail population. Existing laws or local government's orientation may be in support of small retailers and, hence, the conditions can be favorable for small retailers to enter the market and survive. However, much of the time, both at the state and the federal levels, though lip service is given to small businesses, favoritism prevails toward large businesses. Large businesses receive a lot of favors from local communities, including better financing, a substantial degree of leniency if there are financial problems, and so forth.

Substantial increases in fees to practice in the downtown or permission to allow rents to go up exorbitantly may determine if retail establishments remain in the same location, relocate, or discontinue. Special assistance to small retailers also has significant impact on the size and performance of particularly small retail populations. Assistance to small business can be government instigated, government operated, or privately encouraged. Certainly all of these could take place simultaneously. As funds, advice, and suitable conditions are made available, the number and performance of small retail establishments change.

Perhaps one of the major trends during the past decade or so is the increasing number of foreign-made products in American retail stores. Apparel made in Italy and France, furniture made in Sweden or Norway, T-shirts and other cheap textiles from Pakistan and Sri Lanka, sports shoes from Taiwan and Malaysia, and many other products are imported and made available to American consumers. In fact, in some cases foreign companies or countries have developed their retail outlets. For instance, Payless Shoes exclusively sells shoes made in the People's Republic of China, and Benetton is owned by an Italian company. There are also many Chinese- and Japanese-owned retail outlets in Hawaii and California.

In Exhibit 3.10, emerging new opportunities are specified. These new opportunities and the factors influencing them are specific in the exhibit. Much of our discussion thus far has covered most of these areas. It is clear that the strength of the factor would indicate retailing opportunities. Prospective or existing retail establishments that are planning to expand must explore similar factors and corresponding new retail opportunities very carefully.

Internal Factors

Though there are many internal factors that are helping retailers to succeed, this section deals with the factors whose lack causes small retailers to fail or discontinue. These points are emphasized because they provide guidance for opportunities to enter the marketplace and survive.

Particularly in the case of small retailers, poor choice of location is rather common. As is discussed in various sections of this book, traffic is the backbone of a retailer. If, therefore, the retailer does not choose a good location for some reason, this creates an irreversible, negative impact. If the location does not provide the necessary traffic, the retailer's probability for success is seriously reduced. Of course, the retailer must understand that some locations are, by definition, not very good and others, in time, become poor. There was a time when fashionable downtown areas became old and dilapidated. Today, the same thing is happening to the earlier suburban shopping complexes. This aging process causes many failures among retailers and is subsequently reflected in total retail population.

Poor management is, unfortunately, a part of the freedom to enter the market. Whereas the American dream of being one's own boss is still a strong motivator, this also creates big problems if there is not enough managerial know-how. Freedom of entry is balanced with freedom of exit. Often, when inexperienced and inadequately prepared owner–managers start their businesses, they mismanage and fail in a short period of time. Along with poor management, poor marketing strategy must also be mentioned. Most of the time retailers, particularly small retailers, do not have a clear-cut marketing program specifying the implementation of a carefully designed marketing strategy. Without an effective marketing strategy, the retailer cannot succeed.

Undercapitalization and poor management go hand in hand. This is a common problem, particularly among small retailers. Less than adequate capital quite often leads to failure because the business cannot do what needs to be done to "delight" its customers. If large sums of money are to be made, large sums of money must be spent. Because of lack of capital, small retailers may be located in submarginal sites. They may have inadequate stocks, they cannot undertake critical promotional activity, and they may have inadequate internal layouts. Perhaps the most critical aspect of deficient capitalization is that even if the retail establishment is not undercapitalized at the beginning, if it does not manage the business well it becomes undercapitalized.

If a retail establishment is undercapitalized and mismanaged, it is logical that it also suffers from inadequate information. Most retailers, particularly small retailers, make decisions based on experience and gut feelings. Without proper information based on research, this situation can be detrimental. Not only is good information typically not available, even if it is, small retailers seldom know how to use it. As a result of the absence of good information and the knowledge to use it, the probability of making poor decisions increases.

Almost all of these internal factors lead in the direction of not having an adequate marketing strategy. Inadequate marketing strategy, in the case of many small retailers, refers to not having a marketing strategy at all. Regardless of size and kind of retailing it is engaged in, every establishment must have a game plan to survive, to fulfill its objectives, and to develop a competitive edge. This game plan that is being referred to as the marketing strategy is essential for survival in the marketplace.

THEORETICAL EXPLANATIONS OF CHANGES
IN RETAIL INSTITUTIONS

Thus far this chapter has presented a discussion of the factors influencing retail population changes. Though there are a number of trends behind these factors that are discussed, these trends have led in the direction of theory development. At a higher plateau, there are certain theories explaining the changes in retail institutions. Exhibit 3.10 lists seven such theories. Though these are constructed as theories, they may also be treated as working hypotheses. Such hypotheses provide a foundation for further research and exploration. However, regardless of whether they are called theories or hypotheses, these concepts attempt to explain why and how retail institutions and indeed the retail population change. Such general explanations can lead in the direction of providing guidance to retail decision makers as well as public administrators. In both cases, analyses based on these theories can lead to predictions that can be utilized for planning both at the enterprise level and in the public decision area. The seven theories are as follows: (1) the wheel of retailing, (2) natural selection in retail institutions, (3) the general–specific–general cycle, (4) the dialectic process, (5) the retail life cycle, (6) the Markin–Duncan adaptation theory, and (7) survival of the fattest (Gist 1968; Markin and Duncan 1981; Samli 1989).

The Wheel of Retailing

As early as 1960, Stanley C. Hollander popularized this concept which was originally posited by McNair (1958). This theory maintains that as new retail establishments emerge, they are typically characterized by low prices, low markup, few or no services at all, austere surroundings, and low status (Samli 1989). These characteristics can be attributed to changes in the value systems of consumers as well as to certain new cost-cutting procedures that will lower operating expenditures. As time passes, they change. They try to differentiate, they trade up their goods and services, they add new services, and they improve their layouts. Hence, they become high-price, high mark-up, multiservice establishments with expensive surroundings and high status. These changes make them quite vulnerable to new retail institutions, and the process continues. Exhibit 3.11 illustrates five such cycles in American retailing. The movement in these cycles is upward, and the institutions closer to the upper end of the cycle are closest to extinction. Studies indicate that similar cycles have also taken place in other countries. Perhaps the most important lesson from the wheel theory is that the retail population does and will always undergo change. Those who understand these changes keep on top of them and are more likely to succeed.

Natural Selection Theory

Charles Darwin's theory of natural selection among the living species has been recognized as the survival of the fittest. In retailing, according to this theory, retail establishments cannot cope with the major changes in their environments. They eventually lose their relative position and disappear. The problems with central business districts, the relative decline of department stores, or the disappearance of "ma and pa" stores are all the result of natural selection. This theory purports that this can happen to any and all retail establishments, in that no retail establishment is guaranteed survival or is immune to environmental change. This suggests that successful retail establishments, in order to survive, must regularly scrutinize environmental changes and must adapt to "unfriendly" changes and take advantage of "friendly" changes (Gist 1968; Samli 1989).

The General–Specific–General Cycle

This theory brings out the fact that American retailing vacillates from general to specific and to general again. For a period of time, consumers patronize general stores. Subsequently, a number of specialty stores enter the market and take away a large chunk of business from general merchandisers. But then general merchandisers enter the picture in a different format and regain a large portion of the market. This sequence of events continues. The American retail system has gone through a wide variety of offerings by retailers. This particular era was followed by a period of significant specialization. But then, with department stores, the period of a wide variety of offerings by general merchandisers reappeared (Hollander 1966; Gist 1968; Samli 1989). A number of forces appeared to stimulate the generalization end of the cycle. Among these are joining complementary lines (such as meat, grocery, and produce) by taking "sure" merchandise from other specialty stores; scrambling merchandise, which means also taking "risky" merchandise from stores and adding full lines from specialty stores; and, finally, growing shopping centers that are making one-stop shopping more plausible.

However, the increasing tendency toward austere behavior on the part of consumers, cost-cutting tendencies of businesses, downtown rehabilitation activity, and further scrambling of population may all be leading in the direction of more specific lines being sold in large quantities. This theory needs further exploration. The emergence of highly specialized small retailers in recent years may provide additional support for it.

The Dialectic Process

The Hegelian philosophy of dialectical logic, which is further reinforced by Karl Marx's "dialectical materialism," implies that there is always a three-stage development. First, there is a thesis; in our case, this may be a new retail establishment such as department stores. Second, an opposite of the thesis emerges, such as discount stores, which is called an antithesis. Finally, the third-stage synthesis emerges, in this case discount department stores. The process does not stop here. The synthesis of one phase becomes the thesis of another cycle and, hence, the whole process repeats itself by generating new types of retail establishments. The significance of this theory is that it provides a specific vision as to the changing institutional make up of retailing.

The Retail Life Cycle

The retail life cycle concept has existed for a long time also (Davidson, Bates, and Bass 1976; Markin and Duncan 1981; Samli 1989). This theory depicts a four-stage life cycle for retail institutions. The first stage describes the emergence of a new retail institution. This new institution may be significantly different from others. This new institution may be able to provide better products or services more efficiently and more conveniently, yielding customer delight.

The second stage deals with the experience of this new institution in terms of rapid growth, both of sales and profits. At this stage, widespread expansion of the new retail institution into new markets occurs. These new entrants are attracted to different geographic areas. At the end of this stage, favorable and unfavorable factors are balanced. Along with popularity and growth, there will be increasing cost pressures because of bigger and better staffs, more complex and expensive store management, more management control, and so forth. Emerging size and increasing number of stores are offset by diseconomies of cost-creating requirements.

The third stage is maturity. As growth and popularity are offset by costs, market share starts declining and managers do a less effective job in controlling their now-too-large organizations. Managers become rather unmotivated, since the excitement of challenge disappears. They also may lack the skills to manage their large organizations (Davidson, Bates, and Bass 1976; Samli 1989). By this time, they develop too much capacity, part of which becomes excess. Thus, the once new retail establishment is now vulnerable to mean, lean, efficient new entrants.

The fourth and final stage is death. The market share shrinks rapidly, profits dissipate, and the institution may approach extinction. It may be difficult, if not totally impossible, to reverse this undesirable cycle. However, some thinkers posit that early managerial action can avoid this particular stage (Markin and Duncan 1981; Dhalla and Yuspeh 1976).

The Adaptation Theory

Markin and Duncan (1981) have interpreted differently the Darwinian approach to the transformation of retailing institutions. They claim that these institutions maintain their existence through adaptation. They put forth a doctrine that the functional processes of retail institutions and their resultant transformation gain value only if they survive (Vanderpool 1973; Samli 1989). Those retailers that cannot adapt to the pressures of changing environments are replaced by those that are more adaptable. It may be further stated that it is this adaptation and accommodation on the part of retailers which explains why the retailing sector is extremely diverse. Hence, there is a wide variation among retailers. In addition to the Darwinian component, this theory also has a classical economic component in that the retail institution's functions are determined by the institution's structure which, in turn, is conditioned by market forces (Stigler 1951). Thus, when market forces change, retail institutions are pressured to adapt and accommodate or simply discontinue.

When a large number of firms change their functions or themselves because of market force pressure, the structure of the retail sector becomes modified. For instance, a series of social, technological, and economic forces caused the emergence of supermarkets and Radio Shack.

Thus, according to this theory, what survives is appropriately adapted and therefore fit, at least for the time being. This fitness implies that the retailers' functions and services are deemed valuable by consumers in the marketplace (Markin and Duncan 1981). The retailers' managerial ignorance and deficient capital investments, among other factors, can cause the fit retail establishments of today to become unfit tomorrow. Holdren (1959) maintained that many retailers operate under severe capital shortages. They also suffer from inertia and ignorance. Hence, many retailers are very vulnerable. This vulnerability can be compared with Wiener's (1967) theory of entropy. He posited that there is a statistical tendency for things that are left alone to become run down, to deteriorate, and to change. It stands to reason that retail managers must control or forestall these entropic tendencies in their institutions as they face critical market changes. This can be achieved by meeting requirements that the market is imposing on them and by tolerating minimum and maximum conditions that immediate ecosystems are imposing on them. Facing the requirements and showing tolerance are related to each other as well as to retail institutional survival.

The retail sector is composed of a large variety of establishments. Any one specific type of retail establishment is not singled out to be encountering optimum conditions or functions in its given habitats. Naturally, those that meet the requirements and display a high degree of tolerance are most likely to survive. However, it is not automatic that those who are meeting the requirements and displaying tolerance today will not experience entropic tendencies tomorrow.

Survival of the Fattest

As a variation of the Darwinian theory, this author presents the survival of the fattest theory. This position is based on the discussion presented in Chapter 2, in which the American economy is described as imperfect in terms of monopolistic competition. If the economy is less than perfect, it stands to reason that the businesses that fail are not necessarily inferior or inefficient but simply lacking in sufficient resources to survive. Similarly, a very large retail establishment such as Sears can survive adverse economic conditions for a long time even though it may not be efficient or profitable. Thus, the fat has a greater probability to survive than the lean, regardless of efficiency levels. Of course, this should not be construed to mean that large retailers never fail. They just do not fail as often as their small retailer counterparts.

These seven theories are not mutually exclusive. Rather, they overlap. Therefore, it is necessary for retailers and retail academicians to understand all of them so that they may be able to predict the future more effectively and understand the complex phenomenon of retail population.

INTERNATIONAL CORNER

Retailing, historically, has been local because it required knowledge of the needs and habits of specific groups of local consumers. With the opening of global markets, some retailers are forced to go global just to stay competitive. Modern technology can be used to better understand what customers like and what sells well in each store as if it were a local store. In so doing, stores can be differentiated by their merchandise assortment and their making the store more accessible and more effective in serving customer needs. Many retailers use electronic data interchange, transmitting data electronically to replenish their stocks automatically.

Among the top ten international retailers, supermarkets, diversified companies, department stores, discount stores, and hypermarkets are predominant. Hypermarkets are particularly noticeable in the global arena. These are very large department stores that include a supermarket (Howard 1994).

As many countries are making economic progress, they find themselves forced to develop their retailing sector and become more consumer oriented. Though in almost all countries retailers are typically very small (less than four employees), this situation is changing fast in those countries where there is noticeable economic progress. While small retailers in Japan comprised more than 85 percent of the total retail population in the late 1970s, their number was below 80 percent in 1988 (Czinkota and Woronoff 1991). It is too early to predict if large-scale international retailing will replace local small retailers. It is also not clear if some of the same trends that have been experienced in the United States will hold true in the world markets.

SUMMARY

This chapter explores various key trends that the retail population is experiencing, and the factors behind these trends. In order to understand retail population trends, two groups of variables are identified: external and internal. External factors include economic conditions, changing consumer needs, sociological factors, the nature of competition, and political environment. Internal factors include poor location, poor management, undercapitalization, inadequate information, and inadequate marketing strategy.

Finally, seven theories explaining retail population trends are presented in this chapter. These theories are the wheel of retailing, natural selection, the general–specific–general cycle, the dialectic process, the retail life cycle, adaptation theory, and survival of the fattest. Without an adequate understanding of the macro aspects of retailing population trends, a retailer may limit his opportunity for survival. The trends and patterns that exist in the marketplace are good indicators of opportunities. Capitalizing on these opportunities always enhances the probability of success.

Exhibits

Exhibit 3.1
Retail Establishments per 1,000 Population for Selected Census Years

Year	Establishments per 1,000 population
1929	12.13
1958	10.36
1982	8.29
1987	9.96
1992	10.45

Source: Computed from U.S. Bureau of the Census Data.

Exhibit 3.2
Retail Sales per Establishment

Year	Number of Establishments	Total Retail Sales Volume	Sales/ Establishment
1967	1,763,000	$310,214,000,000	$175,958
1972	1,912,871	457,400,000,000	239,117
1977	1,855,068	723,134,221,000	389,815
1982	1,923,000	1,065,900,000,000	554,290
1987	2,419,641	1,540,263,330,000	636,567
1992	2,671,715	1,959,100,000,000	733,274

Source: Computed from U.S. Bureau of the Census Data.

Exhibit 3.3
Per Capita Retail Sales and Per Capita Income

Year	Sales per Capita	GNP per Capita
1967	$1,561	$4,125
1972	2,242	5,791
1977	3,392	9,055
1982	4,592	13,694
1987	6,343	18,712
1992	7,680	23,665

Source: Computed from U.S. Bureau of the Census Data.

Exhibit 3.4
Incorporated Retail Establishments and Sales

Year	Number of Corporations	Percent of the Total Retail Establishments	Corporate Retail Sales as a Percent of Total
1967	451,050	25.6	68.3
1972	565,970	29.6	76.7
1977	695,440	37.5	79.8
1982	820,538	42.7	84.6
1987	1,031,910	42.7	88.9
1992	1,044,800	39.1	86.9

Source: Computed from U.S. Bureau of the Census Data.

Exhibit 3.5
Retail Chains

Year	Number of Establishments*	Total Sales (000,000)	Sales per Establishment	Retail Chains as a % of Total	Retail Chain Sales as a % of Total
1967	220,000	123,000	559,091	12.5	39.7
1972	291,000	201,000	690,722	15.2	43.9
1977	331,697	340,650	1,026,992	17.9	47.1
1982	415,000	567,000	1,366,265	21.6	53.2
1987	498,000	844,000	1,694,779	20.6	54.8
1992	528,179	1,136,607	2,151,936	19.8	58.0

Source: Computed from data presented in different issues of U.S. Department of Commerce, *Statistical Abstract of the United States*.

*Number of establishments depicts the number of chains and not the number of stores.

Exhibit 3.6
Independent Retailers

Year	Number of Establishments	Total Sales (000,000)	Sales per Establishment	Independents as a % of Total Establishments	Independent Sales Volume as a % of Total
1967	1,543,000	$187,214	$121,331	87.5	60.4
1972	1,621,871	256,400	158,089	84.8	56.1
1977	1,523,371	382,484	251,077	82.1	52.9
1982	1,508,000	498,900	330,836	78.4	46.8
1987	1,921,641	696,263	362,327	79.4	45.2
1992	2,143,536	822,492	383,708	80.2	42.0

Source: Computed from U.S. Bureau of the Census Data.

Exhibit 3.7
The Roles of Department Stores and Discounters

Year	Department Store Sales (000,000)	As % of Total Retail Sales	Discount Store Sales (000,000)	As % of Total Retailing
1967	$32,344	10.4	$16,561	5.7
1972	51,083	10.1	29,000	6.3
1977	75,909	10.1	39,211	5.4
1982	107,163	10.0	56,657	5.3
1987	153,679	10.0	74,648	4.8
1992	190,785	10.1	106,201	5.4

Source: Computed from data presented in different issues of U.S. Department of Commerce, *Statistical Abstract of the United States*.

Exhibit 3.8
The Share of Department Stores of Total Retail Employment

Year	Total Retail Trade Employment	Department Store Employment	As % of Total Retailing
1967	10,081,000	1,324,000	13.1
1972	11,705,000	1,594,000	13.6
1977	12,968,000	1,519,000	11.7
1982	14,468,000	1,515,000	10.5
1987	17,780,000	1,651,000	9.3
1992	18,407,000	1,719,000	9.3

Source: Computed from U.S. Bureau of the Census Data.

Exhibit 3.9
Performance of Eating and Drinking Places

Year	Number of Eating and Drinking Establishments	As % of Total Retail Establishments	Total Sales (000,000)	Sales per Establishment
1967	276,740	11.7	23,843	115,328
1972	359,524	18.8	36,868	102,546
1977	368,066	19.8	63,276	171,914
1982	318,765	16.6	104,400	327,514
1987	490,383	20.3	153,462	312,942
1992	433,608	16.2	202,078	466,041

Source: Computed from U.S. Bureau of the Census Data.

Exhibit 3.10
Factors Influencing Retail Trends

EXTERNAL FACTORS	EMERGING NEW OPPORTUNITIES
1. Economic Conditions	Emergence of discounting
2. Changing Consumer Needs and Lifestyles	Direct marketing; specialized retail opportunities
3. Sociological Factors	Slow deterioration of first inner city and then the regional shopping centers
4. The Nature of Competition	Increasing variety, price and service benefits for consumers
5. Political Environment	Emergence of more foreign-made products; more inner city minority retailing

INTERNAL FACTORS	
1. Poor Location	Location consultants
2. Poor Management	Management consultants; incubators
3. Undercapitalization	Various financial institutions
4. Inadequate Information	Emerging information technologies
5. Inadequate Marketing Strategy	Retail management consultants

THEORIES EXPLAINING RETAIL INSTITUTIONAL CHANGES

1. Wheel of Retailing
2. Natural Selection
3. The General-Specific-General Cycle
4. The Dialectic Process
5. The Retail Life Cycle
6. Adaptation Theory
7. Survival of the Fattest

Source: Adapted and revised from Samli (1989).

Exhibit 3.11
Wheel of Retailing in the United States

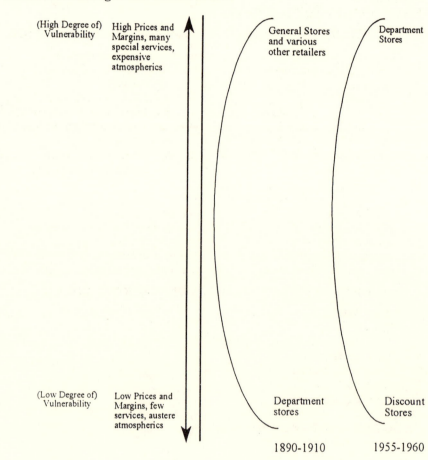

(High Degree of) Vulnerability · High Prices and Margins, many special services, expensive atmospherics

General Stores and various other retailers

Department Stores

(Low Degree of) Vulnerability · Low Prices and Margins, few services, austere atmospherics

Department stores

Discount Stores

1890-1910

1955-1960

Exhibit 3.11 (*continued*)

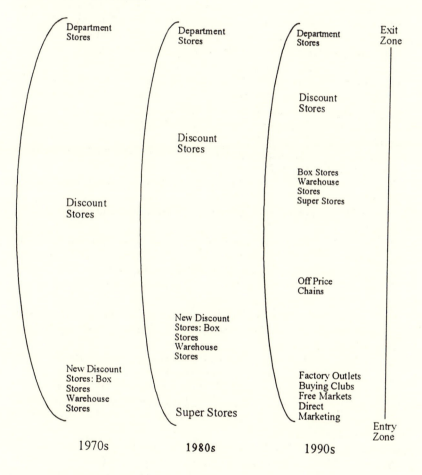

Department Stores	Department Stores	Department Stores	Exit Zone
		Discount Stores	
	Discount Stores	Box Stores Warehouse Stores Super Stores	
Discount Stores			
		Off Price Chains	
	New Discount Stores: Box Stores Warehouse Stores		
New Discount Stores: Box Stores Warehouse Stores		Factory Outlets Buying Clubs Free Markets Direct Marketing	
	Super Stores		Entry Zone
1970s	1980s	1990s	

67

References

Berman, Barry, and Joel R. Evans. 1995. *Retail Management*. Englewood Cliffs, N.J.: Prentice Hall.

Chamberlin, E. 1977. *Monopolistic Competition*. Boston: Harvard University Press.

Chandler, Susan. 1995. "An Endangered Species Makes a Comeback." *Business Week*, 27 November.

Czinkota, Michael R., and Jon Woronoff. 1991. *Unlocking Japan's Markets*. Chicago: Probus.

Davidson, William R., Albert D. Bates, and Stephen J. Bass. 1976. "The Retail Life Cycle." *Harvard Business* Review (November–December): 89–96.

Dhalla, Nariman K., and Sonia Yuspeh. 1976. "Forget the Product Life Cycle." *Harvard Business Review* (January–February): 102–122.

Duncan, Delbert J. 1965. "Responses of Selected Retail Institutions to Their Changing Environment in Marketing and Economic Development." In *Proceedings from the Conference of the American Marketing Association*. Chicago: American Marketing Association.

Gist, Ronald R. 1968. *Retailing: Concepts and Decision Making*. New York: John Wiley and Sons.

Holdren, Bob R. 1959. *The Structure of a Retail Market and the Market Behavior of Retail Units*. Englewood Cliffs, N.J.: Prentice Hall.

Hollander, Stanley C. 1960. "The Wheel of Retailing." *Journal of Marketing* (July): 37–42.

———. 1966. "Notes on the Retail Accordion." *Journal of Retailing* (Summer): 38–47.

Howard, Kim. 1994. "Global Retailing 2000." *Business Credit* (February): 22–25.

Markin, Rom. J., Jr., and Calvin P. Duncan. 1981. "The Transformation of Retailing Institutions: Beyond the Wheel of Retailing and Life Cycle Theories." *Journal of Macro Marketing* (Spring): 58–65.

McNair, M. P. 1958. "Significant Trends and Developments in the Postwar Period." In *Competitive Distribution in a Free High-Level Economy and its Implications for the University*, ed. A. B. Smith. Pittsburgh: University of Pittsburgh Press.

Samli, A. Coskun. 1964. "Role of Business Failures in the Economy." *University of Washington Business Review* (February): 53–63.

———. 1989. *Retail Marketing Strategy*. Westport, Conn.: Quorum Books.

———. 1993. *Counterturbulence Marketing*. Westport, Conn.: Quorum Books.

Silverman, Edward R. 1989. "Catalogers Turning New Pages." *Newsday*, 9 October, Business 8–9.

Stigler, George J. 1951. "The Division of Labor Is Limited by the Extent of the Market." *Journal of Political Economy* (June): 185–193.

U.S. Department of Commerce. Annual. *Statistical Abstract of the United States*. Washington, D.C.: U.S. Government Printing Office.

Vanderpool, Harold Y. 1973. *Darwin and Darwinism*. Lexington, Mass.: D. C. Heath.

Wiener, Norbert. 1967. *The Human Use of Human Beings*. New York: Avon Books.

Chapter 4

Intermarket Shopping Behavior

Retailing takes place within given spaces and population movements. As early as 1957, Alderson stated that marketing creates place utility. It is dependent on offering products and services in close proximity to consumers so that they do not have to travel long distances to search for them. Thus, a firm's location is an extremely critical ingredient to generate sales (Goldstucker 1965). These statements are particularly critical for retailers. Location is the lifeblood of retailing. Two principles move the retailers in the direction of location. First, retailers must follow the population to get as close to their customers as possible. Second, retailers, by grouping together and motivating customers, try to bring them to a specific location.

Though these two principles appear on the surface to be opposing each other, they need to be balanced. In other words, while retailers need to locate conveniently regarding their customers, they also expect certain population movements among different shopping complexes. Indeed, this movement of consumers from one shopping area to another makes a retailer's location "good" or "bad." In some cases, consumers travel from one urban complex to another. This means they go out of town to shop. Thus, intermarket shopping patterns must be understood by the retailer as a significant factor behind retail location decisions (Samli 1979, 1989).

Intermarket shopping behavior is generated and modified by a series of factors. These factors create the forces that underlie population movements among different shopping complexes. It is necessary for retailers to understand these forces and intermarket shopping patterns so that they can work with them. The intermarket shopping process may need to be stopped. A series of retailers may get together and try to reserve the prevailing patterns or reinforce them. Perhaps the most important point this chapter makes is that the location of a retailer is not as rigid as it once was. It must be evaluated vis-à-vis changing intermarket shopping patterns and, if necessary, changed accordingly.

This chapter presents a construct which is a general model explaining inshopping and outshopping patterns. It examines a community's staying with the local retailing facilities or going outside the community. Any retailer must have an understanding of the forces causing intermarket shopping patterns.

RETAIL GRAVITATION MODELS

During the past three decades or so in the United States, the emergence of major shopping centers has been observed. One sees, for example, the sudden development of a major shopping center or a mall, perhaps located among three small towns. Typically this shopping complex is not equidistant from these three towns. According to retail gravitation models, the location of this facility can be optimized. These models are among the oldest marketing theory development attempts. The law of retail gravitation was developed on the basis of J. W. Reilly's analysis of retail trade (1931). It subsequently has been referred to as Reilly's Law. It was later revised in an attempt to establish optimal locations and to improve the measurement of retail trade among cities (Converse 1949).

In Reilly's (1931) words, "Two cities attract trade from any intermediate city, or town in the vicinity of the breaking point approximately in direct proportion to the population of the two cities and in inverse proportion to the square of the distances from these two cities to the immediate town."

This particular concept is analyzed more closely in Chapter 6. Subsequent attempts to revise Reilly's Law were in the direction of determining the breaking point of intercity shopping. This breaking point was approximated between any two cities by the intermediate community that divides its retail trade shopping equally between these two cities. If properly used, such an approach could establish a town's normal trading area (Converse 1949). Though other subsequent studies did not reject this law, it did not provide enough direction and guidance to communities, Chambers of Commerce, or other local development groups to understand and use retail gravitation as the basis for the development of local retail complexes. This particular law can only be used to explain the dynamics of intermarket purchase behavior in very general terms. However, later on, additional models were generated and used as planning tools for regional shopping-center location, which was a critical concern, particularly in the 1960s (Schwartz 1963).

Once again, questions concern issues of how cosmopolitanism and outshopping relate. Who are the people that are most likely to be engaged in shopping out of the home-front retailing facilities? And what are the types of products and services that they typically seek? These questions were not completely answered. The answers to these and similar questions are the qualifiers for Reilly's law in evaluating the nature and the scope of intermarket shopping behavior. More knowledge of these issues would enable local planners to improve their retail trade facilities in a macro sense, and for individual retailers in a micro sense.

RETAIL LEAKAGES AMONG MARKETS

Having retail gravitation implies that consumers are shopping out of their home fronts. In other words, they are outshopping and thereby creating intermarket leakages. In earlier research efforts, outshopping was defined as the frequency of going out of town to shop, as reported by the respondents themselves (Thompson 1971). On this basis, an outshopper is the person who shops out of town at least once a year. Herrmann and Beik (1968) also used frequency figures to identify outshoppers, but stipulated that the shopping trip must be in at least a five-mile radius of the downtown shopping area of the home town. Reynolds and Darden (1972) concluded that there should be at least twelve out-of-town shopping trips per year to consider the individual an outshopper. Instead of frequency or the distance traveled, Samli and Uhr (1974) maintained that the relative proportion of purchases as a percent of total should be the criterion indicating outshopping. They divided consumers into four groups: heavy outshoppers, who buy 75 percent or more of their purchases out of town; outshoppers, who buy 50 to 74 percent of their purchases out of town; inshoppers, who buy 50 to 74 percent of their purchases in town; and, finally, loyal inshoppers, who buy 76 to 100 percent of their purchases in town (Samli and Uhr 1974).

Though earlier studies indicated that there are significant differences between inshoppers and outshoppers in respect to age, income, and education (Reynolds and Darden 1972), other studies did not support these findings conclusively. Thus, the makeup of the people who are heavily engaged in outshopping and their purchase behavior are still not well known. Studies have used demographics, psychographics, and psychometrics as the bases of analyses in these earlier efforts. There is obviously much which remains to be done in this area.

POPULATION CHARACTERISTICS

Earlier studies of intermarket shopping emphasized the premise that populations are not homogeneous. They attributed outshopping to the existence of different groups in different populations. Among others, they posited that certain groups that are highly educated, more sophisticated, and have higher incomes are more likely to be engaged in intermarket shopping. This approach, however, is less than adequate in explaining the outshopping phenomenon that is prevalent in small communities where populations are likely to be more homogeneous than in large metropolitan areas.

In an earlier study by Samli, Riecken, and Yavas (1983), it was shown that actual retail sales in small communities are much less than their estimated potentials. The potentials were estimated by the Sales and Marketing Management Buying Power Index, which is discussed in Chapter 6. However, larger communities realized actual retail sales that are far beyond their estimated potentials. Thus, in general terms, larger communities have certain drawing power over the citizenry of neighboring smaller communities. These analyses necessitated a better explanation for the outshopping phenomenon by developing a general model (Samli 1989).

A MODEL OF INTERMARKET SHOPPING

A general model of intermarket shopping is developed here. The model is based not only on the previous research findings but on some other finer points of consumer behavior and store patronage knowledge. Such a model must start with consumers' needs and wants for both goods and services relating to the retailing sector. These needs are primarily formulated by the lifestyles of the consumers. Lifestyles surface in the form of a number of variables, among which the following are particularly critical (Berman and Evans 1995):

- Cultural values and norms that are important to consumers
- Consumers' social class
- Reference groups with which they identify themselves
- Class consciousness
- Time utilization preferences
- How important the goods and services are that are being offered
- Social status and performance

All these and others are related to three key modifiers of lifestyles: background, education, and sophistication.

Lifestyle characteristics have been explored as determinants of outshopping patterns (Reynolds and Darden 1972; Herrmann and Beik 1968; Darden and Perrault 1976; Samli 1989). The lifestyle typologies or configurations may lead the individual to patronize certain retail facilities. If, for instance, the individual's lifestyle is likely to be specified as "jetsetter," then that person is not likely to patronize any other retail establishment than upscale retail stores. Similarly, if the lifestyle is likely to describe the individual as a member of Generation X, then clothing that is made of recycled materials and sold in second-hand stores is more likely to be purchased. By the same token, the individual's brand preference is formulated by lifestyle. This factor, as discussed elsewhere in this book, is crucial in the individual's store selection process. If, for instance, a female consumer's preference is the Liz Claiborne brand of apparel, she will patronize an apparel shop that will carry this line of products. Similarly, Guess jeans may attract many young teenage girls who may, for this reason, frequent certain trendy apparel shops.

Background of the individual is one of the factors conditioning or modifying lifestyle. It may be a critical determinant of outshopping behavior. For instance, if an individual is used to shopping in large shopping centers or regional malls and is accustomed to choosing from a very large variety of choices, that background is likely to influence that individual's lifestyle. Where the individual grew up is quite critical. If, for instance, the individual has lived primarily in large communities and currently resides in a large community, outshopping may not be a consideration. However, if the same individual is reassigned to live and work in a small community, then outshopping becomes a critical factor, since that individual tries to seek out shopping facilities that he or she is used to in neighboring towns. Samli (1977) found that people who are used to large communities but who presently live in small communities tend to outshop. If, for instance, a professional person were to be transferred from San Francisco, California, to Murphysboro, Illinois, he or she would seek out the nearest large shopping center to shop, regardless of distance. Such an individual may go as far as St. Louis, which is about 100 miles away from Murphysboro. Maintaining a certain lifestyle, therefore, is partly a function of the background of the individual. It must be realized that in time the background changes. Exhibit 4.1 illustrates this phenomenon. A series of outshopping studies has indicated that more than 30 percent of the people who lived in a small town less than two years are prone to outshopping. By the same token, if they have lived in the small town more than ten years, they do not have the same zeal for outshopping. In fact, in time they may become loyal inshoppers.

Part of this transition has to do with the changing retailing sector in the town itself. If the local retailers are sensitive to outshopping tendencies of consumers, they may attempt to improve their overall services. Exhibit 4.2 illustrates one such experience. After the earlier study, the town's merchants got together and discussed the study findings. There appeared to be critical deficits, particularly in selection, prices, and parking areas. Product knowledge, service, and appearance also fared less than 50 percent. Some seven years later, a similar study indicated that significant improvement was displayed by the local merchants. The deficient areas, particularly selection, improved significantly. There still appeared to be areas remaining that needed improvement, such as prices, product knowledge, and parking, but obviously the local merchants were on their way toward stopping the outshopping tendencies of local consumers.

In the general model, in addition to the backgrounds, degrees of education and sophistication are shown as modifiers of lifestyle. The degree of education implies the consumers' alertness to good quality merchandise, their ability to identify good values, and their openness to new products and innovations (Hart 1989). The degree of sophistication, though related to education, relates to preference on the basis of rational and far-reaching knowledge. For instance, sophisticated consumers not only may know the major brands, but also may know the orientation of these manufacturers toward the environment.

Once needs and wants are basically established in the minds of consumers, primarily an unconscious process, Exhibit 4.3 illustrates that there are two modifiers of these needs and wants: attractiveness of other shopping complexes and satisfaction with local retailing facilities.

Attractiveness of Other Shopping Complexes

Attractiveness of other shopping complexes is primarily related to the general knowledge of the consumers who are prone to outshopping as to the offering of other shopping complexes and the quality of the offering. Again, this information is filtered through the consumer's degrees of education and sophistication. Part of this attractiveness is related to net promotional efforts of other shopping complexes and the local shopping complexes. If other complexes out-promote the local facilities, the attractiveness of these outsiders is likely to increase (Exhibit 4.3). Attractiveness is further related to proximity.

Proximity of Other Complexes

Closely related to attractiveness is proximity. If the other complexes, in the minds of consumers, are too far, then the attractiveness is reduced or nullified. These facilities are not perceived as viable alternatives to the home shopping complexes.

Satisfaction with the Local Retailing Complexes

The degree of satisfaction is already touched upon in this chapter. An overall improved sentiment toward local shopping facilities is most likely to cut down the outshopping tendencies of consumers. Outshopping, therefore, is very strongly influenced by what merchants (both in town as well as out of town) are doing.

GENERAL IMPLICATIONS

The spatial dimension of marketing is closely related to consumer movements and retailers' behavior in an effort to delight their customers. If the population movements in search of goods and services within markets are understood, then the retail location decisions can be optimized in terms of both the retailers' benefit and the consumers' satisfaction. If retail locations are congruent with consumer movements and the level of satisfaction of consumers with the local retailing facilities, then consumers will patronize these facilities and will benefit from having their needs taken care of. Understanding intermarket purchase behavior, therefore, provides a special insight into perhaps one of the most important aspects of retailing, the spatial dimension.

But as populations increase or move around, intermarket purchases become more noticeable and, for individual retailers, this situation can become unsurmountable. No one retailer can singlehandedly reverse intermarket consumer movements. However, organized and coordinated retailers can make a significant impact. In recent years, more small communities are emerging throughout the country, and their retail facilities are less and less consistent with each other and among themselves. As these facilities are more fractured, in that they do not offer all the necessary goods and services, outshopping increases. The general lack of planning and coordination in the development of retail complexes is not helping individual retailers.

If there are not studies such as the one illustrated in Exhibit 4.2, and if there is no leadership that provides direction to local retailing facilities, then retailers that are mushrooming somewhat indiscriminately will have difficulty fulfilling their goals, delighting their markets, and surviving. Even if there is help offered by the local Chambers of Commerce, retail merchants associations, or city or town planning offices, many retail merchants do not quite benefit. This is at least partially due to not having any coordination and leadership among the retailers. Much of the time these merchants are very independent people and are not trained for team play. In other words, these merchants do not know how to collaborate with some other merchants who are, otherwise, competitors. However, without such collaboration they cannot counteract the outshopping tendencies of consumers.

It must be pointed out that between the two studies mentioned in Exhibit 4.2, the outshopping dollars were estimated to have dropped by one-third. The reason was the merchants' efforts to satisfy customers guided by the local town's planning office, Chamber of Commerce, and local university. Thus, if local retailers can remain sensitive to local consumer needs, monitor the increase or decrease in outshopping, coordinate their efforts to cater to customer needs, organize efforts to periodically determine consumer satisfaction, and learn to work together to promote the community, the results are likely to be very satisfactory for all parties concerned.

It is implied throughout our discussion that the model presented here is not exclusively a macro model, in that it takes into consideration the micro factors such as consumers' lifestyles, their backgrounds, and the like. Our knowledge about inshopping and outshopping is still less than adequate. For instance, what happens if out-of-town shopping conditions improve faster than in-town shopping facilities? How much advertising should in-town shopping facilities and out-of-town shopping facilities undertake? Is outshopping a relative or an absolute concept?

However, one particular point stands out. Local retailers must know the attitude of their customers toward their retail offerings. They furthermore must be aware of the nature and the scope of prevailing outshopping activity. In other words, they should undertake research projects systematically and periodically.

The impact on the individual retailer must particularly be kept in mind. If, for instance, the local auto parts retailer realizes that most of the people in town are going out of town about twenty miles to a regional shopping center to purchase auto parts and related products, then that retailer needs to examine its offering, prices, and service. But, by the same token, if outshopping is stopped and reversed, all local retailers will benefit. There is, therefore, an important area of *synergism* that needs to be cultivated by the local group of retailers.

A new entrant to the retailing scene must have an understanding of the intermarket shopping behavior of local consumers. Without such knowledge, assessing market opportunities is almost impossible.

INTERNATIONAL CORNER

At present, international tourism and tourism-related industries are the second largest employer in the world. The tourism industry is expected to grow in very substantial proportions. In one sense, tourism can be considered some form of outshopping. Certain groups of tourists are likely to shop around and buy certain products. They may be searching for internationally known retailers or internationally recognized brands. Other types of tourists particularly go for local products that are not at all available at home. In either case, international retailing appears to be very promising. It is important for retailers to understand tourism-related outshopping and use it to their advantage.

There is one other type of international retailing that is pertinent to our topic here. That is retailing in national border cities or towns. Some locations are free trade areas, where there are no tariffs or taxes and, hence, products are cheaper and more plentiful. In such cases, people from neighboring areas and regions are likely to outshop. Once again, retailers must understand the nature and the magnitude of all this potential.

SUMMARY

The general topic of this chapter, outshopping, provides a valuable understanding of the importance of spatial dimension in retailing. Earlier intermarket purchase studies have been too general and primarily macro in scope. These studies fall short in explaining the reasons behind outshopping behavior and the nature of such behavior. Earlier micro studies, on the other hand, explained the whole phenomenon by the differences in populations. They identified the characteristics of outshoppers and stated that the young, highly educated professional consumers with relatively higher income are primarily the care group in the outshopping process. In this chapter, we posit that outshopping is even more prevalent in small communities, where the populations are rather homogeneous. In order to explain the reasons behind this widespread phenomenon, a general model is presented. The model is both macro and micro in nature. In the model it is posited that outshopping is primarily a function of the degree of satisfaction or dissatisfaction with the local shopping facilities.

Exhibits

Exhibit 4.1
Tenure in the Small Community

Tenure in Small Town	Heavy Outshoppers	Outshoppers	Inshoppers	Loyal Inshoppers
Less than 2 years	Large proportion	Medium proportion	Small proportion	Small proportion
2 to 5 years	Medium proportion	Large proportion	Medium proportion	Small proportion
5 to 10 years	Medium proportion	Medium proportion	Large proportion	Small proportion
More than 10 years	Small proportion	Medium proportion	Large proportion	Large proportion

Source: Samli and Uhr 1974; Samli 1979; Samli 1977; and other unpublished studies by the author.

Note: Large proportion is larger than 30 percent; medium proportion is between 20 and 30 percent; small proportion is less than 20 percent.

Exhibit 4.2
Attitude toward Local Shopping Facilities

	First Study	Second Study (7 years later)	Net Change
Quality of Goods	67.8	69.0	1.2
Selection	-14.8	9.8	24.6
Prices	-13.3	-2.0	11.3
Product knowledge of salespeople	25.7	40.5	14.8
Ease of shopping	59.3	72.8	13.5
Ease of parking	-16.8	31.7	14.9
Service	44.8	53.3	8.5
Appearance of stores	48.0	58.3	10.3
Store hours	51.7	62.7	9.0

Source: Adapted and revised from Samli (1979).

Note: Figures are calculated by subtracting "poor" and "very poor" categories from "good" and "very good" categories on a five-point scale.

Exhibit 4.3
A General Model of Intermarket Purchase Behavior

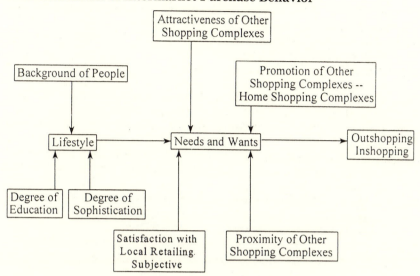

Source: Adapted and revised from Samli (1989).

References

Alderson, Wroe. 1957. *Marketing Behavior and Executive Action*. Homewood, Ill.: Richard D. Irwin.

Berman, Barry, and Joel R. Evans. 1995. *Retailing Management*. Englewood Cliffs, N.J.: Prentice Hall.

Blackney, Vicki L., and William S. Sekely. 1993. "A Product Specific Examination of Shopping Mode Choice." *Journal of Marketing Management* (Spring–Summer): 23–38.

Casparis, R., Jr. 1969. "Shopping Center Location and Retail Store Mix in Metropolitan Areas." *Demography* 6 (May): 125–131.

Clark, W. A. V. 1968. "Consumer Travel Patterns and the Concept of Range." *Annals of the Association of American Geographers* 58 (June): 386–396.

Converse, P. D. 1949. "New Laws of Retail Gravitation." *Journal of Marketing* 14 (October): 378–384.

Darden, William R., John J. Lennon, and Donna K. Darden. 1978. "Communicating with Interurban Shoppers." *Journal of Retailing* 54 (Spring): 51–64.

Darden, William R., and William D. Perrault. 1976. "Identifying Interurban Shoppers." *Journal of Marketing Research* 13 (February): 81–88.

Getis, Arthur. 1963. "The Determination of Location of Retail Activities with the Use of a Map Transformation." *Economic Geography* 38 (January): 14–22.

Goldstucker, Jac L. 1965. "Trading Areas." In *Science in Marketing*, ed. George Schwartz. New York: John Wiley and Sons.

Hart, Peter. 1989. "Showcase of Shoppers." *Wall Street Journal*, 19 September, 84.

Herrmann, Robert D., and Leiland L. Beik. 1968. "Shoppers' Movement Outside Their Local Retail Area." *Journal of Marketing* 32 (October): 45–51.

Huff, David L. 1964. "Defining and Estimating a Trading Area." *Journal of Marketing* 28 (July): 24–29.

Lillis, Charles M., and Delbert I. Hawkins. 1974. "Retail Expenditure Flows in Continuous Trade Areas." *Journal of Retailing* 50 (Summer): 30–42.

Mazze, Edward M. 1974. "Determining Shopper Movement Patterns by Cognitive Maps." *Journal of Retailing* 50 (Fall): 43–48.

Reilly, J. W. 1931. *The Law of Retail Gravitation*. Austin: University of Texas Press.

Reynolds, Fred D., and William R. Darden. 1972. "Intermarket Patronage: A Psychographic Study of Consumer Outshopping." *Journal of Marketing* 36 (October): 50–54.

Reynolds, Fred D., William R. Darden, and Warren S. Martin. 1974. "A Multivariate Analysis of Intermarket Patronage: Some Empirical Findings." *Journal of Business Research* 2 (April): 193–199.

Samli, A. Coskun. 1977. *A Look at Consumption Patterns in Blacksburg, Virginia 1976–1977*. Blacksburg, Va.: Virginia Polytechnic Institute and State University Extension Division.

———. 1979. "Some Observations on the Intermarket Shopping Behavior as It Relates to the Spatial Dimension." *AMA Educators Conference Proceedings*. Chicago: AMA.

———. 1989. *Retail Marketing Strategies*. Westport, Conn.: Quorum Books.

Samli, A. Coskun, G. Riecken, and U. Yavas. 1983. "Intermarket Shopping Behavior and the Small Community." *Journal of Academy of Marketing Science* (Winter): 43–52.

Samli, A. Coskun, and Ernest B. Uhr. 1974. "The Outshopping Spectrum: Key for Analyzing Intermarket Leakages." *Journal of Retailing* 50 (Summer): 70–78.

Schwartz, George. 1963. *Development of Marketing Theory*. Cincinnati: Southwestern.

Thompson, John R. 1971. "Characteristics and Behavior of Outshopping Consumers." *Journal of Retailing* 47 (Spring): 70–80.

Chapter 5

Downtowns, Shopping Centers, and Local Clusters: The Retail Evolution

As we analyzed intermarket shopping behavior in Chapter 3, it became clear that the population is mobile and the retailing sector must remain in close proximity to the population. As retailing moves from intramarket to intermarket situations, it is moving from one pivotal locale, central business districts (CBDs) or downtown, to another pivotal location, shopping centers. In this retail evolution, the movement can also be described as from unplanned to planned.

As the society changes, consumer behavior also changes. With the alterations our society is currently undergoing, retail competition adjusts to changes in consumer behavior. During the past twenty-five years or so, downtowns throughout the country have experienced difficult times. However, shopping centers are beginning to experience the same type of hardship. Both institutions are losing sales, and shopping centers are beginning to look like ghost towns, or the way some downtowns looked for a long time.

Both CBDs and shopping centers are in desperate need of carefully planned, deliberate marketing activity. CBDs in particular need to be revitalized fast. In the meantime, small neighborhood shopping centers, or strip malls, are mushrooming. In the opinion of many, the retailing sector is overbuilt. These considerations point to the fact that both downtowns and shopping centers need to do a better job of marketing themselves for survival. This chapter explores the specific problems of downtowns and shopping centers, and then explores how retailing can be more responsive to population movements and to changing consumer needs.

CBDs ARE IN TROUBLE

Historically, American retailing revolved around downtowns. In many parts of the world, this is still the case. CBDs are the focal point of retailing activity. However, in the United States, downtowns historically emerged as an "amorphous and uncoordinated conglomeration of groups of stores" (Samli 1989, 61). There were never plans for CBDs, their general offerings, their appearance, their general appeal, or their overall marketing activity. The plight of downtowns can be analyzed in terms of five major trends: (1) population dispersion, (2) uncoordinated marketing, (3) emergence of shopping centers, (4) decreasing accessibility, and (5) inertia.

Population Dispersion

The American population has been very mobile. It has been stated that one-fifth of all Americans move every year. The major population movements have been from the Northeast to the Southwest, and from the South to the Southeast. That is, primarily from rust belt to sun belt. Equally important, people moved from the city to the suburbs. Thus, the American population is not only mobile, but also dispersing. As the population disperses, the retailers need to move also to remain reasonably close to the population. But dispersing markets makes it difficult for retailers to stay abreast of consumers and to satisfy their needs. In general terms, as populations move out, downtowns no longer have the economic base they once drew from.

Uncoordinated Marketing

Downtown shopping facilities are composed of many independent entrepreneurs who own their own stores and run their business as they see fit. This is, perhaps, one of the major problems CBDs are facing. These independent businesses usually have difficulty getting together with others and agreeing on a general strategy to promote downtown business as a whole. Not only are they not too willing to get together with others and develop an overall strategy, they are not even willing to coordinate their activities so that some synergism in promoting the downtown can be realized. For instance, they could coordinate special sales, advertising, or a special event.

In addition, since downtowns are typically not planned, the effectiveness of their merchandise mix in time may become questionable. If the merchants are not interacting, they may have little opportunity to improve the situation.

Emerging Shopping Centers

Retailing's answer to population movements and changing needs in the United States for the past forty years or so has been shopping centers. If we recall the dialectic process discussed in Chapter 3, shopping centers are the antithesis of central business districts. Planned suburban shopping centers emerged about the same time American suburbia started mushrooming. This retailing phenomenon first came into being at the beginning of the 1950s. Unlike the central business districts that dominated the retailing scene up to that time, shopping centers enjoyed at least four major features that established superiority for them over downtowns. These were (1) accessibility, (2) modern and well-planned facilities, (3) plentiful parking, and (4) coordinated merchandising and marketing (Samli 1989).

Accessibility of shopping centers is a critical feature and exhibits itself in various ways. First and foremost, they are conveniently located, since they follow the population dispersion. They invariably locate adjacent to newly emerging population centers, catering to more than two or three such population centers. Since they are connected to population centers by superhighways and bypasses, they avoid traffic bottlenecks and traffic lights in the middle of the city. They cater to the fast vehicular traffic of major highways. Even if they are equidistant, they are much more accessible than downtowns. They can be reached easily by using superhighways and by avoiding all complications of inner-city traffic.

Shopping centers are generally modern and well planned. The word "generally" is critical here because some of these shopping centers are becoming old, and what was well planned and modern in the late 1950s cannot be considered as such in the late 1990s. Thus, it will not be a big surprise if some of the earlier shopping centers are experiencing the plight of downtowns. However, the fact remains that they are planned and, therefore, their problems can be encountered and most often reversed more easily than downtowns. Unlike a typical central business district, shopping centers have architectural unity and a theme that would be appealing to their customers. A theme can be ultramodern, Mexican, early American, patina, or underground, among many others. This architectural theme provides special attraction and cultivates a general image that is being projected by the whole shopping complex. Again, unlike downtowns, modernity involves a well-designed layout of the total shopping facility. The entrances, exits, parking facilities, and store locations are all carefully designed to accommodate traffic patterns and overcrowded conditions.

Again, an important strength of shopping centers is that their merchandise and service mixes are also carefully planned. They provide a balanced offering of goods and services in such a way that they make it worthwhile to customers to drive a long distance. Carefully balanced merchandise and service mixes make a strong contribution to the shopping center's drawing power, which is essential for survival.

As downtowns become more and more cluttered, plentiful parking becomes the most attractive feature of shopping centers. Many downtowns were not originally planned for heavy traffic. This feature is painfully noticeable, particularly in the glorious historic cities of the Old World, such as Rome, Paris, and so forth. During the heavy traffic hours, the whole day in some cities, downtown driving becomes so discouraging that shoppers are willing to go five or ten miles extra but in an uninterrupted manner to buy things. In a shopping center, they are guaranteed a parking space. As a result, downtown underground facilities, parking ramps, and pedestrian malls are emerging in downtowns. This may be a part of the synthesis in the dialectic process (Chapter 3). However, they are not quite the answer to the traffic bottlenecks that are becoming more common. Nor are they eliminating the perception that going downtown is more of a hassle than it is worth. Furthermore, pedestrian malls have not been carefully conceptualized and, therefore, do not have a widespread appeal, and newly developed parking facilities in downtowns are too concentrated, forcing some people to walk long distances in order to shop.

Coordinated merchandising and marketing are unique strengths of shopping centers. All businesses in a specific shopping center participate in general marketing plans and specific promotional activity. There are coordinated efforts planned by experts for the whole mall that require cooperation on the part of individual merchant members. These members not only ask to participate and cooperate but at times are also asked to perform certain specific tasks in a planned effort. Giving door prizes, displaying wares outside, providing entertainment, and preparing special signs and displays are among these special tasks. In addition to this type of coordinated activity, there are regular promotional themes; for example, an education awareness day, a travel extravaganza, and so forth. All merchants need to participate in partially institutional (image-building attempts for the whole mall) and partially promotional advertising for particular merchants to attract heavier consumer traffic. Similarly, much of the public relations work is coordinated and planned for synergistic impact.

Difficulty in Downtown Accessibility

Most downtowns in the United States emerged when people used to walk to stores or use public transportation. Indeed, in many parts of the Old World this pattern still continues. However, in modern days practically nobody uses public transportation or walks to stores. Thus, downtowns were not built for modern-day American vehicular traffic. In time, inner cities became more crowded, traffic became heavier and heavier, and downtowns became less and less accessible. People, particularly those who lived in the suburbs, started avoiding downtown shopping. This avoidance became stronger and more noticeable as people continued moving further and further away from downtowns (Samli and Prell 1965). The quality of shopping started changing as those who avoided downtown shopping most rigorously were primarily higher socioeconomic groups who lived at the outskirts of the city and were located only slightly further from shopping centers than the CBD. They preferred going to the shopping center in a fast and uninterrupted manner. Downtowns, in time, lost their upper socioeconomic clientele.

In summary, downtowns throughout the country are in some degree of trouble. If a certain concerted effort is not made, they are likely to get worse. Considering the fact that the population is growing and the available land is the same, some things need to be done with CBDs. In order to gain more insight as to what to do with downtowns, an analysis of the evolution and current status of shopping centers is presented in the following section.

FROM CBDs TO PLANNED SHOPPING CENTERS

Planned shopping centers emerged as an answer to population movements and changing needs. They also are the antithesis in the dialectic process (Chapter 3). However, planned shopping centers do not necessarily come in one size and shape. Exhibit 5.1 illustrates four types of shopping centers. There are no specific theories about the emergence of these shopping complexes and the time sequence of their appearance; however, it is proposed here that the first was the move from totally unplanned (CBD) to carefully planned (regional shopping center). As population continued dispersing, shopping centers felt the need to get closer to people. However, by this time, planning the shopping complex had become quite attractive and, hence, the other types of shopping centers started emerging.

In Exhibit 5.1, a distinction is made between neighborhood shopping centers and neighborhood clusters. Whereas neighborhood shopping centers are mainly strips with some combination of shopping and convenience goods, neighborhood clusters are just a group of a few stores with primary emphasis on convenience of basic goods and services. They are also called strip malls. In this sense, neighborhood clusters are much less planned than neighborhood shopping centers. This is somewhat justified, since every neighborhood is different. However, such lack of planning brings them closer to the dilemma that central business districts are in, being less effective and arbitrary vis-à-vis changing profiles of their immediate markets.

As the population increases and becomes denser in areas where it was sparse in the past, there will be more neighborhood clusters located near high-density condominium complexes. As Chandler (1995) stated, a shopping trend is the moving away of stores from large malls to smaller shopping centers. Experiences of the past forty years or so indicate that the more planned the shopping facility, the greater its chances for survival and success. Hence, it is predicted that there will be more planning at this level. It is not clear that at this point in time we know how the planning should take place so that neighborhood clusters can be optimally satisfactory for the customers and also become financial successes for prolonged periods of time.

One of the most important features of Exhibit 5.1 is the goods and services mix. It is very clear that the regional shopping center must bring customers in. This calls for a strong appeal and drawing power. The types of products and services that can create such effects are shopping and specialty goods and services. These shopping centers are very big. They offer very large assortments of shopping and specialty goods, as well as specialty services such as food courts, movie theaters, and other entertainment-related services. All in all, they must (and many do) offer a goods and services mix that will enhance the shopping experience and attract consumers accordingly. On the other end of the product and service spectrum, neighborhood clusters almost exclusively deal with convenience goods and services. As stated in Exhibit 5.1, they are typically composed of a convenience store, bakery, barbershop, video store, and perhaps a fast-food facility.

Shopping centers are primarily planned and, as such, are in a much better position to satisfy ever-changing consumer needs. The planning can go as far as totally controlling the goods and services offerings, coordinating promotional activity, trying to project a uniform image for the whole shopping complex, and other activities. Typically, shopping centers are doing better than central business districts. One of the reasons for this is that most shopping centers have special budgets and marketing managers.

Marketing Malls or Shopping Centers

Most regional malls or shopping centers have marketing managers. They are in charge of joint promotional activities of the mall. These activities have a twofold purpose. First, they enhance the name recognition and the image of the mall. Second, they help stimulate the traffic to the mall. Of course, these managers also see that the tenants of the shopping center or the mall are maintaining certain image-building activities, such as customer service, quality maintenance, and overall appearance features.

At a different level, these marketing managers are responsible for bringing in new tenants as some of the existing tenants discontinue or fail. Developing criteria for new tenants and promoting the shopping center among prospective tenants is a critical activity that needs regular and systematic attention. The marketing director must be working on these points regularly so that the center will not be without tenants for prolonged periods of time.

Though mall marketing is not a part of the academic curriculum or even a part of regular retailing courses, there may be more attention and more research emphasis required for this very critical position.

More and Better CBD Studies

As can be seen, shopping centers are quite ahead of CBDs. The key question here is, what can be done at the CBD level? Though, particularly in the 1980s, there have been many downtown revitalization projects that have cost millions of dollars each, the CBD problems have not been resolved. These projects did not prove to be altogether useful (Spalding 1983; Stark 1980; Samli 1989).

Perhaps one of the key problems in downtown renovation activity is that these projects are undertaken as architectural undertakings rather than retailing-related marketing projects. It is very critical that the causes of CBD problems are understood and that downtown renovation projects are developed accordingly. This situation first and foremost calls for carefully designed CBD studies.

Samli elaborates on the projects that were based on CBD studies:

- In a large western city, two large city blocks were converted into pedestrian malls. Much money was spent on brick, mortar, and waterfalls for physical appearance enhancement. However, these "improvements" had nothing to do with consumer satisfaction, merchandise mix, and so on. Shoppers did not think that this was an improvement and, hence, the project failed.

- A revitalization project in a small town invested much money in a face-lift of the downtown. However, the merchant mix and resultant merchandise and service mixes did not change. The end result was that the downtown's status did not improve.

- Though the physical appearance of downtown in a small city was altered noticeably, this change in appearance was not followed by attitudes. The store managers', owner–managers', and retail clerks' attitudes and behavior patterns were not altered.

These types of experiences are not only costly, but ineffective. CBD studies have become more necessary than ever before. Such studies can identify the directions that the downtown can choose from and the implications for all of the individual retailers. CBD studies can explore the present and future potentials of the total downtown area and develop detailed programs, based on consumer needs and preferences, that would enable the whole area to capitalize on existing market potentials. Offering changes that would be preferred, desired, or at least acceptable to the local consumer groups provides hope for the central business district.

Past Trends

In order to conduct an effective downtown marketing study, it is necessary to understand the past trends in the area. The changing patterns of the merchant mix, the changing products, and the service mixes must be analyzed and compared to the changes in the needs, shopping patterns, and socioeconomic status of the consumers.

Patterns of change in the industrial profile of the area and the economic base analyses will provide a better understanding of the pressures on and the demands of the CBD. If the industrial profile of the area is changing and industries are leaving the area and the economic growth along with population appears to be dispersing, then it would be reasonable not to expect a major growth in CBD. Instead, it would be more meaningful to think of a series of local shopping centers or neighborhood clusters to emerge. The downtown in such cases might take a more specific character, catering to local consumers or becoming an entertainment or a service center dealing with financial or medical services.

ANALYZING SUPPLY AND DEMAND

In order to rescue CBDs and develop them, a basic research framework is needed. Such a framework can be constructed by analyzing supply and demand. Behind supply there are at least eight key variables to consider. These are listed in Exhibit 5.2. The CBD must work with all of these variables, create a cohesiveness among them, and provide an overall acceptable shopping experience for the consumers.

However, in order to manage the supply in an optimal manner, the key demand modifiers need to be taken into consideration (Exhibit 5.2). There are at least seven such modifiers that need to be carefully analyzed. Once both supply and demand are analyzed simultaneously, major areas of agreement can be established. These areas of agreement provide certain options that would be reasonable to use for the CBD in order to get out of the negative situation that it is in. If, for instance, merchants think that it is the parking that is causing a major problem, but consumers are complaining about the selection offered by the CBD and field research confirms that, then the emphasis must be put on the merchandise mix. It is necessary to have the correct merchandise mix in downtown development plans.

Supply Modifiers

Of the eight supply factors identified in Exhibit 5.2, the most important one or the relative importance of each factor is not known. Though all factors are basically important, different shopping complexes may have different points of emphasis regarding the nature and the development of the central business district. The growth and rehabilitation of a downtown shopping complex is closely related to understanding the different supply elements.

Physical Structure

Physical facilities, including stores, highways, parking, warehousing, and proximity to other commercial and industrial buildings, have a twofold impact. First, the status of physical surroundings is a key determinant of what can be done with the downtown. Thus, this factor can be a hindrance as well or a boon for the future development of the complex. Second, the physical conditions of the shopping complex would encourage or discourage the demand factor. If certain developmental plans cannot be implemented because of the lack of space, additional appeal to consumers will not materialize, and additional consumers will not frequent the facility.

Merchant Mix

This is a very important supply factor. If the retail facility does not have the types of businesses that would lure consumers, then nothing can be done about it. This is parallel to the shopping center discussion presented earlier. The regional shopping centers need to have exciting specialty and shopping goods and services to attract consumers from long distances. If the merchant mix is good, then merchandise and service mixes can be adjusted. But many CBDs may be missing the most typical types of businesses, such as eating and drinking places, apparel stores, and so on. In such cases, the problem becomes obvious. Comparing a CBD that is doing poorly with a regional shopping center that is doing well can point out the direction to improve the CBD. Thus, it can be stated that analyzing the merchant mix and the merchandise mix is an effective diagnostic tool to pinpoint relative weaknesses of the CBD in question.

Physical Facilities

Parking and accessibility are among the worst problems CBDs have. Hence, analyzing how people can go to the CBD and what kind of parking is needed are critical areas to consider.

Overall Attitude

How merchants see the shopping complex and its future, and what kind of bonding exists among merchants themselves as well as merchants and property owners, are areas that should also be explored. If merchants do not have a positive attitude and do not think much of the CBD's future, it would be very difficult to elicit their cooperation for improvement plans. Furthermore, if the property owners let the whole complex deteriorate, very little, if anything, can be done to improve the CBD.

More on Attitudes

The prevailing attitude toward the CBD is so critical that it needs to be explored more carefully. Samli (1989) stated that indolence, traditionalism, or lack of knowledge on the part of businessmen interferes with the growth or revitalization of the CBD. He goes on to suggest a six-point analysis of the merchants (Samli 1989, 66):

1. The degree of commitment must be examined by analyzing the efforts that merchants put into expansion, remodeling, and development attempts.
2. The merchants' own plans for expansion and development must be understood.
3. The leasing arrangements the merchants have with the landlords is a key question indicating the long-range commitment (or lack thereof) of the merchants to the area.
4. Assessing the merchants' feelings, likes, and dislikes toward the CBD is critical.
5. Similarly, their feeling toward the buildings they occupy must be understood.
6. Understanding the relationship between merchants and property owners would indicate the expected cooperation (or its absence) toward the development plans.

In many downtown situations, the owners of the buildings and facilities, who do not live there, play a very critical role. If they are enthusiastic and looking forward to a developed CBD, they may be very helpful. But if they manage their properties like slums and allow them to deteriorate, they become a major hindrance to downtown shopping revitalization.

Demand Modifiers

The size and scope of the downtown revitalization process depends substantially on the potentials. These potentials are determined by studying the shopping patterns of people who actually patronize the CBD and those who have a tendency to patronize. Contrasting these two groups with those who do not patronize the CBD will provide critical direction in planning downtown revitalization. In this sense, it is necessary to study on-the-spot shoppers as well as households. These two are the most critical sources of information.

Shoppers

It is critical to know the socioeconomic class of typical CBD patrons. In time, the socioeconomic class of typical CBD patrons often changes. The income levels, education, occupation, age, and residence of shoppers need to be known. Then it will be possible to determine if the CBD is still appealing to the same group of people or to other socioeconomic groups. If the CBD is primarily frequented by people who live nearby, then it becomes clear that the CBD is not drawing a lot of people from other parts of the metropolitan area. Thus, the CBD is becoming primarily a local convenience shopping center. Just knowing this provides a critical starting point. At this stage, it becomes possible to formulate future objectives of the CBD. These objectives can be generating more drawing power and attracting people from further distances for exciting shopping experiences. Similarly, the CBD may continue becoming a convenience shopping center. How often do shoppers come to the CBD, what do they purchase, and how much do they spend are all important bits of information that would supplement this process of establishing objectives. Similarly, the goods and services the customers cannot find at the CBD provide more refinement to revitalization plans. Shoppers must be contacted a number of times to ascertain such information. Similarly, studying the license plates of a number of cars parked in the CBD and tracing these license plates to their addresses provide further evaluation of the drawing power (or the lack thereof) of the CBD.

Households

If the households that are located in the area were to be studied carefully, additional information could be obtained about the strengths and weaknesses of the CBD. Practices of households regarding patronizing the CBD and purchasing there could provide additional information about the strengths or the weaknesses.

An early study (Samli and Prell 1965), for instance, determined that consumers who are located in the immediate vicinity patronized the CBD about 75 to 90 percent of the time. These people were relatively less educated, earned relatively less money, and worked primarily as unskilled blue collar workers. There was a relatively higher proportion of unemployment in this group. They rated the stores, merchandise, services, and convenience very highly.

Another sample was taken from neighborhoods located at about a five-minute driving distance. It was found that the residents patronized the shopping facility about 50 to 75 percent of the time. Analyses indicated that this portion of the total sample were slightly younger and somewhat better educated. They were primarily employed as skilled blue-collar workers. Unemployment in this group was lower than the first portion of the sample. This group's attitude toward downtown shopping facilities was not nearly as positive as the previous group. They found multiple gaps in the merchandise and service mixes of the CBD. They were not happy with the stores or their personnel.

Finally, a third sample was taken from suburbs that were about twenty-minutes driving distance from the CBD. They patronized the CBD less than 50 percent of the time. This sample was composed of younger professional people who made much more money that the first two groups. They were well educated and there was almost no unemployed among them. They disliked the CBD. Whenever they had a chance, they went to a regional center for shopping that was located some ten miles further than the CBD in the opposite direction. These findings clearly identify the CBD's options. It could try to lure those who are in the third sample group, it could concentrate more on appealing to the second group, or it could stay with the first group. Each of these alternatives would call for a different revitalization plan.

Specialty Retail Centers: Another Alternative?

Specialty retail centers (SRCs) have become another alternative used by CBDs to respond to the suburban shopping center challenge (Maronick and Stiff 1985). SRCs focus on entertainment facilities and eating and drinking places as anchors (Samli 1989). They emphasize natural settings or uniform architectural designs that unify the whole CBD. They further utilize the old and well-known buildings as special attractions (Maronick and Stiff 1985). These institutions, by protecting the entertainment-center image, had a distinct influence on the old CBDs by doing the following:

- Stimulated consumer traffic by being an entertainment center.
- Managed to attract consumers from high-income suburbs, again by projecting the image of an entertainment center.
- Gave support to cultural activities in the area.
- Enhanced the existing merchants' opportunity to profit by improving their product and service mixes (Maronick and Stiff 1985).

A more specific version of specialty retail centers is outlet malls. These are projected to be company outlets simply selling expensive and well-known products at real bargain prices. Even though some of these establishments may be trying to live up to this image, in reality they simply are selling cheaper versions of expensive and well-known products. As such, they are planned and are an answer to the CBD plight.

Our discussion in this chapter indicates that downtowns are in trouble and that shopping centers are also changing. But in order to improve downtowns there must be specific plans based on CBD studies. CBD studies provide information on supply and demand. By examining the common denominators between supply and demand, the CBD can develop strong revitalization programs. We only explore the general orientation here; each CBD has its own opportunities and limitations. Unless these opportunities and limitations are brought into focus and analyzed on the basis of supply and demand, there cannot be very constructive revitalization programs.

One last point that needs to be carefully explored is the implications for individual merchants. If a prospective retailer in the CBD does not understand the big picture and cannot relate the prevailing opportunities and threats to its specific needs and conditions, there will be no opportunity for success and profit.

INTERNATIONAL CORNER

The United States, being a relatively young country, has had different retailing experiences than other industrialized parts of the world, such as Western Europe and the Scandinavian countries. In most industrialized countries and all major cities of the world, downtowns or central business districts have been, are, and most likely will be the most prevalent parts of retailing. While there is a movement away from downtown to suburbs in the United States, giving rise to suburban shopping centers, people in many major cities of Europe have for generations bought at the same groups of small stores in downtowns and other convenient clusters. Perhaps one of the key differences is the automobile versus the availability of public transportation. As automobiles became more commonplace, Americans left the downtown's congestion and moved to suburbs. As this happened, retailing followed population to suburbia and later to neighborhoods. In most other countries, public transportation and the super-advanced stature of downtowns created a much more prolonged loyalty to downtowns than in the United States. In other words, population in these countries either followed retailing or moved with it. But retailing was the pivotal force in such moves. Of course, in other countries there has also been suburban development and resultant emergence of shopping centers. However, this is a very recent development. In most cases, loyalty to small stores in the neighborhood and in downtowns is still very much prevalent in Europe and other countries such as Japan and Russia. These stores treat their customers almost like family members, since the store owners or managers have grown up together with their customers for generations. Thus, in many countries, retailing is somewhat uneventful and quite traditional.

SUMMARY

This chapter examines the key macro developments in the retailing sector. From the central business district, which has naturally evolved into planned regional shopping centers, there have been a few critical changes. Though regional shopping centers have been creating very critical competition for CBDs, they are also facing competition from community shopping centers, neighborhood shopping centers, and neighborhood clusters. Most of these also are cutting into the downtown's retailing business.

This chapter posits that CBDs need to be planned on the basis of prevailing demand and potential supply. These shopping complexes must analyze supply and demand and the factors behind these two in order to plan a revitalization activity for the CBD. These revitalization plans are based on detailed CBD studies. These studies will identify the most important alternatives for the downtown by analyzing the common denominators between demand and supply forces.

Exhibits

Exhibit 5.1
Types of Shopping Centers and Their Specific Features

FEATURES	TYPES				
	Regional Shopping Centers	Community Shopping Centers	Neighborhood Shopping Centers	Neighborhood Clusters	
Location	Outside central city at the edge of town on major highway or expressway	Close to populated residential areas (preferably more than one)	Along a major thoroughfare in one residential area	A group of stores in a residential area	
Proximity	30 minutes or more driving time	15 to 20 minutes driving time	5 to 10 minutes driving time	3 to 5 minutes walking distance	
Economic base necessary to support the facility expressed by the number of people living in the area.	100,000	20,000 to 100,000	3,000 to 20,000	3,000 or less	
Size in square feet rented to various retailers.	400,000 to 2,000,000+	100,000 to 400,000	30,000 to 100,000	Less than 30,000	
Number of stores	50 to 150+	15 to 25	10 to 15	Less than 10	

Exhibit 5.1 (*continued*)

FEATURES	TYPES			
	Regional Shopping Centers	Community Shopping Centers	Neighborhood Shopping Centers	Neighborhood Clusters
Goods and services mixes	Very large assortment of shopping and specialty goods; specialty services that would enhance the shopping experience	Moderate assortment of shopping and convenience goods and services	Limited assortment of convenience goods and services with some shopping goods.	Total emphasis is on convenience and basic goods and services
Principal tenant	One, two or more full-sized traditional department stores	One discount department store and/or category killer store	Supermarket or drug store	No principal tenant, a convenience store, bakery, barber shop, etc.
Layout	Mall, often enclosed with anchor stores at major entrances	Strip or L-shaped	Strip	A group of stores
Planning status	Always carefully planned	Carefully planned with some unplanned features	Somewhat planned with much unplanned flexibility	Barely planned

Source: Adopted and revised from Berman and Evans (1995).

Exhibit 5.2
The Supply and Demand Analysis in Planning CBDs

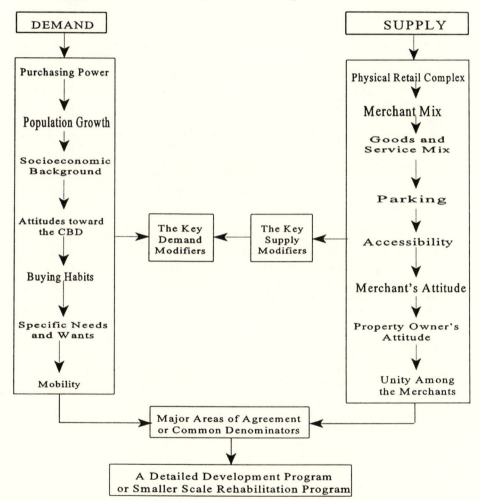

DEMAND		SUPPLY

Purchasing Power → Population Growth → Socioeconomic Background → Attitudes toward the CBD → Buying Habits → Specific Needs and Wants → Mobility

Physical Retail Complex → Merchant Mix → Goods and Service Mix → Parking → Accessibility → Merchant's Attitude → Property Owner's Attitude → Unity Among the Merchants

The Key Demand Modifiers ← The Key Supply Modifiers

Major Areas of Agreement or Common Denominators

A Detailed Development Program or Smaller Scale Rehabilitation Program

References

Berman, Barry, and Joel R. Evans. 1995. *Retail Management*. Englewood Cliffs, N.J.: Prentice Hall.

Chandler, Susan. 1995. "Where Sears Wants America to Shop Now." *On Line Proquest*, 6 November.

"Chicago Brings Loop Back to Life." 1981. *Engineering News-Record*, 2 July, 29–35.

Gobisborough, R. G. 1983. "Downtown: Good Views and Bad Views." *Advertising Age*, 21 March, 32–39.

"Heart of Atlanta Gets Transfusion." 1982. *Engineering News-Record*, 23 December, 65–72.

Lewis, Stephen E. 1980. "Every Downtown Is Different Says Developer, but All Urban Malls Require Viable Existing Market." *The National Real Estate Investor* (May): 10–19.

Maronick, Thomas J., and Ronald M. Stiff. 1985. "The Impact of a Specialty Retail Center on Downtown Shopping Behavior." *Journal of the Academy of Marketing Science* (Summer): 292–306.

Peterson, Eric C. 1983. "Centers That Serve a Downtown Function." *Stores* (March): 35–39.

Samli, A. Coskun. 1989. *Retail Marketing Strategy*. Westport, Conn.: Quorum Books.

Samli, A. Coskun, and Arthur E. Prell. 1965. *The Challenge to Regionalism*. Herrin, Ill.: Southern Illinois University, Business Research Bureau.

———. 1966. *The Challenge to Regionalism, Granite City, Illinois*. Herrin, Ill.: Southern Illinois University, Business Research Bureau.

"Saving Downtown: Government Courts Retailers." 1981. *Chain Store Age Executive*, 27 July, 39–44.

Sloan, S. H. 1982. "Boston's Fasevilk Hall: A Rousing Success." *Chain Store Age*, March, 25–31.

Spalding, Lewis A. 1983. "Some Proof There Is Life After Death: Downtown." *Stores* (October): 33–38.

Stark, Morton S. 1980. "Shopping Center Future." *Stores* (March).

"St. Louis Downtown Makes Slow Comeback." 1981. *Engineering News-Record*, 12 November, 24–31.

Sutler, Gregg. 1982. "City Toils Over Seeds of Growth." *Advertising Age*, 11 January, 55–63.

Chapter 6

From Market Potentials
to Capitalization

It must be realized that unless macro and micro conditions of retailing make a good fit, the retailer may be facing a major risk of premature failure or discontinuance. In either case, the costs to the retailer as well as to society are very high. Earlier studies have shown that more than 30 percent of new retail establishments survive less than six months (Samli 1989). Thus, the risk of premature failure or discontinuance must be reduced. This chapter attempts to establish a fit between the macro and micro conditions and, hence, reduce the risk of failure that will cost both the individual and society. Three preliminary activities are proposed to meet this goal (Samli 1989, 75): assessing market potentials, evaluating the feasibility of the retail establishment, and determining the capital needs. Thus, the risk-reducing preliminary planning moves from macro to micro in a sequence of three steps (Exhibit 6.1). This chapter explores this sequential process.

GEOGRAPHIC DIMENSION OF MARKET POTENTIALS

In order to understand retail market potentials, it is necessary to connect these potentials to a specific area. Store location is not a very flexible factor in a retail strategy plan, since stores cannot simply pack up and move from one location to another on a moment's notice. Hence, location must be studied carefully in advance. Once the decision is made as to where to locate, there cannot be any major adjustments (Berman and Evans 1995). In order to assess market potentials and translate them into feasibility and capital needs, trading areas must be defined so that retailers can locate their establishments successfully.

Geographic delineation of an area containing potential customers for a prospective retailer or a retail complex such as a shopping center is extremely important. Such a geographic identity is called a *retail trade area* (Huff 1962; Goldstucker 1965; Samli 1989). Ideally, trading area would minimize the cost of contact between consumers and retailers. This means that the retailers have the greatest access to the market with the most potential. Similarly, consumers will have the greatest access to the best retailing facility.

Being able to single out such an area that is beneficial to both parties is based on a successful market potential analysis. Samli (1989) posited that identification of a trading area has three distinct points:

1. The critical mass of population who are likely to be customers of the retail store (or the retailing complex).

2. The proportion of those who are likely to be customers who live in the immediate area. For instance, if 55 to 70 percent of the store's customers live in that area, this will be identified as the *primary trading area*. By the same token, if 15 to 25 percent of the customers are located in the area, it will be identified as the *secondary trading area*. The remainder of the market is typically identified as the *fringe trading area*.

3. The proportion of the purchases that will take place in the store or the retailing complex in question; in other words, the store's competitive effectiveness.

These three points can be made operative if additional information about the people and the retailing in this particular area is obtained. This information needs to be related to (1) demographic or socioeconomic characteristics of the store's or the retailing complex's customers, (2) the future growth or decline of the area, and (3) the number of stores the area can reasonably handle without becoming overcrowded (Berman and Evans 1995). Delineating the trading area starts out with retail gravitation models.

RETAIL GRAVITATION MODELS: EARLY EFFORTS

The original versions of retail gravitation measurements were begun by Reilly (1931) and later expanded by Converse (1946). These efforts were based on two key variables: population and the distance to be traveled. Reilly's original retail gravitation hypothesis was formulated as follows: Two cities attract retail trade from any intermediate city or town in direct proportion to the population of the two cities in question and in inverse proportion to the square of the distance from the intermediate city or town to either one of the two cities. Reilly expressed this hypothesis with the following formula:

$$\frac{B_a}{B_b} = (\frac{P_a}{P_b}) \, (\frac{D_b}{D_a})^2$$

Where

B_a = the proportion of the trade from the intermediate city attracted by city A
B_b = the proportion of the trade from the intermediate city attracted by city B
P_a = the population of city A
P_b = the population of city B
D_a = the distance from the intermediate city to A
D_b = the distance from the intermediate city to B

Assume, for instance, that city A has a population of 100,000 and city B 400,000. The intermediate city X is 40 miles from A and 60 miles from B.

$$\frac{B_a}{B_b} = (\frac{100,000}{400,000}) \, (\frac{60}{40}) = 1/4 \times 9/4 = 1/9$$

City A has a drawing power which is one-ninth of B. This drawing power is interpreted as about 11 percent of that of B.

An extension of Reilly's Law is the breaking point between A and B. This is the optimal point. It is also referred to as the point of indifference. In other words, this will be the best location for a proposed new retail facility. It also can indicate that an existing facility is in the right or wrong location.

$$\text{A's breaking point miles from B} = \frac{\text{Miles between A and B}}{1 + \sqrt{\dfrac{\text{Population of B}}{\text{Population of A}}}}$$

Assume, for instance, that cities A and B have populations of 100,000 and 900,000, respectively. The distance between these two cities is 80 miles. The breaking point can be computed as follows:

$$B_b = \frac{80}{1 + \sqrt{\dfrac{900,000}{100,000}}} = \frac{80}{1 + \sqrt{9}} = \frac{80}{1 + 3} = \frac{80}{4} = \text{Approximately 20 miles}$$

If the breaking point between cities A and B is 20 miles, then the best place to locate a new shopping complex is about 20 miles outside of A and 60 miles from B. If a new shopping complex were to be located here, it will optimize the business coming from both A and B, without favoring one or the other.

Further revision of the gravitation model was performed by Curtis Publishing Company. The revised approach substituted population with the square footage of each retailer and substituted the distance between cities by the actual travel time to these cities (Huff 1962; Samli 1989).

Substituting the population with the square footage stems from the thinking that larger retailing facilities that offer greater variety and choice are likely to have greater drawing power. It is difficult to explain Reilly's reasoning exactly. It is quite feasible that he thought that larger population centers attract more people because they actually do have greater options for shoppers and prospective shoppers.

The second portion of this revision is related to actual travel time. This is related to distance versus accessibility of a retail complex. Assume, for instance, the retail complex is located at a five-mile distance, but there are twenty-five stoplights on the way. Similarly, another retail complex is located about ten miles away. However, the second facility does not have any stoplights; it is simply located at the end of a major highway. Chances are that because of accessibility the second complex will be preferred. Furthermore, in reality, the actual driving time to the second complex will be less than the first.

Based on these revisions, Exhibits 6.2 and 6.3 illustrate how the delineation of the trading area for a new shopping center can be achieved. Exhibit 6.2 illustrates the major competition to the proposed shopping complex A. This exhibit points out that between A and B, for instance, the seven-minute travel time indicates what A's drawing power is likely to be in that particular direction. A may wish to promote itself within this area according to what B offers, and may wish to establish a competitive advantage over B by matching or excelling what B offers or does. The same practice can be repeated in all other areas according to travel time and breaking points and what each center has to offer.

In recent years, two specific developments have contributed to the advancement of gravity models. First, attempts have been made to generate simulation models based on the gravity concept (Samli 1989). Second, various applications of multiple regression techniques have been used to improve these models.

Exhibit 6.3 is a hypothetical illustration of the data presented in Exhibit 6.2. Such an illustration is quite useful in terms of connecting the drawing power of A (the proposed shopping complex) to population data put out by the Bureau of the Census. Census tracts that are covered in the exhibit provide certain information. This information is related to housing units, number of people, income, education, and other basic information. The Bureau of Labor statistics give information regarding what proportion of income is spent on which general product categories by different income groups. By combining census tract data with Bureau of Labor statistics, estimates can be generated regarding market potential in the geographic areas identified within the census tracts.

One additional bit of information is also necessary; an approximation of outshopping by the people who reside in census tracts 1, 2, 3, and 4. In Exhibit 6.2, the last column gives some hypothetical figures on this. Assuming little or no outshopping around the proposed shopping complex A and proportions of outshopping as depicted in Exhibit 6.2, the last column of Exhibit 6.3 is calculated. If A is proposed to be adjacent to all of these census tracts and does not have a census tract of its own, it may be able to generate $4.1 million. The same procedure needs to be repeated for all key merchandise and service lines that A is planning to offer. Such analyses will indicate how many stores and what merchandise and service mixes are to be offered by A. The last columns of Exhibits 6.2 and 6.3 are obviously quite critical. They require additional information. Exhibit 6.4 illustrates a simple questionnaire that is used in a situation where such information is generated. Outshopping is determined indirectly without referring to such criteria as how often one goes out of town or how much of total purchases are done in a shopping complex located out of town or at a certain distance. As seen in Exhibit 6.4, the questions indirectly indicate proximity or distance, mode of transportation, respondent's degree of shopping complex loyalty, and, finally, socioeconomic status.

Thus far, an attempt has been made to identify and evaluate the trading area. But it must be realized that the trading area is not homogeneous, and the impact of competition varies from one part of the trading area to another. In other words, those who are closer to the retail complex may frequent it more often and, if there are other shopping complexes nearby, they may cut into the original trading area. Samli (1989) discusses primary, secondary, tertiary, quadrinary, and the rest (or fringe) of the trading area. As was stated earlier, proximity can be construed as distance or accessibility, or perhaps it is a combination. However, within this context it is necessary to identify these primary and other components of the trading areas. This identification is made on the basis of distance and time (both driving and walking time). But a critical subjective dimension can be added to this in the form of proportion of the store's total business in this area. As stated (Applebaum 1966), the primary trading area may be the people who live in the geographic core from which a store obtains about 55 to 70 percent of its business. The secondary trading area is the geographic area from which the store gets between 15 and 25 percent of its business. One may add the tertiary trading area, that may account for 5 to 10 percent of the store's business. The remainder may be around 5 percent or so. The fringe may be somewhere around 2 percent or less, and perhaps some unexpected sales from one of the remote areas.

Since there are both subjective and objective dimensions to the trading area identification, it is necessary to combine the two. For instance, the breakdown of the trading area may be achieved by drawing circles on the map of the total trading area and identifying zones with radii of one-fourth, one-half, three-fourths, and one mile walking distance, or, five-, ten-, fifteen-, or twenty-minute driving distance, based on whichever orientation appears to be most appropriate. Subjectivity of the approach is based on interviewing consumers in each of the identified zones.

Applebaum (1966) attempted to establish what he called value indexes by multiplying the total purchases of interviewees by the number of visits they paid to the particular shopping complex. These value indexes approximated the purchases of consumers in the primary, secondary, tertiary, and quadrinary markets. His attempts led to development of population dot maps identifying the zones where customers come from and sales per capita for each zone.

It is quite possible that about 55 percent of the store customers are spotted within a zero to one-fourth mile zone. If the store's weekly volume is $40,000, then it is expected that 55 percent of this amount will be generated in this primary trading area zone. The secondary trading area zone may be bringing in about 20 percent, and so on.

Thus, the total trading area can be broken into primary, secondary, tertiary, quadrinary, and the remainder of the market zones. In conjunction with this total trading area analysis, additional information can be gathered by using a questionnaire such as the one displayed in Exhibit 6.4. With this attempt, customer profiles can be established. These profiles can be compared to total population densities in the primary, secondary, tertiary, and so on markets in the total trading area. Trading area zones, combined with customer profile and population density analyses, can yield a good approximation of the total market potential.

There are at least three additional information sources available to retailers. These are all called geographic information systems (GIS). One has been developed by Urban Decision Systems. In addition to population density and income distribution, this system provides future population change projections (Robins 1993). Another GIS system is offered by Strategic Mapping, Inc. This is a more interactive computer mapping system that responds to some of the retailers' "what if" types of inquiries (Berman and Evans 1995). Another GIS activity is presented by Thompson Associates. This group provides sophisticated area forecasts along with store performance analyses (Berman and Evans 1995).

Thus far, the trading area has been identified and evaluated. However, there is more to evaluating the trading area. In order to choose the best site, it is necessary to evaluate some of the other features of the area. This process requires at least four specific steps: (1) evaluating the traffic and history of the site (Gist 1968; Samli 1989), (2) evaluating access to the site and parking facilities (Gist 1968), (3) determining legal aspects of the site, and (4) deciding on a particular site.

Traffic and History

It is has been mentioned a number of times that traffic is the lifeblood of retailing. If a site is in a mall or a shopping center, then pedestrian traffic must be explored. However, if a location is considered for a group of stores or a solo-standing store, then vehicular traffic must be analyzed.

The individual store and location must be considered according to the particulars of the case in hand, and traffic counts must be performed accordingly. When using pedestrian traffic counts, supplemental information can be and indeed needs to be obtained through interviews. Information that can be generated by surveying prospective customers can be of particular value. Finding out how far the consumers will go to buy home electronics and computers, for example, is another approach to determining the chances of the proposed store to succeed. Thus, a combination of traffic counts with interviews is a better source of information than simple traffic counts or only interviews with consumers.

The history of the site needs to be taken into consideration. In the 1950s and 1960s, for instance, not only were there gas stations on every corner, but they constantly changed hands. There appeared to be an approach on the part of the new owners reflected in the words, "That poor guy who owned this place could not make it, but I can do it." Naturally, such an orientation was not sufficient for success. Without a desirable site, success is impossible. Thus, part of the history is related to who occupied that site previously and for what purpose. Another part of the history of the site in question is the legal aspects of the land-use pattern in that and adjacent areas. If, for instance, city planners change the land-use patterns in the area often, this can be a critical factor for the prospective retail establishment. If the city government keeps on changing its position regarding this particular site or its position on the redirection of the traffic, the desirability of this site is questionable.

The Site's Accessibility

Much of the time, a site is erroneously assessed on the basis of its proximity rather than its accessibility. Even though the site might be in good proximity, it might have excessive traffic congestion. Hence, it may not be very accessible at critical times.

If vehicular traffic is critical for the site in question, a number of issues must be clarified:

1. The site's ability to create traffic.
2. The specific features that would enhance the attractiveness.
3. The safety of the area for pedestrians.
4. The potential growth in the traffic patterns within walking distance.

Within these given areas of examination, there are many questions. Since each case is different, individuals who are involved in this preliminary site-selection activity can develop their own checklists. Such an attempt is made in Exhibit 6.5.

Though areas of examination have been identified as vehicular versus pedestrian traffic, one must not forget that every area has both vehicular and pedestrian traffic dependencies. Hence, both areas of examination must surface as the area is evaluated.

Legal Aspects of the Site

Every site has certain legal dimensions that need examination. Among these are zoning laws, landlord responsibilities, renter responsibilities, rent values (Samli 1989), and land ownership.

If the area zoning laws are very changeable, the prospective retailer cannot plan against future competition, nor can the market potentials be predicted accurately. Certain land in the area can be easily converted from residential to commercial, and hence bring about unexpected and unplanned competition for the retailer.

There are other points indirectly related to the legal aspects of the site. If zoning laws for housing are tightened in such a way that housing in the area becomes scarce, then the expected market growth for the planned retail establishment will not materialize. Also, zoning laws can favor economic growth of one part of town at the expense of other parts. This may have an extremely adverse influence on the proposed retail establishment.

There are certain landlord responsibilities. Since most retailers are more likely to lease than to build, it is critical to determine if the landlords are committed to upkeep, maintenance, and improvement of buildings and grounds. Similarly, the town management and/or property owners may be unrealistic in their demands about rent, maintenance, and other related areas. These can bring about unanticipated hardship on the proposed retail establishment.

Rent values can be or can become very unrealistic. If, for instance, property owners are leaving the area or the properties are already owned by absentee owners, then it is quite possible that they may ask exorbitant rental rates. Some absentee property owners are known to use the national consumer price index as the basis for their rental increases, but economic growth is far below such index increases. The prospective retailer must also be able to judge a reasonable rental rate based on the strengths and weaknesses of the location.

Finally, land and/or property ownership may create a legal hassle. If the owner passes away and multiple heirs cannot agree on certain terms, life for the retailer can become very difficult. In order to handle the whole area of location, Exhibit 6.6 presents a checklist. Assuming there are four sites that are being considered, Sites 1 and 2 appear to be substantially better than Sites 3 and 4. Of course, the individual retailer can generate a more specific checklist with more details reflecting the conditions that are particularly pertinent to the case. Though the factors are given equal weight, the individual retailer may find it necessary to use different weights if some of these are more important for the case under consideration.

ASSESSING MARKET POTENTIALS

Though trading-area analyses and market-potential assessment are considered interchangeable, here a distinction is made. It is more realistic to identify and measure (or approximate) the trading area before a site is selected. Once a decision is made regarding the site, it is still critical to identify the proposed store's market and to determine its potential so that the sales potential of the proposed store can be estimated and the feasibility of this whole project assessed. In identifying the market and determining its potentials, Samli (1989) proposes a three-stage analysis: (1) examine economic and business activity, (2) assess the strength of competition, and (3) analyze the prospective customers.

Examining the Economic Activity

When the site is decided upon, it is necessary to undertake a detailed analysis of the economy of the area. The economy of the area can be analyzed from the perspective of two dimensions: commercial structure and business activity. These two dimensions are equally important for the retailer. The commercial structure is related to the number of stores in the area. As such, this dimension can be evaluated on the basis of two critical phases: (1) the degree of store saturation, and (2) the proper number of establishments in the particular area that is being evaluated. Store saturation answers the question of just how crowded the retailing sector is in this area. It is measured as follows:

$$S = \frac{C \times RE}{RF}$$

Where

C = number of customers
RE = average expenditures in retailing by these customers
RF = number of retail establishments
S = store saturation

In this formula, if the numerators C or RE increase and/or the denominator decreases, then the retail saturation is becoming more attractive. Certainly, it is possible to compare the saturation rate of a number of areas if these are being compared, and the higher the S, the better the area.

Determining the adequate number of establishments is more complicated. Three separate equations have been developed for this purpose. Equation (1) deals with the total expenditures for current consumption on the part of the local residents:

$$E = (C)\,(I)\,(a)\,(b) \tag{1}$$

Where

E = expenditures for current consumption in the marketplace
C = the number of consumption units (composed of families and unrelated individuals)
I = median family income before taxes
a = tax ratio
b = ratio of expenditures

Equation (2) deals with the total expenditures for current consumption based on data generated from shopping. This formula facilitates the calculation of estimated annual expenditures in retailing and service establishments in the area that is being examined.

$$T = (d)\,(E)\,(e)\,(f) \tag{2}$$

Where

T = expenditures in retail and service establishments in the market area

d = percentage allocation of expenditures for current consumption (E in For mula [1]) by store type

e = shopping pattern ratio

f = trade flow ratio

Equation (3) deals with the recommended number of retail establishments for each line of product and service trade.

$$S = \frac{T}{gh} \tag{3}$$

Where

S = recommended number of establishments for each retail and service line

g = dollar sales per square foot for each trade line

h = recommended average establishment size in square feet for each trade line

Combining these three equations provides a good assessment of the identified trading area and the opportunities therein.

The number of the local retail facilities (RF) can be greater, equal, or smaller than S in Formula (3). If RF is less than S, there are a lot of opportunities in the area. If RF equals S, the area is properly represented by retail establishments, but not saturated. If RF is greater than S, then the area is oversaturated.

Business activity in the area where the site is selected is critical. If, for instance, estimated sales volume for apparel is more than $1 million and The Limited store needs about $1 million to open up a new store, then this becomes a good match. There are a number of approaches that would help determine the level of business activity. Samli (1989) identifies four different approaches that can be used to examine the level of business: (1) physical observation of the area, (2) buying power index analysis, (3) quality and sales activity index examination, and (4) using indicators.

Physical Observation

Observing the area and its physical features can reveal much information about the level of business activity. The number of homes, their price range, and their age and density are all indicators of the level of business activity. One simple way of approaching this matter has been to take aerial photos of the area. Such photos indicate the highway network, household density, and accessibility and proximity to the specific trading area. In recent years, very sophisticated computer systems have also been used for this purpose. Early in this chapter, various geographic information systems were briefly discussed. These computer systems, in the near future, are likely to become a very powerful tool to use in the assessment of the physical analysis of the area (Robins 1993; Berman and Evans 1995).

Buying Power Index

One of the oldest and most widely used techniques to evaluate the level of business activity is the buying power index (BPI). It is available for all towns and counties larger than 10,000 population. Three specific components make up the buying power index: effective buying income, retail sales, and population. The technique was developed by the *Sales and Marketing Management Journal*. In addition to business-level analysis, this technique has provided a sound base for historical analysis, since it has been in existence for about half a century. The three variables, effective buying income, retail sales, and population, are weighted by 5, 3, and 2, respectively. Thus, the effective buying power index of a city, for example—Jacksonville, Florida—is calculated as presented in Exhibit 6.7. Jacksonville's effective buying power is estimated to be 0.64 percent of that of the national total. By using a total national sales figure, such as total auto tire sales, and multiplying it by 0.64, we could approximate the number of auto tires to be purchased in this city. The same procedure is applicable for all of the major product and service lines.

The Quality Index

This particular measure provides additional insight into the existing opportunities in the area that is being studied. By dividing the buying power index that is calculated for this city by Jacksonville's population as a percentage of the national total, we develop a quality index figure. The figures are presented in Exhibit 6.7. Dividing 0.64 by 0.50, we get 1.28. This figure indicates that the area still has unused potential. There could be more sales in this city. Another approach is an index of sales activity. This can be calculated by dividing the population percentage by the retail sales percentage. In this case, 0.5 divided by 0.3 equals 1.67. Once again, the resultant sales activity index indicates that there is substantial additional sales potential in the area.

Indicators

The local business-level activity can be measured by one or more indicators. A certain type of consumption activity—for example, grocery purchases—can be explored by tying the calculations to per capita or per household consumption figures. It is, of course, necessary to have the population and household numbers in the area. Exhibits 6.8 and 6.9 illustrate one such attempt. In an effort to determine the market potential for groceries in Jacksonville, income of households and number of households in each income range are determined. The proportion of grocery purchases in each category is also presented in Exhibit 6.8. These grocery purchase proportions are national averages and considered to be homogeneous throughout the country.

Exhibit 6.9 is based on the data presented by the previous exhibit. This particular exhibit illustrates how an approximation of total income in each income category looks and the amount of money that is spent on groceries. The total grocery consumption (or purchase) figures presented in the exhibit can be used to determine the market opportunities in Jacksonville for grocery retailing. Assume, for instance, the average sales volume for a supermarket is $12 million; the area would then support about 724 supermarkets. Assuming there are only 650 supermarkets already, there is room for about 74 more. It must be reiterated that this indicator approach provides a crude approximation of the market potential. It will be necessary to go beyond this point and examine the consumption patterns, brands, and product preferences in each income category. These patterns most assuredly vary between income groups.

Another illustration of the indicator approach is presented in Exhibit 6.10. It evaluates the level of business activity in the area of gas stations for Jacksonville. By using the number of cars, number of gas stations, and cost of driving one mile as indicators, it determines that, on average, about $5 million revenue is generated for each service station. Needless to say, the total potential is not equally distributed among the service stations. However, the averages indicate that, for instance, there is much money to be made if the average revenue of service stations is around $2 million. It means that there is room for a number of additional service stations in the area.

Customer Analysis and Sales Potentials

Once an area's potential is established, then it becomes necessary to determine just how much of this total potential can be obtained by the proposed retail store. Here, identifying certain characteristics of consumers in the area is important. Such analyses emphasize two additional dimensions: (1) further analyses of demographic and income levels, and (2) examining attitudes and habits of those who are most likely to be customers, through customer surveys. These two approaches are complementary to each other, not substitutes for one another.

Evaluation of demographic data has already been discussed in this chapter. Further analyses relating to the specific trading area must take place before the store's sales potential can be realistically approximated (Exhibit 6.5). Market potentials must be revised with the socioeconomic makeup of the market so that this goal can be realized. However, it is necessary to go even further in these analyses. Additional survey inputs will identify if consumers like the existing shopping complex where the proposed store is to be located. Basically, consumers' likes and dislikes relating to the particular area and their shopping patterns regarding where they go, how often they go there, and approximately how much they buy need to be understood. The whole exercise leads to the proposed store's sales potential, which leads to capital needs.

Sales potential estimation can be achieved by following six steps (Samli 1989), as identified in Exhibit 6.11. They are based on (1) number of households, (2) average annual income, (3) proportion of annual income spent on certain product lines, (4) the proportion of total that is likely to be spent in the proposed store, (5) competitor's negative impact, and (6) sales potential. The whole process is illustrated in the numerical example section of Exhibit 6.11. Assuming, for example, that a new supermarket requires a sales potential of $2 million, in the proposed area there is a very substantial sales potential for another supermarket. Thus, the proposed store is very feasible (Exhibit 6.5).

CAPITAL NEEDS

Thus far we have discussed the amount of revenue that the proposed store may receive. It is now necessary to determine how much capital it would take to get the store started. Therefore, all of the steps presented in Exhibit 6.5 up until the last step are the means to an end. A true assessment of a store's feasibility must necessarily include its capital needs.

Quite often, when businesses fail, it is claimed that they were undercapitalized. It is critical to realize that unless there are adequate funds, a business should not enter the marketplace. It must also be realized that when a business fails because of financial status, it may be called undercapitalized for inadequate funds; however, inadequate funds can be an afterthought or simply an outcome, but not the cause.

Exhibit 6.12 illustrates some of the key statistics that may be used in determining the pre-opening expenses along with capital requirements. Assuming cost of operations, including cost of goods sold plus personnel costs and other immediate transactions, and assuming (hypothetically) that inventory turnover rate, which indicates just how many times the average inventory is sold in the course of a year, is about three, a number of analyses can be performed.

First, let us assume 75.9; 60 percent is the actual cost of goods sold. It is customary in practice to have six months revolving credit. Therefore, 60 percent of $2.7 million (Exhibit 6.12) is $1.6 million divided by 3, yielding roughly $530,000. One-sixth of $530,000, since there is six months revolving credit, yields an approximate $88,000 as what may be needed for the two-month inventory.

Assuming that the first three months are not likely to yield any profit, at least two of these must be covered. Again, 40 percent of $2.7 million divided by two (two months) is likely to yield the second part of capital requirements. This portion will yield about $180,000.

On top of the first two portions of the analysis (inventory costs, operating costs for two months), there are pre-opening expenditures. Pre-opening expenditures are not usually excessive because the land and buildings are included in the rent. The site is made operational by the landlord(s). The pre-opening expenditures include some of the store layout, display windows, signs, and promotional and other expenditures. Anywhere between 10 to 50 percent of the monthly expenses can be allotted for exterior and interior fixtures and other promotional expenses. About $225,000 is monthly sales ($2.7 million divided by 12). About 10 percent of this amount is $22,500, the estimated pre-opening expenditures. Thus, by combining the three components of these analyses—$88,000 plus $180,000 plus $22,500 equals $290,500— we find the amount necessary to start this supermarket. Assuming the net profit is about 3.3 percent of $2.7 million sales, approximately $89,100, the return is expected to be actualized. This is slightly above a 30-percent return on investment and, hence, appears to be quite an attractive investment proposition.

INTERNATIONAL CORNER

Wherever the retailer plans to expand in the world markets, it cannot proceed with a business-as-usual approach. International markets present special challenges in terms of merchandising, labeling, logistics, labor unions, employees, and customer cultural sensitivity (Redman 1995).

Merchandising presents differentiation possibilities that may be critical for the retailer to gain competitive advantage. Sometimes the name of the company may also be its special brand. Ann Taylor stores, for instance, have been promoting the Ann Taylor name as a special name particularly in women's specialty apparel retailing (Wilson 1995). Benetton has done this internationally for years. Some countries' laws require certain features of merchandise labels. In Canada, for instance, they are required to be bilingual.

Building a large assortment of goods in a 100,000-square-foot store, for instance, is a formidable logistics challenge, along with merchandising and marketing. Finding and developing suppliers to obtain the necessary merchandise calls for hands-on experience and a lot of time. It is critical that the international retailer find proper vendors and establish a partnership with them.

A model such as the one presented in Exhibit 6.10 can be used in international retailing. But it has to be repeated for every site and every market. In establishing capital requirements, the retail establishment must factor additional promotion costs so that the retail establishment can be properly introduced. These promotion costs are also likely to vary in each and every market.

Finally, the international retailer must be extremely sensitive to local culture, not only to treat its employees right, but to appeal to its local markets effectively.

SUMMARY

This chapter deals with market potentials. Any prospective retailer must be able to evaluate the overall market potential. This way it can be decided if this a feasible proposition. The chapter dwells upon assessing market potentials, determining sales potential, evaluating feasibility, and assessing capital needs. These four areas are all based on a series of macro and micro analyses.

It is pointed out that if market potentials cannot be converted into capital needs, a retail investment project cannot be objectively evaluated. The chapter deals with different aspects of trading areas. The important concept of determining the level of business activity in a given area is analyzed carefully. The chapter provides guidance and gives encouragement to retailers and prospective retailers to use existing data and to undertake additional marketing research.

Exhibits

Exhibit 6.1
Risk-Reducing Preliminary Plans

Assessing Market Potentials	Macro
Determining Sales Potential	Macro
Evaluating Feasibility	Micro
Determining Capital Needs	Micro
Risk Reduction through Planning	Micro

Exhibit 6.2
Delineating the Trading Area of a Proposed Shopping Center

Shopping Center	Located in Census Tract	Square Footage of Selling Space	Travel Time From A	Breaking Point from Shopping Center to A	Estimated Proportion of Outshopping (%)
A	1	500,000	0	0	--
B	2	125,000	7	7.5	15
C	3	250,000	18	10.8	10
D	4	100,000	15	3.8	20
E	5	500,000	28	14.9	5

Source: Adapted and revised from Samli (1989).

Exhibit 6.3
Census Tracts and Market Potentials for Apparel within the Trading Area of the Proposed Shopping Complex A

Census Tracts	Population	Per Capita Apparel Purchases*	Potential for Tract ($000,000)	A's Share ($000,000)**
1	7,500	1,500	11.2	1.7
2	10,300	1,700	17.5	1.1
3	5,500	1,300	7.2	.8
4	8,100	1,500	12.2	.5

*Calculated by total income multiplied by national averages of apparel purchases by income groups.

**Calculated by multiplying the outshopping tendency figures and potential for the tract figures.

Exhibit 6.4
Consumer Purchase Behavior Questionnaire

1. What SHOPPING CENTER did you last make your purchases of the following items?

    _____ Clothing   _____ Household Furnishings

    _____ Food   _____ Hardware

    _____ Cosmetics/Drugs   _____ Home Electronics

    _____ Eating out/Entertainment

2. Do you patronize the same places for these purchases or do you change quite often?

    ☐ Same   ☐ Change

3. How many members of your household normally work full time and how many part time?

    _____ Full time   _____ Part time

Exhibit 6.4 (*continued*)

4. What type of work do full-timers do and part-timers do?

Full-timers	Part-timers
1. _____	1. _____
2. _____	2. _____
3. _____	3. _____

5. What are the APPROXIMATE AGES of those persons living in your household?

    Male (_____) (_____) (_____) (_____)   Female (_____) (_____) (_____) (_____)

6. How many CARS in the family? _____

7. At what shopping center do you NORMALLY MAKE THE MAJORITY of the following family purchases?

    _____ Clothing   _____ Household Furnishings

    _____ Food   _____ Hardware

    _____ Cosmetics/Drugs   _____ Home Electronics

    _____ Eating out/Entertainment

8. What is the EDUCATIONAL LEVEL of the adults in your family (adult 21 years or older)?

    Adult 1 (Male) _____   Adult 1 (Female) _____

    Adult 2 (Male) _____   Adult 2 (Female) _____

    Adult 3 (Male) _____   Adult 3 (Female) _____

9. What bracket indicated below most closely fits your TOTAL FAMILY INCOME per year?

    ☐ Less than $10,000   ☐ $60,001-75,000
    ☐ $10,001-25,000   ☐ $75,001-90,000
    ☐ $25,001-40,000   ☐ $90,001-105,000
    ☐ $40,001-60,000   ☐ Over $105,000

Source: Adapted and revised from Huff (1962) and Samli (1989).

Exhibit 6.5
Converting Trading Area Potential to Capital Needs

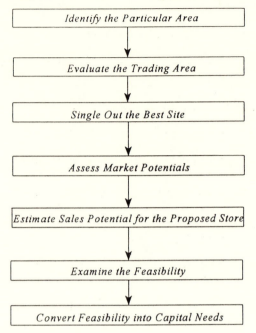

| Identify the Particular Area |
| Evaluate the Trading Area |
| Single Out the Best Site |
| Assess Market Potentials |
| Estimate Sales Potential for the Proposed Store |
| Examine the Feasibility |
| Convert Feasibility into Capital Needs |

Exhibit 6.6
A Checklist of Site Evaluation

Features	Site 1	Site 2	Site 3	Site 4
Traffic congestion (vehicular)	1	4	6	8
Highways connecting to the site	4	4	8	5
Exits are adequate	1	2	3	2
Parking facilities are sufficient	1	1	4	8
Attractive to pedestrians	3	3	8	4
Safe to walk around	3	3	3	3
Density of pedestrian traffic	3	3	8	8
Landlords are responsive	1	1	4	6
Landlords maintain facilities well	2	2	2	2
Landlords will give long term leases	1	5	6	8
Rents increase unreasonably	1	4	4	2
Landlords are not absentee owners	1	1	4	7
Economic and business activity is good	1	3	4	7
Competition is reasonable	1	3	3	8
Customers in the immediate area are a good target	1	1	2	3
TOTAL	25	40	69	81

Note: Each feature is evaluated on a scale of 1 (excellent) to 10 (poor).

Exhibit 6.7
Buying Power Index of Jacksonville, Florida[a]

Income[b]	$0.9 \times 5 = 4.5$
Retail Sales[c]	$0.3 \times 3 = 0.9$
Population[d]	$0.5 \times 2 = \underline{1.0}$
	$6.4 \div 10 = 0.64$

[a]Hypothetical figures

[b]Income as a percentage of the national total.

[c]Retail sales as a percentage of the national total.

[d]Population as a percentage of the national total.

Exhibit 6.8
District of Jacksonville, Florida, and National Distribution of Expenditures on Food

Income per Household	Percentage of All Households	Total Percentage of Expenditures on Food in U.S.
$10,000-14,999	8.8	23.0
$15,000-24,999	19.0	17.4
$25,000-49,999	36.3	13.8
$50,000 & Over	21.8	9.0

Source: Department of Commerce (1993), U.S. Department of Labor (1993).

Note: Total number of households in Jacksonville was 343,043 as of December 31, 1989.

Exhibit 6.9
**Estimated Total Personal Income, Number of Households in Each
Income Category, and Estimated Expenditures on Food, Jacksonville,
Florida**

Income per Household	Number of Units[a]	Total Estimated Income[b]	Total Estimated Expenditures on Food[c]
$10,000-14,999	30,187	373,503,751	85,905,863
$15,000-24,999	65,178	1,358,896,122	236,447,925
$25,000-49,999	124,525	4,326,621,125	597,073,715
$50,000 & Over	74,783	5,886,244,713	529,762,024
		TOTAL	1,449,189,527

[a]Estimates are based on household percentages in Exhibit 6.8 multiplied by the total number of households.

[b]Number of units were multiplied by the midpoint of income per household, with the exception of the last category, in which an estimated average income of $80,000 was utilized.

[c]Total income figures were multiplied by total percentage of expenditure figures in Exhibit 6.8.

Exhibit 6.10
Estimating the Market Potential for a New Service Station

1. Number of automobiles in Jacksonville Beaches area (estimation): 30,000

2. Number of service stations in Jacksonville Beaches area: 40

3. Average market share per service station:

$$\frac{Number\ of\ autos}{Number\ of\ Service\ Stations} = \frac{30,000}{40} = 750\ Autos\ per\ Station$$

4. Costs associated with auto maintenance and operation (including gas, oil, service):

    Cost of driving one mile = 48.9[a]

    Average mileage driven per year = 11,621

    Cost of driving one mile x average mileage driven per year:

    48.9 x 11,621 = 6,683.00 per year per automotive operation and maintenance

5. Estimating market potential for each service station: 750 x 6,683.00 = 5,012,250; on the average $5 million volume per service station.

Note: All estimates are subjective, based on some facts and intuition.

[a]Motor Vehicle Manufacturers' Association (1995).

Exhibit 6.11
Estimating Sales Potential

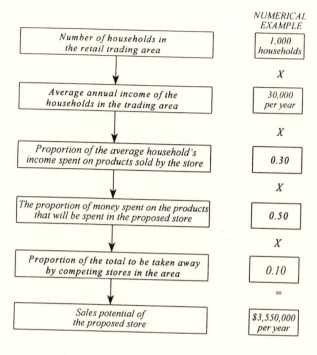

	NUMERICAL EXAMPLE
Number of households in the retail trading area	1,000 households
X	
Average annual income of the households in the trading area	30,000 per year
X	
Proportion of the average household's income spent on products sold by the store	0.30
X	
The proportion of money spent on the products that will be spent in the proposed store	0.50
X	
Proportion of the total to be taken away by competing stores in the area	0.10
=	
Sales potential of the proposed store	$3,550,000 per year

Exhibit 6.12
Operating Expenditures

	Stores with Assets Less Than $100,000	Stores with Assets of $1-5 Million
Net Sales	100.0	100.0
Cost of Operations	75.9	80.0
Rent	2.9	1.4
Interest	0.7	0.5
Depreciation	0.8	0.9
Pensions	0.3	0.7
Other	14.4	13.7
Compensation	3.0	1.0
Taxes	1.3	1.2
Profit Margin after Taxes	3.3	1.4
	(Sales 2,700,000)	(Sales 23,600,000)

Source: Troy (1995).

References

Amato, Henry N., and Evan E. Anderson. 1972. The Location of Retail Activity. Working paper series, no. 75. Graduate School of Administration, Tulane University, New Orleans.

Applebaum, William. 1966. "Guidelines for a Store-Location Strategy." *Journal of Marketing Research* (October): 128–134.

Berman, Barry, and Joel R. Evans. 1995. *Retail Management.* Englewood Cliffs, N.J.: Prentice Hall.

Converse, P. D. 1946. *Retail Trade Areas in Illinois.* Business Study No. 4. Urbana: University of Illinois Press.

Dalrymple, Douglas J., and Donald C. Thompson. 1969. *Retailing: An Economic View.* New York: Free Press.

Department of Commerce. 1993. *1990 Census of Population and Housing Census Tracts and BNAS.* Jacksonville, Fla.: MSA.

Eisenpreis, Alfred. 1965. An Evaluation of Current Store Location. Paper presented at the National Conference of the American Marketing Association, Chicago.

Elmaghraby, Salah F. 1966. "On Generalized Activity Networks." *Industrial Engineering* 18 (November): 75–86.

Enis, Ben M., and Keith R. Cox. 1968. "Demographic Analysis of Store Patterns." In *Marketing and the New Science of Planning,* ed. Robert L. King. Chicago: American Marketing Association.

Forbes, J. D. 1968. "Consumer Patronage Behavior." In *Marketing and the New Science of Planning,* ed. Robert L. King. Chicago: American Marketing Association.

Gist, Ronald R. 1968. *Retailing: Concepts and Decision Making.* New York: John Wiley and Sons.

Goldstucker, Jac L. 1965. "Trading Areas." In *Science in Marketing,* ed. George Schwartz. New York: John Wiley and Sons.

Goldstucker, Jac L., Danny N. Bellenger, and Thomas J. Stanley. 1978. "New Developments in Retail Trading Area Analysis and Site Selection." Georgia State University.

Huff, David L. 1962. "Determination of Inter-Urban Retail Trade Areas." Real Estate Research Program, University of California.

Mason, J. Barry, and Morris L. Mayer. 1987. *Modern Retailing.* Dallas: Business Publications.

Moore, Charles T., and Joseph B. Mason. 1970/1971. "Empirical Behavioristic Assumptions in Trading Area Studies." *Journal of Retailing* (Winter): 31–37.

Motor Vehicle Manufacturers' Association. 1995. *Facts and Figures.* Detroit: Motor Vehicle Manufacturers' Association.

Redman, Mel. 1995. "Preparation and Study Central to International Expansion." *Chain Store Age,* 15 October.

Reilly, William J. 1931. *The Law of Retail Gravitation.* New York: McGraw-Hill.

Robins, Gary. 1993. "Retail GIS Use Growing." *Stores* (January): 46–49.

Samli, A. Coskun. 1989. *Retail Marketing Strategies*. Westport, Conn.: Quorum Books.

Troy, Leo. 1995. *Almanac of Business and Industrial Financial Ratios.* Englewood Cliffs, N.J.: Prentice Hall.

U.S. Department of Labor. 1993. *Consumer Expenditures Survey Series, 1990–91*. BLS Bulletin 2425.

Wilson, Marianne. 1995. "Reinventing Ann Taylor." *Chain Store Age Executive* (January): 26–45.

Chapter 7

Adjusting Retail Marketing
Strategies to Consumer Behavior

Understanding consumer behavior, by definition, implies understanding the underlying factors that would lead the consumer to decide what, where, when, and how he or she will buy apparel (Schiffman and Kanuk 1994).

This chapter presents a general consumer behavior model that directly applies to retailing. The approach that is used in constructing this model is eclectic. The model draws from numerous consumer behavior theories and research efforts to make our knowledge of consumer behavior more applicable to retailing.

The model presented in this chapter explores the consumer behavior principles that are related to store selection and store patronage activities. If the retailer understands these processes, then he or she can attract consumers to his or her store. However, store selection and store patronage decisions are very complex. They are influenced by cultural, socioeconomic, and racial factors, along with lifestyle characteristics and educational backgrounds, among other numerous internal and external factors that influence behavior. It must be understood that the retailer cannot possibly change internal factors, such as personality or cultural background, but he or she can significantly influence (or at least work with) the external variables, such as socioeconomic and racial characteristics.

A CONSUMER BEHAVIOR MODEL IS NEEDED

The retail decision maker is vitally interested in three specific phases of consumer behavior that are related to retailing. The first is pre-purchase behavior: Just how do consumers decide that they need the product or service? The second is purchase behavior: How or why do consumers choose those stores, products, and brands? The third is post-purchase behavior: What is the thought process that will keep them away from our store or bring them back to our store next time? These three phases of consumer behavior are critical for success in retailing.

Consumer behavior, as a discipline, has enjoyed great success during the past thirty years or so. During this time, many consumer behavior models were constructed. Much research either supported these models or helped construct new models. During this period, emphasis on the marketing concept (Kotler 1994) increased and, simultaneously, the increasing voice of dissatisfied consumers also reinforced the emphasis on consumer-behavior-related research. Unfortunately, only a small portion of this research has been focused on retailing. In general terms, retailing as a discipline has been deprived of the use of our ever-increasing knowledge of consumer behavior (Samli 1989).

Since consumer behavior at the retail level is very complex with many phases, dimensions, and influencing factors, any attempt to bring it to the retail level is a very valuable. Purchase-behavior-related theory and information must be systematically organized so that retailers can better serve their customers and enhance their market position and profit picture.

Exhibit 7.1 illustrates a general consumer behavior model that is appropriate for retailing. Retail consumer behavior is functionally related to seven components: (1) cultural background, (2) individual personality, (3) need realization and shopping motivation, (4) shopper characteristics, (5) purchase behavior, (6) store choice, brand choice, and product choice behaviors, and (7) buyer remorse or cognitive dissonance.

Component five of Exhibit 7.1 illustrates and discusses the specific aspects of the consumer behavior model pertinent to retailing. This discussion is particularly important to retailers, since it brings consumer behavior theory and retailing practices together. The main thrust of this model is to distinguish shopping motivation from shopper characteristics and connect them to marketing functions by the retailer. The retailer must take into account the behavior in its target markets and influence this behavior by proactive management practices. It is critical to assume that motivation can be conditioned by external stimuli, whereas shopper characteristics are innate. For instance, agreeable shoppers who are brand loyal and cautious cannot suddenly become status shoppers who are impractical, go for new gadgets, and are impulse buyers. These shopper characteristics can further modify shopping motivation. It is critical to understand them and work with them.

Both internal and external influences must be identified carefully and dealt with effectively. They are discussed in some detail later on in this chapter. Obviously, all external influences in internal modifiers form the consumers' purchase process. Purchase process is vital for the retailer to understand because here the consumer is making a decision to patronize the retail store. Store patronage of regular customers is particularly important because acquiring new customers is estimated to be five times more costly. Therefore, the retailer has much stake in the outcome of the shopping process. In Exhibit 7.1, the outcome of the purchase behavior is depicted as post-purchase behavior, which is discussed further in the specific model. But it must be emphasized here that the retailer is aiming at repeat purchases and continued patronage. Hence, there is no room for buyer remorse or cognitive dissonance (Festinger 1957) that implies a doubtful attitude on the part of customers as to whether or not they have gotten a good deal.

CULTURE, PERSONALITY, AND SHOPPING MOTIVATION

Culture, according to many thinkers and researchers, is the basic force behind consumer behavior. According to Samli (1995), an individual, because of the influence of a culture screen, develops a personality and behaves in certain ways as a consumer. In other words, all people are products of a culture, and that culture, in a broad sense, determines an individual's behavior patterns.

Thus, cultural background and personality must be considered together, and behavioral patterns must be related to them (Samli 1995). America is a multicultural society. There are many minorities, such as Asian Americans, Hispanic Americans, and African Americans. In addition, there are large subcultures among the majority, primarily based on socioeconomic diversities. Though there have been many attempts to classify cultures (or subcultures) from a retailing perspective, an attempt is made here to dichotomize consumer behavior between *individualistic* and *collectivistic* subcultures (Samli 1995). Exhibit 7.2 illustrates the characteristics of these two subcultures for the individual.

Consumers in the collectivistic subculture are influenced by other individuals; they learn from others (cognitive impact). Economic necessities play a critical role in their behavior patterns and values. Immediate groups (such as the extended family) have significant influence on their decision making relating to what, where, and how much. All these influences are still modified by certain beliefs and values (affective factors) that are instilled in individuals by others in their immediate circles (Samli 1995). This overall series of influences have very significant retailing implications. Most minorities in the United States display many aspects of this overall pattern, with shades of deviation.

An individualistic consumer, as a member of the individualistic subculture, at the periphery is influenced by social classes. Closely related to this is a hierarchy of needs that brings about perceived needs in the minds of the consumer. Both the hierarchy of needs and social-class values are nominally passed on to the individual by other people. However, in individualistic subcultures this process is initiated by the individual himself or herself rather than by the groups or other individuals in inner circles. Affective influences (beliefs and values) are not as strong as they are in collectivistic subcultures. The most important influence on the individual in these subcultures is the individual's efforts to explore and learn. Cognition in individualistic subcultures is the most critical factor. Individuals in such cultures reach out and initiate certain information searches and information gathering. The retailer must be there trying to give part of this information with the hopes of bringing them to the store.

While most American minorities appear to be in the collectivistic subculture mode, the American majority may be identified as being close to an individualistic subculture. In these two extreme cultural alternatives, consumer behavior regarding retailing varies and, hence, there must be significantly different retailing practices to cater to each effectively.

Though these two cultural blocks have different approaches to realizing that they have to frequent or patronize certain retail institutions, they both have, in general terms, the same basic shopping motivators. However, these motivators may have significant differences in influencing the subcultures.

NEED REALIZATION AND SHOPPING MOTIVATION

Every retailer should realize that all consumers do not patronize a retail facility for the same reason. People shop for different reasons. It is important for retailers to know first why people shop, and second, and perhaps more importantly, why they shop here or elsewhere.

Need realization, or recognizing the fact that we need to buy certain things, is extremely critical and is discussed in the specific model. It is important, however, to look at just what motivates people to shop, not in terms of need realization, but in terms of shopping information (Assael 1981). An early classical study by Tauber (1972) identified seven shopping motives. Through an in-depth interviewing technique, the following were concluded (Tauber 1972; Samli 1989):

1. Diversion—the need to get away from daily routines and changing pace.
2. Self-gratification—a special stimulation on the individual's psyche that is produced by the shopping process itself.
3. Learning about new trends—since there are new products and services that are entering the market and there are new fashions, individuals can learn much about these by visiting stores.

4. Physical activity—walking around and shopping in large shopping complexes provides exercise and relaxation.

5. Sensory stimulation—by seeing, smelling, touching, or trying the product out, individuals are motivated.

6. Social experiences outside the home—socializing with friends and other consumers or interacting with salespersons provides a special motivation.

7. Pleasure of bargaining—to be able to compare, contrast, and negotiate the terms of the purchase to find the "best buys" can be a very important stimulator (Tauber 1972).

8. Clearly identified needs or wants of the individuals—trying to satisfy the identified needs with shopping around is a critical motive.

9. Specific pressures on individuals to shop—particularly in collectivistic cultures, individuals may be directed to buy certain things from certain places. This is a critical motivation factor for shoppers.

At least two additional factors are added onto Tauber's seven. As seen in Exhibit 7.1, pre-purchase behavior begins with shopping motivation. Each and every one of the nine factors listed will force the consumer to consider where they may go, among numerous alternatives, to satisfy their realized needs. Obviously, the consumer who is seeking diversion is not likely to buy at the same place as of the consumer who is trying to take care of urgent needs. This second consumer may go directly to the nearest specialty store that may provide the best quality of that product line. However, the consumer who is looking for diversion may go to a luxurious mall in the area.

It must be reiterated that, in a general sense, any one of the nine motives may not play a more critical role in the consumer's shopping activity than any other. However, in the case of specific shopper groups or market segments, some of these motives may play a more important role than others. It must also be reiterated that these nine motives are not mutually exclusive, and therefore they may interact with one another. It may be stated that if there are these shopping motives, then there may also be various shopping behaviors. These shopping behaviors can be explored in an effort to classify shopper characteristics. Once again, if the shopping motives and shopper characteristics are understood, then the retailers can do a better job of satisfying (or better yet, delighting) their customers. The following section deals with the various attempts that have been made to classify shoppers on the basis of their shopper characteristics.

GROUPING SHOPPERS

If it were possible that a retailer could group his or her customers on the basis of the identified characteristics and behavior patterns, the retailer could do a better job. If the store is attracting bargain hunters, there may not be any justification to carry mink furs or diamonds and advertise them. But perhaps the customers are attracted to the store because the store does a good job of not detaining them at the checkout counters. Similarly, they are attracted to the store because they do not spend too much time trying to locate merchandise due to the outstanding layout of the store.

One of the earliest attempts to classify consumers was made by Nystrom (1929). This particular typology was replicated and researched by Stone (1954). Stone used a consumer classification by grouping consumers into four categories: (1) economic, (2) personalizing, (3) ethical, and (4) apathetic.

Economic Consumers

These are the people who are primarily inclined to be efficient in their shopping activities. According to them, a store must be judged on the basis of objective criteria, such as price, quality, and merchandise mix. They like to know more about new trends, and need satisfaction, effectively and fast.

Personalizing Consumers

These are the people who need social contact. They are likely to develop strong personal relationships with the store personnel. Such relationships stimulate their loyalty to the store. They are motivated by the intimacy they achieve in the store. They are particularly influenced by diversion, social experience, and self-gratification motives.

Ethical Consumers

These are the people who are motivated by certain idealistic values, such as supporting the local economy by patronizing local businesses. They shop particularly to help the "little guy" who has been there for decades or even generations. They are motivated by social experience and self-gratification motives.

Apathetic Consumers

These people do not like to shop. They are likely to minimize the trouble of shopping by being efficient and emphasizing convenience. They need satisfaction in a fast manner and with minimum interaction with store personnel.

According to Stone (1954), higher socioeconomic groups are primarily ethical consumers, and lower socioeconomic groups are apathetic. In 1971, Darden and Reynolds came up with additional validation of Stone's conclusions. However, Stone's categorization of consumer groups was subsequently found to be inadequate. Darden and Ashton

(1974–1975) posited that there were other consumer groups, and added three different groups to Stone's typology. According to their findings, the typologies may change depending on the phenomenon that is being researched. They illustrated this point by analyzing shoppers in supermarkets. They discovered that there were those who loved shopping stamps (or, in current times, coupon collectors), those who disliked stamps (coupons), and some who simply thrived on convenience (Darden and Ashton 1974–1975).

About the same period, Mochis (1976) came up with his own classification of consumers on the basis of their behavior with cosmetic purchases. He identified six important groups: (1) special sales shoppers, (2) brand loyal, (3) store loyal, (4) problem solvers, (5) specializers, and (6) name-conscious shoppers. The first four are basically self-explanatory, the fourth being a group of people who cannot make up their minds. Members of the fifth group were influenced by peer group behavior, and the sixth group was attached to the store that sells the product (Samli 1989). If Dillards is planning on introducing a new line of cosmetics and if this somewhat upscale department store has customer loyalty, its regular customers are likely to try this new product line.

In 1987, McCammon, Coykendall, and Whitfield developed a new typology. Their classification was composed of five particular groups: (1) transitional shoppers—7.6 percent of the population, who have career aspirations and are very price conscious; (2) impacted shoppers—26.8 percent of the population, who are affected by economic changes and cautious in their shopping practices; (3) dedicated shoppers—24.8 percent of the population, who shop more departments than stores; (4) contemporary shoppers—25.4 percent of the population, who represent the upper class in terms of their education, income, and lifestyle and whose concern is not price but need satisfaction; and (5) social shoppers—15.4 percent of the population, who consider shopping an extension of their normal social life. The best classification of this sort was presented by Hart (1989). Hart developed a seven-group typology. These groups and the particular purchase motivation that is significant for each are presented in Exhibit 7.3. There may not be a perfect classification system, but it is clear that the retailer must be able to group consumers in some logical manner so that a decision can be made about which group to emphasize. No retailer can be all things to all groups.

Between the shopper descriptions and purchase motivation characteristics, Exhibit 7.3 has significant implications for individual retailers as well as the retailing sector in general. If the purchasing behavior of each group is identified and connected to certain purchase motives, then the retailer can cater to these consumer groups and can motivate them the way purchase motives indicate in general terms. K-Mart, for instance, can advertise to lower-middle to middle income people who are agreeable shoppers. In addition to having particular mass media to reach these people, the company must follow through on clearly identified needs, such as back to school, spring cleaning, and the like, or specific pressures, such as managing a home economically or developing a casual-wear wardrobe within a limited budget.

Individual, proactive retailers must generate their own information about need perception, product preferences, brand recognition, store loyalty, and other factors influencing their customers' behavior patterns. It is also quite likely that existing research typologies regarding shopper groups are not comprehensive and universal. Thus, retailers will (and must) always be on the lookout for additional groups and changing purchase motivation.

It must be reiterated here that the pre-purchase, purchase, and post-purchase activities or behavior patterns are extremely important to retailers. It is quite possible that these three major phases of shopper behavior may be at least nominally modified for every retail establishment. Nominal modification describing shopper behavior may be the key for survival if the retailer understands the specific nuances of the total behavior pattern.

THE SPECIFICS OF PURCHASE BEHAVIOR

It is necessary to explore the specifics of consumer behavior as it relates to retailing. Such exploration will provide the retailer with specific and effective marketing approaches. Exhibit 7.4 illustrates the specific steps involved in purchase behavior. These steps are applicable to all consumers regardless of buyer motivation and shopper characteristics.

In addition to the pre-purchase and purchase processes, there are two groups of modifiers. External stimuli includes lifestyle, social class, and popular trends. These are givens for the retailer. These stimuli are modified by cultural background and personality characteristics of the individual. They all lead to shopper behavior, which is further stimulated or modified with purchase motivation. Finally, retailers' efforts in terms of establishing certain store attributes and promoting brand, product, and store images form the overall behavior patterns. Even if all consumers were to go through the same purchase process, because of these modifiers the actual behavior pattern becomes different.

Retail Buyer Behavior

Retail buyer behavior is expressed in terms of the specifics of the purchase process as depicted in Exhibit 7.4. The process begins with an individual's perception, which means the degree of exposure to the mass media and other types of information and promotion (Lambert 1970; Enis and Stafford 1969; Bettman 1973; Samli 1989). Each individual uses an individual perceptual encoding process (Bettman 1973), which indicates a personal interpretation of a stimulus, the information, or promotional messages. This perceptual encoding process can either enhance a purchase need recognition of a product or a brand, or a store patronizing need recognition. In many cases, all three may materialize (product, brand, and store), which indicates a powerful job of retail marketing. The enhancement of the purchase need can be both at the conscious and the subconscious levels (Cohen and McCann 1978; Samli 1989). When a consumer receives a stimulus that is related to shopping, it is received at a threshold. This is the level at which an effect of the stimulus begins to occur (Wilkie 1994). If the stimulus is received at the conscious level but penetrates only the absolute threshold, then it may establish an image for the product, brand, or store. However, if the penetration of the stimulus takes place at the level of differential threshold, the stimulus is more likely to enhance the image of that product, brand, or store (Samli 1989; Cohen and McCann 1978).

If the stimulus is perceived at the subconscious level, this would be a questionable way of providing stimuli for the retail buyer (Cohen and McCann 1978; Samli 1989). First, it is very difficult, if not impossible, to send messages to the subconscious of the consumer, and second, and more important, this type of subliminal approach has many legal implications. This particular approach is only used for antishoplifting practices in retailing. It is beyond the scope of this chapter.

Exhibit 7.4 illustrates the purchase process, which begins with perception. The perception process, in turn, begins with acquiring some information or receiving certain incoming messages. It is necessary for the retailer to understand just where shoppers go to receive general information. The availability of new model suburban utility vehicles (SUVs) in the community could be the first bit of information that would trigger the total process displayed in Exhibit 7.4. Since information is critical for the retail buying process to commence, it is important for the retailer to understand the consumer's information search process. Before the actual information search, individuals perceive certain information that triggers the whole activity.

Information regarding local retail shopping, for instance, comes from various sources. An earlier study has shown that the use of different sources of information has something to do with the individual's tenure in town (Samli 1989). Those who are new in town receive signals more from radio and much less from neighbors, job associates, and relatives than those who have been in one area for a long time. Friends and relatives play a more important role as a source of information among the people who live in an area for twenty years than among those who live in that area two years or less.

It must be reiterated that an individual's perception system will detect influences on the differential threshold. Weber's Law, which deals with "just noticeable difference" (JND) states that "as stimulus intensities get larger, it takes more of a change in the stimulus to be detected as a change" (Wilkie 1994, 211). In order for the consumer to reach the stage of problem recognition, there must be at least a just noticeable difference reaching the individual's differential threshold. This can be the opening of a new store, remodeling a retail establishment, introduction of a new line, seasonal changes, total remodeling, or other retailing activity.

The second step in Exhibit 7.4 is problem recognition. Based on the perception and internal interpretation of the perceived information or the message, the recognized problem may have different degrees of intensity. The high degree of intensity of the recognized problem is an indicator of successful retail marketing. The problem needs to be sufficiently intense that the consumer feels the necessity to buy, for instance, a camcorder. Along with the intensity of the problem, the intensity of the brand of the product and particularly the intensity of the store recognition (store image) must have penetrated the individual's differential threshold. If the problem is not strongly enough recognized for the consumer to stimulate the desire to purchase this product, then the brand and store image intensities of the problem do not even become a consideration. However, if the problem recognition is intense, then product or brand image and store image factors become a reinforcer of the degree of intensity. This intensity would automatically lead to the product brand and store choice; or it will lead to the recognition of the information needed to solve the problem. Thus, the intensity of the recognized problem, in general, is directly related to the perception process itself as the perceived message filters through a host of modifiers (Samli 1989).

These modifiers, among others, are related to the shopping motives discussed earlier. The individual who, for instance, is seeking diversion or sensory stimulation is likely to perceive the intended message in an exaggerated intensity, if the message is designed accordingly. In this case, the individual would recognize the problem as an extremely acute one.

The third step in the retail consumer behavior model is the information search. Again, a proactive retailer can be quite effective in this area to help accelerate this search process and to influence the consumer to make decisions in favor of the retail establishment. All buyers search for certain information. This search can be conscious or unconscious. Since the shopping behavior is mainly a learned behavior, shoppers must experience a basic learning process. This process conditions the individual to develop certain loyalties toward buying groceries at Kroger, appliances at Sears, or shoes at Payless. In order for this learned behavior to take place, information is needed. Before learning, therefore, individuals search for information. However, depending upon the cultural backgrounds and culture-triggered behavior patterns, individuals have different search processes. As depicted in Exhibit 7.2, individualistic consumers have a different way of receiving information than collectivistic consumers. Both information search and information processing vary. As indicated in Exhibit 7.2, information is received from different sources and filters through in a different way. Again, it is critical for the retailer to understand the difference. Both individualistic and collectivistic consumers are searching for information. The intensity of this search process depends on how seriously the problem is recognized and the cultural background of the shopper (Samli 1995). If the problem recognition leads to a major purchase that would take a large chunk of the shopper's budget, or if it is an important and particularly complicated product, the search process for information is likely to be intensified.

Assael (1981) stated the following:

The amount of search for information for a given product is contingent on the nature of the product (high risk or high price will generate more search), the situation (an involving situation will generate more search), the consumer's past experience and characteristics (less experience will generate more search), brand attitudes (weakly held attitudes will generate more search), and group influences (products important to the group will result in more search).

Similarly, the individualistic consumer is more likely to search for information. (p. 493)

It is maintained here that the consumer search process is composed of two separate search activities: internally triggered and externally triggered. Internal search implies a mental recall or a review of what an individual has already learned about the store, product, and brand. The internal search is often the outcome of previous external searches and depicts the linear learning theory (Kuehn 1962; Samli 1989).

The linear learning theory holds that the pattern of store selection probabilities is conditioned by the knowledge of past decisions regarding top-store choice. The theory posits that a customer's store selection is not a random process. The consumer exhibits bias in the area of store choice. The more recent the purchase experience in a particular store, the more likely the consumer will frequent the same store to purchase the same or similar products again. An early study by Kuehn (1962) formulated the application of linear learning theory to brand and product choice processes.

External search is the actual process of seeking information from various sources. Among these are mass media, other people, store employees, a store itself, product information, and brand information.

The internal search and external search processes can be either internally triggered or externally triggered. Exhibit 7.5 illustrates both internal and external information sources and search process. As can be seen, internal information sources provide information to the consumer from previous sources and personal experiences (and perhaps personal biases). External information sources are basically the retailer and the manufacturer, both of whom are seeking to create linear learning and penetrate the differential threshold. But "internally triggered search process" and "externally triggered search process" mean different things to the retailer.

Internally triggered means the individual is self-motivated to either go back to the store (having had positive experiences) or to seek out more information about the store, product, and brand. This situation is akin to cognitive influences, particularly among individualistic consumers. They are quite likely to be mainstream, upper-middle-class WASPs.

Externally triggered means the individual is motivated by others to go back to the store (having been told by certain opinion leaders) or to seek out more information about the store, or is influenced particularly by store features. This situation is closer to having affective influences, particularly among collectivistic consumers. They are more likely to be minority subcultures.

Exhibit 7.6 illustrates these options. As can be seen, if internal search is internally triggered, then the individual is relying heavily on cognitive influences. The whole activity here revolves around the individual relying on acquired experiences and information. If the individual pursues an external search which is internally triggered, then that person will rely heavily on cognitive influences received primarily through mass media. The lower left quadrant of Exhibit 7.6 illustrates that collectivistic consumers motivated by affective influences acquired through interpersonal experiences undertake an internal search that is externally triggered. Finally, an external search that is externally triggered again creates affective influences gained by interpersonal experiences. In each of the four quadrants, the retailer plays a different role.

In the first quadrant, the retailer must make sure that the customer's experiences were very positive, because here consumers rely on their own efforts and experiences. The retailer must somehow indirectly relate the message that there are new and better reasons to renew these experiences. In the second quadrant, the retailer directly tries to communicate with the consumer. Here the consumer carries the responsibility of seeking information, primarily from mass media. The informative nature of the message by the retailer is particularly critical. In the third quadrant, the retailer tries to appeal to certain subcultures, elders, or groups. These groups, in turn, will influence the individual who is a member, but this process is indirect and takes place over time. The individual develops certain values and behaviors that are learned and last a long time. Finally, in the fourth quadrant, the retailer will make the store particularly attractive to certain given subcultures. The store personnel will do a good job of selling the product by emphasizing certain cultural values and tastes.

As can be seen, Exhibit 7.6 demonstrates important guidelines regarding information source and the nature of information that the retailer should consider regarding different consumer groups. Much research is needed here to give more precise information to the retailer so that better communication and persuasion can take place to benefit both consumers and the retailers.

Information processing is the fourth step in the consumer behavior model presented in Exhibit 7.4. Consumers do not process information the same way. The retailer's message is encoded and transmitted through mass media and through the actions of sales people and a store's physical properties. The consumer receives and processes this message, and this processing activity begins with decoding. The retailing literature about decoding the message is quite weak. It is maintained here that the cultural dichotomy presented in Exhibit 7.2 and the perception process depicted in Exhibit 7.6 indicate significant differences in decoding. It is, above all, conditioned by the cultural values of the individual. A key question in the decoding area is related to whether the store, product, and brand messages are perceived simultaneously or separately. Naturally, the next question relates to whether these three are received separately, which is the most important consideration for the retailer. Again, research is critically needed in these areas.

The total decoding process involves at least five specific stages: exposure, attention, evaluation, comprehension, and retention (Exhibit 7.7) (Samli 1989). Different cultural orientations lead to different types of exposure. Individuals with collectivistic cultural backgrounds are more readily exposed to certain cultural and group values. Their exposure comes more readily from cultural values and resultant likes and dislikes. Individuals with individualistic cultural backgrounds are more exposed to the mass media and other information sources (Samli 1995). In both of these cases, exposure and attention go hand in hand. Certain cultural patterns, by definition, create preferences for information sources as well as the messages themselves. From the retailer's perspective, an attempt is made in both cases (in different ways, however) to reach the individual's differential threshold by creating JND.

A number of earlier studies have explored the evaluation stage somewhat carefully. Evaluation may mean either evaluating the source or evaluating the message itself. Studies have posited that the perceived credibility of the source is closely related to the acceptability of the message. Hence, if the source is more credible, the message enjoys greater acceptability (Miller and Basehart 1969). The retail activity here revolves around determining the credibility of different media. Again, individualistic versus collectivistic cultural orientation has a significant impact on the credibility of different media.

Subsequently, other studies indicated that source credibility is related to message acceptance only for low-involvement products. These are the types of products the consumer would buy routinely. These products do not posit a risk and, therefore, consumers repeat purchases. However, when the consumers do not agree with the message, it is rejected even if the credibility of the source is not questioned. These occurrences take place in the cases of greater involvement. If the consumer is exploring the product in great detail because of its relative importance, cost, or significance, then the message receives greater scrutiny. Hence, the message is more critical than the messenger (Cohen and McCann 1978; Samli 1989). We must reiterate here that retailers can increase the believability of their message by enhancing their own credibility in low-involvement cases. In high-involvement purchase cases, the retailer must make doubly sure that the message is credible. It may be posited here that individualistic consumers are more likely to be involved in message credibility, whereas collectivistic consumers pay more attention to source credibility. Future research is needed in this area.

The remainder of the decoding activity is related to how the message is evaluated. Comprehension and retention of the message is a function of how the message is received and evaluated. As shown in Exhibit 7.7, the consumer receives multiple messages from different stores through multiple media. If the message achieves exposure and attention, then evaluation takes place. Naturally, comprehension and retention follow suit. The outcome of this process is brand, product, and store evaluation, which is expected to lead to purchase in that particular store (Samli 1989). On the basis of this discussion, Sears hopes that middle-class Americans will have exposure to its advertisements. If these advertisements communicate well (that is, they are decoded effectively), consumers will pay attention to these advertisements and will evaluate Sears's brands, products, and stores. All these may lead to shopping at Sears stores.

A serious question can be raised regarding evaluative criteria. They are, in addition to the believability of the message and the messenger, attributes or characteristics used to compare existing alternatives by consumers. The information needs to be processed before a sale is ultimately made.

Store selection is the fifth phase of retail consumer behavior. In the final analysis, the whole behavior model presented in Exhibit 7.4 revolves around store selection. A purchase in our store cannot be achieved unless our store is selected. Two paths leading to store selection are identified and labeled critical. These are attribute orientation and activity orientation (Monroe and Guiltinan 1975; Samli, Tozier, and Harps 1980; Samli 1989). Attribute orientation implies a greater role for store characteristics in the store selection process. Store attributes include layout, color combination, design, sales clerks, displays, special sales, brands, and other special buyer information (Exhibit 7.8). Activity orientation means preoccupation with the selection process itself, based on information search and processing. Here there is more likely to be a pre-store selection planning. More emphasis is put on the budget of the consumer and product and brand features. The whole process implies individuals taking more initiative in the search process for information. It is posited here that the emphasis on the attribute characteristics of store selection is more appealing to the collectivistic consumer. Similarly, activity orientation is what the individualistic consumer is likely to exercise.

In activity orientation, the individual takes it upon himself or herself to search, sort, and process information partially before the purchase and partially during the purchase process. Attribute orientation, on the other hand, implies stronger predisposition or preconceived notions toward the store. These notions are reinforced by the specific attributes of the store if a sale is to take place. Exhibit 7.8 distinguishes these two critical and divergent search processes. Two early studies dealing with the store selection process discussed these two concepts. They implied that attribute orientation is more prominent among African American consumers, whereas activity orientation is more attributable to white Americans (Samli, Tozier, and Harps 1980; Monroe and Guiltinan 1975; Samli 1989).

During the purchase phase, the individual may display behavior patterns categorized as autonomous, semiautonomous, and dependent decisions. Autonomous is considered here as the continuation of activity orientation. Careful plans have been prepared in advance through information search and information processing. Therefore, the consumer can purchase in a retail store without needing any sales pitch from retail sales clerks and other internal stimuli. However, the individual follows another information search process in the store. Titus and Everett (1995) have constructed seventeen propositions that have valuable insights into this topic; however, they are not as yet carefully researched. They maintain that certain retail environments are symmetrical designs which are more legible but not as stimulating. It may be further hypothesized that legible or more visible store layouts would appeal to activity-oriented people, since they put more emphasis on the search for products and information itself. Stimulating environments are not symmetrical and are more likely to appeal to attribute-oriented behavior.

At the other extreme of the spectrum, purchase behavior for those who have attribute orientation involves dependent purchase decisions. The sales clerk's help and advice, among other store features, makes the purchase process feasible. These people are more stimulated with asymmetrical layouts.

Semiautonomous purchase behavior implies the partial adoption of attribute orientation and activity orientation. There is no research evidence, but it is quite likely that more people may be in this middle position. These individuals may use an attribute orientation in purchasing clothing or small appliances. They may use an activity orientation in shopping for more expensive or more involved products, such as an automobile, a camcorder, or a personal computer.

Purchase behavior may also vary depending upon differences in retail stores. For instance, Bloomingdale's in New York may thrive on attribute orientation leading to dependent purchase decisions. The sales people would stimulate purchase decisions by elaborate sales pitches. People who shop at Sears may be quite activity oriented, looking, exploring, and comparing. On the other end of the spectrum, a boutique in the inner city may attract consumers because of its attributes and sales people's personal knowledge of the store's customers.

An ideal situation would be for a store to have its attributes established in such a way that attribute orientation would be natural. Those who are inclined in the direction of activity orientation will also shop in the store because the store may facilitate the information search and process activities as well. However, such an orientation may not be practical for all retailers. Hence, a retail store may find itself in a position to choose one of these two approaches.

POST-PURCHASE ACTIVITIES IN RETAILING

The last stage of the general consumer behavior model presented in Exhibit 7.1 is post-purchase behavior. Peters (1989) stated that it is five times more costly to get new customers than to keep current ones. Thus, the retailer must make sure that customers are happy. Festinger (1957) generated the theory of cognitive dissonance. This theory, as stated earlier, relates to buyer's remorse. If a customer develops second thoughts about the recent purchase he or she made and does not feel good about shopping in Store A or about the merchandise that was purchased, then there is cognitive dissonance.

This situation, if common among the store's customers, reflects a serious problem. The problem may come from pressure-selling tactics, less-than-adequate customer services, or questionable quality merchan-

dise. Regardless of what might be causing it, if there is cognitive dissonance, the store's post-purchase policies are deficient. If a post-purchase
survey of store customers reveals that most of those who are questioned are planning on coming back to the store to shop again and an
equally large group would recommend the store to their friends, these
results indicate the absence of cognitive dissonance. However, if a similar study were to indicate that most of those questioned are not planning on coming back and even a larger proportion of the respondents
would not recommend the store to their friends, then there is a very
serious problem with the store's post-purchase policies.

It is critical to determine if there is customer attrition based on after-
the-fact dissatisfaction. Such a customer attrition quotient can be a
good indicator of the success of the store's marketing practices. Dissonance can be caused by a product or a product mix, certain brands,
sales force, customer services, the store as a whole, or any other related retail feature. If the attrition quotient is high, the retailer must
determine the real reason behind the dissonance and remedy the situation. Such an early indicator could provide important direction to the
retailer to improve marketing practices. The retailer should make sure
that (1) the customers are satisfied after a purchase transaction, (2) if
there is dissonance, customers must realize that they can return the
merchandise, (3) the attrition quotient is measured periodically, and
(4) customers have recourse, such as complaining about a store practice or sharing an opinion with the management.

Of course, it must be reiterated that all purchases do not end up
with cognitive dissonance. Indeed, many consumers are happy with
their purchases and would go back to the same store. But it is up to the
retailer to know what proportion of its customers are happy and how
happy they are.

PLANNED VERSUS UNPLANNED SHOPPING

It has been stated that activity orientation typically implies early
planning, whereas attribute orientation means a lot more, including
allowing oneself to be impressed by the attributes or shopping conditions. It is also discussed earlier that activity orientation is common
among individualistic consumers and attribute orientation is more
common among collectivistic consumers.

Consumers, particularly individualistic consumers, learn to plan for
the purchase. They decide where to buy, what to buy, or both, in advance. If and when consumers plan a purchase, they are quite likely to
plan where this product is to be purchased and what brand or make it
is going to be.

However, collectivistic consumers, who are likely to be impressed
with the attributes of the shopping facility, are not likely to plan. Ex-

hibit 7.9 illustrates four pre-purchase planning points. These represent four distinct points on a purchase-planning spectrum:

1. Collectivistic consumer who prefers attribute orientation realizes the existence of a shopping problem, but has not decided on the store or the brand and product. This could be a situation where the intended purchase is a VCR.

2. Collectivistic consumer becomes cognizant of a shopping problem and has decided on the product and brand but has not yet decided where the product will be purchased. Since the store decision has not been made, there will be a search of the stores that carry this product that is already planned. For instance, purchasing a GE washer and dryer may lead the consumer to a number of places where such an appliance is sold.

3. Individualistic consumer becomes cognizant of a shopping problem and, after some research and analysis, decides on the store but has not yet decided on the brand and the make of the product. The person may be considering a couple of suits for a forthcoming business trip. He is likely to go to the apparel shop where he knows the people but, more importantly, where he can move around freely without sales pressure and try on a large variety of suits.

4. Individualistic consumer becomes cognizant of a shopping problem, and has decided on the store, product, and brand. He and his family decide on a new car. After some research and analysis, the individual decides on a medium-sized Japanese car. Further analyses indicate that a Honda Accord will be the product. After contacting some of the Honda dealers in the area, a decision is made on the dealer also.

Thus, the purchase behavior stage can be longer if the consumer is shopping in an unplanned manner, or shorter if the shopping is done in a totally planned manner. Cultural background, shopper characteristics, and purchase motivation together form a planned or unplanned shopping event.

Knowing that consumers are coming to the store either pre-planned or unplanned and also knowing that they are motivated by certain shopping motives, the retailer must be cognizant of the existence of many alternatives that need to be considered. Exhibit 7.10 illustrates important retail marketing practices. These are only some general observations. Obviously, the retailer must make specific provisions in each and every purchase motive area. Again, it is necessary to check the effectiveness of all of these practices periodically and one by one. Much research is needed in these areas of market practices and their effectiveness. Some of these practices may be more important to one retailer than other practices.

As we move further away from shopping motives to shopper characteristics (Exhibit 7.2), a new set of critical considerations surface. It is clear that retailers can use the shopper profiles presented in Exhibit

7.2. These shopper profiles, in conjunction with shopping motives, provide critical guidelines. The retailer must consider which of the shopper descriptions are more suitable to their needs and how they can be put to use. The applicability of buyer typology presented in the exhibit is almost self-evident. It is up to the retailer to move on the specifics of these guidelines.

The planned versus unplanned purchase spectrum presented in Exhibit 7.9 will also provide direction. Lower- and medium-price-range discount stores such as Wal-Mart (low price) and Target (medium price) may rely on good name brands being sold at reasonable prices. By doing so, they are emphasizing brand and product satisfaction rather than store satisfaction. Similarly, some upscale department stores and specialty stores emphasize the store name rather than the merchandise. Evidently, in such cases, even convenience goods such as men's underwear can become like a specialty good. The manufacturers would find this to be a very desirable situation, because their products receive a higher value than they otherwise would have.

Retailers will find that the most desirable situation occurs when brand and store loyalties overlap. The upscale apparel stores, for instance, carry most exclusive brands. The practice here is consistent with the theory constructed earlier, in that if the upscale store emphasizes specialty goods with strong appeal, it will develop strong monopoly power. This is a very desirable situation for the retailer, and enhances the retailer's viability, longevity, and profitability.

INTERNATIONAL CORNER

It is difficult to reach consumers all over the country. Consumers are different, with different needs, preferences, and buying behaviors. Internationally, this is even more the case. While, for instance, German consumers respond well to factual and rational advertising, the French respond to emotion and symbolism. British consumers, on the other hand, respond well to humor ("Who Is the Exclusive Global Consumer?" 1993). While American and British consumers buy their food products in bulk and less frequently, continental Europeans (French, Spaniards, and Italians) buy fresh produce, meat, and bread daily. Thus, entering world markets by retailers is costly, but also quite profitable. Well-developed retailers from the United Kingdom, such as J. Sainsbury Plc and Marks & Spencer, have been successfully expanding into international markets. For these large firms, locating and understanding local markets in different countries and catering to their particular needs have brought about substantial dependency on sophisticated database marketing ("The Cost of Entry Is High but Profit Margins Are High Too" 1995).

Value retailers such as Wal-Mart have entered world markets with their selection, price, and value combinations. However, the Coin department stores from Italy have done well by using community-oriented merchandising techniques. They have designed their stores to blend with the historic beauty of their specially selected sites. They thrive on strong relationships built on loyalty and mutual trust (Krienke 1996).

Much research needs to take place before more can be accomplished in international retailing. At this point in time only large global retailers may be able to compete with traditionally strong local retailers. Understanding consumer behaviors and catering to them is a must.

SUMMARY

Retailers *must* know their customers. Understanding consumer behavior is perhaps the only way for success in retailing. In this chapter, a basic consumer behavior model is presented. This model is composed of four specific areas: need realization, shopper behavior, shopper characteristics, and post-purchase behavior. All of these are considered within the constraints of the individualistic versus collectivistic consumer dichotomy. Purchase motivation and shopper profiles are analyzed so that their implication to retail marketing management can be understood.

Seven shopper groups are identified and connected to nine purchase motives. A detailed purchase process model follows. Six specific components are discussed in conjunction with this model: perception, problem recognition, information search, information processing, store selection, and purchase.

Consumer information search is critical to the retailer. There is internal and external information that is generated. How this information is perceived is equally critical. Individuals search for information internally and externally. Furthermore, these search processes are internally and externally triggered. Once the information is received, it will be processed. The retailer's understanding of this process is critical so that the consumer will prefer that store.

Store selection by the consumer determines the retailer's success or failure. Consumers use an activity orientation or an attribute orientation to select the store. These options provide clear-cut alternatives to the retailer regarding marketing practices.

Store selection can be planned or unplanned. In either case, the retailer may try to influence the consumer's decisions.

Finally, a discussion regarding retail practices in conjunction with shopping motives and buyer typology is presented. Throughout the chapter, critical research areas that are missing are pointed out.

Exhibits

Exhibit 7.1
Consumer Behavior Implications for Retailing Strategies

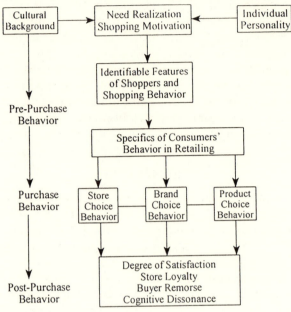

Source: Adapted and revised from Samli (1989).

Exhibit 7.2
The Two Cultural Extremes as They Relate to Retailing

Individualistic Consumer	*Collectivistic Consumer*
Influenced primarily by cognitive influences. Makes up his or her mind based on the information gathered.	Influenced by the group and its culture. Affective influences are more prominent.
Has the initiative to search for goods and services until he/she finds them.	Economic necessities articulated by the group are critical.
Influenced more by hierarchy of needs and social class than to the group to which he or she belongs.	The initiative lies with the outsiders. Certain opinion leaders or family elders relate the need for purchase and the details regarding how, what, where, when, etc.
Sensitive to information about store, product and brand.	Sensitive to opinions and values regarding store, product and brand.
Not necessarily to store, brand, or product loyal.	More store, brand, and product loyal.

Source: Adapted and revised from Samli (1995).

144

Exhibit 7.3
Shopper Characteristics and Purchase Motives

	Shopper Description	*Purchase Motivation*
Agreeable Shoppers 22%	Lower middle income, shopping at discount stores, much mass media exposure. Brand loyal for everything.	Clearly identified needs and wants; specific pressures.
Practical Shoppers 21%	Research purchases in advance, looking for best deals, middle income, younger, better educated, women. Buy modern frills. Not too brand loyal.	Pleasure of bargaining, learning about new trends.
Trendy Shoppers 16%	Impulse buyers. Go for latest fads. Go to fashion boutiques. Mostly young. Not much brand loyalty. Need many products. Prefer foreign products.	Self-gratification, sensory stimulation.
Value Shoppers 13%	Cost conscious. Brand loyal. Go for old, accepted products and brands. Frequent department stores. Older, higher than average income. Consider shopping a chore.	Clearly identified needs.
Top-of-the-line Shoppers 10%	Shop at upscale department stores. Equate quality with reputation. Older, highest median income. Prefer foreign goods.	Social experiences, diversion, self-gratification.
Safe Shoppers 9%	Prefer familiarity. Traditional. Do not like shopping. Go to well-known mass merchandisers.	Clearly identified needs. Specific pressures to shop.
Status Shoppers 5%	Impractical. Go for new gadgets. Second highest median income. Spend much time on shopping but also buy on impulse.	Physical activity, social experience, self-gratification, learning about new trends.

Source: Adapted and revised from Hart (1989), Samli (1989).

Exhibit 7.4
The Specific Steps in the Purchase Process

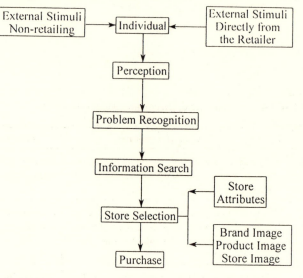

External Stimuli   Purchase Process   Retailer's Efforts

Source: Adapted and revised from Samli (1989).

Exhibit 7.5
Consumer Information Search Process

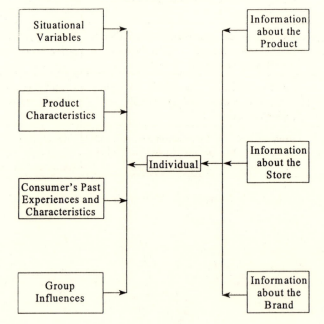

146

Exhibit 7.6
Perception of the Searched Information

	Internal Search	External Search
Internally Triggered	Individualistic consumer motivated by cognitive influences generated by self (personal) 1	Individualistic consumer motivated by cognitive influences (mass media) 2
Externally Triggered	Collectivistic consumers motivated by affective influences with self (interpersonal) 3	Collectivistic consumers motivated by affective influences by others (interpersonal) 4

Exhibit 7.7
Information Processing by Retail Consumers

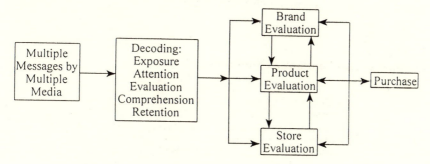

Exhibit 7.8
Store Selection

Source: Adapted and revised from Samli (1989).

Exhibit 7.9
Planned versus Unplanned Shopping

| | Product/Brand | | |
Unplanned Shopping	Planned Shopping[a]	Store Planned Shopping[b]	Totally Planned Shopping[c]
Product/Brand Purchase Unplanned	Product/Brand Purchase Planned	Product/Brand Purchase Unplanned	Product/Brand Purchase Planned
Store Selection Unplanned	Store Selection Unplanned	Store Selection Planned	Store Selection Planned

[a]The likelihood of product/brand loyalty.

[b]The likelihood of store loyalty.

[c]The likelihood of both product/brand and store loyalty.

Exhibit 7.10
Connecting Retail Practices to Shopping Motives

Shopping Motives	*Retail Practices*
1. Diversion	Making shopping exciting.
2. Self-gratification	Helping the consumer to make good purchase decisions by giving them choice and information.
3. Learning about new trends	Carrying most up-to-date products and having good information about them.
4. Physical activity	Giving consumers an opportunity to walk around freely and safely so they can look at products and try them on, etc.
5. Sensory stimulation	Attractive arrangements and appearances, but also providing opportunity for the consumers to feel, try on, or try out the products.
6. Social experiences	Having an opportunity to socialize in the store with the personnel as well as other customers. Maintaining a high level of traffic in the store.
7. Pleasure of bargaining	Providing an opportunity to negotiate, analyze the merits and demerits of the product, and discuss the characteristics of key substitute products.
8. Clearly identified needs and wants	Making sure that certain products are always available and the shopper can get adequate information anytime. The shoppers can move fast and get out of the store quickly.
9. Specified pressures on the individual	Establishing rapport with the customers who know that the store has certain products and the purchase process is easy and reliable.

Source: Adapted and revised from Samli (1989).

References

Aaker, D. Jones. 1971. "Modeling Store Choice Behavior." *Journal of Marketing Research* 8: 46–54.

Assael, Henry. 1981. *Consumer Behavior and Marketing Action*. Boston: Kent.

Berman, Berry, and Joel R. Evans. 1995. *Retail Management*. Englewood Cliffs, N.J.: Prentice Hall.

Bettman, James R. 1973. "Perceived Risk and Its Components: A Model and Empirical Test." *Journal of Marketing Research* 10 (May): 184–190.

Cohen, Samuel Craig, and John M. McCann. 1978. "Assessing Communication Effects on Energy Conservation." *Journal of Consumer Research* 5 (September): 82–88.

"The Cost of Entry Is High but Profit Margins Are High Too." 1995. *Chain Store Age Executive*, 15 December, 20–23.

Darden, William R., and Dub Ashton. 1974–1975. "Psychographic Profiles of Patronage Preference Groups." *Journal of Retailing* 50 (Winter): 99–112.

Darden, William R., and Fred D. Reynolds. 1971. "Shopping Orientations and Product Usage Rates." *Journal of Marketing Research* (November): 505–508.

Dash, Joseph F., Leon G. Schiffman, and Conrad Berenson. 1976. "Information Search and Store Choice." *Journal of Advertising Research* (June): 35–39.

Edmunds, Linda. 1979. Clothing Buying Practices and Life Style Differentials between Employed Black and White Women. Ph.D. diss., Virginia Polytechnic Institute and State University.

Edwards, Allen L. 1957. *Edwards Personal Preference Schedule Manual*. New York: Psychological Corp.

Enis, Ben M., and James E. Stafford. 1969. "Consumer's Perception of Product Quality as a Function of Various Informational Inputs." In *Marketing Involvement in Society and the Economy*, ed. Phillip R. McDonald. Chicago: American Marketing Association.

Festinger, Leon. 1957. *A Theory of Cognitive Dissonance*. Stanford: Stanford University Press.

Hart, Peter. 1989. "Showcase of Shoppers." *Wall Street Journal*, 19 September, 84.

Kotler, Philip. 1994. *Marketing Management: Analysis, Planning and Control*, 5th ed. Englewood Cliffs, N.J.: Prentice Hall.

Krienke, Mary. 1996. "Piergiorgio Coin." *Stores* (January): 144–146.

Kuehn, A. 1962. "Consumer Brand Choice as a Learning Process." *Journal of Advertising Research* 210.

Lambert, Zarrell V. 1970. "Product Perception: An Important Variable in Pricing Strategy." *Journal of Marketing* (October): 68–71.

Lusch, Robert F. 1982. *Management of Retail Enterprises*. Boston: Kent.

McCammon, Bert C. Jr., Deborah S. Coykendall, and Mary B. Whitfield. 1987. Structure and Strategy in Retailing. A special presentation at the AMA Faculty Consortium in Retailing, July, University of Alabama, Tuscaloosa.

Miller, G., and J. Basehart. 1969. "Source Trustworthiness, Opinionated Statements and Response to Persuasive Communication." *Speech Monographs* 36: 1–7.

Mizerski, Richard W., James M. Hunt, and Charles Petri. 1978. "The Effects of Advertising Credibility on Consumer Reactions to an Advertisement." In *Proceedings of the American Marketing Association Educators' Conference*, ed. Subhash C. Jain. Series 43. Chicago: American Marketing Association.

Mochis, George P. 1976. "Shopping Orientations and Consumer Uses of Information." *Journal of Retailing* (Summer): 61–70.

Monroe, Kent B., and Joseph B. Guiltinan. 1975. "A Path-Analytic Exploration of Retail Patronage Influences." *Journal of Consumer Research* 2 (June): 17–28.

Nystrom, Paul H. 1929. *Economics of Consumption*. New York: McGraw-Hill.

Peters, Tom. 1989. *Thriving on Chaos*. New York: Alfred A. Knopf.

Samli, A. Coskun. 1989. *Retail Marketing Strategies*. Westport, Conn.: Quorum Books.

———. 1995. *International Consumer Behavior*. Westport, Conn.: Quorum Books.

Samli, A. Coskun, Enid Tozier, and Yuette Harps. 1980. "Social Class Differences in the Store Selection Process of Black Professional Women." *Journal of the Academy of Marketing Science* (Winter–Spring): 138–152.

Schiffman, Leon G., and Leslie Kanuk. 1994. *Consumer Behavior*. Englewood Cliffs, N.J.: Prentice Hall.

Stone, Gregory P. 1954. "City and Urban Identification: Observations on the Social Psychology of City Life." *American Journal of Sociology* 60 (July): 36–45.

Tauber, Edward M. 1972. "Why Do People Shop?" *Journal of Marketing* 36 (October): 46–49.

Titus, Philip A., and Peter B. Everett. 1995. "The Consumer Retail Search Process: A Conceptual Model and Research Agenda." *Journal of the Academy of Marketing Science* (Spring): 106–119.

Walters, C. Glenn. 1978. *Consumer Behavior*. Homewood, Ill.: Richard D. Irwin.

"Who Is the Exclusive Global Consumer?" 1993. *Chain Store Age Executive*, 15 December, 28–30.

Wilkie, William L. 1994. *Consumer Behavior*. New York: John Wiley and Sons.

Chapter 8

Heterogeneity of Retail Markets

Many retailers realize that no one store can cater to all segments of the market simultaneously and satisfy their customers adequately. A market, any market, whether it be for automobiles, apparel, or carpeting, is not homogeneous. It is composed of many different groups with different incomes, tastes, values, and motives. If we consider what has been discussed in Chapter 7, we have to take into consideration shopper characteristics and shopping motives as well. This type of diversity in the marketplace necessitates grouping the market into its components. These are market segments. They must be (1) identifiable, (2) measurable, (3) significant, (4) accessible, and (5) actionable (Kotler 1994).

Since the market system is very competitive, the retailers must understand their markets well and cater to the prevailing needs and wants of these markets so that they can survive and succeed. Being able to cater to these heterogeneous markets represents the retailer's greatest challenge. Those who can accomplish this successfully are rewarded by the market system by gaining a positive store image and a commensurate store loyalty, both of which lead to a favorable market share and, ultimately, greater profits (Samli 1968, 1969, 1975, 1989).

A segment (or a portion) of the market is worth cultivating if the five criteria listed are met. Identifying market segments can be done on the basis of many different sets of criteria, but it is all based on classifying consumers. As discussed in Chapter 7, there are different and identifiable consumer behavior patterns. Segmentation, in essence, is being able to group like consumers with like purchase behavior so that the retailer can satisfy their needs better. However, it is necessary that the segment can be measured, otherwise it is not possible to make realistic decisions about it. Once the segment can be identified and measured, it becomes easier to determine if it is significant enough to be worthwhile for the retailer to pursue. The segment can be classified, measured, and found significant, but if the retailer cannot cater to it properly, or if it is already taken up by competitors, then it is not useful.

For a retailer to be successful, a store must first identify the segments that it will consider before aiming at them. Here, at the starting point, it is necessary to classify consumers (or prospective customers). Wilkie (1994) proposed to classifying consumers at three distinct levels: personal characteristics, benefits sought, and behavioral measures. These three levels of classification lead to segmentation by personal characteristics, benefit segmentation, and behavioral measures segmentation, respectively.

Exhibit 8.1 presents an example of these three levels of consumer classification. Let us assume that Mr. Williams (or at least Mrs. Williams, if there is one) and Ms. Winterling are rather typical in the trading area we expect to reach. How can we segment this market? We can identify the people and group them on the basis of personal characteristics. In Chapter 6, it is argued that at least some of these demographic features are known and others can be improved by surveys or observations.

But it is equally critical to know the benefits sought by Mr. Williams. Therefore, just having socioeconomic criteria is not adequate. We must, therefore, understand the benefits sought by Mr. and Mrs. Williams, as well as Ms. Winterling. The third level of classification relates to behavioral measures. Unlike the first two, this level attempts to classify consumers on the basis of their product ownership, quantities used, and store brand loyalties. Exhibit 8.1 illustrates some behavioral information about Mr. Williams and Ms. Winterling. Once again, it is important for us to know some of these behavioral measures and, more important, to connect such specific behavior patterns to purchase motivation and buyer behavior groups (Chapter 7).

It is important to note that, though these three levels of consumer classification may be used for segmentation separately, given the opportunity, they can reinforce each other. For instance, the segment can be defined on the basis of personal characteristics and may be evaluated by the benefits sought or behavioral measures.

BASIS FOR SEGMENTATION

Markets are not homogeneous. Economists such as Joan Robinson and Edward Chamberlain acknowledged this early on and made important contributions in bringing imperfect market systems into focus. On the other end of the spectrum, it was sociologists such as Lloyd Warner who provided a workable path for marketing practitioners by asserting that our society is composed of different classes. Warner and his associates analyzed the heterogeneous American markets by using a tool they coined Index of Status Characteristics (ISC). Subsequently, marketing researchers like Pierre Martineau (1958) have explored specific consumption patterns of the groups that Warner and his associates identified. Early analyses concentrated on rather tangible and easy variables such as demographics to segment the market. In addition to ISC, age, sex, income distribution, geographic location, educational and occupational background, and stage in the life cycle are all utilized for segmenting markets. These individually, as well as combined in some manner, can help the retailer to make better marketing decisions.

Numerous researchers have posited that demographics are not entirely adequate to analyze markets. Yankelovich (1964, 84), in his classic article, stated that "important differences in buyer attitudes, motivations, values, usage patterns, aesthetic preferences, or degree of susceptibility," must be studied. This is necessary, he further asserted, because "We are not dealing with different types of people, but differences in people's values." Gottlieb (1958), among others, examined concepts such as compulsiveness or punitiveness as criteria for segmenting the market for antacids and analgesics. He further asserted that it does not follow that a man who drives an expensive car may not prefer cheap whiskey. Another scholar tried to analyze market segments on the basis of demand elasticities or the reaction of different consumer groups to changes in prices. Others used price quality relationships to segment the market (Myers 1967; Samli 1989).

More creative and perhaps more functional techniques of segmentation have been used by many researchers. As mentioned, benefit segmentation is one of them. According to this technique, different groups of consumers derive different benefits from the use of a service, product, or store. The degree of benefit here is the key criterion by which segmentation can be accomplished (Bahn and Granzin 1985; Samli 1989; Dubow 1992).

Exhibit 8.2 illustrates the most important segmentation criteria for retailers. Some seven basic criteria are presented in the exhibit: (1) ethnic and cultural, (2) demographics, (3) sociological, (4) behavioral measures, (5) store loyalty, (6) benefit, and (7) geography. The examples presented in the exhibit make these criteria self-explanatory, and the literature in consumer behavior covers these topics in great detail.

As can be seen, these are important criteria, and much effort has been made to segment the market on the basis of these or other similar criteria. It is important to realize that these criteria create an opportunity to segment the market "before the fact." Such an attempt to segment the market on the basis of one of these criteria makes the total segmentation effort somewhat arbitrary and quite unidimensional. It is arbitrary because it is before the fact or before the retail establishment is in full swing. It is not quite clear if such a segmentation effort will really succeed. It is unidimensional because this type of segmentation implies or encourages the retail store to try to attract the people in that particular segment only, or at least somewhat exclusively. It is quite possible that the store's customers, in reality, come from a variety of segments rather than only one.

MULTIPLE SEGMENT AFFILIATION

If the consumers of certain products or the customers of certain retail establishments were to be analyzed to determine certain common denominators and be categorized accordingly after the fact, the segmentation efforts of retailers will be more realistic.

In their analysis of supermarket patronage, for instance, Hartman et al. (1990), posit that patronage characteristics cross different segmentation lines. Customers from different walks of life value distance, low prices, quality of products sold, and atmosphere. They further suggest that segments need to be refined to provide better information about patronage behavior and the factors influencing such behavior.

Kopp, Eng, and Tigert (1989), in their analysis of market segmentation for retail apparel shoppers, discovered that store choice variable is not for an individual retailer but rather competitive groups of retailers by customer choice. Hence, grouping competitors as well as customers provides good retail management guidance. The results of the study indicated that a high degree of multistore patronage is present among female fashion shoppers. This further indicates that retailers must attempt to draw customers from multiple and sometimes incompatible market segments.

Kamakura and Novak (1992) used the list of values (LOV) for segmentation. They maintain that human beings hold more than one value and these values carry different levels of relevance in determining the motivation of shopping for each individual. They attempted to segment the market according to these LOVs. In a way, this orientation comes close to benefit segmentation; however, this approach draws from more distinct groups in a more sophisticated manner.

Finally, Steenkamp and Wedel (1991) proposed to segment the retail markets based on store-image attribute importance by different consumer groups. Store-image attribute importance is considered to be the critical factor for the retailer to accommodate consumer behaviors.

Users or consumers of certain products share certain characteristics, benefits sought, or behavioral measures. To the extent that any or all of these can be detected and measured, segmentation is achieved. If, for instance, it is found that, on the average, BMW owners are between the ages of thirty-five and fifty, belong to the upper socioeconomic category, and are achievers, it may be possible to develop, change, or continue the market strategy for BMW. All aspects of a marketing plan—pricing, promotion, product characteristics, and distribution—can be planned accordingly.

Applying the same way of thinking to retailing, the demographic and behavioral characteristics of the existing market appear to be of great significance, not only because they are determinable and quantifiable, but also because they are there. These are the givens for an ongoing retail store to work with. Though some degree of heterogeneity always exists in the markets it is drawing from, a high-status retail establishment such as Neiman-Marcus appeals primarily to an identifiable and quantifiable market. This quantification lends itself more readily to demographic and behavioral criteria. But the situation is more blurred when the customers of a discount store such as Wal-Mart or a department store such as Sears are considered. This is because they do not appeal to only one segment. Rather, they draw from a number of different segments.

In the case of ongoing retail establishments, it is more important to determine the segments that already patronize the retail outlet rather than to identify the market segments that are most suitable for that retail outlet. On this premise, Samli (1968, 1975, 1989) has developed a tool that combines several important variables and examines the commensurate retail behavior patterns. The tool is called the *segmentation index* (SI).

SEGMENTATION INDEX: AN ILLUSTRATION

Given the ongoing nature of the retail store, and assuming that the store draws from one market segment only, it is critical to determine if the store's clientele is significantly different than those of competitors. The segmentation index is a tool that is used for this purpose. Exhibit 8.3 illustrates the basics of this tool, and is based on a number of studies (Samli 1968, 1975, 1989).

Assume Store 1 is an upscale carpeting store, Store 2 is a department store that sells carpeting, and Store 3 is another department store that sells carpeting. Finally, our store is a discount carpeting store. Survey data provide detailed information on the six categories of variables. Each element in every category is weighted by a series of weights. As pointed out in Exhibit 8.3, the segmentation index indicated a significant difference from other stores. It is now critical to attach certain aspects of buying behavior to SIs.

THE RELATIONSHIP BETWEEN SI
AND BUYING BEHAVIOR

The survey results revealed that Store 1 customers valued good selection, recommendation of friends, and good reputation, in that order. On the other side of the coin, our store's customers preferred sales, right price, and good selection, in that order. The two department store respondents were quite similar.

Problem recognition here is related to the occasion on which the respondents bought carpeting. Whereas Store 1 customers moved into their "dream home," our store's customers were refurnishing or remodeling. Again, the two department stores were in-between these two extremes. Finally, purchase behavior among Store 1 customers was predominantly not self-initiated personal and interpersonal cognitive orientation, which implies activity orientation to the point that they brought their interior decorators (store salespeople) home. Since our store customers appeared to be leaning in the direction of more personal and self-initiated cognitive orientation, they did the information-seeking aspects of the total process themselves; they read the newspaper ads. Thus the two groups' behavior patterns are not altogether different. However, the purchase motivation factors and shopping behavior patterns appear to vary.

In terms of seeking information, Store 1 customers relied on the recommendation of friends or just walked into the store. Our store's customers relied very heavily on manager advertisements. The other department stores were in-between Store 1 and our store. In this case, our store's customers belonged to a relatively lower socioeconomic group, and their buying behavior appeared to be consistent with this socioeconomic status. They were more price oriented, more attracted to bargains, and did not shop around. They came to our store and bought there rather than having the salesperson come to their home. They paid more attention to bargain-oriented advertisements than to the reputation of the store or word-of-mouth advertising from friends. They appeared to be more economy-minded, practical people who made up their minds and then acted accordingly (Samli 1975, 1989).

THE PROFILE OF LOYAL CUSTOMERS

The core of the retail store's clientele is its loyal customers. If SI is not different at this core level, it is not likely to be at the fringe, because the fringe group is composed of transients who buy only occasionally. They may be considered a plus factor, but the business' well-being depends on the loyalty of its core market.

Thus, store loyalty is a very critical area of study, both for researchers and for retailers. Since local customers are the essence of the retailer's survival, they must be identified and understood. In so doing, the retailer improves its chances of keeping them satisfied and bringing them back to the store. Furthermore, if it happens that the core target market is not large enough or shrinking, this information provides new opportunities to the retailer to explore other target markets before it is too late.

Loyal customers of a store can be identified in a number of ways: first, by determining if the customers shop around extensively, somewhat, or not at all before they buy in a particular store; second, by determining where the individuals do most of their shopping (Cunningham 1962); third, by finding out how often individuals frequent the store within a given period of time (Samli 1975). By using this third method, some earlier studies have indicated that there are noticeable differences between the SIs of loyal customers and occasional (or nonloyal) customers. If the SIs of loyal customers are significantly different than the others, then it is clear that the retail store is performing well for this group. Such loyalty is essential for retail survival. Finally, the fourth way of determining store loyalty is related to whether the customers plan on coming back and if they would recommend the store to friends.

It must be reiterated that the loyalty factor is essential for retail survival and prosperity. If we reconsider Peters's (1987) concept that obtaining new customers is five times more expensive than maintaining current customers and keeping them happy, it becomes more clear where retailers should concentrate their efforts.

USING THE SEGMENTATION INDEX FOR RETAIL STRATEGY DEVELOPMENT

Though in our discussion of SI a carpeting example is used, any retail store should have a good understanding of the market segment that it is serving. Developing an SI is going one step beyond this. It will facilitate the development and implementation of the store's strategy. It is critical to emphasize the importance of SI in terms of identifying the customers of the store and connecting them to the store's marketing practices; in other words, adjusting the store's marketing practices accordingly. SI is primarily important for the retailer who has been in business for a while but does not know for sure the store's target markets.

The method discussed here for the construction of such a managerial instrument is by no means fixed. Factors used in the index and weighting system are all flexible and can be changed depending on the store and the conditions surrounding its marketing practices. The key point here is that an index must be sensitive enough to distinguish one store from its competitors and give an understanding of the market segment(s) we are dealing with.

The followup, of course, is dependent on how much the retailer knows about its customers' purchase behavior patterns. A sensitive SI is not important when buyer practices cannot be related to each other. Market segment matching and buyer behavior is unique to each and every retailer. Therefore, we are concerned about the purchase behavior of our customers as a group and how they differ from those of our competitors. These distinguishing characteristics of our customers must be kept separately from the buying habits of a national, large subsector in the economy; for example, senior citizens or Generation X. Thus, very specifically, by matching the store's key segments and consumer behavior specifically to the store's marketing practices, the firm can carve its niche in the marketplace.

Exhibit 8.4 illustrates a logical flowchart for the retail establishment to segment its market and cater effectively to this segment. This procedure is applicable to manufacturers as well as to retail stores. This exhibit does not illustrate the details of what the key factors are and how the SI is developed, but it does provide the picture of an orderly, sequential process that can be used by any retail establishment. The model is composed of a series of questions and the necessary actions that are connected to these questions. Proper sequencing of these questions and actions provides a logical order for the strategy development. Such models can also be computerized, and certain simulation models may be constructed accordingly.

As has been stated repeatedly, the model here deals with an existing retailing firm. It then provides a direction to identify the prevailing strategy. Similar models can be developed for any other retailer as well. For a beginning firm or a new product line that is just being considered, a different model needs to be developed. Since the image of the firm or the product is now known, activities to identify the market and specify the practices to satisfy this market are more likely to be arbitrary than research based. In time, as the retail establishment or the product gains acceptance, the proposed model becomes necessary to determine the firm's appeal in the marketplace (Samli 1989).

STRATEGIC IMPLICATIONS

The model presented in this chapter is a tool which reinforces the fact that retailing practitioners must learn to identify their markets. Such identification is necessitated by the lack of homogeneous demand that is the function of customers who are very different from each other by desire for variety or desire for exclusiveness, or by basic differences in customer needs caused by cultural and socioeconomic differences.

If the retailer can identify the immediate market segments and thus understand the customers better, a more effective marketing plan can be formulated. This marketing plan gets its strength from matching the segments and consumer behavior within the segments with what the retail establishment can do best. The result of this endeavor is satisfaction for both the retail marketing practitioner and his or her market.

This practice of identifying the market and catering to it adequately is the essence of marketing and in retailing is the process of carving a niche in the market. If done properly, this enables the retail establishment to survive and prosper. It is not the total environment as much as it is certain well-defined components that are crucial to the particular retailer's survival.

This well-defined slice of the market which is the retailer's segment or niche, coined "foothold" or "footing" by Alderson (1957), can be analyzed effectively through socioeconomic and demographic criteria. As seen in Exhibit 8.4, if these criteria do not identify the store's segment, we go to Level 2, benefits sought (Wilkie 1994). If the benefits sought do not make a difference, then Level 3 is suggested (Exhibit 8.1). If the proposed behavioral measures do not work, then there is serious doubt that the firm has an identifiable place in the market or indeed any place at all.

But if the retail establishment can successfully develop a segmentation index, Exhibit 8.4 suggests that this SI should be contrasted to the retail establishment's loyal customers. If the loyal-customer segment that is the core of the retail store's survival is large enough, then the store is in good shape. To the extent that this core segment is stable or growing and is satisfied, the store will continue to thrive. The retail establishment utilizes all its competitive tools—merchandise mix, promotion mix, price mix, and human resource mix—to reach out to this core segment even further to delight its loyal customers. Thus, the firm manages to carve a deep and well-defined slice of the market as opposed to a superficial and blurred one.

However, analyses could also show that the core market segment of the retail establishment is shrinking and, if the firm is to survive, it will have to aim at other market segments. If this is not done, the retail establishment could die as its core market segment continues to shrink.

It must be emphasized here that it is not developing a segmentation index per se, but understanding the market segment(s) that the retail establishment is serving that is the critical point. A small retail establishment may not need to develop an official SI to know its market. Similarly, a large retail establishment can go beyond the simplicity of developing an SI as described here. At the beginning of this chapter, some of the most recent and sophisticated segmentation efforts were discussed. The retail establishment must be able to find a way to understand its market segments and how they differ (if at all) from those of competitors. SI is discussed here because it is practical and, based on numerous research projects, it works. However, again, the focus of discussion here is not SI but understanding and coping with the heterogeneity of retail markets.

One last point needs to be reiterated. If the retail store is just starting, it makes some critical decisions up front as to which segment (or segments) it can reasonably draw from and what it would take to do so successfully. Once the store becomes operational, then a segmentation index such as the one described here can be developed and checked periodically to see if there are significant changes in the clientele.

INTERNATIONAL CORNER

International retailing is not a recent phenomenon. Woolworth, for example, opened its first store outside America in Liverpool in 1909. It set up shop in Germany in 1911 and in England in the 1920s. However, until recently, not many retailers tried to internationalize their operations. This situation has changed dramatically in the 1990s.

Food retailers, discounters, hypermarket operators, and category killers are particularly inclined to internationalize. On the other end of the spectrum, the British-style agile continental food discounters are showing special vitality. They sell a small range of manufacturer brands (about 500 products) in their no-frill stores. Despite their low prices, they make a profit because of their fast turnover, low capital and operating costs, and deep discounts from manufacturers. These discount stores have taken up 15 percent of England's grocery market and, in Germany, 29 percent of the total. Their share in Italy, Spain, and France is growing fast.

One of the trends in international retailing is European and American retailers going to other continents. Thus, a new breed of transcontinental retailers is emerging. But transplanting a retail business to international markets is a very complex undertaking. The firms, in addition to increased capital, time, and management requirements, must adapt a successful retail format to local consumer tastes. This latter is perhaps the most critical consideration. Some of the more successful international retailers, such as IKEA, Macro, Aldi, and Toys 'R Us, emphasize variations in different local markets on a number of continents. In order to cope with the prevailing heterogeneity in the world markets, they propose a six-point program:

1. Study the market. IKEA and Toys 'R Us look at a market several years before they enter it or decide against entering.

2. Decide on your pace. Different retailers have different paces in expanding their operations in different world markets. It is important to expand at a pace most appropriate for that retail establishment.

3. Think about local partners. Many international retailers use joint ventures to help them deal with local markets and their unique problems.

4. Adapt to local conditions. Buying some products from local suppliers and adjusting supplies and practices to fit local tastes and constraints must be seriously considered for success in these foreign markets.

5. Stick to core skills. Retailers must make sure that their logistics and computer systems can be made to work in these new international markets. They must maintain their reputation for quality, low prices, or service. They must do what they do the best.

6. Develop local management. Transferring the retailer's corporate culture across the national cultures requires some local managerial competency ("All the World's a Shop" 1995).

SUMMARY

This chapter posits that segmentation is extremely critical for the modern retailer. It presents a discussion of what specific criteria are used and how retail markets are segmented. Unlike the standard treatment of market segments, in retailing a store may appeal to a variety of well-defined segments. In such cases, the retail establishments must get away from conventional segmentation activity and move into a situation where they can identify their customers, particularly their loyal customers, who are the core market.

On this basis, the chapter presents the segmentation index. By attempting to quantify the characteristics of the store's customers, the retailer can determine if the particular retail store has a significantly identifiable market segment (or customer profile) that would enable that retail store to reach out and satisfy that definable market with greater zeal. Such an effort would undoubtedly improve the firm's ability to survive and prosper. SI is applicable to any size business. All retailers can benefit from the development and proper utilization of such a tool.

Exhibits

Exhibit 8.1
The Three Levels of Consumer Classification

Personal Characteristics	*Benefits Sought*	*Behavioral Measures*
Steven Williams is	Steven Williams seeks	Steven Williams
<ul><li>60-year-old male</li><li>Married</li><li>A semi-retired attorney</li><li>A homeowner in an upscale area</li><li>White</li><li>An $85,000-a-year earner</li><li>A convenience-oriented shopper</li><li>Interested in more leisure-related activities</li></ul>	<ul><li>High quality casual wear</li><li>Good information for good choices</li><li>Making life easier</li><li>Better products and equipment</li><li>Style and power in his automobile</li><li>An image of success and leisure</li></ul>	<ul><li>Prefers brands that imply quality</li><li>Buys more through catalogs</li><li>Buys expensive cars Jaguar or BMW, no compacts</li><li>Buys expensive sports equipment</li><li>Spends heavily on travel and leisure</li><li>Is not too loyal to stores</li></ul>
Mary Winterling is	Mary Winterling seeks	Mary Winterling
<ul><li>48-year-old female</li><li>Divorced, living with her 25-year-old daughter</li><li>An executive in a public relations firm</li><li>White</li><li>A $65,000-a-year earner</li><li>Very active in travel and entertainment areas</li></ul>	<ul><li>High quality and brand recognition in casual clothing</li><li>Expensive travel-related products and services</li><li>A stylish business image at work</li><li>Reasonably expensive service in home and dining out</li><li>An active life with some support from out of home</li></ul>	<ul><li>Prefers status brands in leisure wear</li><li>Buys fine professional clothing</li><li>Eats out often</li><li>Purchases ready made good food</li><li>is likely to be loyal to a few stores</li></ul>

Source: Adapted and revised from Wilkie (1994).

Exhibit 8.2
Retail Segmentation Criteria

Criteria	Examples
Ethnic or Cultural	
Ethnic groups	Spanish-speaking shopping facilities
Certain cultural subcultures	An overall oriental shopping complex
Demographics	
Income	High-income market vs. low-income market
Age	Elderly market, children's market
Education and Occupation	Highly educated sophisticates
Sex	Male or female consumers
Sociological	
Subcultures	Yuppies, WASPs, Generation X
Racial differences	African Americans, Asian Americans
Behavioral Measures	
Life Styles	Jet setters
Life Cycles	Empty-nesters, young married couples
Attitudes	People who are more prone to new products
Store Loyalty	
Heavy users	Those who buy more often
Regulars	Those who come to store regularly
Loyals	Those who try to buy from the same place as often as possible
Benefit	
Benefits sought	Expected satisfaction by patronizing the store
Direct benefits received	Satisfaction from the store or the products directly
Indirect benefits received	Satisfaction delayed as in gifts, health foods
Greater vs. lesser benefits	Those who experience greatly improved health from a health spa
Geography	
Distances	Those who live nearby vs. those who travel a distance
Reputation of the location	Fashionable areas
Inshoppers vs. outshoppers	The area's ability to attract from neighboring communities

Source: Adapted and revised from Samli (1989).

Exhibit 8.3
Segmentation Index Components

	Store 1	Store 2	Our Store	Store 3
Income	High	Medium	Low	Medium
Education	High	Medium	Low	Medium
Occupation	High	Medium	Medium	Medium
Monthly House Payments	High	Medium	Medium	Low
Ownership of Valuables	High	Medium	Low	Medium
Car Ownership	High	Medium	Low	Medium
Segmentation Index*	High	Medium	Low	Medium

*Calculated by using a simple weighting system based on percentage distribution of each store's detailed data. For instance, the percentage of car ownership is weighted by 3 if the car is high price range, by 2 if medium price range, and by 1 if low price range. Segmentation index points of Store 1 subsequently are converted into an index of 100. Other stores express some percentage figure less than 100. For instance, Store 1's segmentation index is 100, our store is 78.

Exhibit 8.4
A Logical Flowchart to Develop a Segmentation Index

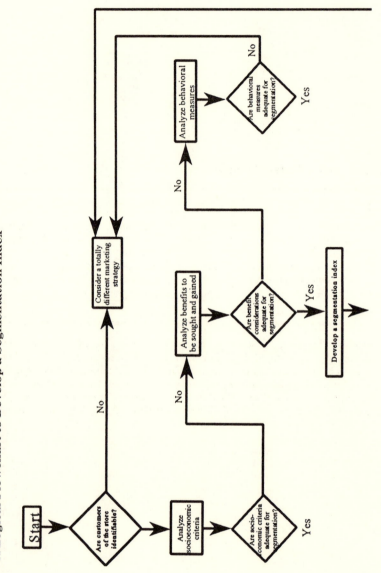

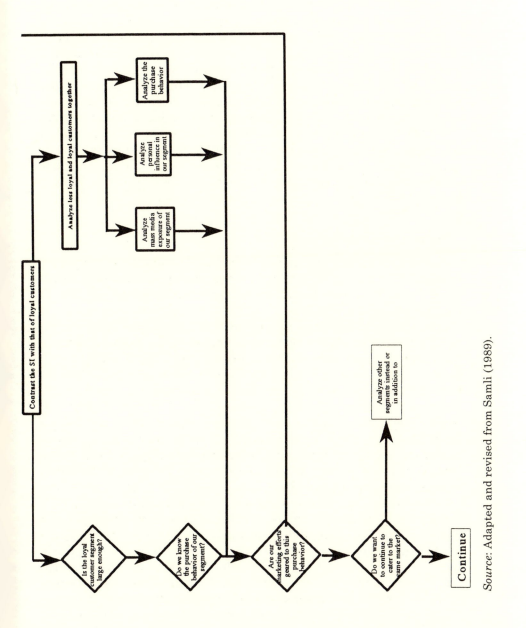

Is the loyal customer segment large enough?

Do we know the purchase behavior of our segment?

Are our marketing efforts geared to this purchase behavior?

Do we want to continue to cater to the same market?

Analyze other segments instead or in addition to

Contrast the SI with that of loyal customers

Analyze less loyal and loyal customers together

Analyze mass media exposure of our segment

Analyze personal influence in our segment

Analyze the purchase behavior

Continue

Source: Adapted and revised from Samli (1989).

167

Appendix: Carpet King, Inc.

Carpet King (fictitious name) is located in one of the major cities on the West coast. It is a major discount carpeting store with a very large variety of selection and low prices. In the data presented here, this store is identified as Store A. Store B is a high-status specialty carpeting store, and Store C is an upscale department store. All three stores are located in the same city. The data, in this case, were obtained through a survey of 294 families in the metropolitan area where these stores are located.

The samples for the study were drawn from random lists of customers of both carpeting stores. An additional list was constructed based on information from respondents who built homes in the area and/or who purchased carpeting in the past two years. In addition, a number of randomly chosen neighborhoods were canvassed so that a number of families who recently purchased carpeting can be pinpointed.

Socioeconomic Analysis

An analysis of the respondents by income distribution (Exhibit 8.5) indicates that Store A had the smallest percentage of customers in the top three income categories. Store B respondents were the highest in the highest income categories.

Educational background (Exhibit 8.6) indicates that Store B customers on the average are better educated, with 29.1 percent having a bachelor's degree or more. The monthly house payments of the Store A customers appeared to be slightly lower than the other two (Exhibit 8.7). Thirty-eight percent of the Store A customers paid $800 or less per month, whereas only 28.5 percent of Store B customers paid that much. This proportion was 34.5 percent for the Store C. Exhibit 8.8 illustrates that Store A customers were more heavily composed of skilled and unskilled workers and government employees, whereas the Store B customers were primarily composed of supervisory, white-collar, and self-employed people. Store C had more supervisory and white-collar customers than Store A, but much less than Store B.

Ownership of certain items considered "luxuries" indicates the lifestyles of people. Four products were singled out for this study. These are PCs, home entertainment centers, boats, and CD player sound systems. In all cases, a lower proportion of Store A respondents owned these products. Exhibit 8.9 illustrates that in all cases a smaller percentage of the Store A respondents owned these items.

Car ownership was kept as a separate entity in the ownership area since, for most Americans, automobiles mean more than just transportation; they mean status, accomplishment, lifestyle, and so on. As seen in Exhibit 8.10, Store A customers primarily own low-price cars (68 percent). Store B was the highest in terms of expensive car ownership.

As can be seen, Store B respondents were significantly higher in all of the criteria considered in this section.

Developing the Segmentation Index

By using the weights displayed in Exhibit 8.11, for each category a segmentation index was developed. Exhibit 8.12 illustrates the outcome of this attempt. As can be seen, Store A had the lowest and Store B had the highest totals. Assuming Store A has an SI of 100, then the SIs of Stores B and C are 125.8 and 110.5, respectively. As can be seen, there were significant differences in SI figures.

As expected, the customers of the discount specialty store (Store B) are of a higher socioeconomic status. If it were possible to connect the relative status to buying behavior, then important advice could be given to the management of Store A. Exhibit 8.13 illustrates that the store's customers had different reasons for buying carpeting. One missing factor in the exhibit is that Store B customers were primarily moving to their "dream home" and appeared to have different motivation for buying carpeting. Store A customers emphasized refurnishing, deciding to buy new carpeting, or replacing old carpeting.

At least two more points are important in this analysis: First, how loyal are the customers, and second, where do they get their information. Exhibit 8.14 illustrates that Store A customers did not shop around as much as Store B customers. They appeared to have read newspaper ads and to have gone for special sales. Store B customers shopped around the most. They received their information from friends and relatives (Exhibit 8.15), a combined 34.8 percent. Store A customers showed a tremendous inclination toward newspaper ads, at 63 percent.

The final aspect of these analyses is the customer's methods of purchase. Exhibit 8.16 indicates that Store A appeared to be very appealing to its customers by its special sales and prices. Store B customers relied on selection and their friends' recommendation. Finally, quite consistently, Store B customers put more emphasis on working with the interior decorator salesperson of the store (Exhibit 8.17). Store A customers just read the ads, went to the store, and bought carpeting.

The owner–manager of Store A asked your advice as a key marketing consultant. He wanted to accomplish two things:

1. Compete better with Store B in terms of better marketing practices.
2. Improve Store A's image and make it more compatible with Store B.

Carefully comment on these two goals. Analyze the above data in detail. Indicate if you need additional information. However, you must realize that "do more research" is not an answer to any question.

Appendix Exhibits

Exhibit 8.5
Income Distribution

Income	Store A Respondents (%)	Store B Respondents (%)	Store C Respondents (%)
Under $20,000	6.2	--	2.8
20,001-30,000	6.2	4.2	2.8
30,001-40,000	8.6	4.2	8.3
40,001-50,000	11.1	4.2	--
50,001-60,000	16.0	8.3	11.1
60,001-70,000	28.3	29.1	30.6
70,001-80,000	22.1	41.6	36.1
Over 80,000	1.2	8.3	8.0

Source: Adapted and revised from Samli (1968, 1975, 1989).

Note: Updated based on basic economic changes.

Exhibit 8.6
Education of Respondents

Education	Store A Respondents (%)	Store B Respondents (%)	Store C Respondents (%)
Less than 8 years	4.9	--	--
8 to 12 years	49.2	29.1	41.7
Some College	32.0	41.6	38.9
Bachelors Degree	8.6	16.6	16.6
Beyond Bachelors	2.5	8.3	2.8
Masters Degree	2.5	4.2	--

Exhibit 8.7
Respondents' Monthly Home Payments

Monthly Payments	Store A Respondents (%)	Store B Respondents (%)	Store C Respondents (%)
Below $500	8.2	--	--
$501-650	14.1	7.1	13.9
$651-800	16.5	21.4	30.6
$801-950	24.7	35.8	13.9
$951-1,100	21.2	17.9	19.4
$1,101-1,250	4.7	7.1	13.9
Over $1,250	4.7	3.6	--
House paid for	5.9	7.1	8.3

Exhibit 8.8
Occupations of the Respondents

Occupation	Store A Respondents (%)	Store B Respondents (%)	Store C Respondents (%)
Managerial	8.6	14.3	20.0
Clerical	2.5	--	5.7
Other White Collar	13.5	33.3	20.0
Professional	11.1	14.3	11.4
Skilled Workers	24.6	4.8	14.3
Unskilled Workers	7.4	4.8	--
Government Employees	17.2	4.8	8.6
Self-Employed	7.4	14.3	5.7
Retired	7.4	9.5	14.3

Exhibit 8.9
Ownership of Various Luxury Items

Item	Store A Respondents (%)	Store B Respondents (%)	Store C Respondents (%)
PC	9.3	21.4	11.1
Home Entertainment Center	54.1	70.4	55.5
Boat	14.0	25.0	14.9
CD Player Sound System	61.9	75.0	63.9

Exhibit 8.10
Car Ownership

Price Range	Store A Respondents (%)	Store B Respondents (%)	Store C Respondents (%)
High	3.5	12.5	1.3
Medium	28.3	37.5	36.2
Low	68.0	50.0	57.6

Exhibit 8.11
Criteria and Weights Used in Segmentation Index

Categories	Weighted by
Income	1-8
Education	1-6
Monthly House Payment	1-7
Profession:	
White Collar	3
Blue Collar	1
Luxury Items:	
PC	2
Home Entertainment Center	3
Boat	4
CD Player-Sound System	5
Car Ownership:	
High-Priced Car	5
Medium-Priced Car	3
Low-Priced Car	1

Exhibit 8.12
Segmentation Index

Socioeconomic Criteria	Store A	Store B	Store C
Income level distribution	502.9	611.5	589.1
Education of Respondents	261.2	216.1	280.5
Occupation of Respondents	151.3	200.1	182.8
Monthly House Payment	351.8	378.9	355.6
Ownership of "Luxury" Items	393.3	571.8	413.5
Car Ownership by Price Ranges	170.4	225.0	202.7
Total	1,830.9	2,303.4	2,024.2

Note: Points are calculated by the scoring system shown in Appendix.

Exhibit 8.13
Occasion on Which Respondents Bought Carpeting

Occasion	Store A Respondents (%)	Store B Respondents (%)	Store C Respondents (%)
Moving	15.3	50.0	25.0
Remodeling	14.1	17.9	8.3
Refurnishing	27.1	17.9	19.4
Family Event	1.2	--	5.6
Purchasing New Furniture	1.2	3.6	2.8
Decided to Buy Carpeting	14.1	--	8.3
Replacing Old Carpeting	12.9	10.7	13.9
Other	14.1	--	16.7

Exhibit 8.14
Shopping before the Purchase

Customers of	Did not shop around (%)	Shopped one store (%)	Shopped two stores (%)	Shopped three stores (%)
Store A	54.1	12.9	17.6	16.4
Store B	32.1	5.6	21.4	32.1
Store C	55.6	14.2	16.7	22.2

Exhibit 8.15
Where Respondents Heard about Store

Sources of Information	Store A Respondents (%)	Store B Respondents (%)	Store C Respondents (%)
Recommendation - Friends	11.3	30.4	40.0
Recommendation - Relative	3.8	4.4	--
Saw the Store	13.8	26.0	20.0
Newspaper Advertisement	63.0	17.4	40.0
Friend Worked There	6.0	--	--
Radio	--	4.3	--
Other	5.1	2.5	--

Exhibit 8.16
Factors That Made Customers Decide to Buy

Factors	Store A Respondents (%)	Store B Respondents (%)	Store C Respondents (%)
Reasonable Price	8	5	7
Good Selection	3	1	3
Close to Home	7	6	9
Newspaper Advertising	5	11	9
Advertising	9	6	9
Right Price	2	6	7
Best Buy Available	4	6	2
Recommendation of Friend	6	2	9
Recommendation of Relative	9	6	9
Sales	1	11	5
Good Guarantee	12	11	5
Good Reputation	9	3	1
Better Service	12	4	4

Exhibit 8.17
Customers' Methods of Purchase

Method of Buying	Store A Respondents (%)	Store B Respondents (%)	Store C Respondents (%)
Visited the Store	83.0	65.8	75.0
Had Salesman Come to Home	11.0	23.7	13.9
Both	6.0	10.5	11.1

References

"A&P Looks like Tengelmann's Vietnam." 1982. *Business Week*, 1 February, 29–30.

Alderson, Wroe. 1957. *Marketing Behavior and Executive Action*. Homewood, Ill.: Richard D. Irwin.

"All the World's a Shop." 1995. *The Economist* (March): 15–16.

Bahn, Kenneth D., and Kent L. Granzin. 1985. "Benefit Segmentation in the Restaurant Industry." *Journal of Academy of Marketing Science* (Summer): 226–247.

Bass, Frank M., Douglas J. Tigert, and Ronald T. Lonsdale. 1968. "Market Segmentation: Group versus Individual Behavior." *Journal of Marketing Research* (August): 264–276.

Berkowitz, Eric N., Roger A. Kerin, and William Rudelius. 1986. *Marketing*. St. Louis: Times/Mirror Mosby.

Berman, Barry, and Joel R. Evans. 1986. *Retail Management*. Englewood Cliffs, N.J., Prentice Hall.

Bucklin, Louis. 1973. "Retail Strategy and the Classification of Consumer Goods." *Journal of Marketing* (February): 45–54.

Cunningham, R. 1962. "Customer Loyalty to Store and Brand." *Harvard Business Review* (December): 127–137.

Davidson, William R., Albert D. Bates, and Stephen Bass. 1976. "The Retail Life Cycle." *Harvard Business Review* 54 (November–December): 89–96.

Dubow, Joel S. 1992. "Occasion-Based versus User-Based Benefit Segmentation: A Case Study." *Journal of Advertising Research* (March–April): 11–18.

Frank, Ronald E., and William F. Massy. 1965. "Market Segmentation and the Effectiveness of a Brand's Price and Dealing Policies." *Journal of Business* (April): 186–200.

Gottlieb, Morris J. 1958. "Segmentation by Personality Types." In *Advancing of Marketing Efficiency*, ed. Lynn H. Stockman. Chicago: American Marketing Association.

Green, Norma. 1977. "Furniture Makers Adjust Marketing to Hit Less Home Oriented Life Styles." *Advertising Age*, 17 January, 3.

Hartman, Sandra McCurley, Arthur W. Allaway, J. Barry Mason, and John Rasp. 1990. "Multisegment Analysis of Supermarket Patronage." *Journal of Business Research* 21: 209–223.

Joyce, Mary, and Joseph B. Guiltinan. 1978. "The Professional Woman: A Potential Market Segment for Retailers." *Journal of Retailing* (Summer): 59–70.

Kamakura, Wagner A., and Thomas P. Novak. 1992. "Value-System Segmentation: Exploring the Meaning of LOV (List of Values)." *Journal of Consumer Research* (June): 119–132.

Kopp, Robert J., Robert Eng, and Douglas Tigert. 1989. "A Competitive Structure and Segmentation Analysis of the Chicago Fashion Market." *Journal of Retailing* (Winter): 496–515.

Kotler, Philip. 1994. *Marketing Management Analysis, Planning and Control.* 5th ed. Englewood Cliffs, N.J.: Prentice Hall.

Lincoln, Douglas, and A. Coskun Samli. 1981. "Evolution in Retail Marketing Strategies." In *Academy of Marketing Science Conference Proceedings.* Miami: *Academy of Marketing Science.*

Martineau, Pierre. 1958. "Social Class and Spending Behavior." *Journal of Marketing* (October): 121–130.

McCarthy, E. Jerome, and William Perreault. 1987. *Marketing Management.* Homewood, Ill.: Richard D. Irwin.

Mochis, George P., Roy L. Moore, and Lawndes F. Stephens. 1977. "Purchasing Patterns of Adolescent Consumers." *Journal of Retailing* (Spring): 17–28.

Myers, John G. 1967. "Determinants of Private Brand Attitude." *Journal of Marketing Research* (February): 73–81.

Ohmae, Kenichi. 1982. *The Mind of the Strategist.* New York: Penguin.

Peters, Tom. 1987. *Thriving on Chaos.* New York: Alfred A. Knopf.

Porter, Michael. 1985. *The Competitive Edge.* New York: Random House.

Reynolds, William. 1965. "More Sense About Market Segmentation." *Harvard Business Review* (September–October): 107–114.

Roberts, Alan A. 1961. "Applying the Strategy of Market Segmentation." *Business Horizons* (Fall): 65.

Samli, A. Coskun. 1966. "Marketing Segments—A Key to Marketing Strategy Development." *Business Perspectives* (Winter): 21–26.

———. 1968. "Segmentation and Carving a Niche in the Market Place." *Journal of Retailing* (Summer): 35–49.

———. 1969. "Segmentation Index and Store Image in Retail and Service Establishments." In *Proceedings of ESOMAR Seminar XXIX on Research That Works for Today's Marketing Problems, 1976.* From talk delivered before the X ESOMAR Seminar, 2–5, at Lucerne.

———. 1975. "Use of Segmentation Index to Measure Store Loyalty." *Journal of Retailing* (Spring): 51–60.

———. 1989. *Retail Marketing Strategies.* Westport, Conn.: Quorum Books.

Samli, A. Coskun, and Douglas Lincoln. 1981. Comparative Advertising and Evolution in Retailing. Paper presented at Southwest Marketing Association meetings, Atlanta.

Satow, Kay. 1977. "Some Comments on Changing Life Styles among Single Young Adults." In *Advances in Consumer Research*, Vol. 4, ed. William Perreault. Chicago: Association for Consumer Research.

Smith, Wendell R. 1956. "Product Differentiation and Market Segmentalion as Alternative Marketing Strategies." *Journal of Marketing* (July): 3–8.

Steenkamp, Jan-Benedict E. M., and Michel Wedel. 1991. "Segmenting Retail Markets on Store Image Using a Consumer-Based Methodology." *Journal of Retailing* (Fall): 300–320.

Sweeney, Daniel J., and Richard C. Reizenstein. 1972. "Developing a Retail Market Segmentation Strategy for a Women's Specialty Store, Using Multiple Discriminant Analysis." In *Combined Proceedings*. Chicago: American Marketing Association.

Wilkie, William L. 1994. *Consumer Behavior*. New York: John Wiley and Sons.

Yankelovich, Daniel. 1964. "New Criteria for Market Segmentation." *Harvard Business Review* (March–April): 83–90.

Zikmund, William. 1977. "A Taxonomy of Black Shopping Behavior." *Journal of Retailing* (Spring): 61–72.

Chapter 9

Retail Marketing
Strategy Alternatives

The game plan for the retailer is designed so that an establishment can cater to the market in the most favorable manner and in so doing have competitive advantage and customer loyalty. This, in essence, is saying that the retailer is trying to shift the demand curve to the right and make it more inelastic. This is what is meant by differential congruence.

Consumers are all different and act differently. In order to use this variety and heterogeneity to his or her advantage, the retailer must have a game plan. This game plan will enable the retailer to do the best possible job by taking into consideration the diversity that exists in the market and being proactive about it.

This chapter explores the development of retail marketing strategy in three different dimensions. First, an evolutionary point of view is used to explore retail marketing strategies. Second, the retail establishment's stage of the life cycle is taken into consideration. Third, the concept of retail marketing strategy is analyzed from the perspective of developing congruence between product classification and retail store classification.

HISTORICAL EVOLUTION

A marketing strategy is a plan of action or a game plan used by the retailer to achieve the company's goals or objectives, to compete in the marketplace, and to survive progressively adverse market conditions (Ohmae 1982; Samli 1989). Our society, just as others, has gone through times when the seller called the shots. A seller's market of this type implies that demand exceeds supply, and, therefore, the seller can have limited variety, high prices, unreasonable terms, and take advantage of consumers. In such cases, the seller obviously does not have to consider consumer differences and individual needs. One might generalize that retailing basically started this way and unfortunately is still this way in many less-developed countries. Until the demise of the USSR, this pattern prevailed in most of the Russian republics.

In the United States, this picture presented itself early on in the form of general merchandise stores that treated the entire market as a single, undifferentiated, homogeneous mass (Berkowitz, Kerin, and Rudelius 1986). Thus, the whole market was treated in basically the same way, regardless of obvious or not-so-obvious differences which prevailed among consumers. Sears and Montgomery Ward had, for instance, a very large chunk of the American market in the 1930s and 1940s and even in the 1950s.

As competition became keener, mass retailers started differentiating their overall orientation, services, merchandise mix, and other related areas. But the general orientation of all consumers was basically alike and remained the same. Sears and a number of other department stores in the 1950s tried to differentiate themselves without very significant (or detectable) results.

Moving away from this market aggregation strategy or being a general merchandiser (or a mass retailer) took place as competition stiffened and supply started not only catching up with but somewhat exceeding demand. Retailers recognized that the total market for products was too heterogeneous to rely on differentiation strategy only. Upscale retailers such as Neiman-Marcus, upper-middle retailers such as Jacobsons, and more economic retailers such as Kresge's appear to have segmented their markets in terms of merchandise quality, prices, and geographic location. These were early attempts to segment. Economically speaking, the retail establishments moved within the theoretical framework of monopolistic competition (Chapter 2). In so doing, they tried to control some degree of customer loyalty. Advertising was used extensively for such outcomes. Here we were taking the total heterogeneous market for retailing and trying to divide it into submarkets or segments that are identifiable, measurable, significant, accessible, and actionable (Kotler 1994). These submarkets tend to be homogeneous in all significant aspects, such as socioeconomic criteria, benefits sought, and the like. Advertising, location, merchandise mix, and store features all played critical roles in segmenting the retail establishment. The theory of product differentiation and market segmentation was already in place (Alderson 1965; Smith 1956).

Around the early 1970s, Trout and Ries (1972b) heralded the coming of a new era in marketing strategy. They named it the "Era of

Positioning." Their concept was emphasizing the product's form, package size, and price as compared to its competition. They assumed, however, that this would apply to the company as well. Brown and Sims (1977) viewed positioning as an extension of product differentiation. Positioning in the 1970s called for comparative advertising. This approach compares two or more specifically named and/or recognizably presented products, services, or establishments (Wilkie and Farris 1975; Lincoln and Samli 1981; Nickels 1978).

Partly because our understanding of consumers had become sharper and partly because some market segments became more crowded in the middle, in the 1980s niching became a concept to consider. There appeared to be certain specific corners in the marketplace that were somewhat neglected. Special services, products, and retail establishments started going in these directions.

By this time, supply exceeded demand and, hence, competition in retailing became even keener. At this stage in the game, some major retailers started combining segmentation, differentiation, and mass retailing. The outcome was the category killer. This was an especially large specialty store that featured a very wide selection in its product category at quite low prices. Toys 'R Us, The Limited Express, Gap, and Barnes and Noble are among these (Berman and Evans 1995; McCune 1994).

THE KEY RETAIL PLAYERS

Perhaps one of the most important considerations in the retail evolution process is that new institutions coexist with old ones for an indefinite period of time. It is clear that at least six types of retail institutions entered the picture during the first half century or so. They all reflected the practice of certain retailing strategies. Exhibit 9.1 illustrates the orientation and goals of these retailing strategy users. These are (1) mass retailer, (2) differentiator, (3) segmenter, (4) positioner, (5) nicher, and (6) category killer.

Whereas Exhibit 9.1 identifies the basic orientation of each one of these and articulates their specific goals, Exhibit 9.2 presents a comparative discussion. This discussion is based on five key areas: (1) starting point, (2) general orientation, (3) view of the market, (4) competitive emphasis, and (5) treatment of the market. The following discussion combines Exhibit 9.1 and Exhibit 9.2 material and presents a brief critical analysis of the six retailing strategies that surfaced in time.

Mass Retailing

The retailer in this instance dwells upon market aggregation strategy. Mass retailers start with similar marketing mixes as those of competitors. They assume the market is large enough and that they can capture a portion of this large market by imitating others. Sears, Montgomery Ward, and others thrived on convenience, variety, and ease of shopping. These retailers attempted to serve the total market by making a wide assortment of products available at accessible locations so that one-stop shopping and scrambled merchandising would take place. For them, advertising played an informative role. It emphasized the variety, prices, events, and store-location variables. Advertising messages were basically the same for all segments, as the retailer appealed to the total market. All customers were viewed as basically alike. Differential congruence was only partially achieved and not deliberately. These retailers are basically imitators. They do not develop any unique characteristics.

Differentiating

Even though the differentiator starts out by thinking that all consumers are basically alike, it tries to appeal to them with different retail mixes for the mass market. It develops a competitive edge by being different from competitors. Many department stores and discount department stores are following such a strategy. This helps them to enhance their monopolistic competitive skills which means, again, shifting the demand curve to the right and making it more inelastic (Chapter 2). In other words, they expand their demand and build customer loyalty. In addition to retail mixes, the stores may add such features as credit, gift wrapping, delivery, extended store hours, liberal return policy, restaurants with fashion shows, and the like. They use advertising to dwell upon these features. Most important, they will try to create and promote the store image that will distinguish them from their competitors. However, this type of differentiating does lead to differential congruence. A differentiator does not think of matching the store's unique features with the target market's self-image (Samli 1989).

Segmenting

Once retailers realize that markets are not homogeneous, they also realize that neither their customers nor their trading areas are homogeneous. They further realize that their trading areas are composed of several heterogeneous submarkets within which there is some homogeneity of needs, purchase motives, and behavior patterns. It becomes clear that some retailers need to segment their markets and use a segmentation strategy (Samli 1968, 1975, 1976, 1989), though retail segmentation has not been as rapid and as sophisticated as manufacturers' segmentation (Sweeney and Reizenstein 1972). Market segmentation is still not very common among retailers.

Segmenters begin with the orientation that consumer needs are diffused and that it is not possible to cater to all of these needs. Therefore, consumers need to be categorized and these categories need to be prioritized. The segmenter expects to excel by catering to these identifiable, measurable, significant, accessible, and actionable portions of the total market. Their goal is to adjust their supply to heterogeneous demand (Exhibits 9.1 and 9.2). They view all customers as being different, and they emphasize their competitive advantage by offering a unique marketing mix to each of a few segments on which they are concentrating. They are geared to satisfy only certain specific needs. Many of the specialty stores are examples of segmentation in retailing. The Limited, Gap, and Payless Shoes are all examples of specialty retail chains that appeal to carefully defined market segments. Some department stores also are trying to segment: Bloomingdale's, Marshall Fields, and Target are examples. While Bloomingdale's is aiming at the upper socioeconomic class, Marshall Fields is aiming at the upper middle class, and Target stores are appealing to the middle class. Though these retailers originally may not have planned it this way, they still appeal primarily to these segments. Needless to say, proactive segmentation (i.e., intentional and planned segmentation) is much more desirable than de facto segmentation (i.e., unintentional and after-the-fact segmentation). Because segmentation is still a very important research and practice area in retailing, much emphasis is put on it in Chapter 8 of this book. Segmentation is a necessary ingredient for differential congruence, but it is not sufficient by itself to generate such congruence. Successful segmentation must generate congruence between the way the store is perceived by consumers and these same consumers' self-image.

Positioning

Exhibit 9.1 indicates that the positioner starts with orienting itself in the marketplace vis-à-vis a specific competitor. Originally, Wal-Mart positioned itself somewhat below Sears, with the intention of appealing to the fast-growing lower middle class as opposed to the somewhat shrinking middle class. Subsequently, Target stores appear to have positioned themselves somewhat above Wal-Mart and somewhat below Sears. Obviously, Target stores are attempting to take some customers away from Sears and some from Wal-Mart. They might think that there is a void in the market and that they will capture that particular portion of the market. The positioner believes that there are some differences between its customers and the competitor's customers. Hence, the positioner approaches the market with a different marketing mix than the competitor and segments the market differently than the same competitor. It has to assume that its customers are clearly different than those of the key competitor. As a result, it tries to offer each segment a retail mix that is different and better than the key competitor. The positioner has an even better chance of creating a differential congruence than does the segmenter, if it can position itself just right and cater to that portion of the market successfully.

Given the realities of the American markets in the late 1990s, it is extremely critical that the retailer think in terms of positioning. The increasing competition and sharp changes in the retailing environment are bringing about an acute need to move beyond the market segmentation strategies that well-known retailers have been following for some time. Chances are that the historical position occupied by already established retailers will erode as market conditions change dramatically. Developments that are likely to dramatically change the retailing environment include the following:

1. New demographics—A continuation of shifts of population to the Southeast, Southwest, far West, and Rocky Mountain states; changing age distribution, with great increases in the fifty-year-old and above sector and particularly in the elderly sector (age sixty-five and over). Birth rates also started increasing since the late 1970s.

2. New values—Examples include a growing concern with environmentalism, green products, consumerism, women's liberation, and increasing recycling.

3. New economic realities—There is a decline in the income of the middle class; new jobs that are created are not high-paying jobs, and consumers want more value for their dollars (Samli 1993).

4. Escalating competition—Retail competition is increasing. In addition to both intra- and intertype competition (Chapter 2), new developments are making conditions for the traditional retailers even more difficult. Among these new developments are telemarketing, TV marketing (direct), catalogs, other types of nonstore retailing, and the like (Bates 1976; Doyle and Sharma 1977; Berry and Wilson 1977; Samli 1989; Ellsworth 1993).

5. New realities—In addition to the fragmentation of consumer markets as the middle class disappears, scarcity of time and differences in lifestyles and shopping patterns create problems as well as new opportunities (Bates 1989).

In order to cope with these changes and still thrive, retailers may find it necessary to use more carefully planned and extensively implemented positioning strategy. It must be understood that a retailer who is segmenting can simultaneously be positioning as well. In fact, in a different context, Cappel and colleagues (1994) maintain that those retailers using more than one strategy simultaneously and in congruence are likely to outperform their competitors using only one strategy.

Niching

According to Exhibit 9.1, niching begins with a very carefully defined corner of the market. The nicher assumes that it can do the best job of satisfying the needs here, and profits by catering to this well-defined corner of the market. By doing a good job, it preempts competition. The nicher is a very specific segmenter. General Nutrition Centers (GNC), catering to the health and bodybuilding component of the market, the New Life Bookstores, that cater to the religious sector with special books and other paraphernalia, and, finally, Payless Shoe stores, that cater to the portion of the market with limited purchasing power, are all nichers. They appear to adjust their offering very sharply to the needs of very well-defined corners of the market.

Category Killing

Category killing as a strategy is very recent. The category killer starts with the orientation that regardless of their differences, consumers truly go for bargains and some product lines are desired by people from all walks of life. Category killers expect to capture a large portion of the market by doing everything better than anybody in the field and at lower prices (Exhibit 9.1). The category killer maintains better merchandise mixes with better variety at lower prices, and believes that whatever the competitors do, he or she can do better and cheaper (Exhibit 9.2). Retail chains such as Home Depot, Blockbuster Videos, and Books-a-Million are all category killers. Certainly, their efforts are likely to generate and maintain a very successful state of differential congruence.

Considerations Relating to Guerrilla Fighters

Guerrilla fighting may be considered a strategic posture that is most appropriate for small retailers who have limited budgets but great willingness to survive. It has been stated that today, more than ever before, there have been more entrants into the market as small retailers (Samli 1993). These establishments primarily have a willingness to serve their customers and provide convenience. These establishments are fighting for existence and would do many things to extend their survival. Not much has been done systematically to identify the specifics of the guerilla fighting strategy. There will be much more on this topic in the near future (Levinson 1989).

Baum's experience may be considered to be a cross between niching and guerilla fighting. Baum's is an 8,500-square-foot women's specialty store in Morris, Illinois. The store has been in existence since 1874. It started as a dry goods operation to sell fabric and home furnishings. The store managed to survive because of hands-on management and determined guerilla tactics. Over the years, the store changed and sold everything from china to children's wear. About ten years ago, the decision was made not to carry anything but ready-to-wear clothing. The store emphasized differentiating itself and specializing heavily on larger sizes and older women. The management felt that chain stores in malls do not have the flexibility to cater to such a market. The store made significant promotional efforts to reach older customers. It started a fifty-plus club and sent birthday presents to its members. It also gave members back a percentage on all credit cards (Bredin 1993).

MARKETING STRATEGY IN DIFFERENT STAGES OF THE RETAIL LIFE CYCLE

Retail establishments have a life cycle that must be considered in terms of strategy implementation (Davidson, Bates, and Bass 1976; Alderson 1965; Samli 1989). In the preceding section, six generic retail marketing strategies are identified. However, it is also important to explore how these strategies are implemented and what kind of changes take place at different stages in the retail life-cycle development. Strategy implementation variations in different stages of the life cycle must be carefully examined. Exhibit 9.3 illustrates some of the key highlights of this examination. There are four stages in the retail life cycle: innovation, accelerated development, maturity, and decline.

Innovation

At this introductory stage, the retail establishment is making its first appearance. This phase must be carefully planned, since the first impression could be very critical in the minds of consumers. The retail establishment may have positioned itself right and, hence, it may not have many competitors. Though it may be growing reasonably fast, its profitability is likely to be low to moderate. Since the risks are rather high, management is likely to search and experiment with almost all aspects of the business. Only a minimal number of management control techniques are used.

The management style is entrepreneurial. An extensive amount of informative advertising is used. Product mix must be unique, innovative, and suitable for the market. Prices are likely to be extra low for introductory efforts of the establishment. Finally, to be consistent with the entrepreneurial orientation, the personnel must be outgoing, understanding, and accommodating.

Accelerated Development

At this stage, the retail establishment is facing increasing competition. The sales are growing at a rapid rate. The profit level progresses from low to high. During the early part of this stage, increasing sales volume generates economies of scale. This increases the firm's profitability. Toward the end of this stage, competition gets very keen, while cost pressures and increasing complexities of doing business create the need for larger staff, a more complex inventory system, and more extensive controls. Near the end of this stage, both growth and market share, as well as profits, approach their maximum level. Product and service mix, by the help of a sophisticated inventory system, is adjusted and its strengths reinforced. Promotional activity is still extensive. Here, the emphasis is more on persuasion. Prices, due to increasing costs, are higher, and there are fewer bargains. Finally, the personnel try to promote the store and sell more.

Maturity

At this stage the retail store stops making progress and starts losing ground. There are a number of factors that cause these adverse conditions. First, entrepreneurial managers start having difficulties controlling their organizations, which, by now, have become large and complex. The managers who are very proficient in maintaining the vitality and excitement that were instrumental in the success of their organizations in the first two stages are no longer effective. They often lack the management skills that are necessary to direct their now large organizations in turbulent markets. Hence, the overall quality of their operations begins to decline.

Second, the capacity that is developed in the first two stages becomes a problem. Retailers, encouraged by the growth rate in the first two stages, often expand beyond the levels justified by the size of the total market. They expand the store's square footage, the inventories, and the merchandise mix to unprofitable levels.

Third, management finds itself facing direct and indirect competition from new forms of retail institutions. The challengers manage to capture some portion of the firm's market and hence create profit reduction and decline in the sales volume.

Thus, the maturity stage is characterized by strong competition and moderate to slow growth. The management of the retail establishment at this stage needs to employ extensive management control techniques so that numerous operational problems can be resolved. In this stage, specifically trained professional management becomes a necessity rather than a luxury.

Since the store is by now quite well known, advertising efforts are likely to be somewhat reduced. Prices are likely to be high to offset the adverse impact of excess capacity and declining profits. It must be realized that our discussion here does not reflect a normative retail management procedure. Rather, the practice of running a retail establishment is being presented here. Finally, the merchandise mix at this stage is likely to have great depth and breadth. This deep and broad merchandise mix can be both part of the problem and part of the solution. It is part of the problem, because such a merchandise mix may have too many unprofitable lines leading to unnecessarily large levels of inventories. But it is also part of the solution, because if the product mix does not have slow moving, unprofitable lines, it could be a true competitive tool for the retail establishment.

Decline

This final stage in the retail life cycle is to be avoided or at least postponed. At the end of the maturity stage, the retail management must be sensitive enough to realize that there is need for a major revitalization activity, and some drastic changes are necessary.

Many years ago, two brothers owned and operated an Italian restaurant in Detroit. The restaurant had reached its decline stage and was not doing well. One of the brothers left the business. The other brother decided to change the menu and emphasize home delivery of pizza. This is how Domino's was born. At the decline stage, it is not possible to reverse the trend by taking a position of "business as usual." A total modification of operations may be necessary. The retail establishment may reposition itself and use a totally new product–service mix, catering to a different market segment with a different product and service choice. However, it is not always possible to implement such a critical and risky undertaking and make it successful. Hence, many retailers fail at this stage.

During the decline stage, the firm will experience major losses in its market share, its profits become very marginal, and its ability to compete in the marketplace deteriorates. K-Mart appears to be in this stage. This $30-billion retailer is experiencing losses and appears to have lost its focus. Many of its stores are old and are not located in the best possible places. The new CEO realizes that the problem cannot be resolved with a "Band-Aid"; it requires "surgery." The need to resolve K-Mart's core merchandising problems is acute. The company appears to be stockpiling goods better suited for a department store than a discounter. As a result, K-Mart is stuck with huge inventories it can sell only at deeply discounted prices ("Kmart: Who's in Charge Here" 1995).

Thus, in this last stage, the rate of growth is low or negative, and profitability is low or negative. Retail establishments, at this stage, refrain from reinvesting capital in this particular venture. Central management experiences a fatal inability to compete in the market-place. Control techniques are no longer functional and are not used extensively, primarily because of administrative layoffs and the administration being out of touch. The management style can be primarily seen as caretaking, which means still continuing as business as usual. Advertising is used only moderately. Many prices are likely to be reduced, but many are still high and not responsive to the target market needs.

As can be seen, marketing strategies, as well as their implementation, vary on the basis of the stage in the life cycle. The life-cycle process implies that the firm must be cognizant of the stage of the life cycle it is in and, accordingly, how the firm should modify the implementation of its strategy in view of this stage in the life cycle. The descriptive detail in Exhibit 9.3 is not ideal but practical, and mainly indicates how firms behave in each stage. "Correct or incorrect behavior notwithstanding, all retail establishments go through a life cycle, and at each stage of this cycle retail marketing strategy components must be evaluated and changed" (Samli 1989, 167).

RETAIL MARKETING STRATEGY MODIFIED ON THE BASIS OF PRODUCT AND STORES

Consumer products are categorized as convenience shopping and specialty (Kotler 1994). Similarly, authors in retailing attempt to use the same classifications for retailing (Bucklin 1973). No attempt is made here to discuss them, as any retailing book discusses them (Berman and Evans 1995). But the congruence between these two categories is very critical and must be carefully discussed. The three product and three store categories give us a three-by-three matrix or nine strategic alternatives (Exhibit 9.4). This discussion does not focus on which of these should be chosen. Instead, it emphasizes that congruence between the products and stores should be carefully examined. Obviously, a specialty store such as Tiffany's thrives on a good balance of a specialty store that carries upscale specialty merchandise. On the other end of the spectrum, most drug stores are a combination of convenience goods and convenience store.

Though there are no cut and dried formulas or clear-cut rules, a few dos and don'ts can be extremely useful:

1. If the combinations are two degrees removed from each other, the result may be quite ineffective.
2. Instead of one of the nine cells, two side-by-side cells may be very appropriate.
3. The general positioning of the store is critical in the choice of one of these strategic cells.

If the classifications are two degrees removed, then a specialty store may be emphasizing convenience goods or a convenience store may be pushing some very special products and brands. Tiffany's selling cheap costume jewelry or the corner drug store emphasizing expensive diamonds are examples. These are not likely to be successful strategic options. People do not go to Tiffany's to buy cheap costume jewelry. Similarly, buyers do not go to the corner drug store to buy an expensive Rolex watch.

However, a retail establishment does not have to be a store where you buy only convenience products. It may handle some shopping goods as well. Similarly, specialty apparel stores may have some accessories that are more likely to be shopping goods. This type of diversity can be quite useful.

Finally, positioning of the store must be decided on before choosing a strategy or a combination strategy. If, for instance, there is a very upscale, expensive female apparel store in the area that carries expensive products and brands, another store may wish to position itself somewhat below the first store. This is still a specialty store, but it may have some upscale shopping goods alternatives as well as slightly lower-priced brands. Thus, carrying some cheaper specialty and some shopping goods is necessary for this store, based on its original positioning decision.

The implementation of the six generic retail marketing strategies (Exhibits 9.1 and 9.2) needs to be modified on the basis of the stage in the life cycle. However, all of these considerations are going to be expressed in terms of the product–store match choice. It is implied here that the generic strategies stage of the life-cycle strategies and product–store match strategies may coexist. K-Mart, for instance, is using a category-killer strategy modified somewhat by maturity, a beginning decline strategy, and a shopping store with shopping and convenience-good strategy simultaneously. Management must understand how all three can be used simultaneously to the best advantage.

IMPLEMENTATION OF THE STRATEGY

Strategic decisions are basically all encompassing and far reaching. They are game plans put into practice to enhance the retailer's market position. They will also change the store image. However, it is necessary to realize that, at the lower levels of the store's decision-making process, there are policies and tactics. Exhibit 9.5 illustrates differences among strategies, policies, and tactics.

For instance, XYZ is an elegant women's apparel store. It caters to middle-aged professional or upper-middle-class married women who are slim and who follow the latest fashions. It provides its customers an opportunity to "learn about new trends," enjoy "sensory stimulation," and have "enriched social experiences" by carrying up-to-date merchandise, good color combinations, and attractive ambience. The store makes these experiences a part of the store policy, which is used to implement a niching strategy. The store is visited by a steady stream of loyal customers who are upper middle class and know each other reasonably well. The store understands the importance of personalizing customers (see Chapter 7 for details).

At the more specific tactical level (Exhibit 9.5), the store or perhaps the manager and assistant manager make a practice of giving some of their best customers the post-Christmas sale prices on before-Christmas purchases, especially during the period just before Christmas and when a customer has purchased quite a bit and wants to buy more but is hesitating because of some personal budget restrictions. Other special tactics may be meeting a competitor's price if customers complain or placing the store brand on the shelves next to the most expensive competing brand, alerting the customer to the price differential.

Storewide policies and tactical decisions are a part of the total implementation of the store's strategy that has been decided upon. Many aspects of the strategy are partially based on the consumers' behavior patterns discussed in Chapter 7. Store-level policies and tactics are more specific implementation points that can be initiated and used. An example of store policy is Winn Dixie giving a customer a gallon of free ice cream if there are more than three people in line at the check-out counter.

THE USE OF STRATEGIC BUSINESS UNITS (SBUs) AND PROFIT CENTERS (PCs)

SBUs and PCs are standard terms in marketing strategic or marketing management books; however, in retailing these concepts are not widely used. Strategic business units are comprised of groups of products that have a common market base. The managers of these units typically have complete responsibility to integrate all functions into a strategy to fulfill certain goals or compete with readily identifiable competitors (Jain 1993). The manager of the sporting goods department at K-Mart is certainly competing with similar departments in other discount and department stores as well as sporting goods stores. SBUs are very critical in establishing a competitive advantage for a retail store. It is quite possible, for instance, that one supermarket is very well known for its deli center, whereas another is well known for its fresh produce section. These unique departments or sections are the sequel to SBUs in marketing.

Profit centers, on the other hand, are the units, product groups, or departments that are most profitable for that particular retail establishment. It must be pointed out that SBUs and PCs are not necessarily the same, nor do they necessarily overlap. It is quite possible that in retailing the SBU may enhance the image of the store, may bring in more customers, or may increase customer loyalty. However, none of these imply that SBUs make the most money. Naturally, if SBUs and PCs are overlapping or close to each other or carefully chosen and promoted, then the firm is managing its merchandise mix and its interior resources well. Exhibit 9.6 illustrates the relationship between SBUs and PCs. If the two are the same or chosen carefully so that proper attention is paid to both, this is called *good management*. If the strategic business units of the firm are not carefully chosen, but its profit centers are chosen well, this is called *questionable management*. If the strategic business units are chosen carefully, but the profit centers are not doing well, this would be *borderline poor management*. Finally, if both SBUs and PCs are poorly chosen and poorly treated, this is definitely *poor management*. Exhibit 9.6 indirectly makes a very questionable statement. It posits that if PCs are different than SBUs, then the retail store should opt for short-run profit rather than long-run competitive advantage. This is illustrated in Exhibit 9.6 by indicating that it is better to have a good choice in PC than SBU.

Questions might be raised about how SBUs and PCs are identified. The following list shows some of the key variables and considerations in choosing SBUs:

General Characteristics of the Department or Division

    The department has a unique appeal

    It has a clear-cut market

    It has identifiable external competitors

    Its appeal is stronger to the target market than others

    There is control over its functional activities

Key Considerations

    How many SBUs should be considered?

    The size of SBUs (individually and collectively)

    How meaningfully markets can be separated or combined

    Is it okay for SBUs to overlap?

    Selecting the competitors' SBU for comparison (Adapted and revised from Jain 1993).

It is necessary for SBUs to have a unique appeal. If the department or division does not have certain unique products or service—if it cannot be identified as interesting, appealing, and attractive—it cannot have the basic ingredients to become and remain an SBU. The SBU must have a clear-cut market and a determinable impact. Similarly, the SBU has identifiable external competitors, and it is possible to compare the characteristics and performance of these competitors with those of the SBU. If, however, the SBU does not have some degree of autonomy, then it cannot be managed in such a way that it can be part of the overall strategic posture of the retail establishment. It certainly must be in the position to make certain changes and adjustments to stay in the forefront of the strategy implementation. If, for instance, the sporting goods department is the SBU but it does not have the freedom to counteract the promotional advances and/or merchandise mix changes of its competitors, then it cannot maintain its status as an SBU. The point raised earlier must be further explored. Given a choice, should the retail establishment opt for a PC or SBU? It may be hypothesized that small retailers may need more profit in the short run because of a lack of financial resources. However, large retailers may be better off putting more emphasis on SBUs than PCs. In this way they improve their competitiveness, which has positive long-run implications.

One of the critical questions is just how many SBUs should be in existence. There are no clear-cut answers, but obviously all of the departments or other divisions cannot be SBUs. Only a few key aspects of the retail establishment can be promoted as SBUs. Their number certainly will depend on specific circumstances surrounding the retail establishment. Among these, two are particularly important. First, could the total market of the retail establishment be broken into specific components that are identifiable and significant? Second, could the markets of SBUs overlap? The first question is very specific to the nature of the retail establishment. If, for instance, Toys 'R Us were to develop SBUs, it would be much more difficult than Sears or K-Mart. It is necessary to analyze the situation carefully and undertake careful market analysis.

The second question is not necessarily a matter of an overlap but of how much. Again, in the case of Toys 'R Us it is critical to realize that whatever SBUs are utilized, they are going to overlap in the total market of the retail establishment. It will be much more difficult to determine the impact of SBUs on the market demand and variations in it.

Profit Centers

Some departments, divisions, or product–service groups are more profitable than others. In retailing, it is necessary to bring more traffic in so that these profit centers will generate more profit. It is also necessary to keep the customers happy and loyal so that the contribution of these PCs will be more prolonged.

As illustrated in Exhibit 9.6, coordinating SBUs and PCs is essential for good management and resultant profitability. At least two problems occur in this area. First, firms do not necessarily do a good job in identifying their SBUs and PCs. Second, almost all retailers expect all the departments to be equally profitable. Quite often the firms may confuse their SBUs and PCs. The department that may be quite effective as an SBU may be used as a PC and vice versa.

Though it is possible for SBUs and PCs to be the same, quite often they are different. Particularly where the two are different, coordination of SBUs and PCs is of the utmost importance. Sears, for many decades the nation's biggest retailer by far, around the mid-1980s started treating its credit and other consumer finance activity as a major profit center. As a result, unfortunately, it moved away from its core competency—merchandising. A few years later, Sears was no longer the largest retail establishment in the country. The company had lost its focus and gotten into major financial difficulties. In this case, consumer credit could have been an SBU and could have promoted all of Sears's general business.

This particular discussion is also related to the fact that retailers expect all departments to yield a certain acceptable return. In the case of Sears, or any retailer, if making good credit available can boost the profit from merchandise by 10 percent, the company certainly can afford to not make money from the credit department. In this case, the credit department becomes a critical SBU but not at all a PC.

A similar case can be made for any retail establishment. A supermarket, for instance, has a very good deli. This department can be a very good SBU, but simultaneously forcing it to make a lot of money may be self-defeating. Once again, SBUs and PCs are usually separate entities. Identifying them properly and making them part of the overall strategy are extremely important for success in retailing. This aspect of strategic planning in retailing is likely to receive much research attention.

CATEGORY MANAGEMENT

In recent years, closer cooperation between retailers and suppliers has led to the emergence of a concept known as "category management." This concept implies development and merchandising of a line of goods through mutual understanding and agreement by both the manufacturer and the retailer. Developing categories and managing them call for the following areas of consideration:

1. What should be included in the product category?
2. How should the category be positioned in the total product mix?
3. How should this category be promoted?

4. What is the target market for this category?

5. What should the promotion budget be?

6. What is the projected demand?

Many retail buyers are becoming category managers. Categories are broader than what typical buyers handle. More important, retail professionals who, as buyers, thought in terms of short run and buying, now, as category managers, think in terms of long-term planning and consumer needs along with strategic planning. One may assume that some of these categories were created for use as PCs or SBUs (Balevic and Mancuso 1996).

THE TQM CRAZE

During the 1980s, total quality management (TQM) swept the United States's corporate boardrooms. It is critical to think of TQM as proactive marketing that encourages the retailer to provide better service. Both SBUs and PCs of the retail establishment must keep in mind six principles of TQM: (1) know what customers require, (2) identify problems and opportunities, (3) examine the sources of problems, (4) develop plans to satisfy customer needs better, (5) implement these plans, and (6) monitor your results (Samli 1996). The example of Von Maur department store illustrates these points. The customer can have his or her purchases wrapped and shipped via UPS for free. If his or her desired size or color is not available, the store will search other units of the chain and have it shipped. The customer does not even pay interest on his or her store charge account. This particular chain loses money willingly on gift wrap, labor, and postage. It tracks down merchandise, moves freely from store to store, and foregoes profitable interest income. But its customers are happy with the quality of the service they receive (Hazel 1996).

SUMMARY

Strategy for a retailer is developing a game plan to fulfill its objectives. The retail establishment must understand critical strategic alternatives. It must also make a deliberate attempt to develop a strategy and implement it successfully.

First, in this chapter, six different generic retail marketing strategies are discussed. These are general merchandiser, differentiator, segmenter, positioner, nicher, and category killer. These are important alternatives for the retailer. They need to be understood and used appropriately.

In addition, the retailer must realize where the store is in its life cycle. In different stages of the retail life cycle, different strategies and different implementation of these strategies need to be considered.

Another key modifier (or retail strategy option) of retail strategies is the store–product combination. Three types of stores—convenience, shopping, and specialty—and three types of consumer products—convenience, shopping, and specialty—are discussed. There are nine combinations of these two groups, and these combinations are key strategy modifiers.

It is emphasized that all three groups of strategic options can be considered simultaneously, and the store may have a game plan that borrows from all three groups (i.e., generic strategies, life cycle strategies, and store–product combination strategies).

Finally, a discussion regarding strategic business units and profit centers is presented. These two are not the same, and they play a critical role in the firm's well-being. This is an area of retail strategy that needs much research.

Exhibits

Exhibit 9.1
The Elements of Historic Evolution

Retail Strategy	Basic Orientation	Goals
Mass Retailer	Starts with basically similar marketing mix to everyone, appealing to all consumers' desire for convenience and ease of shopping.	Tries to capture a large portion of the total market by not doing anything different than competition.
Differentiator	Starts with the orientation that all customers are basically alike but we must be different than our competitors.	Expects to develop a competitive edge by being different than competitors.
Segmenter	Starts with the orientation that consumer needs are diffused and all of them cannot be treated equally.	Expects to excel by catering well to a few well-defined segments.
Positioner	Starts with the orientation of positioning itself vis-á-vis a specific competitor. This could be above, below, or head on.	Attempts to profit by either taking a good portion of the market away from a competitor or using a void in the market.
Nicher	Starts with an extremely well-defined section of the market. Assumes that it can do the best job of satisfying the needs here.	Profits by catering to a well-defined corner and by preempting competition.
Category Killer	Starts with the orientation that, regardless of other differences, consumers truly go for bargains, values and variety.	Expects to capture a large portion of the market by doing everything better than anybody in terms of variety and values.

Exhibit 9.2
Alternative Retail Marketing Strategies

	Mass Retailer	Differentiator	Segmenter	Positioner	Nicher	Category Killer
Starting Point	Starts out with similar marketing mix.	Starts with different marketing mix.	Starts with market segmentation.	Starts with specific position aimed at a competitor.	Starts with well-defined corner of a market.	Starts with best mix and lowest prices.
General Orientation	Tries to capture a very large part of the mass market by imitating.	Tries to develop better mixes for the mass market.	Attempts to match supply and demand more carefully in a segment.	Attempts to take away a good portion of the market from the well established competitor.	Tries very carefully to cater to the well-defined corner of the segment.	Tries to undercut with greater variety and aggressive marketing.
View of the Market	All customers are basically alike.	All customers are basically alike.	All customers are different.	There are differences between our customers and competitors' customers.	Some customers are uniquely identifiable.	Customers are different but they all like bargains and variety.
Competitive Emphasis	Emphasizing marketing mix similarities, convenience, and prices.	Emphasizing marketing mix differences.	Market segmentation and mix differentiation when necessary.	Market segmentation and mix differentiation from a competitor.	Very specific market segmentation.	Better merchandise, better variety, lower prices.
Treatment of the Market	Tries to offer something for everyone, expects customers to adjust their needs to its.	Tries to offer something different than competitors to everyone. Expects customers to adjust their needs to its offering.	Tries to offer a unique marketing mix to each segment. Tries to adjust its supply to customer needs.	Tries to offer each segment a marketing mix which is better than the specific competitor's.	Adjusts its offering very sharply to a well-defined market.	Whatever the competitors do, it can do better and cheaper.

Exhibit 9.3
Stages in the Retail Life Cycle

Subject of Concern	Stage of Life Cycle Development			
	1. Innovation	2. Accelerated Development	3. Maturity	4. Decline
Competition	Innovation; light level of competition	Moderate level of competition	New direct and indirect competitors	Moderate direct and heavy indirect competition
General Management Concerns	The store concept refinement through adjustment and experimentation	Establishing preemptive market position	Prolonging maturity and revising the store concept	Harvesting or total renovation
Product-Service Mix	Innovative, unique, and forward-looking	New features added and strengths are reinforced	Need to explore new segments, repositioning the product mix, making it narrow and deep	Totally new mix, looking at different segments with different offering
Promotion Mix	High promotion; informative	Promotion for acceptance and purchase	Increased promotional activity	Complete change in appeal and image remanagement
Pricing Mix	Overall lower introductory prices	Higher prices in the strength areas, fewer loss leaders	Higher prices, trying to reemphasize price competition	Very aggressive low prices, regenerating volume
Human Resource Mix	Friendly, outgoing, people oriented	More sale and promotion oriented	Somewhat disappearing service and friendliness	Completely new start, few but dedicated

Exhibit 9.4
Strategic Alternatives Based on Product and Store Combinations

Patronage	Convenience Goods	Shopping Goods	Specialty Goods
Convenience Store	Consumers are driven by convenience. They buy whatever is available in the most accessible stores. *Brand loyalty and store loyalty do not exist.*	Consumers prefer to buy at the most accessible store. But they choose somewhat carefully from the existing assortment. *Brand loyalty and store loyalty do not exist.*	Consumers are driven by brands. But they will buy them at the most accessible store. *Brand loyalty exists.*
Shopping Store	Consumers shop at different stores in order to get the best service or the best price. But, they are not influenced by the brand or product. *Brand loyalty and store loyalty do not exist.*	Consumers are likely to compare both stores and the merchandise mixes. They will buy the best price from the best store. *Brand loyalty and store loyalty do not exist.*	Consumers product and brand drive. But they will buy these from the best store. They will compare stores. *Strong brand loyalty, no store loyalty.*
Specialty Store	Although they are indifferent to product or the brand, consumers prefer to shop at a specific store. *Store loyalty exists.*	Consumers clearly attached to the store. They will carefully compare and examine the products. *Store loyalty exists.*	Consumers strongly prefer the store as well as the product. *Both brand and store loyalty exist.*

Source: Adapted and revised from Samli (1989).

Exhibit 9.5
Implementation of Strategies at the Lower Levels

The Nature of Retail Decisions	Scope of Retail Decisions	Impact of Retail Decisions
Strategic Decisions	Overall, far reaching, competitive advantage long range	Enhance or deter differential congruence, develop or modify image, enhance or harm store's outreach to its target markets
Policy Decisions	More limited than strategy, storewide practices to implement strategy, unique to each store in a multistore setting, relatively shorter lived	More concentration on purchase motives, catering to idiosyncratic behavior, *using special policies to attract target customers.*
Tactical Decisions	Very limited storewide or even department wide. Shortlived local (departmental) interpretation and implementation of strategies	Developing specific practices that are unique to stores or departments to satisfy special consumer needs, being flexible and interactive about it, *providing them with special favors*

Exhibit 9.6
The Relationship between SBUs and PCs

Strategic Business Units

	Good Choice	Poor Choice
Good Choice	Good Management	Questionable Management
Poor Choice	Borderline Poor Management	Poor Management

Profit Centers

References

"A&P Looks Like Tenglemann's Vietnam." 1982. *Business Week*, 1 February, 29–30.

Alderson, Wroe. 1965. *Dynamic Marketing Behavior*. Homewood, Ill.: Richard D. Irwin.

Balevic, Betty V., and Jennifer Mancuso. 1996. "The Changing Role of the Retail Store Buyer." In *Proceedings of the Fiftieth Congress of IMDA*, ed. E. Kaynak, D. Lascu, and M. Beyer. Hammelstown, Pa.: IMDA.

Bates, Albert D. 1976. "The Troubled Future of Retailing." *Business Horizons* (August): 22–28.

———. 1989. "The Extended Specialty Store: A Strategic Opportunity for the 1990s." *Journal of Retailing* (Fall): 379–388.

Berkowitz, Eric N., Roger A Kerin, and William Rudelius. 1986. *Marketing*. St. Louis: Times/Mirror Mosby.

Berman, Barry, and Joel R. Evans. 1995. *Retail Management*. Englewood Cliffs, N.J.: Prentice Hall.

Berry, Leonard C., and Ian H. Wilson. 1977. "Retailing: The Next Ten Years." *Journal of Retailing* (Fall): 5–28.

Bogard, Leo. 1973. "The Future of Retailing." *Harvard Business Review* (November–December): 16–18.

Bredin, Alice. 1993. "Kudos to Jim Baum." *Stores* (January): 72–74.

Brown, Herbert E., and J. Taylor Sims. 1977. "Market Segmentation, Product Differentiation and Market Positioning as Alternative Marketing Strategies." In *Proceedings, American Marketing Association Educators' Conference*. Chicago: American Marketing Association.

Bucklin, Louis P. 1973. "Retail Strategy and Classification of Consumer Goods." *Journal of Marketing* (January): 45–54.

Cappel, Sam D., Peter Wright, David C. Wyld, and Joseph H. Miller, Jr. 1994. "Evaluating Strategic Effectiveness in the Retail Sector: A Conceptual Approach." *Journal of Business Strategy* (October–November): 209–212.

Davidson, William R., Albert D. Bates, and Stephen J. Bass. 1976. "The Retail Life Cycle." *Harvard Business Review* (November–December): 89–96.

Doyle, Peter, and Ian Fenwick. 1975–1976. "Shopping Habits in Grocery Chains." *Journal of Retailing* (Winter): 39–52.

Doyle, Peter, and Alok Sharma. 1977. "A Model for Strategic Positioning in Retailing." In *Proceedings, American Marketing Association Educators' Conference*. Chicago: American Marketing Association.

Ellsworth, Dick. 1993. "Time to Do or Die." *Journal of Business Strategy* (September–October): 19–29.

Hazel, Debra. 1996. "Resurgence of the Regionals." *Chain Store Age* (January): 65–70.

Jain, Subhash C. 1993. *Marketing, Planning, and Strategy*. Cincinnati, Ohio: Southwestern.

"K-Mart: Who's in Charge Here." 1995. *Business Week*, 4 December, 104–105.

Kotler, Philip. 1994. *Marketing Management: Analysis, Planning and Control*. 5th ed. Englewood Cliffs, N.J.: Prentice Hall.

Levinson, Jay Conrad. 1989. *Guerilla Marketing Attack*. Boston: Houghton Mifflin.

Lincoln, Douglas, and A. Coskun Samli. 1981. "Evolution in Retail Marketing Strategy." Academy of Marketing Science, *Conference Proceedings.*

Markowitz, Arthur. 1994. "Sears Takes Steps to Strengthen and Revitalize." *Discount Store News* 2 (February): 71.

Mason, J. Barry, and Morris L. Mayer. 1987. *Modern Retailing: Theory and Practice.* Dallas: Business Publications.

McCarthy, E. Jerome, and William Perreault. 1987. *Marketing Management.* Homewood, Ill.: Richard D. Irwin.

McCune, Jenny C. 1994. "In the Shadow of Wal-Mart." *Management Review* (December): 10–16.

Nickels, Williams G. 1978. *Marketing Principles.* Englewood Cliffs, N.J.: Prentice Hall.

Ohmae, Kenichi. 1982. *The Mind of the Strategist.* New York: Penguin.

Porter, Michael. 1985. *The Competitive Edge.* New York: Random House.

Roberts, Alan A. 1961. "Applying the Strategy of Market Segmentation." *Business Horizons* (Fall): 65.

Samli, A. Coskun. 1968. "Segmentation and Carving a Niche in the Market Place." *Journal of Retailing* (Summer): 38–49.

———. 1975. "Use of Segmentation Index to Measure Store Loyalty." *Journal of Retailing* (Spring): 51–60.

———. 1969. "Segmentation Index and Store Image in Retail and Service Establishments." In *Proceedings of ESOMAR Seminar XXIX on Research That Works for Today's Marketing Problems, 1976.* From talk delivered before the X ESOMAR Seminar, 2–5, at Lucerne.

———. 1989. *Retail Marketing Strategies.* Westport, Conn.: Quorum Books.

———. 1993. *Counterturbulence Marketing.* Westport, Conn.: Quorum Books.

———. 1996. *Information Driven Marketing Decisions.* Westport, Conn.: Quorum Books.

Sears, Roebuck and Company. 1994. *Annual Report.*

Sims, J. Taylor. 1970. On Measuring the Long-Run Effects of Product Line Extension. Ph.D. diss., Graduate School of Business, University of Illinois at Urbana.

Smith, Wendell R. 1956. "Product Differentiation and Market Segmentation as Alternative Marketing Strategies." *Journal of Marketing* (July): 3–8.

Stanton, William J. 1982. *Fundamentals of Marketing.* New York: McGraw-Hill.

Sweeney, Daniel J., and Richard C. Reizenstein. 1972. "Developing a Retail Market Segmentation Strategy for a Women's Specialty Store Using Multiple Discriminate Analysis." In *Combined Proceedings, American Marketing Association.* Chicago: American Marketing Association.

Trout, Jack, and Al Ries. 1972a. "Positioning Cuts through Chaos in Marketplace." *Advertising Age,* 1 May, 51–53.

———. 1972b. *The Positioning Era Cometh.* Chicago: Craig. Reprint of a three-part series in *Advertising Age.*

Underwood, Elaine. 1994. "On the Record With the Man Who Turned Around Sears." *Brand Week,* 4 April, 18–22.

U.S. Bureau of the Census. 1986. *Statistical Abstract of the United States.* Washington, D.C.: U.S. Government Printing Office.

Wilkie, William L., and Paul Farris. 1975. "Comparison Advertising: Problems and Potential." *Journal of Marketing* (October): 7–14.

Chapter 10

Developing and Measuring the Store Image

A regular customer of Saks Fifth Avenue decides to visit a factory outlet store. That person is not likely to be pleased with the atmosphere, merchandise, service, and other store features (Samli 1989). The person is most likely to feel uncomfortable and out of place. Of course, the opposite situation is also true. A regular consumer of the factory outlet store may find himself or herself out of place at Saks Fifth Avenue. In both cases, the perceived store images are very different, but also the individual's perception is quite different. The so-called *category-based processing theory* recognizes that individuals do not face a new stimulus (such as a new store) as if this were a completely new experience. They will compare incoming data against the information that they have stored in their memories.

Exhibit 10.1 takes this theory and applies it to an individual who has been in a number of K-Mart stores, but is experiencing a "new" K-Mart store for the first time.

It is clear at this point that the synergistic characteristics of the retail store illustrate the importance of the store's "character," which is known as the store image. A retail store is not only a place where goods and services are purchased, but also a place where a combination of functional and emotional stimuli are perceived (Oxenfeldt 1974–1975; Samli 1989). Thus, in common parlance, there is more to a retail store than meets the eye. A retail store has many personal and impersonal aspects that distinguish it from other stores. From every store many tangible and intangible stimuli emanate. It is clear, therefore, that the retail store is synergistic. This total synergism is depicted by the store image, which is the sum total of the functional qualities, psychological attributes, and symbolic characteristics of the store (Martineau 1958).

The image not only distinguishes the store from all others but also provides the basis for competitive advantage. Thus, there cannot be any question about the importance of the store image to the store's well-being. Particularly in the case of certain fashionable and upscale stores, retail management is managing the store image. In this chapter, we discuss the development, manipulation, and adjustment of the store image, first, by understanding its dimensions and measurement, and second, by managing it.

CONCEPTUALIZING STORE IMAGE

Pierre Martineau was perhaps the pioneer in the exploration and understanding of the retail store image. He was among the first to bring the store image concept into focus and research it. He described the store image as "the way in which the store is defined in the shopper's mind." In analyzing the concept further, he proposed two key components: functional qualities and psychological attributes. The functional qualities of a store include such store characteristics as product assortment, store layout, store location, price–value relationships, and other related features that consumers are capable of comparing, reasonably objectively, to competitors. The second component is the store's psychological attributes. These refer to consumers' perceptions of certain store features, such as friendliness and helpfulness of store personnel, attractiveness of decor, or general ambience. Both of Martineau's image components, functional qualities and psychological attributes, imply the existence of multiple descriptors to which a goodness–badness attitude scale rating can be attached. Though he did not discuss the interaction between the two components or a possible causality between the two, Martineau set the stage for an endless stream of store image research activity (Samli 1989).

Underlying the image concept is that no store can be all things to all people. Hence, different consumer groups are likely to place differing amounts of importance on store-image attributes (Steenkamp and Wedel 1991).

As early as 1961, a study measuring the impact of television advertising on store image defined image as "a complex of meanings and relationships serving to characterize the store for people" (Arons 1961, 1). This definition implies that consumers take a set of factors and reduce them down to manageable proportions, as illustrated in Exhibit 10.1. Arons's definition refers to "meanings," which also implies dimensions and certainly parallels Martineau's definition as well as the definition presented by Steenkamp and Wedel (1991, 301): "the overall attitude toward the store, based upon the perceptions of relevant store attributes."

The customer's perception of store image at the functional level depends on how well the store has met the customer's aspiration level with regard to price, quality, and service. At the psychological level, the consumers' likes and dislikes regarding the store's not so obviously measurable features are accounted for. It may be quite possible to explore certain symbolic characteristics of the store's image which may be the joint product of functional and psychological features of the store.

Oxenfeldt (1974–1975), following the same dichotomy that is created by Martineau (1958), referred to image as "a combination of factual and emotional material." This point of view reinforces the point of view that many customers will hold factually based opinions about the store based on the functional features. They also feel certain ways based on psychological attributes. Berry (1969) approached the analysis of store image with a more systematic technique. He asked whether retail image could distinguish one store from others. Then he explored which aspects of the store's discriminable powers were important enough to establish or enhance the comparative advantage of the retail establishment. Berry defined store image as "the discriminative stimuli for expected reinforcement; i.e., image is the total conceptualized or expected reinforcement that a person associates with a given store" (p. 2). This reinforcement aspect is the crux of successful retail management.

Wyckham (1967, 333) defined store image as "the summation of all the attributes of a store as perceived by the consumers through their experience with the store." Blackwell, Engel, and Kollat (1983) reinforced this point, stating that a critical portion of image is experienced by perception. However, they also reiterated that the objective characteristics of the store contributes to its image.

Cox's (1974) definition of image was similar to those presented earlier. He posited that image is "the combination of stimuli, both tangible and intangible, emanating from a variety of personal and impersonal communication sources which a person associates with a particular store." His contribution to the understanding of the concept was the personal and impersonal dichotomy that is communicated. If the stimuli are not communicated properly, they will not register.

More than twenty years later, Berman and Evans (1995, 546) defined image as "how a retailer is perceived by consumers and others." A critical point here is the word "others," because image reaches both customers and noncustomers alike.

It is clear that the store image concept is complex and extremely important. It reflects the personality of the store as perceived by different publics. The personality of the store is made up of physical attributes, character, and the skill qualities of its personnel. When a customer enters the store, he or she wants the store's displays and ambience to tell what that store is like, and the cues must be up-to-par in terms of expectations.

The image that the store is attempting to project must be realistic enough that it will be immediately obvious and quickly accepted by the targets for which it is designed. It is obvious that the store needs to be deliberate in making statements like the following:

- The friendliest place you have ever been.
- The best values for the most reasonable prices.
- Cutting edge of technology to improve your life.
- Ultimate in female underwear.

An image is projected deliberately through personal and impersonal communicators, in the form of a combination of tangible and intangible features, all of which are leading in the direction of providing an overall symbolic impression. In the simplest sense, this symbolic impression says, "Hey! This is what I am." Of course, it is also obvious that the store may not live up to its claims. To the extent that there is a critical gap between the store's claims and customers' perception of it, the store is not succeeding, and its future is questionable.

Finally, as stated earlier, no store can be all things to all people. Therefore, it is next to impossible to expect that the store will project the same image in a variety of different market segments. The store deals with a number of publics. Among these are loyal customers, occasional buyers, loyal customers of competitors, the rest of the community that does not buy at the store nor at the competitors' stores, the store's management itself, and competitors' managements. Clearly, the image projected to local customers is bound to be different than the one it projects to those who dislike the store. The critical point, of course, is the ability to project the desired (or necessary) image in the target market from which the store expects purchases and loyalty in terms of repeat purchases. Similarly, the store must be in a position, if necessary, to manipulate, modify, and sometimes even dramatically change that image. It must be reiterated that the key concepts here are being proactive and deliberate. The store projects and/or modifies the image in advance, and it does so intentionally, accurately, and, preferably, exactly the way it should be.

IMAGE DIMENSIONS

Since image is a complex and synergistic concept, it is important that the retailer understand it. If the retailer is to manipulate the store image as a key weapon to achieve competitive advantage, its dimensions and the respective relative importance of these dimensions need to be known. Again, it must be kept in mind that the store image is composed of multiple dimensions and is synergistic, which means that, positive or negative, it is more than all of these dimensions put together.

Though store image definitions differ somewhat and different stores have different images, it is critical to remember that the store exists in the perception of consumers. The impact on this perception is achieved by the psychological and objective characteristics of the store. Thus, store image researchers must be able to identify the critical dimensions of the store. These dimensions, both psychological and factual, when put together will compose and project the store image (Samli 1989).

Different researchers have taken different positions regarding the dimensions of the store image. Martineau (1958) described the store image in terms of four dimensions: symbols and color, layout and architecture, advertising, and sales personnel. Obviously, this was a somewhat limited orientation. Retailers need numerous additional dimensions so they can manipulate the image more effectively.

Kunkel and Berry (1968) compiled an image dimension list based on consumers' statements. From 3,737 statements describing what consumers like and dislike about the retail establishments, they identified twelve categories derived from a total of forty-three individual dimensions.

Upon his review of nineteen studies, Lindquist (1974–1975) synthesized the store image framework into nine image–attribute dimension categories. These are (1) merchandising, (2) service, (3) clientele, (4) physical facilities, (5) convenience, (6) promotion, (7) store atmosphere, (8) institutional factors, and (9) past transactions. The details of these are presented in Exhibit 10.2.

It is clear that all these nine broad categories do not have equal weight in the composition of total store image. Marketing scholars, based on various research activities, have explored the relative importance of these dimensions. On the basis of how often these variables are mentioned by scholars, Lindquist (1974–1975) concluded that merchandise-related considerations (i.e., assortment, quality, and prices, along with location-related convenience) are considered among the most critical image dimensions. Mazursky and Jacoby (1986) conclude that the most important components of store image are merchandise-related aspects, service-related aspects, and the pleasantness of shopping in the store.

It is more critical to evaluate the image dimensions in terms of their relative success. After all, if store image is generated by discriminative stimuli, it is necessary to determine the relative success of the image dimensions. This success can be measured by using analysis of customer-oriented measures directly, rather than by using management judgments and other indirect measures. These direct analyses have become possible with the advancement of causal modeling in marketing research.

Once again, it is necessary to develop an adequate list of store image dimensions. This list should not be too excessive nor too limited. A comprehensive list is presented in Exhibit 10.3. Though somewhat arbitrary, a distinction is made in the list between the physical attributes and psychological attributes. This list cannot be considered complete, but it does include most of the variables that have been used in retail store image studies. The critical point here is that different types of retailers may emphasize different image attributes as a part of their merchandising and promotional strategies (Jenkins and Forsythe 1979).

In studying the store attributes that are likely to determine patronage, Bearden (1977) identified seven store characteristics. Four of these characteristics were significantly different for downtown patrons versus shopping center customers. The implications of these findings are that different marketing strategies must be used for different market segments, if possible, based on patronage determinants.

The store image component may not be as important or even reliable in different markets. A study investigating the intermarket reliability of store image components found that the major dimensions underlying store image vary from market to market (Hirschman, Greenberg, and Robertson 1978). This finding implies that the retailer has to determine the major image dimensions within each different market in order to assure that the store has a functional and profitable image within a given market.

As can be seen, there is much involved in exploring the dimensions of a retail store. Images vary by store types, from one segment to another as well as from one market to another. The retailer must be in a position to understand, evaluate, and use the key image dimensions so that proper images are not only constructed under certain circumstances, but also can be carefully manipulated if needed.

MEASURING STORE IMAGES

If the store image cannot be measured, it cannot be managed. It cannot be revised or redirected in a deliberate manner. If, for instance, an attempt is to be made to change a store's image, unless it is possible to measure the old and the new images and compare the two, no progress can be made in this area. It is necessary to determine the impact of the attempts to project the new image, and it must be compared to the old image so that progress (or lack thereof) can be measured.

Different approaches can be used to measure the store image. Specific approaches to measuring the store's image are a function of how the researcher defines the store image and what key components of the store make up the image. However, it is important to note that if the new and old image measurement activity is not done in the same way, then the comparability element in the concept disappears. Once the store image is measured in a specific way, then it must be continued to be measured the same way so that continuity is established regarding the image and its impact.

All store image measurement approaches can be classified in two distinct categories, structured or unstructured (Exhibit 10.4). Unstructured approaches include word association tests, nondirective questioning, and other projective techniques (Samli 1996, 1989).

Numerous studies were done during the 1970s. An unstructured psycholinguistic technique was used where individual consumers provided names of stores (nouns) and bases of similarity and dissimilarity (adjectives) among stores (Cardozo 1974–1975). Muse (1974–1975) attempted to explain why consumers left the store in question without making a purchase (walk-outs). Others used an unstructured store image measurement approach by asking walk-outs what thoughts or concepts came to their minds when they thought of the particular store they had just left (Myers 1960). Different projective techniques, such as cartoon tests, were utilized to explore the image variations among different units of major retail institutions in Los Angeles (Marcus 1972). Open-ended questions were suggested as a better alternative to other store image measurement techniques. This technique, however, requires very strong verbal skills for the respondents and very strong interpretive skills for the researcher. A major shortcoming of the technique is that it yields almost no information from nonpurchasers (McDougall and Fry 1974–1975).

Though the techniques used for store image measurement are grouped into two categories, it does not mean that these groups are mutually exclusive. It is quite possible that the unstructured techniques can allow the determination of critical image dimensions. They can be used to develop lists and concepts of image dimensions that are to be used in structured analyses which, for the most part, are more sophisticated and have special applications as well as advantages in analysis (Kunkel and Berry 1968).

Exhibit 10.4 lists four major techniques that are used in store image measurement. These are (1) semantic differential, (2) multidimensional scaling, (3) multiattribute attitude modeling, and (4) multivariate techniques. Of these four, semantic differential is the most popular (Mindak 1961).

Semantic Differential

Perhaps the most popular tool of attitudinal research that has been used in assessing store image is semantic differential. It has been used in many studies and in many different ways:

- To identify the factors underlying consumer patronage decisions (Kelley and Stephenson 1967).
- To measure department store image (May 1974–1975; Wyckham 1967).
- To investigate possible differences in customers' versus retailers' department store image (Arons 1961; Pathak 1972).
- To measure the impact of television advertising on department store image (Wyckham 1967).
- To determine the differences between symbolic and functional store images (Sirgy and Samli 1989).

Marketing scholars have traditionally used this particular technique to measure a store image. The technique is easy to administer and tabulate. It allows the presentation of the processed data in a format that is easily understood and made visual. It does not require extensive verbal skills on the part of the respondents. Furthermore, it is quite reliable, in that the same type of results can be generated under similar circumstances (Arons 1961; Weale 1961; Wyckham 1967; Samli 1996).

Two serious problems need to be eliminated for a better use of semantic differential. First, the researcher needs to determine the attributes (or dimensions) of the semantic differential that are necessary for the store image measurement. Second, the researcher has to select a large number of attributes to be scaled. The question that arises, then, is just how many of these attributes are interrelated in the minds of the consumers and the relative importance of each with regard to its relationship to the total image (Marks 1974; Wyckham 1967; Samli 1996).

Multidimensional Scaling

Multidimensional scaling (MDS) is a newer and, perhaps, a little more sophisticated tool which is also used to measure store image. It has been used to measure the image of several discount department stores (Doyle and Fenwick 1974–1975), and has also measured differences in store images held by consumers as these differences relate to store loyalty.

The important characteristics of MDS are, first, the technique makes the fewest necessary assumptions regarding the respondent's reaction; and, second, it gives the respondents a chance to make minimally structured judgments. As a result, in using MDS respondents are given a chance to be objective in a very subjective attitudinal questioning situation. This technique allows management to evaluate the store's image in comparison with the competitor's store image. But, on the other end of the spectrum, MDS is a difficult technique to administer and it is equally difficult to analyze its data (Blackwell, Engel, and Kollat 1983). Interpreting the dimensions and deciding on the axis are particularly difficult as the researcher attempts to develop a perceptual map. Finally, it is difficult to assess statistical significance by using MDS (Marks 1974).

Multiattribute Models

Multiattribute models rectify some of the major deficiencies in the semantic differential method. Since in semantic differential all of the variables used have the same equal weight, the technique fails to determine which of the variables used in the study are more important based on respondent perception. For instance, in semantic differential one item may concern traditional versus modern, and another may concern salespeople being knowledgeable versus uninformed. Whereas in semantic differential these two variables will have equal weight, in multiattribute models there will be an additional question for each so that a different weight can be assigned to each. It may be that customers put a lot more emphasis on the salespeople's knowledge level than on whether the store is perceived to be modern or old-fashioned. Of course, it could also be just the opposite. In either case, the semantic differential will not show that difference, but a multiattribute model will.

Marketers have been applying multiattribute models for the purpose of measuring store image since Fishbein (1967) established an earlier version of this model. Lessig (1973) adopted a multiattribute model to examine the relationship between consumer images of grocery stores and the commensurate degrees of consumer loyalty to these stores. Many others stated that the multiattribute approach is a good predictor of store image (James, Durand, and Drewes 1976). The multiattribute approach is also used for an entire corporate image measurement rather than for just one store. It is also used to identify and single out the best market segments among a number of choices (Marks 1974; Stephenson 1969).

Multiattribute models enable the researcher to determine which of the variables are particularly important in store image (salience) and their respective degrees of importance (valence). Thus, multiattribute models retain the advantages of the semantic differential while correcting its shortcomings. However, some issues of concern remain in this technique just as in the semantic differential: (1) specification of the multiattribute model (there are some major variations in the application of the model), (2) attribute generation and inclusion (in both semantic differential and multiattribute models, which variables or dimensions to use is a critical issue), (3) determining how the importance of the component should be measured, (4) how the belief components should be treated as opposed to the physical components, (5) how the importance of the belief component should be scored, and (6) the halo effects (the interrelationship of the store attributes with each other and the creation of unwanted bias).

Multivariate Techniques

There are a variety of techniques in this group (Samli 1996), all geared for different types of analyses. Marks (1974) was among the earliest to use multivariate techniques for their benefit in measuring and evaluating store image. He used two different techniques: factor analysis and multiple regression. By using factor analysis, he reduced to eight the thirty variables that were used in the semantic differential. This simplified the total process. Subsequently, by performing multiple regressions, he was able to determine that only four of the eight factors identified by factor analysis were important to responding consumers in evaluating the overall image of the store. Of these, it was concluded that fashionability was the most important factor in forming the image of the apparel store in the study. The other three variables, in order of their importance, were salesmanship, outside attractiveness, and advertising. It must be reiterated that, not only in absolute terms but also in relative terms, this combination of factor analysis and multiple regression techniques is powerful. She used this approach to compare the image factors of three men's apparel shops. Though multivariate techniques are quite powerful, they have not been used extensively in retailing research (Samli 1989).

IMAGE MANAGEMENT

As seen from our discussion, much effort has been made to determine the nature, characteristics, strengths, and weaknesses of the store image. It may be said that managing the retail store well is managing its image effectively. This way, the probability of retail success is likely to be increased. Properly managed store image within the store's target markets can lead to increased sales and profitability. A retailer's repeat business can be considered as a function of the positive image customers have of that store (Marks 1974; Samli 1989). The relationship between the store image and store loyalty indicates that the two are related (Lessig 1973; Sirgy and Samli 1989).

Earlier research indicates that the store image sometimes is more important than the image of the merchandise bought (Dalrymple and Thompson 1969). For example, a study found carpet samples from an upscale store to have a more favorable product image than the same samples from a low-scale store (Enis and Stafford 1969). Obviously, in this case, the consumers' evaluation of products purchased is influenced by the store image of where they were purchased. Another study indicated that store image is used as a method of risk reduction. If the customers believe in the store where they are shopping, then they feel more secure that the product is good (Roselius 1975). Thus, the store image is used as a surrogate indicator of product quality. All in all, the store's image is very important in attracting certain target markets and keeping them loyal (Sirgy and Samli 1989).

It is obvious that the retailer must have a proactive approach to constructing and managing the store's image. Exhibit 10.5 displays a five-step store image management paradigm: (1) evaluate the current store images, (2) evaluate the image of the key competitor, (3) determine the changes or enhancements that are needed, (4) assess the changes in the store image, and (5) relate the changes to the performance of the store.

Evaluating the Current Store Image

If we do not understand the current or existing image, how can we make any progress? In order to gain this understanding, the present image needs to be properly defined. Its important variables or dimensions are critical. They must, first be identified and, second, their relative importance must be determined with regard to the contribution they make to the total store image (Exhibit 10.5). Once the salience and valence of these variables are established, then the firm is, by definition, keenly aware of the present store image and its key component. At this point the retail establishment is ready (if necessary) to manipulate this total image. Understanding the valence, or the weights, of the salient characteristics of the store image will indicate the alternatives regarding other directions for these and perhaps other dimensions of the total image. If, for instance, through a multiattribute analysis the retailer realizes that the store personnel is the most important strength and this feature carries more weight than any other feature of the store indicated in the research study, then it is obvious that the retailer has the options of keeping this feature as is, strengthening it further, or putting more emphasis on some other features of the store. Much of this activity of choosing options depends on the second step of the process.

Evaluation of Competitor's Image

In order to obtain a real understanding of the store's critical strengths, a comparison needs to be made with other stores. If K-Mart, for instance, wants to upgrade its image and be somewhat above Wal-Mart, it must understand its strengths vis-à-vis Wal-Mart's strengths. Only then will it be possible to determine where K-Mart can put emphasis that would distinguish it from Wal-Mart. If K-Mart people find out that Wal-Mart has an image of good merchandise value, all American-made products, and good locations, then K-Mart must decide how to go beyond this overall image and make itself more attractive. K-Mart needs to know just which features are at par and which are above par when compared to Wal-Mart.

At this point it is clear that analyses of this second stage provide the key ammunition for developing a new strategy or revising the old one. Dynamic comparative retail image research described in these first two stages is critical for the well-being of the retail store. This research leads to adjustments in retail marketing mixes and hence helps implement the changes that are desired or necessary. When such marketing changes are implemented, it is critical that consumers perceive the image change efforts exactly the way management intended. However, these image change efforts cannot be measured in isolation. They must be evaluated vis-à-vis other changes and developments in the retailing environment (Downs and Flood 1979). As the changes are planned, a timely and direct evaluation of the new strategy can bring about success.

Designing and Implementing Image Enhancements

Once management understands its store's weaknesses and strengths, and once it has investigated similar criteria about the competitors, then careful analysis will follow.

Assume, for instance, that Circuit City is known for its product variety, quality, and the knowledge level of its employees. But image studies and comparisons, based on customer response, indicate that its location and atmosphere are not admired. Furthermore, customers may not be comfortable with the "deals" they get from the stores. Now it is up to management to consider the relative importance of these pluses and minuses. Just which of these dimensions are particularly critical in the establishment's target markets and which ones will put the company in a more favorable competitive position? The company may decide that in the target markets where it is strong, the existing image features are more important than others. Hence, it may go ahead with a plan to further strengthen these image dimensions rather than to promote others.

The last part of the specific tasks of this stage is designing the retail mixes so that the plans can be implemented. The revised retail mixes must project the store image that is needed to be targeted to the market segment the store is attempting to influence.

Assessing the Impact of the New Store Image

Once the planned changes in the strategy are implemented through the revised retail mixes, the differences between the previous image and the present image must be carefully examined. Image-related research data are necessary for this activity. If the retail establishment is involved in a before–after analysis, then it is essential that these two sets of data be comparable. The data-collection techniques, instruments, and data-analysis methodology must be all consistent on the two different occasions. Once the earlier image is contrasted to the new image, within the constraints of validity and reliability of the data generated, it becomes clear if the attempts to improve the image are paying off. Here, of course, the difference between the previous and current image must be in the direction that the changes were intended. If, for instance, after changing the store layout, it turns out that customers do not like the new layout, then the difference is not in the direction that was desired. Continuing with the earlier example of Circuit City, if the new image data show that customers think that the knowledge base of the personnel has declined, then, obviously, attempts to strengthen the image are not going in the right direction. Thus, the direction and the intensity of the changes as a result of the new strategy are extremely critical to quickly and accurately measure.

Relating the Changes to the Performance

In the final analysis, unless the changes in the image reflect improvements in the store's performance, the store is wasting a lot of time, effort, and resources. Thus, the real success of the first four steps is to be seen in the way the retail store is performing in the marketplace. This market performance can be measured in at least four different ways (Samli 1989). First, changes in sales volume and market share are measured and compared to the same periods in the past. Second, the change (if there is any and if it can be measured) in the degree of store loyalty is evaluated. Third, the outreach of the store is examined. As the retail store attempts to reach out to the market, if it brings in customers from further distances and broader trading areas, then the store is doing well. Finally, the profitability of the store is examined. If the results of strategy changes and improved image are bringing in more profits, then market performance is improving.

It is important for the reader to realize that all retailers do not work on the image problem with such technical sophistication. Many retailers are so intimately involved in their activity that they almost intuitively know the changes to effect.

For example, Bonomo's, an upscale women's apparel and accessories store in a small Southeast university town, had been doing well. In the same mall, at the other end, Dana's, a very upscale women's apparel store was opened. Dana's appeared to be very elegant and expensive. The salespeople appeared to be very proper, but somewhat distant. The store was attracting slightly younger and more fashion-oriented ladies. Bonomo's decided to improve the sales effort and the store atmosphere. It hired some prominent ladies in the town as part-time salespeople. These ladies were popular local leaders, and they were well known for their taste in clothing. In addition to regular customers, Bonomo's started attracting the friends of the part-time salesladies. As the friends dropped in, the store developed a very warm atmosphere with the feeling of an ongoing party. The owner–manager knew her market and her clientele. The store did very well, and changes in the strategy worked even though there was no in-depth research.

COMBINING THE PHYSICAL
AND PSYCHOLOGICAL ATTRIBUTES

Forty key variables indicating the store image are presented in Exhibit 10.3. These variables (or dimensions) are identified in two separate groups: physical attributes of the store and psychological attributes of the store. Instead of using all forty of these attributes and others that would make the list even longer, a series of symbolic features of the store may identify the image more clearly by combining the essentials of physical attributes and psychological attributes. In order to understand the symbolic dimensions which are the product of combined psychological and physical attributes, a comparison is presented in Exhibit 10.6 between Gap and The Limited, two major apparel retail chains.

On the basis of the exhibit, The Limited is considered to be more trendy than Gap. Basically, The Limited appeals to the younger generation. This particular generation is more flashy and follows trends, fads, and current developments. Thus, The Limited is more in with the "now" generation. Similarly, The Limited's lines are also seen as more current and less classically casual. Gap lines are not quite so trendy and almost not at all faddish. Even though some Gap lines are considered current, they are still quite classical.

Perhaps the most significant distinction between the two stores is that Gap deals with lines that have substantially more longevity than trendy fashion lines. Similarly, Gap aims at a more upscale market segment. Hence, it manages to isolate itself somewhat from the fluctuations of fashion changes as well as negative business-cycle impact. Furthermore, it manages to appeal to a larger age segment than The Limited. In a recession, for example, The Limited's customers cut down their purchases slightly, or need to be stimulated with more advertising and lower prices than the Gap customers (Samli 1993).

As can be seen from Exhibit 10.6, seven symbolic characteristics can reflect the retailer's segmentation efforts. It may be possible to expose these dimensions instead of physical and psychological attributes. Much research is needed in this area.

INTERNATIONAL CORNER

Consumer behavior is typically related to the prevailing culture. International retailing is particularly challenged in terms of developing and managing an image that is suitable for the local culture. One of the most critical issues regarding image is related to international versus local image. Some companies, such as Bulgari and Benetton, are known internationally. To the extent that they are aiming at the same segments in different societies, they need to maintain the same image. If Benetton is a status symbol in country A, it cannot simply be just another product in country B. However, others may need to adjust their image to local conditions and be part of the total local scene.

The need to manage a proper image causes international retailers to use different entry strategies. Exhibit 10.7 illustrates a variety of entry strategies for international retailers to expand into international markets. If the company starts a joint venture, it may gain the ability to adjust its image locally as well as to start a totally new image. If the retailer enters by acquiring a local business, it may have a chance to maintain its image as is and use exclusively the local image. In the case of a partnership, the international retailer can slightly modify its image to cater to the local market.

In the examples given, it is clear that much research and thinking must precede the entry process. The retailer must understand the local culture and how the retailer will fit or fail to fit into this culture. Of course, the original image decision is not quite enough when the expansion process is a reality. The retailer must pay very close attention to the image and must make the necessary adjustments.

SUMMARY

This chapter posits that managing a retail store well is managing its image. Four key areas of store image are explored in this chapter: (1)

definition, (2) dimensions, (3) measurement, and (4) management. Though most definitions imply the perception of a combination of, first, functional characteristics, and, second, psychological attributes, both of these areas are combined at a higher level of store image perception based on symbolic image characteristics. Thus, whether we are dealing with functional characteristics, psychological attributes, or symbolic features, image is all perceived and synergistic. The sum total of all of its attributes and characteristics is still less than the total store image.

Though there are no universally agreed-upon list of dimensions, various authors have suggested the presence of some key dimensions. Images vary by store types, by consumer types, by segments, and by various constituencies.

In order to measure the store image, a series of unstructured and structured techniques are discussed. The unstructured measurement techniques are word association, nondirective questioning, cartoon tests, and open-ended questions. Among the key structured techniques are semantic differential, multidimensional scaling, multiattribute models, and multivariate techniques.

A detailed discussion is presented about store image management. This paradigm is composed of five major steps: (1) evaluating the current image, (2) evaluating the image of the key competitor, (3) determining the changes or enhancements that are needed, (4) assessing the changes in the store image, and (5) relating the changes to performance.

Finally, in an effort to combine the physical and psychological attributes of the store image, it is proposed that a series of symbolic dimensions may be used. To illustrate, an attempt is made to compare Gap and The Limited stores.

Exhibits

1. The store must match a previously defined category of stores.

   (Oh! Here is the new K-Mart store; I wonder how it compares to other K-Mart stores I have known.)

2. The store must give out cues that will match information about this category of stores.

   (The consumer enters. Well! It seems pretty much the same merchandise and the same layout.)

3. If the store is perceived to match an existing category of stores, it means we activated the criteria used to describe that category.

   (I wonder if this K-Mart is better about giving out information on sporting goods and electronics.)

4. If the set of criteria is activated, all the information is transferred to this store.

   (It appears that these salespeople don't know much about sporting goods and electronics, just as the others.)

5. If the set of criteria is activated, this set will determine the relevance and consistency of the information about the store.

   (Gee! This K-Mart is exactly the same as the others; let me get out of here or let me buy.)

Exhibit 10.2
The Key Dimensions of Store Image

Dimension	Description
Merchandise	There are five identifiable subdimensions: quality, selection or assortment, styling or fashion, guarantees, and pricing. Merchandise itself means the goods and services offered by the retailer.
Service	The areas included are general service, sales clerk service, presence of self-service, ease of merchandise return, delivery service, and credit policies.
Clientele	Social class appeal, self-image congruency, and store personnel are included as dimensions of this factor.
Physical facilities	Included in this dimension are elevators, lighting, air conditioning, and washrooms. It may also include store layout, aisle placement, identification of sections, carpeting, and architecture.
Convenience	Three key subdimensions are identified: general convenience, location convenience, and parking.
Promotion	In this group are sales promotion, advertising, displays, coupons, symbols, and colors.
Store atmosphere	This is an intangible category. Included are congeniality, customers' feelings, and ambience.
Institutional factors	This is also an intangible category. It deals with reliability, reputation, and modernness.
Post-transaction satisfaction	Merchandise in use, returns and adjustments, and receptability to complaints are all included in this category.

Source: Adapted and revised from Lindquist (1974–1975).

Exhibit 10.3
A Comprehensive List of Store Image Dimensions

Factor Number	Physical Attributes	Factor Number	Psychological Attributes
1	Dependable Products	21	Courteous Salespeople
2	High Quality	22	Helpful Salespeople
3	High Value for Money	23	Adequate Number of Salespeople
4	Wide Selection	24	Store Is Known by Friends
5	Fully Stocked	25	Store Is Liked by Friends
6	Numerous Brands	26	Store Is Recommended by Friends
7	Well-Known Brands	27	Many Friends Shop There
8	High-Fashion Items	28	Easy to Move through Store
9	Low Prices vs. Competition	29	Easy to Find Items You Want
10	Many Specially Priced Items	30	Store Located Nearby
11	Layaway Available	31	Short Time to Reach Store
12	Knowledgeable Salespeople	32	Convenient to Other Stores
13	Store Is Clean	33	Attractive Decor
14	Fast Checkout	34	Advertising Is Informative
15	Company Operates Many Stores	35	Advertising Helps Planning
16	Easy to Park	36	Advertising Is Appealing
17	Company Has Been in Community a Long Time	37	Advertising Is Believable
18	Company Is Well Known	38	Friendly Store Personnel
19	Easy to Get Credit	39	Easy to Exchange Purchases
20	Easy to Get Home Delivery	40	Fair on Adjustments

Source: Adapted and revised from Hansen and Deutscher (1977–1978).

Exhibit 10.4

Store Image Research and Measurement Techniques

Technique (Unstructured)	*Description*
Word Association	Trying to determine the word which comes to the customer's mind first.
Nondirective Questions	If I wanted to shop good quality I would go to _____.
Cartoon Test	Describe the customers of the store you see in the picture.
Open-ended Questions	What do you like the most about shopping at XYZ store?

Technique (Structured)	
Semantic Differential	Old fashioned - - - - - Modern
Multidimensional Scaling	Comparing stores on a perceptual map.
Multiattribute Models	Semantic differential with weights to establish relative importance of each factor.
Multivariate Techniques	Modern statistical analyses techniques, including clustering, discrimant analyses, factor analyses, and canonical analyses.

Source: Samli (1996).

Exhibit 10.5
Specific Steps in Store Image Management

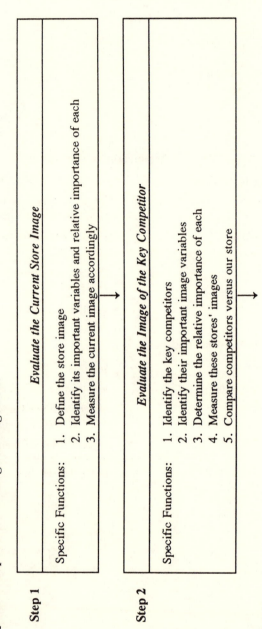

Step 1

Evaluate the Current Store Image

Specific Functions:
1. Define the store image
2. Identify its important variables and relative importance of each
3. Measure the current image accordingly

Step 2

Evaluate the Image of the Key Competitor

Specific Functions:
1. Identify the key competitors
2. Identify their important image variables
3. Determine the relative importance of each
4. Measure these stores' images
5. Compare competitors versus our store

Step 3

Determine the Changes/Enhancements That Are Needed

Specific Functions:
1. Identify the store's strengths and weaknesses
2. Determine importance of image dimensions within the store's market segments
3. Decide what is needed to be done to accomplish the desired enhancements

Step 4

Assess the Changes in the Store Image

Specific Functions:
1. Examine the changes since step 1
2. Evaluate the impact of these changes in your competitive posture
3. Determine if the changes are in the desired direction and how intense they are

Step 5

Relate the Changes to the Performance of the Store

Specific Functions:
1. Measure the changes in sales and market share
2. Measure customers' store loyalty
3. Assess the changes in loyal customers vs. new customers
4. Evaluate the changes in profitability

Exhibit 10.6
Symbolic Characteristics of Gap versus The Limited

Symbolic Characteristics	Gap	The Limited
Trendy	-	+
Faddish	-	+
Flashy	-	+
Current	-	+
Current with classical lines	+	-
Casual	+	-
Appealing to a larger age group	+	-

Source: Adapted and revised from Samli (1993).

Exhibit 10.7
Retail Expansion Activity

Company	Entry Activity	Retail Image Impact
Asko Deutsche Kaufhaus AG Germany	Expanded into Bulgaria through joint venture	Ability to adjust the image locally
Tesco United Kingdom	Entered the French market by acquiring local retailer	Keeping the local image totally local
Carrefour France	Set up a joint venture with Metro for expansion into Italy	Ability to adjust the image locally or start a new local image
Marks & Spencer United Kingdom	Formed partnership to set up operations in Spain	Slightly modified image or keeping images as they are
Ahold Netherlands	Acquired supermarket chains to enter Portugal	Keeping the local image totally local
Rewe Germany	Acquired a stake in a chain to open discount stores in the U.K.	Opportunity to start totally new image
Asprey United Kingdom	Acquired a Swiss upscale watch retailer to expand into Europe	Ability to upgrade the existing image

Source: Adapted and revised from "Globalization of the Retail Industry: A Strategic Imperative" (1995).

References

Arons, Leon. 1961. "Does Television Viewing Influence Store Image and Shopping Frequency?" *Journal of Retailing* 37 (Fall): 1–13.

Bearden, William O. 1977. "Determinant Attributes of Store Patronage: Downtown versus Outlying Shopping Center." *Journal of Retailing* (Summer): 15–22.

Berkowitz, Eric N., Terry Deutscher, and Robert A. Hansen. 1978. "Retail Image Research: A Case of Significant Unrealized Potential." *Proceedings of the American Marketing Association Educators' Conference.* Chicago: American Marketing Association.

Berman, Barry, and Joel R. Evans. 1995. *Retail Management.* Englewood Cliffs, N.J.: Prentice Hall.

Berry, Leonard L. 1969. "The Components of Department Store Image: A Theoretical and Empirical Analysis." *Journal of Retailing* 45 (Spring): 3–20.

Blackwell, Roger D., James F. Engel, and David T. Kollat. 1983. *Consumer Behavior.* 4th ed. Hinsdale, Ill.: Dryden Press.

Cardozo, Richard N. 1974–1975. "How Images Vary by Product Class." *Journal of Retailing* (Winter): 2.

Cox, Charles E., Jr. 1974. An Analysis of Infrequent Shopper Attitudes towards Department Store Appeals. Master's thesis, University of Tennessee.

Dalrymple, Douglas J., and Donald C. Thompson. 1969. *Retailing: An Economic View.* New York: Free Press.

Downs, Phillip E., and Richard G. Flood. 1979. "Dynamic Comparative Retail Image: An Empirical Investigation." In *Southern Marketing Association Proceedings.* Atlanta: Southern Marketing Association.

Doyle, Peter, and Ian Fenwick. 1974–1975. "How Store Images Affect Shopping Habits in Grocery Chains." *Journal of Retailing* 50 (Winter): 46–55.

Enis, Ben M., and James E. Stafford. 1969. "Consumer's Perception of Product Quality as a Function of Various Information Inputs." In *Marketing Involvement in Society and the Environment,* ed. Philip R. McDonald. Chicago: American Marketing Association.

Fishbein, Martin. 1967. "A Behavior Theory Approach to the Relations between Beliefs about an Object and the Attitude towards the Object." In *Readings in Attitude Theory and Measurement.* New York: John Wiley and Sons.

"Globalization of the Retail Industry: A Strategic Imperative." 1995. *Chain Store Age Executive,* 15 December, 6–22.

Hansen, Robert A., and Terry Deutscher. 1977–1978. "An Empirical Investigation of Attribute Importance in Retail Store Selection." *Journal of Retailing* 53 (Winter): 58–72.

———. 1977. "Measure Validation in Retail Research Image Research." In *Proceedings of the 1977 Conference of the Southern Marketing Association.* Atlanta: Southern Marketing Association.

Hirschman, Elizabeth C., Barnett Greenberg, and Dan H. Robertson. 1978. "The Intermarket Reliability of Retail Image Research: An Empirical Examination." *Journal of Retailing* (Spring).

Hollander, Stanley C., and Delbert J. Duncan. 1983. *Modern Retailing Management*. Homewood, Ill.: Richard D. Irwin.

James, Don L., Richard M. Durand, and Robert A. Drewes. 1976. "The Use of a Multi-Attribute Model in a Store Image Study." *Journal of Retailing* (Summer): 23–32.

Jenkins, Roger L., and Sandra M. Forsythe. 1979. "Retail Image Research: State of the Art Review with Implications for Retailing Strategy." In *Developments in Marketing Science* 3:189–196, ed. V. V. Bellur and B. G. Gnaudi. Miami: Academy of Marketing Science.

Kelley, R. G., and Ronald P. Stephenson. 1967. "The Semantic Differential: An Information Source for Designing Retail Patronage Appeals." *Journal of Marketing* (December): 43–47.

Kunkel, John H., and Leonard L. Berry. 1968. "A Behavioral Concept of Retail Image." *Journal of Marketing* 32 (October): 21–27.

Lazer, William, and Eugene J. Kelley. 1961. "The Retailing Mix: Planning and Management." *Journal of Retailing* 37 (Spring): 32–44.

Lessig, V. P. 1973. "Consumer Store Images and Store Loyalties." *Journal of Marketing* 38 (October): 72–74.

Lindquist, Jay D. 1974–1975. "Meaning of Image: A Survey of Empirical and Hypothetical Evidence." *Journal of Retailing* 50 (Winter): 29–38.

Marcus, Burton H. 1972. "Image Variation and the Multi-Unit Retail Establishment." *Journal of Retailing* (Summer): 29–43.

Marks, Ronald B. 1974. A Multi-Attribute Approach to the Store Imagery Problem. Ph.D. diss., University of Missouri.

Martineau, Pierre. 1957. *Motivation in Advertising*. New York: McGraw-Hill.

———. 1958. "The Personality of the Retail Store." *Harvard Business Review* (January–February): 47–55.

Mason, J. Barry, and Morris L. Mayer. 1987. *Modern Retailing: Theory and Practice*. Dallas: Business Publications.

May, Elenor G. 1974–1975. "Practical Applications of Recent Retail Image Research." *Journal of Retailing* (Winter): 15–20.

Mazursky, David, and Jack Jacoby. 1986. "Exploring the Development of Store Images." *Journal of Retailing* (February): 145–165.

McDougall G. H. G., and J. N. Fry. 1974–1975. "Combining Two Methods of Image Measurement." *Journal of Retailing* 50 (Winter): 53–61.

Mindak, William A. 1961. "Fitting the Semantic Differential to the Marketing Problem." *Journal of Marketing* (April): 28–34.

Muse, William A. 1974–1975. "Using Word Association Tests to Develop a Retail Store Image." *Journal of Retailing* (Winter): 35–42.

Myers, Robert H. 1960. "Sharpening Your Store Image." *Journal of Retailing* (Fall): 129–137.

Oxenfeldt, Alfred R. 1974–1975. "Developing a Favorable Price–Quality Image." *Journal of Retailing* 50 (Winter): 8–14.

Pathak, Devendron S. 1972. A Study of Department Store's Images Held by Customers and Management. Doctoral diss., Michigan State University.

Rachman, David J. 1975. *Retail Strategy and Structure*. Englewood Cliffs, N.J.: Prentice Hall.

Roselius, Ted. 1975. "Consumer Rankings of Risk Reduction Methods." *Journal of Marketing* 35 (January): 56–66.

Samli, A. Coskun. 1989. *Retail Marketing Strategies*. Westport, Conn.: Quorum Books.

———. 1993. *Counterturbulence Marketing*. Westport, Conn.: Quorum Books.

———. 1996. *Information Driven Marketing Decisions*. Westport, Conn.: Quorum Books.

Schiffman, Leon F., Joseph F. Dash, and William K. Dillon. 1977. "The Contribution of Store Image Characteristics to Store Type Choice." *Journal of Retailing* (Summer): 3–44.

Semenik, Richard J., and Robert A. Hansen. 1976. "Low Income vs. Non-Low-Income Consumer Preference Data as Input to Socially Responsive and Economically Profitable Decision-Making." In *Proceedings of the 1976 American Marketing Association Educators' Conference*. Chicago: American Marketing Association.

Sirgy, Joseph M., and A. Coskun Samli. 1989. "Self Image Congruence versus Socioeconomic Status: Predictors of Upscale versus Downscale Stores." In *The Cutting Edge*, ed. William R. Darden. Baton Rouge: Louisiana State University Press.

Soldner, Helmut. 1976. "Conceptual Models for Retail Strategy Formulation." *Journal of Retailing* 52 (Fall): 49–56.

Steenkamp, Jan-Benedict E. M., and Michel Wedel. 1991. "Segmenting Retail Markets on Store Image Using a Consumer-Based Methodology." *Journal of Retailing* (Fall): 300–320.

Stephenson, Ronald P. 1969. "Identifying Determinants of Retail Patronage." *Journal of Marketing* 33 (July): 57–60.

Stern, Bruce L., Ronald F. Bush, and Joseph H. Hair, Jr. 1977. "The Self-Image/Store Image Matching Process: An Empirical Test." *Journal of Business* 50 (January): 63–69.

Weale, Bruce W. 1961. "Measuring the Customer's Image of the Department Store." *Journal of Retailing* (Summer): 40–48.

Wyckham, R. G. 1967. "Aggregate Department Store Image: Social and Experimental Factors." In *Proceedings of American Marketing Association Conference*, 333–337. Chicago: American Marketing Association.

Chapter 11

Retail Image Perceived by Different Constituencies and the Congruence Factor

The retail market is composed of different constituencies, and the image perceived by the market is not likely to be uniform. Therefore, in image analysis it is necessary to determine who is receiving what kind of image. Even though the image perceived by the target markets of the retail establishment is most critical, it must be contrasted, particularly with what is perceived by management itself.

This chapter discusses the usefulness as a diagnostic tool of contrasting the image perceived by the store's customers with the store management's perception. The differential congruence, which is the indicator of overall performance, implies a positive match between the store image and the customer's self-image. Discrepancies between the store image perceived by the market and by the management can definitely be used for diagnostic purposes to enhance the differential congruence that the store enjoys. The diagnostic benefits of contrasting images are applied to congruence considerations in the second part of the chapter.

As discussed earlier, store image is all of the impressions perceived from all of the different publics the store interacts with, directly or indirectly. The store's most important interaction is with its loyal customers. This interaction is the most critical consideration for the survival of the store. Ideally, the store should have one image perceived by everyone, one that is similar to that perceived by the store's loyal customers, which, further, should be the same as the one that management intentionally projects. In a practical sense, this is nearly impossible, primarily because a retail store deals with different constituencies (or publics), each of which perceives the store's features, characteristics, and overall personality quite differently.

From a more practical perspective, the store, first and foremost, must concentrate on the image it is projecting to its loyal customers. It must make sure that this particular image is what the customers like and identify themselves with. By definition, this is the image that will create a high level of congruence between how the customers see themselves and how they see the store. In order to achieve this congruence, which intensifies the concept of differential congruence (Chapter 2), the management must have a realistic view of assessing the store image. Thus, contrasting the management's perception of the store image with the loyal customers' perceptions of the store image is a very critical undertaking. If there are critical differences between the two, then obviously the management, in its attempts to construct and manipulate the store image, is not putting the proper emphases and resources in the right areas. In short, the store is not managed optimally. For instance, if the customers think that the store's layout is attractive and functional, but the management thinks that the layout is one of the prime weaknesses of the store, then the management will be using a lot of resources to fix something that is not even broken. On the other side of the coin, the customers of the store, in general, may feel that the store has a bad return policy, but the management may think that the store has a very good (liberal) return policy. Once again, the store may lose a lot of customers or sales without knowing the reason. Thus, if the two are not exactly the same, the management's perception of the store image must at least be very close to the customers' perception.

The discrepancy between these two images can be a very important diagnostic tool. It would provide powerful feedback as to prioritization of managerial decision areas. This chapter deals with this critical tool and presents a discussion as to how it may be used to the best advantage.

THE EVOLUTION OF IMAGE RESEARCH

In Chapter 10, the concepts of store image, measurement, and management are discussed. In order to understand the use of store image by different constituents as a diagnostic tool, it is critical to explore the evolution of store image research. Exhibit 11.1 presents seven separate evolutionary stages in the development and usage of store image concepts. The last two thrusts imply the use of store image as a strategic tool. The previous thrusts have to take place so that the last two phases can become a reality. These last two phases provide a powerful diagnostic tool that can be incorporated into the store strategy.

Samli–Lincoln Paradigm

The multiattribute model has been used in earlier studies (Fishbein 1967a; Rosenberg 1956; Doyle and Fenwick 1974–1975; Wilkie and Pessemier 1973; Oxenfeldt 1974–1975; Samli 1989). This technique allows store attributes to be differently weighted. This model was further revised with the adequacy-importance concept. This concept is expressed as follows (Samli 1989):

$$A = \sum_{i=1}^{n} P_i D_i$$

Where

A = individual's attitude toward an object.

P = importance of attribute I for the individual.

D = individual's evaluation of object with respect to the attribute I.

n = number of attributes.

It has been concluded that this adequacy-importance concept can be used in predicting consumer attitudes more accurately and, hence, can be useful for developing strategies that will result in certain desired attitude changes toward the store (Maris, Ahtola, and Klippel 1975; Lindquist 1974–1975; Greyser 1973; Isaacson 1964; May 1971; Samli 1989).

The Samli–Lincoln Paradigm is presented in Exhibit 11.2. It emphasizes the ability to contrast the store image by preferably loyal customers with the store image by the management. It further emphasizes that the most significant discrepancies are most critical. Such discrepancies indicate the presence of major problems and guide the management to prioritize these problems. It is critical to emphasize that the management must be concerned with the customers' perceptions and must put its resources into the areas where significant gaps exist in these two images and where these significant gaps indicate the displeasure of customers. Finally, the paradigm states that after the management puts corrective measures into practice, it has to reassess the store image.

A study indicated that this type of analysis pointed out four key problem areas. First, consumers did not think the store was modern, but the management did. Second, consumers did not think that parking was very bad, but the management did. Third, consumers thought that it was difficult to purchase on credit, but the management did not. And, finally, consumers did not think there were adequate salespeople, but the management did (Samli 1989). Under these circumstances, if the management goes ahead and undertakes the major financial project of adding parking while there is an acute need for salespeople, wrong remedies are obviously being used for wrong problems.

This is a version of "Gap" analysis, which deals with the comparisons of what is expected and what is experienced. It is possible for retailers to identify positive gaps which indicate a store's strengths, and negative gaps that point out a store's real weaknesses (Samli, Kelly, and Hunt 1998).

Reemphasizing the Diagnostic Sequence

Adequate diagnosis of problem areas centers around understanding the discrepancy between management and customer perceptions of the image of the store in question (Samli 1989). Though it has already been stated that the two images must be as close to each other as possible, it has not been strongly implied that both also must be positive.

On the basis of the theory put forth in this chapter, there are basically two groups of store features. These are congruent and incongruent features, as shown in Exhibit 11.3. In the same exhibit, a distinction is made between "in favor of the store" and "critical deficiency." If, for instance, the store has a very desirable merchandise mix in the minds of both customers and management, this is reflected in the upper left quadrant of the exhibit. Certainly this indicates a critical strength of the store. Incongruencies in favor of the store indicate discrepancies between the management's perceptions and the customer's perceptions of the strengths of the store that are not known by the store's customers. This situation is depicted in the lower left quadrant of Exhibit 11.3. If, for instance, the customers think that the parking facilities of the store are excellent but the management thinks they are totally inadequate, this is an undiscovered strength of the firm. It must be promoted further and must be used properly as a feature establishing competitive advantage for the firm. If the customers and the management both agree that, for instance, the internal layout of the store is poor, this is an obvious problem area that needs to be corrected. This situation is depicted in the upper right quadrant of Exhibit 11.3. Strong agreement by both parties indicates the gravity of the problem and that it needs to be taken care of as quickly as possible. Finally, the lower right quadrant of the exhibit illustrates how undetected problems can arise from these analyses. If, for instance, the management thinks that their credit service is excellent, but the store's customers think otherwise, then there is a big problem that the management has not even realized. A good part of this chapter deals with this concept. The greater the discrepancy between the two groups, the greater the severity of the problem.

Based on Exhibit 11.3, the management should focus first on the most critical undetected problem areas. The critical deficiencies that both parties acknowledge is the second general area on which the management should concentrate. Of course, the competitive advantage features would make very effective promotional messages that need to be utilized to strengthen the store's existing image or to make it more far-reaching.

FOUNDATIONS OF DIFFERENTIAL CONGRUENCE

Now that we have discussed store image in detail, we must make sure that, as we manage it, we make it more acceptable and likable to our customers. This approach leads to developing differential congruence.

Differential congruence gives viability to a retail establishment. It is achieved by developing a positive balance between the store image and an individual customer's self-image. At this point, the store claims it has features that are unique and that differentiate the store, and these features are consistent with the customer's self-image. Thus, there is congruence between the two images. The stronger the differential congruence, the greater the long-term customer satisfaction and value derived from patronizing the retail establishment.

Unfortunately, many retailers emphasize income-based financial figures. These figures are better at measuring the consequences of yesterday's decisions. As such, they are short-run indicators and do not say much about tomorrow's performance. The crux of differential congruences is connecting the store's performance and the resultant store image to its customers' self-image not only on the basis of yesterday's decisions, but on the basis of long-term customer satisfaction and value (Parasuraman, Berry, and Zeithaml 1991).

It must be reiterated that the store image is a product of the store's functional and emotional (psychological) features. These functional and psychological aspects of the store's personality lead to a symbolic store image. It is important to understand how this process takes place and to what extent the functional and psychological features of the store connect to the total symbolic image. Early studies have concentrated primarily on the store's functional features; thus, there is a gap in research relating to the store's emotional (psychological) features and symbolic features (representing the total store personality) (Darden and Babin 1994).

In stereotypic research of the past, the store image, which encompasses all the impressions about the store that shoppers hold, is looked at primarily on the functional and some part of the psychological side of the store's performance. The symbolic, value-expressive store image, on the other hand, is a combination derived from the two traditional aspects of store image. The symbolic store image characteristics are related to traditional versus modern, classy versus folksy, sexy versus plain, friendly versus formal, and high status versus low status (Samli and Sirgy 1981; Sirgy 1982; Samli 1989; Sirgy et al. 1991). If, for example, a consumer perceives that on the basis of its functional and psychological features a store is patronized by high-class consumers and she sees herself as a high-class consumer, then there is congruence. Such congruence will lead to store loyalty (Sirgy et al. 1991). If the store succeeds in creating such a congruence with all of its customers, then, by definition, the store has created a differential advantage. In the customer's mind, the store does not have many close substitutes. Hence it enjoys strong customer loyalty, which, of course, means repeat sales.

It must be reiterated that when we talk about symbolic image, functional image, and psychological image, we always have the problem of which comes first, a dilemma similar to the the chicken or egg. It is vital for the retailer to know the interaction among the three images. Sirgy and colleagues (1991), for instance, suggested that positive general image congruence has, in turn, a positive influence on the functional image of the store. This particular concept of the positive symbolic image causing a positive functional and psychological image needs additional research. This is why two-way arrows are used in Exhibit 11.4 to establish the connection among these three images.

Consumer's Self-Image

Studies have shown that there is a distinct connection between how the individual sees himself or herself and interprets the store image, and patronage behavior (Sirgy 1982; Samli and Sirgy 1981; Stern, Bush, and Haire 1977). Without becoming involved in a complicated theoretical discussion, it is simply stated here that consumers receive cognitive influences, which result in learning and affective influences, by which values are developed. These influences are connected to thoughts and feelings. All of these interactively form the consumer's self-image.

In addition to learning and developing values, consumers are receiving messages from the store about its functions and psychological features. As illustrated in Chapter 10, the individual who is assessing the features of a new K-Mart store ends up saying something like, "This is a nice, modest place with a vast selection. I am not that far advanced economically, but I like to explore and economize. This is a good place for me," or, "Gee! I never liked K-Mart; none of my friends buy here; their merchandise is simply too cheap for my taste. I don't have anything in common with their salespeople; this place is not for me."

The Resultant Congruence

In the final analysis, if there is no congruence between the customer's self-image and store image, the store may be doing business with first-timers only, so it will not be possible to create store loyalty and keep customers satisfied. The lack of congruence makes the store less effective. Considering that it is five times more costly to bring in new customers than to keep current customers happy, the lack of congruence is obviously very costly.

Positive congruence affects store loyalty through the activation and operation of the self-consistency motive (Sirgy 1982). This motive refers to an individual's need to act in ways that are consistent with his or her self-perception. To do otherwise would cause dissonance, which is a psychological discomfort threatening to invalidate that individual's beliefs about himself or herself. Earlier studies (Martineau 1958) have indicated, for instance, that an upper-class family shopped at a store like Cartier's for their public appearance-related jewelry and, hence, members of the family were motivated by self-consistency. If the members of the same family were to shop for custom jewelry in discount stores, K-Mart or Wal-Mart for example, they would feel quite frustrated, knowing and feeling that they were not in their element (Samli 1989).

In addition to the self-consistency motive, some researchers also discuss the self-esteem motive. This motive refers to an individual's need to act in certain ways that are instrumental in achieving goals that maintain and increase that individual's self-regard. In this book, when we refer to "self-image" we are not making a distinction between self-consistency and self-esteem motives. From a retailing perspective, they are both part of the individual's self-image and are both important for the retailer.

Exhibit 11.5 illustrates how store image and self-image congruence take place and influence store loyalty. As can be seen, when there is incongruence, store patronage or loyalty is low or nonexistent. But there is also a limited side to the picture. The consumers who do not feel good about themselves may be attached to certain stores. Thus, two negatives can create a positive. The question is just how long this alliance will last. The high store loyalty emerging from a relatively questionable self-image and store image should not be looked upon as an undesirable oddity. This situation is common and quite widespread. Perhaps the only concern is that customers in time may "outgrow" the retail institution, but there will still be sufficient numbers of consumers to frequent these stores. Thus, congruence on one end of the spectrum may be a little more limited, but it is necessary and fulfills a major void in the marketplace.

STRATEGIC IMPLICATIONS FOR RETAILERS

It is obvious that the consumer is motivated to patronize a store that satisfies both self-esteem and self-consistency needs. For example, the customer thinks, "This store seems to have an image of high social class which matches my own self-image of being a classy person (high self-esteem); therefore, by patronizing it I will not only satisfy my self-esteem, but I will be in my element." This is differential congruence at its best. This notion is beyond differential advantage, in the sense that here, because of congruence and resultant loyalty, there is a state of equilibrium between the store and its market, with no immediate tendency to change. This situation would result in an optimum amount of satisfaction for customers and profits for the store.

Exhibit 11.5 illustrates four separate components in a retail store's target. The most desirable of these is the high congruence component (Column 3). If the store is in a position to do so, it must concentrate on this portion of its market. When the retail establishment is making a diagnostic attempt to compare store image as perceived by customers with store image perceived by the management, the diagnostic outcome will lead to certain decisions. These decisions will make some changes in the image. These changes must be in a direction to enhance and strengthen the store's differential congruence. Thus, differential congruence and corrective action to eliminate image discrepancies are very closely related.

Retailers must focus on positive congruence situations. In doing so, they should be able to identify the demographics, psychographics, geographics, shopping habits, media habits, and evaluation of store image attributes (both functional and psychological as well as symbolic) and cater to these customers accordingly. The demographic, psychographic, and geographic information about the target market would certainly help the retailer to develop all four of the retail mixes—human resources, merchandise, promotion, and price—that are not only suitable for this market but would also create high positive congruence and high levels of loyalty.

The Case of a Student Gift Shop

A student gift shop in a small Southeastern town suddenly realized that they had limited variety, limited stock for the products they had, and a confusing atmosphere because the store was run by part-time help who did not know how to organize the store and its inventory. This whole scenario was not fully detected by the management. Certain customer reactions, observation, and other similar indicators brought the situation to the fore.

Management had to construct a series of alternatives. Three such alternatives are identified in Exhibit 11.6:

1. Develop a more appealing merchandise mix. Hire a few full-time employees who relate to students well and who can organize the store in a way liked by the students.
2. Make the store more nonstudent oriented. Change its image somewhat and appeal to young adults of the town.
3. Develop the store and its atmosphere to appeal to the upper middle class, with a more mature ambience and total orientation.

It is now necessary to examine each alternative with regard to its possible impact on the store's congruence. The basic thinking in this case is that if most of the store's customers are students, there is no way that Alternatives 2 and 3 could enhance the store's congruence. Any development in these directions is bound to weaken the store's differential congruence with its core market, students.

Implementing Alternative 1 is not necessarily difficult and, at this point, is the only reasonable solution. However, as discussed in Chapter 9, there are policies and tactics that need to be considered. In other words, as this option is implemented and perhaps the store's niche strategy is strengthened, this general orientation has many specific implementation alternatives. For instance, the store may expand the merchandise mix more in the direction of co-eds, but may establish a new policy of intercepting those who come in and leave without buying anything. It may also develop a liberal return policy and certain tactics of grouping the new merchandise in a dorm-room arrangement and displaying the most attractive new lines in the best possible manner.

Finally, evaluating the outcome is essential. If Alternative 1 did not improve the situation, it may mean the following:

1. The alternative was not implemented well.
2. It was the wrong decision to begin with.
3. It discouraged the more mature store customers.
4. It did not strengthen the store's congruence.

Obviously, the store must first have feedback to determine the effectiveness of the decision; second, it must develop other alternatives; and third, it must go through the same basic steps until the situation improves.

A PROACTIVE APPROACH TO CONGRUENCE DEVELOPMENT

From our discussion thus far, it is clear that the retailer should focus on the positive congruence group. In so doing, the retailer must identify demographics, psychographics, geographics, shopping habits, and media habits. Furthermore, the retailer must be able to examine the store image perceived by the core customers and the management to identify strengths and weaknesses. Of course, the core customer group has its own self-image and congruence with store image. All of these would enable the retailer to understand the importance of prices, product assortment, quality, personnel, atmosphere, and promotional activities.

The demographic, psychographic, and geographic information, along with knowledge of consumer behavior, should help the retailer develop an optimal merchandise mix that is most appropriate for its target market. The shopping habit information would help the retailer make optimal location decisions. The information on media habits would help the retailer to develop effective promotional plans to communicate with the market. The information regarding the target market's evaluation of self-image and the store image would help the retailer to make changes in the store image to strengthen the store's differential congruence. If, for instance, a store such as Bloomingdale's projects an image of high status, affluence, and prestige, the shoppers who perceive themselves as having high status and prestige and who would like to be thought of as such will experience a positive congruence. If, further, Bloomingdale's has a good idea about where these people are, how they behave, and how they are motivated, its differential congruence will be strengthened.

LOYALTY TO A RETAIL STORE

If differential congruence of a retailer works properly, a desirable level of store loyalty on the part of the target market has to be present. It is critical to explore the factors accelerating such a loyalty and how such a loyalty factor is measured.

Store loyalty is perhaps the single most important concept for the retailer in regard to successful marketing. It indicates "differential advantage" in Aldersonian (1957) terminology or "monopoly power" in Chamberlainian (1933) terminology. If it is possible to determine the nature and degree of loyalty, then the retailer attempts to strengthen this loyalty by developing better and more effective marketing strategies. Traditionally, identifying the market segment that patronizes the retail store along the lines of the store loyalty factor has been construed as an effective method of market segmentation. Here we go one step further and posit that the true measure of successful differential congruence is also store loyalty.

Over a period of three decades or so, there have been many studies analyzing store loyalty concepts. These studies may be classified into four categories. The first group of studies analyzed the store loyalty concept from an unidimensional perspective. Reynolds, Darden, and

Martin (1974), for instance, connected store loyalty to psychographic variables. Their study showed that the store's loyal customers are time conscious, exposed to entertainment media, and likely to be inshoppers rather than outshoppers (see Chapter 4).

The second group of studies related store loyalty to socioeconomic characteristics (Enis and Paul 1968; Mason and Mayer 1970; Samli 1979; Samli and Sirgy 1981). According to these studies, certain socioeconomic groups display a certain segmentation index that is associated with store patronage and loyalty. Among the salient socioeconomic criteria that are used for such an analysis are income, education, occupation, and ownership of certain luxury items.

The third research thrust dealing with store loyalty examined the determinants of store image (Hirschman 1981). This type of research was initiated by Martineau (1958), who maintained that store loyalty is a function of store image. If the store has a favorable image, a degree of loyalty commensurate with the favorableness of the image is likely to emerge. A large variety of research activity followed in Martineau's footsteps, exploring the finer points of image research (Jacoby and Kyner 1973; Lessig 1973; Lindquist 1974–1975; Nevin and Houston 1980; Darden and Babin 1994).

The fourth research direction has been along the lines of geographic factors. Intermarket shopping or outshopping (see Chapters 4 and 5) research indicates that consumers are more loyal to home-front shopping facilities if they are satisfied. Here, the distance traveled and the shopping area image appear to be critical (Nevin and Houston 1980; Samli 1989).

The fifth research effort is related to establishing a relationship between self-concept and store image interaction and store patronage and loyalty. A number of studies demonstrated that consumers shop at stores whose images are similar to their own (Sirgy 1982; Stern, Bush, and Haire 1977). Some indicated that the congruity that exists between these two images is a significant predictor of store loyalty (Bellinger, Steinberg, and Stanton 1976). Others maintained that it is not the actual, but the "ideal" self-image and store image congruity that is the critical force (Dornoff and Tatham 1972).

All these efforts lead one in the direction of multidimensionality of this very complex topic (Samli 1989). Store loyalty is the single most important factor in retailing success and longevity. Without such a loyalty, any attempt to generate differential congruence is doomed to fail.

Though store loyalty is primarily a function of the level of customer satisfaction with the store, there are at least six modifiers of this relationship. All of these must be taken into account as store loyalty research is undertaken. Exhibit 11.7 lists these modifiers under the heading of *store loyalty factors*.

Habit

This is the first loyalty factor. People go to a neighborhood bank, drug store, or convenience store. Such behavior is based on habit and is not likely to change quickly. As can be seen, there are a number of ways habitual shopping is measured.

Specific Store Attributes

Certain features can make consumers attach to a store and become loyal to it. These features need to be identified carefully. They do not have equal appeal; therefore, their relative importance needs to be explored. Would the customers go back to shop there and why are questions for this area.

Activity-Generating Practices

In some cases, the store appeals to certain consumers who are activity oriented (Chapter 7). By providing specific information, the store can help consumers to shop around. This can be a strong loyalty-generating activity.

Inertia

Some consumers shop in a store on the basis of blind loyalty. "These are local boys," and "We have shopped here for generations," are the types of reactions to shopping in this particular store. This is blind loyalty and could be powerful. It is questionable, however, if it can be generated through retailer effort.

Social Class

As discussed earlier, certain types of stores appeal to certain socio-economic classes. Such a situation can generate strong store loyalty.

Self-Image/Store Image Congruence

As discussed in different parts of this book, this is the essence of differential congruence. It has been found that if these two images are in congruity, there will be a strong level of customer loyalty (Samli 1989).

INTERNATIONAL CORNER

Some people claim that worldwide information dissemination and related trends are contributing to the homogenization of consumer tastes. As a result, consumer groups with similar aspirations and needs are becoming identifiable throughout the world. Indeed, certain groups, such as international yuppies, may be considered a reality. However, there is simultaneously a trend of nationalism or indeed even localism going on throughout the world. Hence, while international markets are opening up, the retailer who wants to go international must not strictly consider the "globalization" of world markets. While on the surface some products may be desired and purchased globally, consumer behavior in different world markets is very different and is not becoming global (Samli 1996). Thus, the international retailer must be aware of local cultures and how they differ from each other. If the retail store is to succeed in developing and managing an image leading to differential congruence, it must understand how to market within these cultural and behavioral differences.

If the retail establishment is projecting an image and expands to use a similar image in different international markets, at least two distinct questions arise: (1) Is this image functional in different world markets, or could it be used in these world markets? and (2) Can we measure the image and pursuant customer loyalty the way we measure them in the United States? Most of the store loyalty measurement criteria presented in Exhibit 11.7 are not altogether usable in many parts of the world. On the other hand, in many parts of the world retailers and consumers live, work, and coexist in close proximity. There is a historic and continuing loyalty factor that the international retailer must take into consideration and even work with. This area of international retailing still needs to be researched extensively.

SUMMARY

This chapter connects two vital areas in retail management. First, it explores the discrepancies between the store image perception by the management and the store image perception by customers. Second, it explores how such a diagnostic tool would improve the store's performance. In this regard, a discussion of differential congruence is presented. These two important concepts are presented in a five-step paradigm, as displayed in Exhibit 11.6. These steps, in a more abbreviated manner, are as follows: (1) becoming cognizant of a problem based on image comparisons, (2) determining alternatives, (3) examining each alternative's impact on congruence, (4) choosing and implementing the solution, and (5) evaluating the outcome. Finally, a special section explores the store loyalty concept and its measurement. Six store loyalty factors are discussed, and the approaches to their measurement are identified.

It must be reiterated that the analyses and the recommendations in this chapter are very critical for the health of the retail store. Systematic analyses must take place periodically so that problems can be prevented before they become serious.

Exhibits

Exhibit 11.1
Major Thrusts of Image Research in Retailing

THRUSTS	SAMPLE STUDIES	FINDINGS	IMPLICATIONS
1. Retail Image Components	Hansen and Deutscher (1977-1978) Martineau (1958) Lindquist (1974-75	There are multiple key dimensions in store image analysis.	It is necessary to understand the extent and implications of store image concept.
2. Comparative Image Analysis	Lessig (1973) Kunkel and Berry (1968)	Consumer store images and store loyalties are related.	By comparing our store's image with those of competitors we can improve our competitive edge.
3. Image Measurement Techniques	Marks (1974) Wyckham (1967) Doyle and Fenwick (1974-75) Fishbein (1967)	There are a number of refined techniques used to measure store image.	Unless we measure the store image accurately, this concept cannot be used for effective managerial decisions.
4. Store versus Area Image	Samli and Sirgy (1981) Sirgy and Samli (1985) Steenkamp and Wedel (1991)	There is a strong relationship between the store image and loyalty to the geographic area.	Location can be an enhancer or detractor of store image.
5. Congruence between Store Image and Self Image	Sirgy et al. in Samli (1989) Stern, Bush, and Haire (1977) Bellenger, Steinberg, and Stanton (1976) Sirgy et al. (1991)	Congruence between store image and self image can be measured.	High degree of positive congruence implies strong store loyalty.
6. Using a Store Image by Different Constituents as a Diagnostic Tool	Samli and Lincoln (1989)	Store image is perceived differently by management and by customers.	Discrepancy between the store customers and store management is a strong diagnostic tool.
7. Classifying Different Degrees of Incongruence as a More Powerful Diagnostic Tool	Samli, Kelly, and Hunt (1998)	Customer-management images are classified into six key categories of incongruence.	Six categories of incongruence provide a powerful prioritization system for management action.

Source: Samli, Kelly, and Hunt (1998).

Note: Though a number of studies cut across more than one thrust, the authors classified them on the basis of their major thrusts.

Exhibit 11.2
Samli–Lincoln Paradigm of Perceived Image Conflict Diagnostics

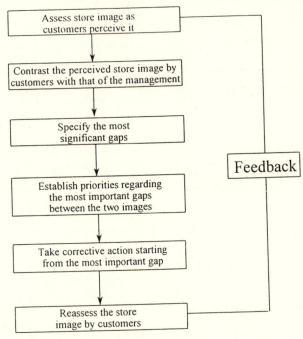

Source: Adapted and modified from Samli and Lincoln (1989).

Exhibit 11.3
The Use of Discrepancies between Management and Customer Perceptions

	In Favor of the Store	Critical Deficiency
Congruence	Competitive advantage feature	Obvious problem areas that need to be corrected
Incongruence	Unknown competitive advantage feature that needs to be promoted	Undetected problem areas that need very special attention

Exhibit 11.4
The Concept of Differential Congruence

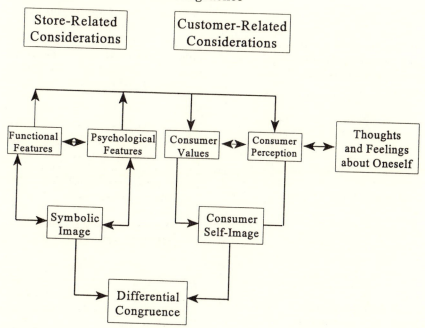

Exhibit 11.5
Self-Image and Store Image Congruence Alternatives

Self Image	Store Image	Congruence	Store Patronage/Loyalty
High	High	High (positive)	High
Low	High	Low	Low
High	Low	Low	Low
Low	Low	High (somewhat limited)	High (somewhat limited)

243

Exhibit 11.6
Solving Image Problems as a Congruence Strengthener

The Case of A Student Gift Shop

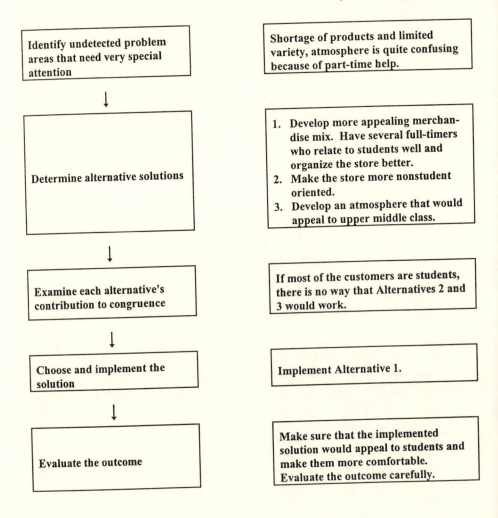

Identify undetected problem areas that need very special attention	Shortage of products and limited variety, atmosphere is quite confusing because of part-time help.
↓	
Determine alternative solutions	1. Develop more appealing merchandise mix. Have several full-timers who relate to students well and organize the store better. 2. Make the store more nonstudent oriented. 3. Develop an atmosphere that would appeal to upper middle class.
↓	
Examine each alternative's contribution to congruence	If most of the customers are students, there is no way that Alternatives 2 and 3 would work.
↓	
Choose and implement the solution	Implement Alternative 1.
↓	
Evaluate the outcome	Make sure that the implemented solution would appeal to students and make them more comfortable. Evaluate the outcome carefully.

Exhibit 11.7
Store Loyalty Factors and Measurement

Store Loyalty Factors	Measurement Criteria
Habit (the simplest form of store loyalty)	Frequency of shopping there Shopping around Proportion of total purchases Preference
Specific Store Attributes	Functional image components Would the consumer go back there
Activity Generating Practices	Different ways of informing the customers while they are shopping in the store
Inertia (blind loyalty)	Loyalty to the area Loyalty to the shopping complex Loyalty to the store
Social Class	Segmentation index
Self Image/Store Image Congruence	Individual self image and store image comparisons Recommending the store to friends

Source: Adapted and revised from Samli (1989).

References

Ableson, R. P. 1976. "A Script Theory of Understanding, Attitude, and Behavior." In *Cognition and Social Behavior*, ed. J. Carroll and T. Payne. Hillsdale, N.J.: Lawrence Erlbaum Associates.

Albaum, G., and J. Dickson. 1977. "A Method for Developing Tailormade Semantic Differentials for Specific Marketing Content Areas." *Journal of Marketing Research* 14 (February): 87–91.

Alderson, W. 1957. *Marketing Decision and Executive Action*. Homewood, Ill.: Richard D. Irwin.

Alpert, Mark I. 1971. "Identification of Determinant Attributes: A Comparison of Methods." *Journal of Marketing Research* 8 (May): 184–191.

Anderson, John R. 1980. *Cognitive Psychology and Its Implications*. San Francisco: Freeman.

Arons, Leon. 1961. "Does TV Viewing Influence Store Image and Shopping Frequency?" *Journal of Retailing* 37 (Fall): 39–47.

Bellinger, D. N., E. Steinberg, and W. W. Stanton. 1976. "The Congruence of Store Image and Self-Image." *Journal of Retailing* 52 (Spring): 17–32.

Bem, Daryl. 1967. "Self-Perception: An Alternative Interpretation of Cognitive Dissonance Phenomena." *Psychological Review* 74: 183–200.

Berry, Leonard L. 1969. "The Components of Department Store Image: A Theoretical and Empirical Analysis." *Journal of Retailing* 45 (Spring): 3–20.

Birdwell, A. 1968. "A Study of Influence of Image Congruence on Consumer Choice." *Journal of Business* 41: 76–88.

Bonfield, E. H., and Michael T. Ryan. 1975. "The Fishbein Extended Model and Consumer Behavior." *Journal of Consumer Research* 2 (September): 118–136.

Boulding, Kenneth E. 1959. *The Image*. Ann Arbor: University of Michigan Press.

Carman, James M. 1970. "Concepts of Brand Loyalty: Some Positive Results." *Journal of Marketing Research* 7 (February): 67–76.

Chamberlain, E. 1933. *The Theory of Monopolistic Competition*. Cambridge: Harvard University Press.

Cohen, Joel B., Martin Fishbein, and Olli T. Ahtola. 1972. "The Nature and Uses of Expectancy–Value Models in Consumer Attitude Research." *Journal of Marketing Research* 9 (November): 456–460.

Coleman, R. P., and L. Rainwater. 1978. *Social Standing in America: New Dimensions of Class*. New York: Basic Books.

Darden, William R., and Barry J. Babin. 1994. "Exploring the Concept of Affective Quality: Expanding the Concept of Retail Personality." *Journal of Business Research* (February): 101–109.

Dolich, I. J. 1969. "Congruence Relationship between Self-Images and Product Brands." *Journal of Market Research* 6: 80–84.

Dornoff, R. J., and R. L. Tatham. 1972. "Congruence between Personal Image and Store Image." *Journal of the Market Research Society* 14: 45–52.

Doyle, Peter, and Ian Fenwick. 1974–1975. "How Store Image Affects Shopping Habits in Grocery Chains." *Journal of Retailing* 50 (Winter): 46–55.

Eccles, R. G. 1991. "The Performance Measurement Manifesto." *Harvard Business Review* 69 (January–February): 131–137.

Ehrenberk, A. S. C. 1972. Multivariate Analysis in Marketing. Paper presented at the annual conference of the Market Research Society, Brighton.

Enis, B. M., and G. W. Paul. 1968. "Store Loyalty Characteristics of Shoppers and Switchers." *Southern Journal of Business* 3: 266–276.

Fishbein, Martin. 1967a. "A Behavior Theory Approach to the Relations between Beliefs about an Object and the Attitude toward the Object." In *Readings in Attitude Theory and Measurement.* New York: John Wiley and Sons.

———. 1967b. "A Consideration of Beliefs and Their Role in Attitude Measurement." In *Readings in Attitude Theory and Measurement.* New York: John Wiley and Sons.

Fornell, C., and D. F. Larcker. 1981. "Evaluating Structural Equation Models with Unobservable Variables and Measurement Error." *Journal of Marketing Research* 17: 39–50.

Frank, R. E. 1967. "Correlates of Buying Behavior for Grocery Products." *Journal of Marketing* 31 (October): 48–53.

Frank, R. E., W. F. Massey, and Thomas M. Lodahl. 1969. "Purchasing Behavior and Personal Attributes." *Journal of Advertising Research* 9 (December): 15–24.

Frank, R. E., W. F. Massey, and Y. Wind. 1972. *Market Segmentation.* Englewood Cliffs, N.J.: Prentice Hall.

Fry, J. N., and G. H. G. McDougall. 1974–1975. "Combining Two Methods of Image Measurement." *Journal of Retailing* 50 (Winter): 53–61.

Greyser, Stephen A. 1973. Making Image Research Work for You. Speech presented at the National Retail Merchants Association Conference, January.

Hansen, Robert A., and Terry Deutscher. 1977–1978. "An Empirical Investigation of Attribute Importance in Retail Store Selection." *Journal of Retailing* 53 (Winter): 58–72.

Hirschman, Elizabeth C. 1981. "Retail Research and Theory." In *Review of Marketing 1981*, ed. Ben M. Enis and Kenneth J. Roering. Chicago: American Marketing Association.

Howard, J. A., and J. H. Sheth. 1969. *The Theory of Buyer Behavior.* New York: John Wiley and Sons.

Isaacson, Lawrence H. 1964. Store Choice. D.B.A. diss., Harvard University.

Jacoby, J., and D. B. Kyner. 1973. "Brand Loyalty versus Repeat Purchase Behavior." *Journal of Marketing Research* 10: 1–9.

Jenkins, Roger L., and Sandra M. Forsythe. 1980. "Retail Image Research: State of the Art Review with Implications for Retail Strategy." In *Developments in Marketing Science*, ed. V. V. Bellur and B. G. Gnaudi. Miami: Academy of Marketing Science.

Kelley, R. G., and Ronald Stephenson. 1967. "The Semantic Differential: An Informative Source for Designing Retail Patronage Appeals." *Journal of Marketing* 31 (December): 43–47.

Kerlinger, F. N., and E. J. Pedhazer. 1973. *Multiple Regression in the Behavioral Sciences.* New York: Holt, Rinehart and Winston.

Kunkel, John H., and Leonard L. Berry. 1968. "A Behavioral Concept of Retail Image." *Journal of Marketing* 32 (October): 21–27.

Lessig, V. P. 1973. "Consumer Store Image and Store Loyalties." *Journal of Marketing* (October): 72–74.

Lincoln, D. J. 1980. The Effects of Comparative Advertising on the Department Store Image: An Experimental Analysis. Ph.D. diss., Virginia Tech.

Lincoln, D. J., and A. Coskun. Samli. 1979. "Retail Store Image: Definitions and Measurement." In *Proceedings of Southern Marketing Association*. Atlanta: Southern Marketing Association.

Lindquist, Jay D. 1974–1975. "Meaning of Image: A Survey of Empirical and Hypothetical Evidence." *Journal of Retailing* 50 (Winter): 29–38.

Maris, Michael B., Olli T. Ahtola, and Eugene R. Klippel. 1975. "A Comparison of Four Multi-Attribute Models in the Prediction of Consumer Attitudes." *Journal of Consumer Research* 2 (June): 38–52.

Marks, Ronald B. 1974. "A Multi-Attribute Approach to the Store Imagery Problem." Ph.D. diss., University of Missouri, Columbia.

Markus, Hazel. 1980. "The Self in Thought and Memory." In *The Self in Social Psychology*, ed. Daniel M. Wegner and Robin R. Vallacher. New York: Oxford University Press.

Martineau, Pierre. 1958. "The Personality of the Retail Store." *Harvard Business Review* 36 (January–February): 47–55.

Mason, J. Barry, and Morris L. Mayer. 1970. "The Problem of the Self-Concept in Store Studies." *Journal of Marketing* 34: 67–69.

May, Eleanor G. 1971. Image Evaluation of a Department Store: Techniques for Conducting the Study. Working paper, Marketing Science Institute, Chicago.

McClure, Peter J., and John K. Ryans. 1968. "Differences between Retailers and Consumers' Perceptions." *Journal of Marketing Research* 5 (February): 35–40.

McDougall, G. H. G., and J. N. Fry. 1974–1975. "Combining Two Methods of Image Measurement." *Journal of Retailing* 50 (Winter): 53–61.

Mindak, William A. 1961. "Fitting the Semantic Differential to the Marketing Problem." *Journal of Marketing* 25 (April): 28–34.

Muse, William A. 1974–1975. "Using Word-Association Tests to Develop Retail Store Image." *Journal of Retailing* (Winter): 35–42.

Neisser, U. 1976. *Cognition and Reality: Principles and Implications of Cognitive Psychology*. San Francisco: Freeman.

Nevin, John R., and Michael J. Houston. 1980. "Image as a Component of Attraction to Intraurban Shopping Areas." *Journal of Retailing* 56 (Spring): 77–93.

Nisbett, Richard, and Lee Rosee. 1981. *Human Inference: Strategies Shortcomings of Social Judgment*. Englewood Cliffs, N.J.: Prentice Hall.

Osgood, Charles E. 1952. "The Nature and Measurement of Meaning." *Psychological Bulletin* 49 (May): 197–237.

Osgood, Charles E., George J. Suci, and Percy H. Tannerbaum. 1957. *The Measurement of Meaning*. Urbana: University of Illinois Free Press.

Oxenfeldt, Alfred R. 1974–1975. "Developing a Favorable Price–Quality Image." *Journal of Retailing* 50 (Winter): 8–14.

Parasuraman, A., Leonard L. Berry, and Valerie Zeithaml. 1991. "Perceived Service Quality as a Customer-Based Performance Measure: An Empirical Examination of Organizational Barriers Using an Extended Service Quality Model." *Human Resource Management* (Fall): 335–364.

Pathak, Devendron S. 1972. A Study of Department Store Images Held by Customers and Management. Ph.D. diss., Michigan State University.

Pathak, Devendron S., William J. E. Crissy, and Robert W. Sweitzer. 1974–1975. "Customer Image versus the Retailer's Anticipated Image." *Journal of Retailing* 50 (Winter): 20–33.

Plummer, J. T. 1974. "The Concept and Application of the Life Style Segmentation." *Journal of Marketing* 38 (Winter): 21–28.

Reynolds, F. D., W. R. Darden, and W. S. Martin. 1974. "Developing an Image of the Store-Loyal Customer." *Journal of Retailing* (Winter): 73–84.

Rich, S. U., and B. D. Portis. 1964. "The Imageries of Department Store." *Journal of Marketing* 28 (April): 10–15.

Rosenberg, Milton J. 1956. "Cognitive Structure and Attitudinal Affect." *Journal of Abnormal and Social Psychology*, 53 (November): 367–372.

Ross, I. 1971. "Self-Concept and Brand Preference." *Journal of Business of the University of Chicago* 44: 38–50.

Samli, A. Coskun. 1968. "Segmentation and Carving a Niche in the Market Place." *Journal of Retailing* (Summer): 35–49.

———. 1975. "Use of Segmentation Index to Measure Store Loyalty." *Journal of Retailing* (Spring): 51–60.

———. 1969. "Segmentation Index and Store Image in Retail and Service Establishments." In *Proceedings of ESOMAR Seminar XXIX on Research That Works for Today's Marketing Problems, 1976*. From talk delivered before the X ESOMAR Seminar, 2–5, at Lucerne.

———. 1979. "Some Observations on Intermarket Shopping Behavior as It Relates to the Spatial Dimension." In *Proceedings, National Educators' Conference*. Chicago: American Marketing Association.

———. 1989. *Retail Marketing Strategies*. Westport, Conn.: Quorum Books.

———. 1996. *International Consumer Behavior*. Westport, Conn.: Quorum Books.

Samli, A. Coskun, Patrick Kelly, and K. Hunt. Forthcoming 1998. "Improving the Retail Performance by Contrasting Management and Customer Perceived Store Images." *Journal of Business Research*.

Samli, A. Coskun, and Douglas Lincoln. 1989. "Management versus Customer Perception of Image." In *Retail Marketing Strategies*, ed. A. Coskun Samli. Westport, Conn.: Quorum Books.

Samli, A. Coskun, and Joseph M. Sirgy. 1981. "A Multidimensional Approach to Analyzing Store Loyalty: A Predictive Model." In *The Changing Marketing Environment: New Theories and Applications*, ed. Ken Bernhardt and Bill Kehoe. Chicago: American Marketing Association.

Schewe, C. D., and W. R. Dillon. 1978. "Marketing Information System Utilization: An Application of Self-Concept Theory." *Journal of Business Research* 6: 67–69.

Sirgy, Joseph M. 1979. Self-Concept in Consumer Behavior. Ph.D. diss., University of Massachusetts, Amherst.

———. 1980. "Self-Concept in Relation to Product Preference and Purchase Intention." In *Developments in Marketing Science*, Vol. 3, ed. V. V. Bellur. Marquette: Academy of Marketing Science.

———. 1982. "Self-Concept in Consumer Behavior: A Critical Review." *Journal of Consumer Research* 9 (December): 287–300.

Sirgy, M. Joseph., and Jeffrey A. Danes. 1982. "Self-Image/Product-Image Congruence Models: Testing Selected Mathematical Models." In *Advances in Consumer Research*, Vol. 9, ed. Andrew Mitchell. Ann Arbor: Association for Consumer Research.

Sirgy, M. Joseph., J. S. Johar, A. Coskun Samli, and C. B. Claiborne. 1991. "Self-Congruity versus Functional Congruity: Predictors of Consumer Behavior." *Journal of the Academy of Marketing Sciences* (Fall): 363–375.

Sirgy, M. Joseph, and A. Coskun Samli. 1985. "A Path Analytic Model of Store Loyalty Involving Self-Concept, Store Image, Geographic Loyalty, and Socioeconomic Status." *Journal of Academy of Marketing Science* (June): 265–291.

Steenkamp, Jan-Benedict E. M., and Michel Wedel. 1991. "Segmenting Retail Markets on Store Damage Using a Consumer-Based Methodology." *Journal of Retailing* (Fall): 300–321.

Stern, B. L., R. F. Bush, and J. F. Haire, Jr. 1977. "The Self-Image/Store Image Matching Process: An Empirical Test." *Journal of Business* 50 (October): 63–69.

Weale, Bruce W. 1961. "Measuring the Customer's Image of the Department Store." *Journal of Retailing* 37 (Summer): 40–48.

Wilkie, William L., and Edgar A. Pessemier. 1973. "Issues in Marketing Use of Multi-Attribute Attitude Models." *Journal of Marketing Research* 10 (November): 428–441.

Wyckham, R. G. 1967. "Aggregate Department Store Image: Social and Experimental Factors." In *Proceedings of the American Marketing Association Conference*. Chicago: American Marketing Association.

———. 1969. "Aggregate Department Stores Images: Special Experimental Factors." Ph.D. diss., Michigan State University.

Wyer, Robert S., Jr., and Donald E. Carlson. 1979. *Social Cognition, Inference, and Attribution*. Hillsdale, N.J.: Lawrence Erlbaum Associates.

Chapter 12

Human Resource Management
in Retailing

With the exception of mail order, direct marketing, automated vending, and a few other types of nonstore retailing, the retailing business is people business. Without proper people and an atmosphere of warm and effective human interaction, retailing cannot survive. Thus, human resource management is a critical determinant of retail performance and profitability.

Human resource mix is one of the four retail mixes that are discussed briefly in Chapter 2. As stated in the Preface, almost 20 million people representing almost 17 percent of the nation's labor force are currently employed in the retailing sector (U.S. Department of Labor 1989).

From all indications, the retailing sector of the labor force will continue to grow in relative importance as the globalization of manufacturing activity continues. Chances are that some of the manufacturing jobs will go south of the border and overseas; the void that is created will be taken with service and retailing jobs.

Although the retailing sector is experiencing employment growth in real terms, serious performance and retention problems with the retail workforce are quite evident. Not only does the retailing sector not pay its employees enough, the turnover among retail workers is so high that it is costing the industry directly and indirectly.

This chapter is adapted from A. Coskun Samli and N. Mehmet Ongan (1996), "Retail Human Resource Management: An Exploration and Research Agenda." *Journal of Marketing Channels* (1 September): 81–99.

THE GRIM PICTURE OF RETAIL EMPLOYMENT

Though every fifth person works in retailing, this sector is not very good in its performance relating to human resource management. Retail workers, on average, make substantially less than the rest of the private sector (Exhibit 12.1), and the relative rate of increase in this average pay in retailing is slower than the rate in the rest of the economy. In addition, while employees in transportation, communication, and utilities have 6.8 median years on the job, in retailing they have only 2.7 years. In other words, the employee turnover rate is more than twice as high. This is also more than 50-percent higher than the national average (Exhibit 12.2). We do not know if the low pay is causing the high turnover rate or vice versa, but it is clear that the retailing sector has a problem. In economic terms, these figures indicate the presence of serious human resource development problems, expressed by a lack of progress in terms of employee pay and employee stability. In 1992, Coopers and Lybrand estimated the median turnover rate in the retailing sector to be around 35 percent. Considering 5 percent for engineers, less than 5 percent for computer programmers, about 7 percent for secretaries, and no more than 10 percent for manufacturing workers, the retail figures are extremely alarming (Samli and Ongan 1996).

Not only does a lack of continuity create less than adequate customer relations, it also does not allow a team spirit to emerge. Furthermore, retail workers may not learn their job as well as they would otherwise. The cost of acquiring new workers and training them properly is another factor. The estimated median cost for hiring replacements in the retailing workforce is about $350. This is considered quite low. However, considering the fact that there were nearly 20 million retail workers in 1992, the total number of retail workers to be replaced was more than 7 million. Seven million multiplied by $350 is about $2.45 billion. Thus, the cost of retail employee turnover ws $2.45 billion in 1992. This is only for one year. Though this volume is less than 1 percent of total retail sales, it is a very large sum. These monies can be used to improve the overall retail labor force by stabilizing, compensating, and training it better. Because the employee turnover in the retail labor force is very high and costly, it has been described as a "key event" in retailing today (Darden, Hampton, and Boatwright 1987). Turnover, particularly involuntary turnover, passes real costs on to both retail establishments and the society. Part of this turnover problem is related to the lack of adequate training in the retailing sector. A study reported in *Training* ("Industry Report" 1992) indicates that retail trade has the lowest numbers of all industries that are devoted to employee training.

From an aggregate economic perspective, turnover reflects an inefficient deployment of social resources, increased welfare rolls, and a decline in quality of life. From a retail management perspective, turn-over is indicative of a failure of the organization's human resource management system. This failure invariably will limit the ability of the organization to serve its markets and achieve a competitive ad-vantage. A somewhat related human resource management issue in retailing is employee theft, which is roughly estimated to be around 0.28 percent of total retail sales, or nearly $15 billion or more per year (Filipowski 1993).

Studies have shown that turnover rate among retail managers, par-ticularly mid- to lower-level managers, is also very high (Good, Sisler, and Gentry 1988). This is likely to enhance the negative impact of turnover activity in retailing in terms of disruption in continuity and lack of leadership, planning, and implementing in store policies and tactics.

Ultimately, failure to address this and other human resource man-agement issues will be reflected in subpar performance in the market-place. Lusch and Serpkenci (1990) note that effective management of human resources in retailing is critically important to achieve a com-petitive market position and a high rate of return. Similarly, retail organizations that are addressing human resource issues adequately will continue to grow and gain competitive advantage.

THE CHANGING STATUS OF RETAIL HUMAN RESOURCE MIX

In recent years, product assortments in different retail stores are becoming more similar. For instance, one can find most standard gro-cery items in Eckerds. Similarly, one finds a lot of health, beauty, and pharmaceutical items in Winn Dixie. The relatively less differentiated product mix necessitates other types of activity to create differential congruence. The way to present the products—service by employees—is becoming more important. In many retailing settings, customer satisfaction is predicated upon the perception of employee performance.

Though many supermarkets and discount stores function on the ba-sis of self-service, which is the efficient way to shop for most custom-ers, some consumers insist on receiving service which can be delivered only by retail employees (May 1989). Consumers' enthusiasm for Nordstrom may be a good example. It is known that employees of Nordstrom stores are expected to go out of their way to service the customers of the store, sometimes over and beyond their work hours. Customers of Nordstrom stores may be willing to pay a little extra for such services as home delivery, running simple errands, and getting certain information or facts about various retailing-related activities.

Time is the major constraint in today's retailing. Consumers and customers of the store want to be served by employees as quickly as possible and with the required level of service (Salmon 1989). Most of the time, consumers who are in a hurry will pay a premium for convenience. To attract consumers, retailers must seek ways to offer the consumer more time efficiency, which requires better trained and more efficient retail employees (May 1989). In addition, in retailing, employees are the ones who get the consumers' reactions for the services offered. Consumers, in such cases, may have useful suggestions to improve both the product and the service offered with it. All these issues bring out the importance of human resource mix in the retailing sector. The human resource management area is gaining more prominence despite general neglect from top retail management. Thus, one of the most critical areas in the retailing sector that would lift the sector's level in the economy to new heights is human resource management. For a retailer, the human resource mix is perhaps the most powerful tool to create competitive advantage.

DEVELOPING A HUMAN RESOURCE MANAGEMENT MODEL

The human resource management process in retailing is basically composed of four key areas: (1) the search process, (2) training, (3) development, and (4) employee loyalty and mutual trust (Pintel and Diamond 1991; Levy and Weitz 1992). In this section, key problems in these four areas are highlighted, and a further attempt is made to connect them to human resource mix to strengthen the competitiveness of the retail establishment.

These particular four areas are the most important topics in human resource management and are studied in most human resource management books (Baird 1992; Cascio 1986; Gordon 1986; Ivancevich and Glueck 1986; Milkovich and Boudreau 1988). But here they are discussed from a retailing perspective. The discussion in this chapter is intended to be provocative. The author believes that this kind of orientation is necessary to bring about much-needed improvement in the retailing sector.

THE KEY PROBLEM AREAS

Exhibit 12.3 illustrates the four areas mentioned and how they are related to the big picture. These four areas are described in the following section.

The Search Process

Locating, acquiring, and retaining qualified employees is basic to effective retailing performance. Employee attributes and qualifications must be objectively established by each retailer. This can be accomplished by having ongoing job analysis and resultant realistic job descriptions. On the basis of the established and revised job descriptions, the characteristics of the prospective employees are established. Reliable sources of employees must be developed, and these sources must be continuously evaluated in terms of the performance of the retail workers they have provided for the business.

It is axiomatic to note that sound recruitment is a prerequisite for effective hiring, training, development, and retention. Retailers, particularly small retailers, are handicapped in their ability to locate and attract quality employees. Even though almost every fifth person works in retailing, this sector has a long-standing reputation for low compensation (including benefits), long hours, and unpleasant working conditions, often involving extensive amounts of customer contact. If the employee is unhappy, these customer contact hours may not be very productive for the retailer. The employee can negatively influence the customers.

Second, as a profession, retailing clearly suffers from major "image" problems. Research has consistently revealed that students rate retailing near the bottom on their list of occupational preferences (Swinyard 1981). The negative image of retailing is particularly significant in that it limits access to quality employees and entry-level management trainees.

Third, many retailers lack the resources that are required to develop an effective human resource management system. Smaller retail organizations, in particular, do not have the personnel and/or organizational strengths needed to systematically recruit and screen prospective personnel. All too often the manager's time is consumed solving daily operational problems, and quite often the crises originate from personnel-related issues. There is simply not enough time or strong inclination for developing powerful strategic human resource planning. Interestingly, this is not a situation that is entirely confined to small organizations. Woolworth's, for instance, suffered from similar limitations for many years (Rose 1989).

Finally, though it is difficult to document, it has been this author's experience that there is an unfortunate bias among many retail managers that tends to discourage high-quality, entry-level prospects from pursuing careers in retailing. Often, this bias is expressed in the statement, "Everyone starts at the bottom and works their way up." This mentality was clearly evident in a series of student-conducted interviews with some of the nation's largest retailers (Samli 1989). When questioned about career opportunities for college graduates (most of the students were pursuing degrees in business administration), the typical response, once again, was, "Everyone starts out the same, unless your degree is in accounting or computer science." Interestingly, this response tended to be most prevalent in the food industry. By implication, this would suggest that supermarkets of the future will not be managed by college graduates, but rather by lesser-qualified persons who worked their way up. Unfortunately, unless trained specifically to eliminate these problems, many of these same individuals will lack the vision and analytical skills needed to effectively manage multi-million-dollar businesses in highly turbulent and competitive environments (Samli and Ongan 1996).

One of the biggest retailers in the United States, Wal-Mart, used to recruit 75 percent of its management people from other retailers, but as traditional sources in the labor pool dried up, Wal-Mart increased its efforts in training and development. Now the company depends on three primary sources to fill its management positions: the ranks of hourly employees (50 percent of all assistant managers began in hourly operations), recent college graduates (35 percent of new hires), and other retailers (15 percent of hires). The company's logic is expressed by the following statement: "If you are not looking at those people who are at the bottom of the line and looking to train and develop them, you are going to continue having employment problems" (Halcrow 1989). This point of view indicates that the company has a good understanding of the importance of training and development processes in the human resource management area. Certainly, some outstanding talent in the lower ranks must have an opportunity to move up, but no retailer can rely solely on entry-level hires for future management talent.

Training

Retailers, by and large, have not done an effective job of training their employees. Expenditures set aside for training in retail organizations, both in absolute dollars and on a percentage of sales basis, have consistently lagged behind other sectors of the economy. Similarly, there is little indication that retailers have committed to new training technology (e.g., satellite networks) on a large-scale basis. Where new technology has been employed, it tends to be found only in the largest organizations (e.g., Wal-Mart), and it tends to be very industry and function specific. For example, automobile retailers are now making extensive use of satellite communication systems for training service personnel. There is little indication that this same technology is being used extensively in other functional areas and/or in other industries.

A related problem can be traced to retail organizations. Not only have retailers been reluctant to invest in training, there are also problems with continuity. If such a lack of continuity takes the retail establishment out of its core competency area, then the establishment could be in real trouble. This can happen to both small and large retailers. Sears experienced such a lack of continuity. The company moved away from merchandising to become a diversified financial institution. This was substantially far away from its core competency. The results were very dramatic and not much in favor of Sears. Thus, the lack of continuity can, intentionally or unintentionally, derail the retail establishment. Part of this lack of continuity is related to the lack of proper training. Certainly, in Sears's case we cannot blame training for the derailment, but if lack of continuity starts emerging, it may lead the company to extremes. Many small and large retailers make statements such as, "We believe in on the job training." This, unfortunately, is in lieu of formal training. There is little evidence of continuity of training throughout defined career paths. This conclusion is reinforced by the fact that training costs are the lowest in retailing, according to one major study ("Industry Report" 1992). The second portion of the lack of continuity is related to the high turnover in the sector. When the employee and particularly the management turnover is high, continuity is impaired.

Though many retailers are facing high rates of employee turnover and extreme pressure on profit margins and are cognizant of the cost of increased training for all employees, the alternatives are considered more costly. Failure to train tends to result in poor employee performance, low morale, job dissatisfaction, and, ultimately, turnover. In effect, retailers are faced with a classic self-feeding cycle, whereby declining productivity associated with marginal employees leads to cutbacks which further lower employee performance (Achabal, Heineke, and McIntyre 1984). On the other hand, training costs increase regardless of the training level the company offers to its employees, due to the high rate of employee turnover. Retail establishments with high employee turnover simply have to give the same orientation and basic training to more employees, which increases their training costs.

If they had offered the appropriate training while it was timely, they might have prevented the duplicated basic training costs for incoming new workers as well as those who just left the company. They might also have decreased the employee turnover rate, and they would have better-trained and therefore better-motivated employees. Thus, the relationship between training turnover and lower labor costs should be made clear to retail managers so that they will consider training a more critical factor in their human resource mix.

Development

The development of employees into good, flexible, knowledgeable, and helpful retail associates is partially dependent on selection and training. If good people are selected to begin with and are trained adequately, their development is reasonably assured. The development process is necessary for personnel to develop high standards and to maintain them.

Though proper selection and effective training are critical, the retailer must have certain programs to develop the skills and professionalism of retail workers. Equally important, this commitment to employee development must be communicated to the retail employee. Indeed, a plausible case can be made that this commitment should be clearly articulated in the organization's mission statement.

As management practices change, special skills that are needed in retailing become better recognized. This will necessitate a change in the employee development process as well. The required skills of a retail employee have been increasing along with the proliferation of technologically complex products and advanced systems and procedures employed by the retailers (Samiee 1990). Thus, either recruiting better employees or training the average employee is not the key to the prosperity desired but simply the key to survival. It has been stated that the skills that are required to achieve excellence in retail execution have changed and are likely to change again (Salmon 1989). At a minimum, more attention must be devoted to better, more precise articulation of required skills and management expectations.

At the management or the supervisory level, turnover rates are equally high. Studies have shown that role ambiguity and role conflict along with work–family conflict are the key factors behind managerial personnel leaving the retail establishment quickly and hence disrupting continuity. Role ambiguity implies not having a good job description and individuals not knowing what needs to be done. Role conflict implies that different people think they have jurisdiction on the situation in question. Finally, work–family conflict implies unrealistic hours that are required of individuals, totally in conflict with the individuals' family lives. In all cases, the result is job dissatisfaction and a high level of turnover (Good, Sisler, and Gentry 1988). Here, among other solutions related to elimination of ambiguity, role conflict, and work–family conflict, experiential retail education programs can be very effective. They may offer special opportunities for skill development and refinement.

It is necessary to have a type of environment within which the individual retail worker can grow professionally. This may take the form of formal and informal in-house discussions, idea generating and exchanging, and information dissemination among the retail workers based on their experiences and observations.

Loyalty and Mutual Trust Cultivation

Without strong loyalty displayed by employees, retail establishments will have difficulty performing satisfactorily. Employees are critical assets in delivering the quality service and satisfaction to customers which, in essence, provides the competitive edge that every retailer is seeking. It has been observed that Machiavellianism, manipulation, and questionable behavior of retail executives results in lower job satisfaction on the part of their subordinates.

In developing loyalty and mutual trust, the same principles apply to supervisors as well as subordinates. Of course, subordinates who have certain Machiavellian tendencies would also cause a breakdown in loyalty and mutual trust. Developing mutual trust based on fairness, understanding, and honesty will quite likely enhance employee job satisfaction and performance. It is essential that both management and employees make an effort in this direction.

The key in this case is to build greater organizational identification, much as the Japanese have done with such remarkable success. The workers or employees identify themselves with the organization. Interestingly, the Japanese have been able to transfer these concepts across cultural and geographic boundaries. Many of the same techniques and practices that have worked so well in the factories of Japan are now working with equal success in the Toyota and Honda factories located in the United States. Unfortunately, there is little indication that these employee strategies have transferred across industries into the retailing sector. However, as indicated by some scholars, the same principles are applicable in retail organizations (Sheth 1983).

To eliminate Machiavellianism in retailing, various strategies may be used. Among these are some very specific ones, such as integrity screening or awareness programs. However, perhaps the most important strategy is to develop loyal employees. This will stop not only Machiavellianism but also lower the turnover rate, eliminate emerging discontinuity, and eliminate employee theft (Filipowski 1993). Treating employees well, offering them a good workplace and a suitable atmosphere, making them feel important, and compensating them appropriately are likely to eliminate employee problems in retailing.

Some authors believe that the empowerment of employees to use their discretion may enhance service delivery in retailing and improve client satisfaction (Kelley 1993). Successful use of discretion is certainly related to the organizational culture of the establishment. If the organization encourages, rewards, and allows it, the employee may be willing to put forth greater effort for the organization.

EFFECTIVE HUMAN RESOURCE MANAGEMENT

Developing an effective human resource management system calls for concentration on three particular areas: (1) employee relations, (2) performance evaluation, and (3) reward system. These topics combined lead to the crux of human resource management in retailing: motivation. Exhibit 12.3 illustrates these focal points, and they are briefly described in the following sections.

Employee Relations

Employee relations consist of some combination of policies, guidelines, and procedures used by the retailer to describe employees' responsibilities toward the firm and vice versa (Samiee 1990). Successful retailers have their integrated package of benefits tied directly to improved productivity of their employees. This package may include such intangible benefits as awards and recognitions, and such tangible benefits as financial awards. This is an area in which the European and Japanese retailers appear very strong, because of tradition (as seen in Japan) and at least partly because of strong labor unions (as seen in Germany).

Unfortunately, in American retailing a general concept of employee relations is a rarity. Very few retail establishments concern themselves with career pathing, career enrichment, skills enhancement, flexitime, and team-building issues. All of these are important in employee relations, but most retailers do not have the type of sophistication to develop these activities. In fact, most retailers are not even cognizant of the fact that a solid employee relations system in their organizations can improve their market performance and, subsequently, their profit picture.

Performance Evaluation

It is estimated that in the United States fewer than 50 percent of all firms have a systematic approach to evaluating employees (Myers 1989). The principal objectives of performance evaluations are (1) to let employees clearly know what is expected of them; and (2) to tell them how well they are performing in relation to those expectations (Little and Myers 1989). The first objective may be achieved by clear job descriptions given to employees. If there are changes in these expectations, they also are clearly communicated to the company's employees. The second objective is achieved by rewarding employees with increases in pay and promotions or by not rewarding them at all.

Reward System

The retailing sector unfortunately is not well respected because of its reward systems and their implementation. Not only do retailers have compensation systems that typically fail to differentiate between good and bad performance, but other rewards are also lacking. Most retailers do not have employee recognition and performance-approval types of positive reinforcements that create a good feeling of belongingness among the employees of the store. Much of the time those employees who are really effective and productive go totally unnoticed. They do not receive a positive word from the administration. However, if they were to make an error they would hear from the administration immediately. Thus, the whole system is quite often managed not by positive reinforcements but by negative reinforcements. This situation is not conducive to hard work and the development of team spirit.

A case can also be made about the retail reward system in that retail managers and the reward system they administer operate with a decided short-run focus (Rosenbloom 1980). In fact, higher-paid employees are subtly encouraged to leave so that they may be replaced with lower-paid employees. Such an orientation does not contribute to the customer service, store image, and team building that are so critical for differential congruence.

In recent years, retail companies have experimented with new pay concepts in an attempt to attract and maintain good employees, to increase productivity, and often to cut costs. Lump-sum bonuses are replacing base wage increases, and gain-sharing plans reward improvements in quality and productivity. According to the 1992 National Retail Security Survey, when employees receive a straight hourly wage or salary the average shrinkage level is 2.1 percent of total retail sales. When a company rewards employees for their individual productivity, the shrinkage level drops to 1.8 percent. Companies that base their employee compensation plans completely on incentives report the lowest shrinkage level in the survey, 1.3 percent (Filipowski 1993). Most programs share two characteristics: They put more of the employee's pay at risk, and they link pay more closely with performance. These objectives will not quite work unless the payment plan is accompanied by some latitude given to the employees to satisfy customers and the organization rewards these employees for their efforts. This is referred to as *enfranchisement* (Schlesinger and Heskett 1991).

Enfranchisement is a way of granting freedom and responsibility to an employee within a franchise without requiring a monetary investment or ownership on the part of the employee. It is achieved through a combination of what has come to be known as empowerment coupled with compensation methods that pay for their performance. Enfranchisement can improve sales and earnings, while at the same time require less direct supervision from corporate management and provide increased employee earnings, job satisfaction, and retention. Employee retention is of particular importance in retailing, because it can have a positive impact on customer retention, which in turn has been found to be an important determinant of profit in many companies (Schlesinger and Heskett 1991).

MOTIVATION

Modern retailing will never reach high levels of performance with-out properly motivated retail workers. Individuals who are working in retailing must be motivated to work harder and smarter. Working harder and smarter basically means better service and, hence, greater customer satisfaction, but because of its deficiency in performance evaluation and its reluctance to pay extra, the retailing sector simply does not provide enough motivation for its workers to work harder and smarter.

Vroom's expectancy theory describes motivation as the joint product of expectancy and valence. Valence is defined as the value attached to specific awards (Vroom 1964). Herzberg, Mausner, and Synderman (1960) also deal with the same concept of motivation. Both Vroom's and Herzberg's treatment of motivation may be interpreted as shown in Exhibit 12.3. In retailing, perhaps more than in other industries, the reward system is the key motivator. Unless this reward system is brought to a point of normalcy, the retailing sector may not be able to improve its overall effectiveness. In other words, the reward system and the performance must have a clearly identifiable relationship. In addition, not all incentives offered result in increased employee per-formance. Managers, therefore, should not make the common mistake of developing employee incentive programs that do not base the re-ward on what the employees value (Nordstrom and Hall 1986).

Managing Quality

Chain-store retailers who are highly successful achieve this success not only by paying attention to the basics of retailing, but by building a team mentality among employees. Building successful teams appears to be critical for them. Successful team building invariably includes good hiring, good communication with employees, and good motiva-tional practices (Redman 1995).

Thus, retailers must invest in their employees by giving them train-ing, benefits, and other support programs. Commitment to employees through such support programs is equivalent to building quality into the retailer's overall performance. Simultaneously, such programs boost employee morale and reduce employee turnover (Parrott 1993).

In recent years, total quality management has emerged as a general orientation in management literature. It has been demonstrated that TQM is successful only when the workforce is adequately trained, edu-cated, and trusted to make informed decisions. These informed deci-sions concentrate not only on how to improve the work process but, in retailing, it also means how to improve the process of satisfying customer needs to the point of delighting them. Thus, the implementation of TQM is related to human resource development and management (Becker 1993; Pennington 1993; Kotler 1994).

It is obvious from our discussion so far that motivation is extremely important to successful retail performance. Unfortunately, there is little evidence that the retailing sector, as a whole, has progressed much beyond traditional approaches. Indeed, a case could be made that the majority of retail managers today still operate under a "Theory X" orientation. Dimensions of this orientation include close supervision, narrow spans of control, reluctance to delegate, and a general "adversarial" relationship with subordinates. In sharp contrast to manufacturing organizations, large numbers of retailers have generally been reluctant to experiment with job enrichment programs, flexitime, employee incentive programs, and other similar activity. Thus, they are not taking advantage of the strengths of the human resource mix. They must make their human resource programs more externally focused, more innovative, and more result oriented (rather than process orientated). They must take some chances with such programs, and they must foster active employee participation, long-term planning, flexibility, and individualism (Jones, Morris, and Rockmore 1995).

Not all retailers are quite as exploitative of their human resources as this chapter may imply. Bernard Marcus, the founder and CEO of Home Depot, stated at a conference in Las Vegas in 1996, "We don't hire our new people at minimum wage. We select them carefully, and we train them with care and help them to develop lifelong careers, rather than giving them a menial job." Certainly, more retailers need to adhere to such a philosophy.

INTERNATIONAL CORNER

Very little is available in the literature on the topic of human resource management in international retailing. However, there is some general information about management styles. In many European countries and Japan, retailing is paternalistic. Whereas in the United States there is a very high turnover rate among retail clerks, it is just the opposite in Europe and Japan. In many countries, the bonding between the retailer and the employees is lifelong and, in fact, sometimes continues through generations. In these countries, the employees of a specific retail establishment may devote their well-being to the well-being of the retail establishment. The paternalistic orientation of the retailer implies that the employees will make a good living and, in return, they will devote themselves to the enhancement of performance in the retail establishment.

SUMMARY

In this chapter, we have discussed how a human resource mix in retailing can be constructed so that it will be a major tool in the retailer's effort to enhance its differential congruence.

The retailing sector is plagued by excessive employee turnovers that are disruptive and costly. It also reflects inefficient deployment of social resources, increased welfare rolls, and a decline of quality of life. Retail human resource management systems must do a better job to eliminate at least a part of these problems. In recent years, retail human resource mix has been considered to be a critical competitive tool, but still, by and large, is neglected.

This chapter presents a human resource management model to overcome the problems. Such a model is composed of four key areas: (1) the search process, (2) training, (3) development, and (4) employee loyalty and mutual trust. In order to develop an effective human resource development program, employee relations and performance evaluation activities need to be included in the equation. Based on a positive reward system, the outcome is a highly motivated workforce in retailing that functions very successfully. The end results are better customer service and better customer satisfaction systems.

Exhibits

Exhibit 12.1
Retail Employment and Earnings

Year	Retail Employee Growth (%)	Retail Pay/Hour [a]	Percent Increase	Private Sector [b] Employment Growth (%)	Private Sector [b] Pay Hour	Percent Increase
1975	-	3.4	-	-	4.9	-
1980	13.5	4.9	45.2	17.6	7.2	47.2
1985	10.4	5.9	21.7	9.0	9.4	30.8
1990	9.3	6.8	13.6	10.5	11.0	17.4
1991	-1.6	7.0	3.7	-1.3	11.4	3.2
1992	.4	7.1	2.0	.1	11.6	2.4
1993	1.9	7.3	2.8	2.0	12.5	7.8
1994	3.0	7.5	2.7	2.9	12.8	2.4

Source: U.S. Department of Commerce, *Statistical Abstract of the United States*, 1993 and 1995.

[a]Current dollars.

[b]Private sector is defined as all industries excluding government, agriculture, and retail.

Exhibit 12.2
Median Years in Job (Tenure) as of 1991

Industry	Years	Total Employment (000s)
Manufacturing	5.8	20,811
Transportation, Communications and Utilities	6.8	8,181
Wholesale Trade	4.4	4,308
Retail Trade	2.7	19,075
Finance, Insurance, and Real Estate	4.1	7,926
Services	4.1	38,737
Total, All Workers	4.4	99,038

Exhibit 12.3
Human Resource Management in Retailing

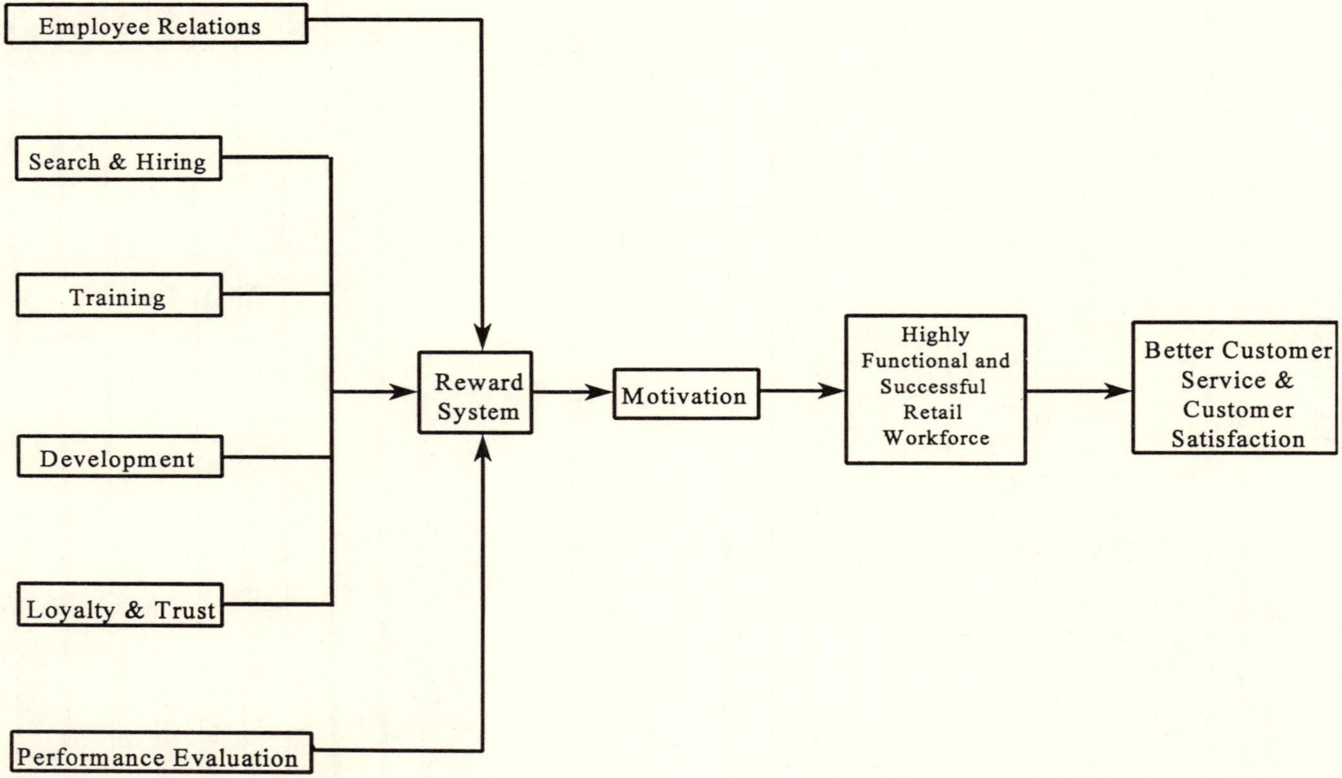

Source: Samli and Ongan (1996).

References

Achabal, Dale D., John M. Heineke, and Shelby H. McIntyre. 1984. "Issues and Perspectives on Retail Productivity." *Journal of Retailing* 60 (Fall): 107–127.

Baird, Lloyd S. 1992. *Managing Human Resources*. Chicago: Business One Irwin.

Becker, Selwyn W. 1993. "TQM Does Work." *Management Review* (May): 30–33.

Berman, Barry, and Joel R. Evans. 1995. *Retail Management*. Englewood Cliffs, N.J.: Prentice Hall.

Cascio, Wayne F. 1986. *Managing Human Resources*. New York: McGraw-Hill.

Darden, William R., Ronald D. Hampton, and Earl W. Boatwright. 1987. "Investigating Retail Employee Turnover: An Application of Survival Analysis." *Journal of Retailing* 63 (Spring): 69–88.

Filipowski, Diane. 1993. "HR Plays a Direct Role in Decreasing Employee Theft." *Personnel Journal* (April): 88.

Good, Linda K., Grovalynn F. Sisler, and James W. Gentry. 1988. "Antecedents of Turnover Intentions among Retail Management Personnel." *Journal of Retailing* (Fall): 295–314.

Gordon, Judith R. 1986. *Human Resources Management*. Boston: Allyn and Bacon.

Halcrow, Allan. 1989. "Voices of HR Experience." *Personnel Journal* (May): 38–53.

Herzberg, Frederick, Bernard Mausner, and Barbara Synderman. 1960. *The Motivation to Work*. New York: John Wiley and Sons.

"Incentive Pay Plan Replaces Wage Hikes." 1989. *Chain Store Age Executive* (February): 78–79.

"Industry Report." 1992. *Training* (October): 25–28.

Ivanchevich, John M., and William F. Glueck. 1986. *Foundations of Personnel/Human Resources Management*. New York: Business Publications.

Jones, Foard F., Michael H. Morris, and Wayne Rockmore. 1995. "HR Practices That Promote Entrepreneurship." *HR Magazine*, May, 86–91

Kelley, Scott W. 1993. "Discretion and the Service Employee." *Journal of Retailing* (Spring): 104–126.

Kotler, Philip. 1994. *Marketing Management: Analysis, Planning and Strategy*. 5th ed. Englewood Cliffs, N.J.: Prentice Hall.

Levy, Michael, and Barton A. Weitz. 1992. *Retailing Management*. Chicago: Richard D. Irwin.

Little, Michael W., and Donald L. Myers. 1989. "Responding to the Youth Labor Shortage." *Journal of Retailing* (Winter): 408–413.

Lusch, Robert F., and Ray R. Serpkenci. 1990. "Personal Differences, Job Tension, Job Outcomes, and Store Performance: A Study of Retail Store Managers." *Journal of Marketing* 54 (January): 85–101.

May, Eleanor G. 1989. "A Retail Odyssey." *Journal of Retailing* (Fall): 356–367.

Milkovich, George T., and John W. Boudreau. 1988. *Personnel/Human Resources Management*. New York: Business Publications.

Myers, Donald L. 1989. *Compensation Management*. Chicago: Commerce Clearing House.

Nordstrom, Rodney, and R. Vance Hall. 1986. "How to Develop and Implement an Employee Incentive Program." *Management Solutions* 40–43.

Parrott, Mark D. 1993. "Employee Top Priority." *Do-It-Yourself Retailing*, June, 10–11.

Pennington, Rand G. 1993. "The Personal Commitment to Quality." *HR Magazine*, March, 100–101.

Pintel, Gerald, and Jay Diamond. 1991. *Retailing*. Englewood Cliffs, N.J.: Prentice Hall.

Redman, Mel. 1995. "The Dynamics of Team Building." *Chain Store Age* (December): 146.

Rose, Don. 1989. "Woolworth's Drive for Excellence." *Long Range Planning* 22 (1): 28–31.

Rosenbloom, Bert. 1980. "Strategic Planning in Retailing: Prospects and Problems." *Journal of Retailing* 56 (Spring): 107–120.

Salmon, Walter J. 1989. "Retailing in the Age of Execution." *Journal of Retailing* (Fall): 368–378.

Samiee, Saeed. 1990. "Productivity, Planning and Strategy in Retailing." *California Management Review* (Winter): 54–76.

Samli, A. Coskun. 1989. *Retail Marketing Strategies*. Westport, Conn.: Quorum Books.

Schlesinger, Leonard A., and James L. Heskett. 1991. "Enfranchisement of Service Workers." *California Management Review* (Summer): 83–99.

Sheth, Jagdish N. 1983. "Emerging Trends for the Retailing Industry." *Journal of Retailing* 59 (Fall): 6–18.

Swinyard, William R. 1981. "The Appeal of Retailing as a Career." *Journal of Retailing* 47 (Winter): 86–97.

Topol, Martin T., and Myron Gable. 1988. "Machiavellianism and the Department Store Executive." *Journal of Retailing* (Spring): 68–84.

"Turnover Rates and Costs." 1992. *Journal of Accountancy* (October): 18.

U.S. Department of Labor, Bureau of Labor Statistics. 1992. *Employment and Earnings*. Washington, D.C.: U.S. Government Printing Office.

Vroom, Victor H. 1964. *Work and Motivation*. New York: John Wiley and Sons.

Chapter 13

Developing a Retail Communication Mix

Though it is typical to discuss retail promotional strategy (Larson, Weigand, and Wright 1982; Dickson 1974; Hartley 1975; Berman and Evans 1995), retail promotional strategy is not a separate entity. As discussed in Chapter 1, the four retail mixes enable the retail establishment to implement a general strategy. One of these critical mixes is the communication mix. This chapter first examines the relative role of promotion (or communication) in general, then it explores how specific retail promotion mixes can be formed to implement different retailing strategies. A special attempt is made to explore the planning, administration, feedback, and control of the total communication mix.

COMMUNICATION FOR RETAILERS

Throughout our discussion in this book thus far, we have asserted that developing a retail marketing strategy and managing it are almost synonymous with store image manipulation. Once we consider the implications of such a statement, the role of communication for the retail establishment becomes obvious. Since "image" means the sum total of impressions perceived by different constituencies, the development and manipulation of retail image can only be achieved through communication. Obviously, if the retailer wants to generate certain impressions about the store, then carefully calculated and tightly controlled communication activity must be planned. The necessary communication mix may change its nature and its components depending on the retail establishment, but the basic need for the communication mix does not change. Regardless of its size, outreach, and specific features, no retail establishment can afford to be a "well-kept secret."

Promoting the Retail Store

When Sears abandoned its special sales and tried to institute an "everyday bargain prices" campaign, it basically abandoned its traditional department store status and came closer to a K-Mart and Wal-Mart type of discount store status. This deliberate attempt to change its status did not help Sears, the number-one merchandiser, to become like Wal-Mart, the number-two merchandiser but a discounter, and the results for Sears were not encouraging. Sears, instead, started promoting its "appliance brand center" as a strategic business unit, its Craftsman tools as a strategic business unit, and its credit card as perhaps a profit center as well as a strategic business unit. Publix, one of the largest grocery chains, has been promoting the idea of "where shopping is a pleasure" to establish an upscale image for the whole chain. In both cases, the companies started the communication process with an image manipulation goal. In the Sears case, the first attempt was not appealing. Sears customers obviously saw themselves somewhat differently from the customers of Wal-Mart or K-Mart. If you claim you are like Wal-Mart or K-Mart we can go and patronize the real thing, customers reasoned. It was a loss in Sears's personality and status. Thus, Sears had to change its orientation. In the case of Publix, it seems the promotional message fits the reality. Publix is continuing this theme in its advertising activity. It is attempting to deemphasize price competition, and the company is doing well.

If the effort put out by all of the promotional and/or communication efforts to manipulate the store image is working, then the store's name recognition in its target markets will also be enhanced. Those, for instance, who are not aiming for grocery bargains and hoping, rather, to feel good about their choice, will find Publix's promotional activity reassuring. Hence, Publix's name will be identified as a good place (not necessarily a low-price place) to shop.

The change in name recognition will create more of a positive attitude toward the customers. Here Publix's assumption is that a certain portion of the upper middle class likes more than just counting pennies and will be attracted to Publix stores. Certainly, in its attempts to manipulate its image, Publix will lose some of the more economy-minded consumers, but the assumption here is that to its target market Publix's appeal is better than purely economic. Thus, in this case the image manipulation may have led to an enhancement in Publix's sales and also its differential congruence. Exhibit 13.1 illustrates that there are a series of events in general for all retailers. However, communicating the image manipulation through promotion is different in every retail establishment.

We have discussed Sears and Publix. A local apparel shop, on the other hand, in order to establish itself as a local fashion leader, ran a series of fashion shows supported by local mass-media advertising and merchandising. The store managed to further enhance its already favorable image. As a result, this promotional activity became an annual event.

Many similar examples can be given. Each retailer may find a way to promote itself effectively. However, the key point is that it is not the size or the nature of the retail establishment as much as proper planning that facilitates image creation and manipulation. If the store's management wants to develop and manipulate the store's image on the basis of the overall strategic plan, it will have to manipulate the total communication mix of the retail establishment accordingly. Promotion is the actual proactive aspect of all of the communication perceived by the market. It is the most deliberate portion of the store's communication activity.

PROMOTIONAL PLANNING

A retail establishment, just as any social and economic institution, communicates with its actual and potential constituencies, both directly and indirectly. Planning this communication activity necessitates the development of a promotional plan and its implementation.

The basic philosophy that is posited here is that managing for a bottom line is more appropriate than managing by a bottom line (Samli 1993). This statement, in essence, implies that the retail establishment must do whatever is necessary to fulfill its objectives. This would include aggressive behavior to establish (or enhance) its competitive advantage by more promotion, better merchandising, and so on. Managing by a bottom line, on the other hand, implies a defensive strategy of cost cutting and modifying competitive advantage forces by toning them down.

Exhibit 13.2 illustrates how such a proactive retail promotional plan is designed and implemented. It illustrates eight specific steps. These steps are identified and discussed briefly in the following sections.

Promotional Objectives

Promotional objectives are essentially established by the marketing strategy that is being pursued by the store. If the store's promotional objectives are not consistent with the image development and image manipulation process, there can be no progress. If, for instance, the retail store wants to project an image as a fashion leader in a particular trading area and it advertises only its prices and its conservative orientation to fashion merchandising, the promotional objectives will not be fulfilled. Similarly, if the store is trying to establish an image of being on the cutting edge in electronics and computers but the salespeople are not well informed about some of the high-tech equipment, the promotional objectives again cannot be fulfilled. On the other end of the spectrum, if Winn Dixie claims "everyday low prices" but actually its customers notice that they are not quite as low as the competitor's prices, then, again, the promotional objectives cannot be fulfilled.

As can be seen, the points of emphasis in the overall promotional activity vary from one retail establishment to another and explicitly or implicitly they reflect promotional objectives. Exhibit 13.3 illustrates how promotional emphases can be and most often are associated with the strategies adopted by the store. An additional component of the exhibit is the media that are likely to be used to implement the promotional emphases that are carefully associated with the chosen strategies. Exhibit 13.3 is not definitive, but suggestive. Each store will still have to decide for itself.

By identifying the points of emphasis and connecting them to media use, Exhibit 13.3 illustrates how an orderly connection among the game plans, goals, and communications can be achieved. In the case of the general merchandiser, for instance, mass information about all the merchandise that the store carries as well as the store itself needs to be promoted. Mass information in this case needs to be disseminated with the most far-reaching mass media. Sears, J. C. Penney's, and other mass merchandisers cannot possibly afford to cut down their advertising activity. In such cases, the least cost and widest amount of information dissemination are essential.

Because strategic options are already discussed in Chapter 9 and promotional emphasis as well as the critical media parts are rather self-explanatory, it is not necessary to discuss each separately in detail. The reader is urged to think along the lines of a well-known retail establishment or a retail store that he or she is familiar with and single out the actual practices of the store versus its ideal strategic options and then evaluate that store's promotional activities.

As mentioned in Chapter 9, a retail store may be pursuing more than one strategy (one from each of the three groups). The areas of emphasis and mass-media considerations must be taken into consideration accordingly. Consider, for instance, a retail establishment that is a differentiator and is at the stage of being a fast grower. Furthermore, this is a specialty store, carrying specialty products (an apparel store carrying top-of-the-line brands for all apparel and accessories). In such a case, the retail store will not only be researching its differences and strengths, but will also enhance these special characteristics by coordinating its three strategic postures (differentiator, fast grower, specialty store carrying top-of-the-line products). As a result, that store will gain further acceptance and will further its differential congruence. Thus, the three strategic objectives can be made to reinforce each other for more effective performance.

Components of the Communication Mix

Retail communication mix (or retail promotional mix) in essence has the same key components of promotional mix in marketing. The difference is not one of kind but one of emphasis. The retail promotional mix differs from typical marketing promotional mixes on the basis of points of emphasis. In retailing, for instance, the local nature of the business and the immediacy of advertising messages imply much heavier emphasis on local radio and local newspaper than on other types of standard advertising. By the same token, because of the advance or lead time required before an ad is to run in a magazine or on network TV, these media are relatively less desirable for the typical retail promotion mix.

At least seven factors must be considered in developing a retail promotional mix (Samli 1989). These factors are (1) strategic objectives, (2) the audience to be reached, (3) the size of the trading area, (4) the message or product that is going to be advertised, (5) the relative cost of available media, (6) the amount of lead time required, and (7) general trade practices.

Strategic Objectives

Whereas the general merchandiser has to use far-reaching mass media, the differentiator, segmenter, or positioner has to use selective media such as local television and local newspapers. If the merchandise in question is related to fashion or well-recognized brands, it becomes particularly critical to use effective visual promotion such as television or special insertions in the Sunday paper, along with some key fashion-related national or local magazines.

In contrast to these two examples, a convenience store promoting convenience products is not likely to use major mass media such as TV or magazines, even at the local level. It will rely heavily on the lowest cost and most far-reaching medium, such as a local newspaper, along with emphasis on its appearance, location, direct mail, and in-store promotion.

The reader should analyze the strategic options presented in Exhibit 13.3 and realize the connection among the strategic options, promotional emphasis, and the critical media use of retail stores that are familiar. It then becomes obvious that there are some notable patterns, which parallel Exhibit 13.3:

1. Major discount drug stores or discount grocery stores that are general merchandisers mostly use newspapers and communicate with the largest possible number of consumers in the most cost-effective manner.

2. Differentiators proceed more readily with specific local media, store appearance, personal selling, and other differentiating characteristics of their store.

3. Segmenters behave basically like differentiators. However, they emphasize the differentiating characteristics of their store, geared specifically to the segment to which the store is aiming. They communicate with their segments by using more specific media, long-lasting print media (magazines), some TV, personal selling, and store ambience.

4. Positioners emphasize comparative advertising. As a result, they rely on visuals (magazines, TV, and newspapers).

5. Nichers must communicate with their specific markets. They are selectively involved in local mass-media use. Their customer services and public relations activities are critical to maintain their differential congruence.

6. Guerrilla fighters have to put forth an all-out effort to promote any and all store features to gain more recognition. Because of limited resources, they have to promote as much as possible for the least cash. Personal customer relations are particularly important.

7. Category killers thrive on overwhelming their competition by the variety and prices they carry. Their critical problem is to get this message out by reaching as many people as possible. They emphasize heavy local and national mass media. They employ a lot of TV, newspaper, and radio advertising. Special sales and other sales promotion activity are critical.

8. Beginning retail stores try to communicate with the market as extensively and as quickly as possible. Local media are particularly important. Specifically, they try to utilize public relations and release news items for public consumption.

9. Fast-growing retailers must maintain momentum. They try to persuade their markets by more long-lasting messages in local magazines, newspapers, store displays, and, again, store ambience. Emphasis is more institutional.

10. The mature retailers continue their promotional activity the way they have been doing all along. Unlike the fast grower, they need more immediate sales results and, hence, they emphasize more promotional than institutional activity.

11. The declining retail store may exercise one of two options: (1) scale down its activities so that the major emphasis is likely to be on low-cost immediate promotion, such as local radio, local newspapers, or in-store promotion, or (2) revitalize, so that the store is almost in the same position as it was as a beginner, trying to get news items in the local newspaper and on radio.

12. The specialty store, regardless of the products it carries, must realize that it is a specialty store and project such an image. Particularly if it is an upscale store carrying prestigious brands of apparel and accessories, in order to create a differential congruence it will use advertising in special media, prestigious magazines, and special newspaper advertising. In ad-

dition, it will capitalize on personal selling, store ambience, and customer satisfaction.

13. The shopping center store, regardless of the product group it concentrates on, must communicate the idea that there are economic gains in coming to the store and comparing prices and merchandise. Therefore, it has to emphasize reaching local media. Local newspapers and radio along with special sales promotions and in-store promotional activity are most commonly used.

14. Convenience stores rely on the traffic developed primarily by neighboring stores. Such a store usually does not have the means to advertise. Cooperative advertising with neighboring stores, promotional efforts, again jointly with other retailers, as well as in-store promotions are typical.

The Audience to Be Reached

Once the strategic decisions have been made, target audiences are identified, and promotional objectives are decided on, an effective media mix needs to be developed. Such a mix identifies the vehicles through which promotional messages are carried.

The retailer has a large variety of vehicles to communicate with the market. Optimizing this communication process with the most effective media mix is critical. There is always a choice among newspapers, telephone directories, direct mail (flyers, newspaper insertions, or coupons), television, magazines, outdoor billboards or posters, and transit media found in buses or taxis. Each of these media can be used to reach a special audience. Each of these has strengths and weaknesses. It is critical for the retailer to have a very good idea about the store's target markets so that it can communicate effectively by using the proper media mix. When Footlocker reinforced their slogan, "Where the gravity stops" at the NBA playoffs on TV, the company certainly connected with its target audience. It is quite well known that local radio stations have their own market segments. Teenagers, senior citizens, African Americans, and Hispanics all listen to different radio stations and watch different TV channels. On the basis of the retailer's knowledge of the target markets and the particular audiences of the retail media, the desired communications can be established.

Based on their needs and objectives, different retailers use different media mixes. It is quite unlikely that Cartier's or Saks Fifth Avenue will advertise a special sale in local newspapers, but Winn Dixie or Krogers emphasizes price-based promotional activity in the local paper every Wednesday.

In order to develop a media mix that will be most suitable to the retailer's needs, an intermedia selection process must take place in an effort to compare and analyze different media classes. There are at least six critical variables that are used for that purpose: (1) quintile analysis, (2) media objectives, (3) audience selectivity, (4) message tone, (5) media sense modality, and (6) geographic dispersion.

Quintile Analysis

By breaking the total market into quintiles, a special market research technique provides important market segment information for each and gives special media exposure data for each quintile. It contrasts, for instance, the 20 percent of viewers who are receiving the heaviest frequency with the lightest viewing in terms of age, education, consumption patterns, and the like.

Media Objectives

Media are critical for the retailer for the broadness of coverage in terms of reach or in terms of depth of the media based on frequency. If the retailer wants to expand its market, it may use the media that has specific reach. Similarly, if the objective is to cultivate the existing market better than before, then the retailer will emphasize frequency and, by doing so, will try to penetrate the existing market further.

Audience Selectivity

Since different media have different audiences, the retailer may choose the media accordingly. It is rather obvious that MTV viewers and *Readers' Digest* readers, in addition to being different from each other, are also quite different than those who read *Scientific American*. Depending on the retailer's target audience, the media classes as well as the medium within each media class can be selected.

Message Tone

The nature of the message that is going to be communicated plays a critical role in the media selection process. The message may or may not be congruent with the media. If the message is incongruent with the media, it may not be received at all or, if it is received, it may be rather ineffective. If, for instance, the retailer wants to project an image of being at the cutting edge of high technology or the leader of fashion, then it should not use media that may be identified by consumers as conservative. In particular, the message tone may not be consistent with the editorials of a magazine or a daily newspaper. By the same token, if the message is highly emotional and carried by a medium that is considered highly rational, the message tone factor is again not in place.

Media Sense Modality

Each medium has a different impact on consumer perception. The medium, for instance, may have a video or an audio effect and sometimes both. The retail establishment must decide on the type of impact it needs to create. While, for instance, a discount drug store may find it adequate to use some visual effect such as the one created by a newspaper, Saks Fifth Avenue may need an audio and video impact with color and ambience. Hence, they may use TV as the vehicle.

Geographic Dispersion

Each and every medium has a different audience that it reaches adequately. This reach can be analyzed both in terms of socioeconomic and geographic dimensions. The retailer must have a good idea of its target markets and its trading area. Once both of these are well known, it is then necessary to match these two by using the most appropriate media. If these two are well matched, then chances are the retailer has the most desirable media mix for its purposes.

This last point needs to be expanded further. The components of the retail media mix which connects the retail store to the market are decided on by the retailer's promotional objectives. Thus, the first two steps that are identified in Exhibit 13.2 are interdependent. If the promotional objectives are not identified, the communication mix cannot be constructed.

A second critical point must also be made. Every retailer communicates with the market. That implies the presence of a communication mix. In some cases, the retailer may not even be cognizant of the fact that it is communicating. By the same token, the presence of communication of the retailer with the market indicates the existence of multiple media. Retailers use a combination of mutually reinforcing media mixes and communication forms. Studies have shown that a combination of media is more effective for a retailer than single-medium advertising (Dickson 1974).

Size of the Trading Area

The size of the trading area that the retail establishment considers its own has a profound impact on the promotional mix of the retailer. In addition to all of the considerations discussed thus far, the size of the trading area determines the media mix. The trading area needs to be covered appropriately. But if the trading area is widespread, the store finds itself facing the quandary of localizing the coverage by emphasizing each locale with local newspaper and radio stations, or covering the area in a blanket fashion by using TV or widespread print media, such as magazines. Also, in such cases, other outdoor media such as billboards and flyers on windshields enter the picture.

The smaller the trading area, the greater the dependence on store signs, appearance, direct mail, and other outside promotional activity, such as sidewalk sales or billboards. The smallness of the trading area is usually related to the nature and size of the retail establishment. A small gift shop or a convenience store such as Lil Champ does not use expensive media such as TV, magazines, or even newspapers. In fact, it often cannot afford advertising in these media. It may use the Yellow Pages, but, above all, by locating conveniently and appearing pleasantly it promotes itself.

The Message and the Product

The need for basic congruence between the message and the media has already been shown. This critical point needs further attention. A new retail establishment may want to establish its credibility. Furthermore, it is trying to position itself in the marketplace. However, if the medium the retail establishment is using or contemplating using does not possess this kind of credibility, the store's message will not get across. By the same token, the retail store that is trying to establish a liberal, forward-looking, or cutting-edge image will never succeed if it advertises on TV next to or during a conservative political or semireligious TV program.

The nature of the message could be particularly important. If the message needs certain visual effects, certain types of media such as radio will be rather useless. Similarly, color may be extremely critical for a store dealing with fashion merchandising; once again, certain media, such as newspapers or radio, become useless.

Congruence between the message and the medium to be used is not sufficient. It is critical that there also be congruence between the product mix and the media. As has been pointed out, certain products, such as fashion goods, or certain types of foodstuffs, such as cakes and frozen gourmet dishes, need visual impact. Therefore, the retailer can use only newspapers, TV, or other print media. Some well-known brands in appliances or well-known stores do not need visual effect. Thus, a special sale or some other promotional activity can be communicated with the market rather easily by using nonvisual media such as radio.

It is necessary to emphasize that each case is unique and must be considered according to its own merits. Generalizations that have been presented thus far in this chapter are useful to enhance the decision maker's awareness and understanding of the factors relating to the store's promotion mix. Every retail store must constantly search to find the most suitable promotion mix for itself. It is also critical to note that in a dynamic market, as conditions change, this promotion mix may also change. The retailer must not have a smug attitude that the promotion mix that is being used is good and there is no need for a change. Similarly, the retail decision maker should refrain from the attitude of, "We tried it already; it simply does not work." What might not have worked in the past may be quite usable now.

Relative Cost

Cost is always a very important factor in making media decisions and constructing a communication mix for the retail establishment.

Most advertising or retailing books discuss different cost factors. The concept of relative cost is critical. It implies that the cost figures must be modified on the basis of the audience outreach. If a one-page ad in a magazine costs $10,000 and if there are two prospective magazines that can be equally useful, then it is necessary to contrast cost-per-thousand figures. In such a case, if Journal A has a readership of 10,000 and Journal B has readership of 50,000, then it becomes obvious that, all things being the same, Journal B has a lower cost per thousand. Another measure is milline rate. It measures the newspaper cost per line by using a simple formula. If, for instance, the rate is $1.80 per line and the circulation is 900,000, then the milline rate is $2.00 (Diamond and Pintel 1996). Again, all things being the same, the lowest milline rate is most desirable.

Amount of Lead Time

In retailing, when advertising is used particularly to generate immediate sales, timing is very important. In such cases there is usually little lead time to prepare ads. Supermarket or discount drug store ads, for instance, appear in local newspapers one day (typically Wednesdays), and are expected to create traffic in the store the next day. Moreover, the specific items that are on sale or the conditions of special sales are always different. They change from one week to the next. As a result, most grocery retailers and others who promote special sales weekly or quite often and who use local media for this purpose do not have enough lead time to prepare ads. They have to work very fast to get these ads ready for the media. Thus, most grocery retailers, discount drug stores, and others who promote special sales for immediate sales increase need to use local media to accelerate the process. They need to act quickly, and they have to have some lead time. Some of the larger retailers have found the solution to be in-house advertising. In fact, in recent years many retailers started using in-house advertising rather than using advertising agencies. In so doing, they have established more control over their overall advertising efforts and costs. In the case of image building or long-lasting impact, as well as those retailers who need illustrations, color, or video and audio combinations, more prolonged lead time is required. In such cases, the retailer may need to go outside and use ad agencies.

General Trade Practice

Trade practices relating to promotion and communication inevitably influence a retailer's communication mix. In most cases, competitors try to match or exceed each other. If one retailer is advertising heavily in the local print media, competitors will feel compelled to match or excel this effort. When, for instance, McDonald's is engaged in massive television advertising, Burger King and Wendy's also accelerate their promotional activity.

These seven factors—strategic objectives, the audience to be reached, the size of the trading area, the message or the product to be advertised, the relative cost, the required lead time, and general trade practice—are all instrumental in determining the detail of the retail promotion mix. Unfortunately, it is not possible to state that one, two, or three of these seven factors are more important than others. There is no research indicating the relative importance of these factors so that they could be evaluated comparatively. Hence, they are not prioritized here. However, it is quite likely that some of these factors are more critical in the development of a promotion mix. Much research is needed in this area. It must also be reiterated that the conditions are different for each and every retailer. It is necessary, therefore, for each retailer to explore the implications of these seven factors on its own operations so that an optimal promotion mix can be developed.

MULTIATTRIBUTE OR SINGLE ATTRIBUTE?

If the retailer wants to establish far-reaching and long-lasting impressions about the store, it will be necessary to use a multiattribute promotional effort. Such an effort is likely to influence the overall store image and enable the retailer to manipulate this image. A multiattribute advertising message includes more than one message. It may indicate, for instance, that the store has unique casual wear, formal wear, and sports wear. In all three cases, the store excels because it carries the best brands and this is its competitive advantage. In such attempts, therefore, a promotional message and an image-building message are combined in one (Lincoln and Samli 1981).

In communicating with multiattribute messages, credibility or believability becomes particularly critical. Since the store has multiple claims establishing credibility, promotion also becomes more difficult. If the claims are not believable and supportable, then the whole promotional effort can become dysfunctional, especially when the multiattribute promotion efforts are developed in the form of comparative advertising. The lack of credibility is likely to support the leader (or the competitor), rather than creating gains for a store.

Single-attribute promotion is necessary for short-run impact and to generate immediate sales results. Advertising a special weekend sale is not likely to do much for the store's overall image in terms of reinforcing or manipulating it, but it can yield significant and immediate sales results.

As can be seen, the retailer must make some very critical decisions as to single-attribute versus multiattribute promotional activity. Both are critical and both are necessary. It will depend on the conditions under which the store is operating to decide if multiattribute or single-attribute promotions should be used and in what proportions. Part of this decision is related to the promotion budget. If the store's budget for promotional activity is limited, then it may make more sense to use more single-attribute promotions and generate short-run sales and cashflow, rather than emphasizing the long run with multiattribute messages.

BUDGETING FOR RETAIL PROMOTION

In standard marketing or retailing books, there are many different approaches to establishing a promotion budget (Anderson 1993). Most of these budgets are based on a *breakdown* principle. In other words, the total figure to be used for promotion is established first, and then it is broken into detailed components in terms of different media coverage. However, though such a budget in terms of total sum to be spent may be quite appropriate, it does not fulfill the goals. When the total budget figures based on a breakdown process are established early in the game, the outcome is usually to ignore the firm's objectives in implementing its strategy. It is critical to connect the strategic and promotion goals to the detailed promotion budget. The author advocates a *buildup* method of budgeting. This is typically referred to as the *task objective* method (Anderson 1993).

Once the promotional objectives are established as a way of implementing the overall strategy, these objectives need to be interpreted in terms of a media mix. It is rather easy to attach a price tag to each component once the details of the promotion mix are determined in terms of time, medium, size, and so on. Thus, based on the details the budget is built up.

REVIEWING THE BUDGET

The budget cannot be finalized without a revision process. The review may, for instance, indicate that the components of the budget may add up to more than the firm can afford. In such a case, the promotion objectives may be questioned. Based on prioritization, some of the low priority items in the tentative budget may be eliminated or reduced so that the whole sum will be more realistic. Of course, it is possible to use other alternatives of budget cutting, such as scaling down all of the items in the budget proportionately.

As mentioned, the review process also takes place on the basis of the seven factors used to develop the parameters of the promotion mix. There may be obvious inconsistencies; for example, the media sense modality may encourage the use of billboards, but the message and the product factor may push in the direction of using more TV. In order to solve this problem, some type of prioritization of the relative importance of the seven factors needs to surface. The management may decide that the message and the product congruence is more critical than media sense modality and, hence, the retail store may go for more TV advertising than billboards.

Budget revision calls not only for evaluation of the budget details and an overall check for consistencies. The final budget must also be consistent with promotion objectives, competitors' activities, and overall strategic plans. Finally, two critical considerations must take place before the budget is finalized: image compatibility and promotional coordination.

Image Compatibility

Earlier chapters in this book dealt with image development and image manipulation. Promotional efforts have significant influence in developing, manipulating, and communicating the image (Hartley 1975). If the store wants to develop and communicate an image of being a pacesetter in professional women's fashions, it certainly cannot imitate its competitors. It must project an image of being a leader rather than a follower. Thus, it cannot use advertising messages that are conveying a "me too" message. Similarly, it cannot use the media that are used by those who take a "me too" orientation.

Promotional Coordination

Since a retail store has a complex promotion mix that is composed of many different components, it is making many claims and offering many products and many prices. When certain promotion efforts are made, in-store backup for these claims and announcements is needed. Delchamps, a national supermarket chain, for instance, initiated the "New Low Price Leader Overall" campaign, which includes suspended signs and shelf tags, particularly in the center of the store. It is very closely coordinated with critical price reductions and intensive local advertising in addition to word-of-mouth communication. The end result has been as much as a 7-percent increase in sales for some stores. Thus, this everyday-low-prices stance combined and coordinated carefully with other promotional activity has been very successful for this 117-store chain (Redman 1996).

In fact, retailers should regularly evaluate their shops from the customer's point of view and make sure that merchandise pricing and quality, the store's interior and exterior design, and its advertising and promotion campaigns are very closely coordinated (Outcalt and Johnson 1995). In addition, when certain merchandise is featured in the intensive promotional activity, sufficient quantities of that particular product or product category must be available. The so-called "bait and switch" practices of some unscrupulous retailers do more harm than good. They create a credibility gap. Finally, if the promotional campaign is going to create unusually heavy traffic in the store, then the management must make sure that an adequate number of salespeople, cash registers, bags, and other support materials and services are made available so that the store will fully benefit from the promotional efforts (Hartley 1975).

IMPLEMENTING PROMOTION PLANS

There is no value attached to promotion plans unless they are implemented properly. These plans gain their value by their successful implementation. Implementation programs specify all the details of the promotion activity. This includes what needs to be done, by whom, and when. Exhibit 13.4 illustrates an advertising budget development process by illustrating the buildup technique. The total implementation program will have the names of the media and the dates when the promotional messages will be conveyed. This particular budget and implementation details reflect strategic and promotional objectives.

Because of the computer information technology revolution, some supermarkets are launching a World Wide Web site that may accelerate the return of home shopping and delivery services. Shaw's Supermarkets, for instance, has been trying to promote its home delivery services through their website (Zimmerman 1996).

CONSISTENCY IN RETAIL PROMOTION

A retail establishment is constantly sending commercial and noncommercial promotional messages. The consistency theory posits that the commercial and noncommercial messages must not be contradictory. While the commercial messages are all part of the total promotion mix, the noncommercial messages are beyond the promotional mix. They are part of the total communications mix, if there is to be a distinction between the promotion mix and communication mix. Throughout this chapter, these two mixes have been used interchangeably. The noncommercial messages are not part of the overall planned promotional activity. Retail establishments, knowingly or unknowingly, are involved in public relations activities. From sponsoring Boy Scouts to being honored by city fathers as the company of the year, the retail establishment is involved in a large variety of activities and, intentionally or unintentionally, gets much recognition. Again, whether it likes it or not, it starts developing a public-civic image.

The consistency theory maintains that if the commercial promotion of the retail establishment is not consistent with its already formulated public-civic image, then most of the promotional efforts of the retail establishment are wasted. This implies that a large proportion of the retailer's promotion budget is also wasted. Ideally speaking, therefore, when the commercial promotion plans are prepared and implementation details are worked out, they must match the noncommercial messages and the resultant public-civic image. This situation will yield optimum results. The retail establishment must try to exert some pressure on noncommercial communications. Without such pressure, there are high risks. This type of pressure can be exerted in at least two different ways.

First, the retail establishment can manipulate certain social and civic activities just enough to implant a certain type of noncommercial messages. When Publix puts together food baskets for the poor, it is manipulating some noncommercial messages. Stix, Baer, and Fuller, a major group of stores based in St. Louis, used to sponsor youth dances and dancing contests. If the store wants to project a dynamic and youthful overall image, such noncommercial promotional activity can contribute significantly.

Second, the retail firm, by using certain marketing research techniques, can successfully monitor the public-civic image that has been formed through its noncommercial communication activity. If as the end result of such a monitoring process the retail establishment discovers a trend that is contrary to what it has been trying to accomplish through its commercial communication, then it may take deliberate action to counteract such a trend.

Though the consistency theory is successfully tested and used in political circles, particularly in election years, as well as in communication sciences, it has not been used in retailing. This particular theory must be tested and implemented if the retailer wants to develop a successful communication mix and subsequently powerful differential congruence. Such research is bound to uncover the details of the consistency theory as well as its successful application and limits. The retailer will be able to operationalize this theory in order to achieve more successful communication.

THE CONTROL FUNCTION

If the Food Lion grocery chain is putting substantial amounts of money and effort into promoting its image as being the lowest-priced grocery chain, and if the consumers do not believe this, it is wasting all this money and effort. This must be stopped and reversed if the company is to have a future. Hence, the control mechanism in this process is a must. If the retail establishment has an information system in place, then it will be in a position to determine the effectiveness of its performance in the marketplace. This information system will yield primary and secondary data, and statistical analyses will enable the retail establishment to realistically assess its marketing performance. From these efforts, decision-oriented models will emerge so that the firm can decide to stay the course or reverse its activities.

Such a control function has at least three specific steps: (1) collecting data continuously regarding market conditions and the company's performance, (2) using statistical techniques to analyze the data, and (3) developing decision-oriented models to decide if the firm should continue as is or deviate from its current course. In controlling the promotional activity, the measuring of effects is essential. The effects or the outcome of promotional activity can be measured at different levels. As illustrated in Exhibit 13.1, there are three different stages where the results of the promotional activity can be measured. In terms of progression, the first step is name recognition. Is the promotional activity enhancing the name recognition of the retail store? This is a critical question that needs to be addressed. It must also be emphasized that if name recognition is not changed, there cannot be significant changes in the customer attitude. Thus, the second step is related to the question of whether customers' attitudes toward the store are changing. Finally, the third stage is related to detecting the changes in the sales volume. Once again, if name recognition is not enhanced and the customer attitude is unchanged, there cannot be a long-lasting sales volume increase.

One final point on this topic is that the proportions also vary. For instance, if the promotional effort has created a 40-percent improvement in name recognition, this may translate to about a 20-percent improvement in customer attitude. This impact on customer attitude may further translate to about a 7-percent sales increase. Thus, the progression here has a downward tendency. It is critical that the retail establishment make attempts to detect the impact of promotional activity at all three stages of the game. Needless to say, the outcome, which actually is the control process, is the adjustment of the communication mix so that a greater differential congruence can be achieved (Exhibit 13.1).

ATMOSPHERICS AND JOINT PROMOTIONS

As early as 1973, Kotler stated that consumers buy the total product. The total product includes the physical entity, service, name, ambience, and more. In this case, the ambience and more are related to atmospherics. Kotler and others have maintained that, in some cases, the place or the atmosphere of the place is more influential in the purchase decision than the product, location, or the name. In fact, in some cases the atmosphere is the primary focus. It implies the aesthetic factor in consumption. It communicates, perhaps somewhat quietly, but as a matter of fact. When a consumer enters a Target store and finds the atmosphere warm and friendly, the merchandise and the layout appealing, and sees families shopping happily and at certain stations adults watching videos with their children, naturally that consumer can conclude that Target is a nice place to shop. Thus, in communicating with its markets, the retail establishment must use the silent language of atmospherics to its advantage. Consider, for instance, a female apparel store that carries merchandise just as good as its direct competitors but provides an extremely friendly and happy atmosphere based on the attitudes of the people who work there, their good taste in apparel, and their personal knowledge of the customers. The store may offer coffee, tea, a home-baked cake, cookies, and, on special occasions, some wine. The atmosphere is elegant but very relaxed, and salespeople are trying their best to satisfy. This store is bound to be considered a fashion leader, a good place to shop, and a fun place to revisit.

A recent development in the promotion area is having tie-in events. Vons, a food chain in California, was engaged in crosspromotion with Shell in Spring 1995. This was considered to be an important traffic builder for both parties. Since Vons is in a food area, it believes that such traffic-building crosspromotional activity is likely to be very effective if it is in a nonfood line. Under the Shell plan, customers who purchased $25 worth of merchandise with Vons received a certificate for $1 off all grades of Shell gasoline (Elson 1995). Such tie-in promotional activity is likely to become more popular in the future.

One additional recent development is related particularly to malls. This is called Mall Perks. All the stores located in that mall give customers purchase points which translate to discounts or free gifts. Similarly, these malls issue credit cards for customers' use in the mall. There are many other similar perks.

INTERNATIONAL CORNER

Retail promotion, in many parts of the world, is very limited. Many small local retailers rely on the loyalty of their local customers and word-of-mouth advertising. Since the population does not move around much, the store's reputation remains the same.

As has been discussed throughout this book, most top-100 retailers in the world are going international. These retailers try to compete with locals through reputation, promotion, merchandise variety, and, perhaps above all, access to data regarding local markets. It is critical for them to be heavily involved in large-scale local, national, and international advertising from these global markets. They must consider if their American name and reputation are good enough that they should be transferred to different national and local markets. Their access to local data may enable them to adjust their retailing mixes and particularly their communication mix to local markets. These international retailers use their size and resources as the tools of competitive advantage in different international markets.

SUMMARY

An eight-step model is presented in this chapter. These steps are (1) establish promotion objectives, (2) construct the communication mix, (3) prioritize the components of the mix, (4) develop an overall promotion budget, (5) review, revise, and finalize, (6) develop an implementation plan, (7) implement, and (8) monitor and control.

All these steps are carefully discussed. Developing the promotion budget by relying on the task-objective method (Step 4) takes into consideration the first three steps. In considering the fifth step, it is necessary not only to adjust the budget according to the retail establishment's capabilities, but also to make sure that the consistency theory is implemented. This latter indicates that there should not be gaps between what the promotional activity claims and what it delivers. The implementation plan is composed of all of the communication activities, their specific media, their timing, and their specific functions. Of course, if the implementation is not successful, the whole effort is wasted.

Finally, monitoring and controlling implies having a functional information system that may generate data regarding the store's name recognition, customers' attitude changes, and increases in sales (if any). This whole activity leads to specific controls based on the lessons learned.

Exhibits

Exhibit 13.1
The Reaching Impact of Retail Communication

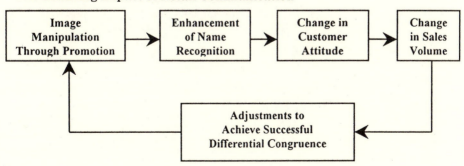

Exhibit 13.2
Retail Promotion and Implementation

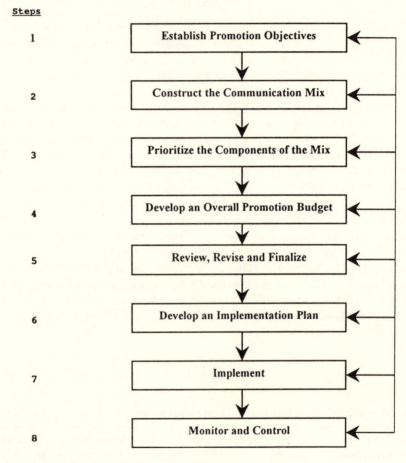

<u>Steps</u>

1 — Establish Promotion Objectives

2 — Construct the Communication Mix

3 — Prioritize the Components of the Mix

4 — Develop an Overall Promotion Budget

5 — Review, Revise and Finalize

6 — Develop an Implementation Plan

7 — Implement

8 — Monitor and Control

Source: Adapted and revised from Samli (1989).

Exhibit 13.3
Strategy Alternatives, Promotional Emphasis, and Media Use

Strategy Options	Areas of Emphasis	Critical Media Use
1. General Merchandiser	Mass information about all the merchandise and the store.	Most far-reaching mass media, heavy TV and radio advertising, heavy concentration on sales promotion, special sales and special events.
2. Differentiator	Emphasis on identifying differences and special strengths of the store.	Selective mass media advertising with local emphasis, critical personal selling, special sales.
3. Segmenter	Emphasis on the key characteristics of the store that will satisfy the obvious needs of the identified segment(s).	Efforts to communicate directly or selectively with the segment, much direct mail and public relations activity.
4. Positioner	Comparative advertising to reassure capturing the position that is being aimed.	Comparative advertising to the target market, mass media, direct mail, special personal selling activity.
5. Nicher	Establishing the fact that the store is the only one in that well-defined portion of the market and it makes its customers happy.	Efforts to communicate directly, special emphasis on customer services. Possible public relations activity.
6. Guerilla Fighter	An all out effort to get name recognition at the lowest possible cost.	Most effort for name recognition with minimum possible cost. Customer services, personal contact and direct mail along with in-store specials are critical. Public relations if possible.
7. Category Killer	Emphasizes mass information about the store merchandise, but above all, prices and variety.	Most far-reaching mass media, heavy TV, newspaper and radio advertising, heavy concentration on special sales. Extensive promotional advertising rather than institutional.
8. Beginner	High level of information dissemination to promote the store (information).	An all out promotional effort of disseminating information about the store in general. Heavy mass media special promotional activity to bring people into the store.

Exhibit 13.3 (*continued*)

Strategy Options	Areas of Emphasis	Critical Media Use
9. Fast Grower	Enhancing the store characteristics to gain stronger acceptance and sharpen its competitive advantage (persuasion).	Accelerating the growth and name recognition with mass media promotion. Emphasizing special strengths of the store with in-store promotion and personal selling. Powerful public relations.
10. Mature	Trying to maintain the successful image and the position in an increasingly hostile market (reminding).	Less mass-media promotion with more pointed message. Renewed emphasis on features that have been neglected lately. Important public relations activity. Important in-store promotion. Special customer service.
11. Declining Store Scaling Down Revitalization Redirection	Overall decline in promotional efforts. All out emphasis on one new feature. Renewed emphasis on certain store features. Developing totally new features.	Promotional efforts are scaled down further. Special emphasis on newly developed feature and emphasis on revising the image. Important public relations activity. Improving sales promotion activity including in-store promotion.
12. Specialty Store Specialty Goods Specialty Goods Shopping Goods Convenience Goods	Maintaining differential advantage and manipulating the image by uniqueness of selection, service, advertising, and people.	Emphasis on special media that will directly communicate with the market segments. Manipulating image by select mass media. In-store personal selling. Efforts to communicate with regular customers. In-store promotion.
13. Shopping Store Specialty Goods Shopping Goods Shopping Goods Convenience Goods	Advertising extensively the prices and values for all critical products and brands.	Extensive mass media activity. Special public relations and sales promotion.
14. Convenience Store Specialty Goods Shopping Goods Convenience Goods	Emphasizing the convenience and practicality of patronizing that store through widespread promotion.	All out effort to bring in traffic. Coupons, direct mail, in-store promotion. Promoting convenience and well-known brand convenience goods.

Exhibit 13.4
A Task-Objective-Based Promotion Budget

Objectives	Task	Cost
Gain awareness of professional women	Use 16 quarter-page ads in four separate successive Sunday editions of local papers. Multicolor super photos.	$16,000
Gain awareness of professional women	Simultaneously with the above there will be announcements inviting professional women to attend jointly sponsored luncheon and fashion show at a very reputable hotel.	8,000
Gain awareness of upper middle class	Four 45-second spots on local TV; heavy image symbols.	12,000
Appeal to regular good customers	Direct mail color brochures. Special mailing with discounts.	8,000 4,000
Overall image continuity	Two local newspaper and two magazine ads combined with improved interior and outside sign.	9,000
Special strategic seasonal advertising	Four seasonal promotional activity combined of flyers.	5,000
	Four newspaper spreads and four promotional TV spots.	4,000 5,000
	TOTAL $71,000	

References

"Advertising for Small Business." 1981. *Bank of America Small Business Reporter* 15 (2).

Anderson, Carol H. 1993. *Retailing*. St. Paul, Minn.: West.

"Attitude Share of Market Predicts Better Than Behavioral Measures." 1980. *Marketing News*, 16 May, 7.

Bendell, C. 1958. "Looking at the Retail Ads." *Advertising Age* 19 (January).

Berman, Barry, and Joel R. Evans. 1995. *Retail Management*. Englewood Cliffs, N.J.: Prentice Hall.

Burton, Philip Ward. 1951. *Retail Advertising for the Small Store*. New York: Prentice Hall.

Cremin, S. 1979. "Stores Urged to Project a Style in Their Ads." *Editor and Publisher*, 27 January.

Diamond, Jay, and Gerald Pintel. 1996. *Retailing*. Englewood Cliffs, N.J.: Prentice Hall.

Dickson, J. P. 1974. "Retail Media Combination Strategy." *Journal of Retailing* (Summer): 61–69.

Eaton, K. 1980. "Retailers Disagree on Ad Philosophy." *Advertising Age* 51 (March).

Edwards, Charles M., Jr., and William H. Howard. 1939. *Retail Advertising and Sales Promotion*. Englewood Cliffs, N.J.: Prentice Hall.

Elson, Joel. 1995. "Vons Said to Be Considering Second Nonfood Tie-In Event." *Supermarket News*, 16 October, 48.

Gilson, Christopher, and Harold W. Berkman. 1985. *Advertising*. New York: Random House.

Gloede, B. 1979. "Department Stores Are Coming Home to Newspapers." *Editor and Publisher*, 29 December, 64.

Gore, B. 1980. "Fifty Years of Retail Advertising: Aim More Direct, Graphics Improve." *Advertising Age* 51 (April): 194–198.

Hartley, Robert F. 1975. *Retailing: Challenge and Opportunity*. Boston: Houghton Mifflin.

Henderson, D. E. 1979. "Radio–Print Ad Mix Could Be Ideal for Retailers." *Advertising Age* 50 (May).

Kamerzura, P. 1980. "Retailers Ask Audio–Visual to Show Way to Higher Sales." *Advertising Age* 51 (June).

Kotler, Philip. 1973–1974. "Atmospherics as a Marketing Tool." *Journal of Retailing* (Winter): 48–64.

Larson, Carl M., Robert E. Weigand, and John S. Wright. 1982. *Basic Retailing*. Englewood Cliffs, N.J.: Prentice Hall.

Levine, Harold. 1979. "Agency Head Urges Retailers to Shift Focus to Marketing." *Advertising Age* 50 (October).

Lincoln, Douglas, and A. Coskun Samli. 1981. "Assessing the Usefulness of Attribute Advertising." *Journal of Advertising* 3: 25–34.

Mandell, Maurice I. 1974. *Advertising*. 2d ed. Englewood Cliffs, N.J.: Prentice Hall.

Marquardt, Raymond A., James C. Makens, and Robert G. Roe. 1975. *Retail Management.* Hinsdale, Ill.: Dryden Press.

Mason, J. Barry, and Morris L. Mayer. 1982. *Modern Retailing: Theory and Practice.* Dallas: Business Publications.

"Measuring How Well Ads Sell." 1976. *Business Week,* 13 September, 104, 107–108.

Moore, Charles Thomas, and T. R. Martin. 1961. *The Extent of Retail Advertising as a Management Tool: Its Scope and Importance in Small Business.* Reno: University of Nevada Press.

"N. Y. B. B. B. Crack Down on Retailer." 1979. *Advertising Age* 50 (September).

Outcalt, Dick, and Pat Johnson. 1995. "Rate Your Store as Shoppers Do." *Gifts and Decorative Accessories* (August): 28–36.

Radolf, A. 1979. "Retailer Seeks Better Service from Newspaper." *Editor and Publisher,* 3 February, 10.

Ray, Michael L. 1982. *Advertising and Communication Management.* Englewood Cliffs, N.J.: Prentice Hall.

Redman, Russell. 1996. "Delchamps EDLP Stance Signing Up Shoppers." *Supermarket News,* 8 January, 21–25.

"Retail Chains Overlook Co-op Pluses, Study Finds." 1979. *Advertising Age* 50 (July): 14.

"Retailers Exhibit Clout in Europe." 1979. *Advertising Age* 50 (July).

Samli, A. Coskun. 1989. *Retail Marketing Strategy.* Westport, Conn.: Quorum Books.

———. 1993. *Counterturbulence Marketing.* Westport, Conn.: Quorum Books.

Zimmerman, Denise. 1996. "Shaws Returning to Home Shopping by Way of Site on World Wide Web." *Supermarket News,* 1 January, 17–19.

Chapter 14

Merchandise Mix Development

The reason for being in retailing is to sell goods and services to specific customers in a given trading area. If these goods and services are not liked, the retailer will not survive. Thus, the retailer must perform numerous functions relating to product assortment so that it can manage the merchandise or service mix well. This whole process is called merchandising.

This chapter deals with four key components of merchandising: buying, planning, managing, and controlling. Buying involves acquiring the necessary merchandise. Planning means developing the proper assortment of merchandise offered by the retail establishment. Managing relates to making sure that the store is not overstocked or understocked and is responding quickly to customer needs as well as market changes. Finally, control procedures are developed and implemented so that the whole process will work smoothly. Much planning goes into the buying activity because it is an extremely critical activity for retail survival. The discussion is divided into four parts: (1) the buying function; (2) planning for buying as well as overall merchandise mix planning for depth, width, breadth, and consistency; (3) developing an efficient customer response model relating to the merchandise planning process (MPP); and (4) the control function, which implies the presence of feedback and corrective action regarding the merchandise mix.

BUYING: THE OTHER LIFEBLOOD IN RETAILING

As discussed earlier, traffic and location are usually referred to as the lifeblood of retailing. If there is less than adequate traffic, a retailer cannot survive. By the same token, there must be something desirable to sell to that traffic. Effective buying makes it possible to have appropriate goods and services to sell. Hence, the buying function is the other lifeblood in retailing. The purpose of a retail establishment is to sell appropriate goods and services to customers who are the traffic. As category killers like Wal-Mart or Toys 'R Us get into fierce competition, some independent retailers thrive by carrying unique products that major stores do not stock (McCune 1994).

There are four merchandise management objectives that supersede and modify retail buying (Samli 1989). These are (1) providing a highly desirable merchandise mix, (2) adjusting the mix to changing customer needs, (3) preplanning merchandise mix, and (4) developing an effective buying plan.

Providing a Highly Desirable Merchandise Mix

This particular objective is the core of merchandise management activity. In fact, the reason for the existence of a retail establishment is to provide a desirable merchandise mix for a specific market segment. As has been mentioned a number of times already, without such a mix the retail store cannot survive. Just what are the characteristics of a desirable merchandise or service mix? The answer to this question varies with the realities of each retail establishment. However, following are some of the key considerations.

The merchandise mix must be different from that of competitors. This difference provides the retail establishment certain monopoly (or market) power (see Chapter 2), and creates an opportunity to enhance its differential congruence. However, having a different merchandise mix is necessary but not in itself sufficient. The particular mix in question must be highly desirable to the market at which it is aiming. Again, the retail establishment must have a well-defined target market or a niche and must know just what would delight this particular market. In fact, this point is most critical in developing a congruence between the store and its clientele. If the customers are delighted, then they become loyal to the store.

In order for the merchandise mix to be different and appropriate, there are five generic dimensions in merchandise planning that need to be considered carefully. These dimensions or continuums are depth, width, breadth, consistency, and flexibility (Berman and Evans 1995; Mason, Mayer, and Wilkinson 1993; Samli 1989; Lusch 1982). Depth means the number of brands and styles within a particular generic product category. A drug store that carries fifteen types of headache remedies may be considered to have a "shallow" assortment if the typical drugstore carries about forty different headache remedies. Width means the number of different classes of products that a store carries. For example, a store selling sports shoes has a narrow line as opposed to a retail store that carries hunting equipment, golfing equipment, and other sports goods. The second store has "wider" lines. Breadth means the number of units in each brand and style within each and every generic class of products. The store that carries ten pairs of shoes in each and every category has more breadth than the one that is carrying only four of each. Consistency means that different types of products that comprise the merchandise assortment are related. Merchandise assortment of the retail store is highly consistent when all merchandise is closely related in value, appeal, use, and quality expressed in perceived image (Markin 1971; Samli 1989). Flexibility means that the retailer has the opportunity to take advantage of good local merchandise buys and adjusts the merchandise mix as deemed necessary.

These five merchandise mix continuums indicate different options in merchandise management and provide general direction for this activity. Understanding the options and directions is a critical starting point for a retailer so that a satisfactory merchandise mix can be constructed. It must be noted that these five continuums do not imply good or bad merchandising policies; instead, they simply identify the retailers' options.

A merchandise mix policy can be developed by using any two of these continuums. In this way, at least six retail merchandising policies are recognized:

1. Deep and narrow assortments—Such assortments are found in specialty stores. Such stores must have numerous brands and styles in their specialty areas.

2. Deep and wide assortments—These are appropriate for general merchandise stores. They represent a good selection of diverse product lines appealing to the general public.

3. Shallow and narrow assortments—Convenience stores follow such merchandising policies. 7-11s and Lil Champs sell only frequently needed lines with little selection or depth in any given line.

4. Shallow and wide assortments—This merchandise mix policy is most suited for discount stores. They typically carry a few brands and styles of a large variety of generic product classes.

5. Consistent assortments—This particular merchandise mix philosophy indicates the presence of consistency within a department or among depart-

ments, as well as within the store as a whole, in the quality, class, and selection of merchandise. Product lines do not show extremes, such as being very good along with very bad. Departments do not show extreme differences in selection, quality, price, and so on. In short, the store's merchandise and its departments are all compatible.

6. Flexible assortments—These assortments typify the old concept of a bargain basement or army surplus store or even second-time-around apparel shops. But, in addition to bargains, flexible assortments indicate the store's autonomy in buying locally available bargains or certain unique products that might cater to certain local markets. Winn Dixie stores have good produce departments that buy the best a community offers.

Merchandise mix is one of the four retail mixes discussed earlier in this book. However, all four of the mixes do not carry equal weight. The merchandise mix carries more weight, and hence it plays a critical role in the implementation of retail marketing strategies. This implementation process is unique to each and every retail establishment. It takes very specific forms, so that the merchandise policies can partially fulfill the retailer's strategic goals with its properly implemented merchandising decisions. Certainly, Wal-Mart cannot have a shallow and narrow assortment when it is trying to differentiate itself as a place to shop for the lower middle class. Similarly, Bulgari jewelry stores carry a deep and narrow assortment, reflecting the very special and exclusive nature of these stores and their pronounced strategy of segmentation.

Adjusting the Mix to Changing Consumer Needs

This objective is related to the retailer's understanding of consumer trends and its ability to swiftly adjust its merchandise mix accordingly. The faster the retailer can make this adjustment, the better off it will be. Exhibit 14.1 illustrates some of the key consumer trends during the past two decades or so and how they impact retailing. If the retail establishment is too old fashioned to pay attention to such trends, it cannot possibly survive and prosper. If consumers want more casual everything, the retailer cannot insist on being formal. It must be reiterated that the trends pointed out in Exhibit 14.1 are national. It is quite possible that there are local trends that are even more critical for the retailer.

How can retailers be sure that they are properly detecting the trends in their markets and trying their best to remain abreast of changes in the marketplace? Keeping up with the market trends means quick and proper adjustments of the merchandise mix to clearly detectable trends. Only effective feedback enables the retailer to make such adjustments.

Preplanning Merchandise Mix

Merchandise preplanning is related to maintaining up-to-date knowledge of the market. It is particularly dependent on feedback and control functions, which are discussed in detail elsewhere in this book. Merchandise mix preplanning reflects the changes in the market, changes in competition, and reaction to past years' merchandise mixes. It must be reiterated that providing a highly desirable merchandise mix is almost an extension of the physical store environment (Babin and Darden 1995). Consistency between the store itself and its merchandise mix has a general appeal to consumers and may even modify their behavior (see Chapter 7). Finally, all these factors influence the overall purchase behavior. Exhibit 14.2 illustrates these relationships. There are two extraneous modifiers that need to be brought into the picture. First is market change, indicating perhaps a demographic change in the immediate trading area, such as when an area's population is growing fast, but unlike the existing older, more mature, and economically established population, the growth is in the direction of young adult families with smaller children. The second modifier is changing competition, such as the emergence of a new shopping center or the entrance of two new competitors into the market.

The retailer, though hoping to alter shopper reaction in its favor by modifying store atmospherics (physical environment) and by modifying the merchandise mix in addition to other promotional activities that are discussed in Chapter 13, varies these effects based on the consumers' original orientation toward the store and their ability to make up their own mind (Babin and Darden 1995). But the changes in the market and changing competition certainly cannot be controlled. Thus, the retailer, while trying to change the disposition of consumers, is also trying to counteract these changes. Merchandise mix preplanning would at least partially enable the retailer to accomplish this.

Laura Ashley, having handled classic floral print varieties of dresses and home furnishings, and having seen an expansion in their number of stores to almost 500 around the world, saw an increase in sales from $53 million in 1979 to $579 million by 1991. By that time, plain, neutral colors became far more popular than busy patterns such as Ashley's. As its competition, such as the Gap and Banana Republic, responded quickly, Laura Ashley continued in its old style. By February 1995, the company said it would lay off 200 employees and close nearly 20 percent of its 190 North American stores. Laura Ashley stores had not had a really good year since 1990. Along with other changes dealing with store restructuring, the company decided to change its merchandise mix. It was planning to make 65 percent of its fashions plain. For instance, the new lines include a "silk sailor dress, plain blue with white strips on the neck and sleeves—for $198, or a plain $138 A-line dress cut above the knee. The home furnishing lines offer cleaner Scandinavian and Mediterranean designs to complement the fluffy looks of its English country style" (Levine 1995, 94).

Considering the changes and problems, it should have been rather obvious that there needed to be a tighter merchandise mix preplanning. Such preplanning must be based on very tight feedback from consumers, such as efficient consumer response. The company has been using comprehensive strategies for electronic data interchange. EDI is a very sophisticated information network, eliminating paperwork, facilitating fast information flow among vendors and retailers, and leading to more efficient ordering and receiving processes. EDI and bar-coding, combined, have given retailers alternative tools to facilitate the rapid flow of information between their organizations (Margolies 1995). This information flow is carefully used for key business processes such as ordering and receiving. This is leading to supplier managed replenishment and automated ordering (Margolies 1995). For nonperishable large-variety and large-volume retailing at some grocery chains, this proposition is very appropriate. Some retailers are making substantial investments in EDI and sharing of product movement data with some selected vendors. Along with automated ordering, EDI and bar-coding are also facilitating automated direct store delivery and paperless receiving.

Finally, EDI and bar-coding are facilitating category management and supplier supported merchandising. This particular process provides greater opportunity for profits for both suppliers and retailers by increasing sales volume rather than only focusing on cost reduction. Many major suppliers, such as Coca-Cola, Procter & Gamble, and Nabisco, are working closely with retailers to initiate category management.

All the EDI and bar-coding initiatives are facilitating efficient customer response. It must be reiterated that these activities or initiatives are primarily activated or utilized by large vendors and large retail chains. There is no question that small retailers will soon also become part of this ECR revolution, but it may take some time and some costly innovations. It must be clarified that all retailers, small or large, can and must develop some type of efficient customer response. Clearly, ECR leads to better merchandise planning.

Merchandise Planning Process

By establishing the direction in which the merchandise mix is to be adjusted on the basis of the last year's results and deviation from the past by efficient customer response, merchandise mix planning can be effectively performed.

The Women's Specialty Retailing Group (WSRG), a nationwide operator of 1,350 women's specialty apparel stores, including August Max Woman, Capezio, Casual Corner, Pappagallo, and Petite Sophisticate, among others, approached the IBM consulting group. WSRG wanted a new information system leading to a better merchandising plan. The IBM consulting group, after analyzing different planning processes by each separate brand, refined and standardized merchandise mix planning.

In an indirect manner, Exhibit 14.2 displays the current use of information technology in merchandise planning; however, a critical point is that the retail establishment must make adjustments to improve its merchandise mix. As preplanning of merchandise mix for the coming year takes place, the actual image and expected image changes of the store need to be considered so that the merchandise mix can be adjusted accordingly. If a retail apparel shop decides to change its image from too "formal, stuffy, and expensive" to more "casual, attractive, and good value for the money," then it must adjust its merchandise mix over and beyond efficient customer response and *merchandise planning process*. Such a dramatic change should not take place in the course of a year. It would take longer than a year to change the image. If the store must make such a change because it is in trouble, then it may do better by modifying its name and promoting itself as if it is new or at least dramatically changed.

If the retailer wants to survive, it must learn to adjust its merchandise mix to changes and trends in the marketplace. If the retailer can play an active role in generating these changes and trends, it is more likely to survive the adversities of the market. In other words, in adjusting its merchandise mix, if the retailer plays the role of being a leader rather than a follower, it has a better chance to survive and prosper. Being such a pacesetter is not so simple. It needs to be established as an objective of the retailer, and then the retail plans must be adjusted accordingly. Liz Claiborne stores, along with Liz Claiborne lines, attempt to make a statement in more traditional and classical elegance in women's wear. They play a leadership role.

Not seen in Exhibit 14.2 is that differential congruence is also in action here. In achieving and maintaining this congruence, the retailer's merchandise mix plays a very critical role. The merchandise mix is a critical extrinsic cue for developing an image for the store which will play a pivotal role in achieving the desired differential congruence.

The effectiveness of the extrinsic cues is dependent on the internal consistency that needs to be displayed by the retailer between its merchandise mix and other variables that play a role as extrinsic cues in the formation or modification of the store image. If, for instance, the retail establishment is trying to establish an image of leadership in women's professional wear, its salespeople must be dressed appropriately and behave professionally. Even the store's exterior must be conservative if the store is to represent the cutting edge of professional attire. In addition, customer services such as credit, merchandise adjustment, and a liberal return policy must be appropriately administered. Without these circumstances, the retail store does not have internal consistency among its extrinsic cues, and the benefits of an appropriate merchandise mix are lost because of this lack of consistency. The store is sending conflicting cues to the market. This situation can be further exacerbated if the store's different departments lack internal consistency. While, for instance, its professional apparel and business casual wear departments are well known for their good value, fashion leadership, and progressive orientation, its shoe and accessories departments may have a reputation of carrying poor quality and cheap merchandise. Such a lack of internal consistency in the overall merchandise mix would send out even stronger conflicting cues and hurt the store's chances of developing the synergistic effect achieved by internal consistency of its merchandise mix that would play a critical role in constructing a uniform image for the firm.

DEVELOPING AN EFFECTIVE BUYING PLAN

Once the features of the most suitable and attractive merchandise mix are established through merchandise preplanning, they must be explored from the perspective of differential congruence objectives and implementation. In other words, attractiveness or adequacy of the merchandise mix must match what the target customers of the store need, want, like, and hopefully will purchase.

It is critical to introduce the store buyers into this picture. Exhibit 14.3 does just that. The merchandise mix, unless it is supplier controlled as in the situations discussed earlier, is put together by a buyer or, most likely, a number of buyers. Exhibit 14.3 reinforces the most important consideration in buying: continuity. Even though the buying function in retailing is a personal creative expression, this creativity cannot be displayed in a direction that is different from those efforts that are trying to construct, maintain, or revise the desired store image leading to a powerful differential congruence.

Exhibit 14.3 illustrates that there are critical store-related points that need to be balanced by critical points that are related to buyers. There are at least three store-related critical points that need to be considered in merchandise mix development. First, merchandise mix development must contribute to the development and maintenance of the store image. As already mentioned, the merchandise mix is a critical contributor to the store image. As the store's merchandise mix is planned and evaluated, consistency with the desired or already existing image must be evaluated and its actual contribution to the overall store image periodically examined.

Inventory control is the second store-related factor. There are numerous ways of controlling inventory. Some of these are computer based and have already been touched upon. Others are further discussed in this chapter. A store's inventory must be controlled within given parameters. Among these parameters are cost constraints, time limits, and, above all, store image goals. There must be an ongoing feedback system leading to inventory control that would guide the buying function for the retailer. For example, XYZ store is a very elegant, well-known, and rather expensive women's clothing store. Inventory controls pointed out that there was a shortage in their lower-price-line merchandise. This was just before Easter. The buyer found a bargain lot from a local superstore which was going out of business. This bargain lot simply did not fit XYZ's image and was substantially larger than the store's needs. By purchasing the lot, XYZ's open-to-buy budget was spent, and the newly acquired lot took up much space. The company lost money because it was not quite ready for Easter and the newly acquired merchandise did not appeal to XYZ's core market. The whole process went against the image XYZ had been projecting. In this case, the buying function did not meet the budgetary and image constraints.

The third factor is coordinated buying. Continuing with the XYZ example, assume, for instance, that XYZ has three buyers. These three buyers have different perception of the store's image. One of them thinks that the store should carry more bargains, the second is buying the most expensive formal and evening wear, and the third believes that XYZ is truly a middle-class store. These three buyers will not coordinate their activities unless there is a general understanding. Without such coordination, the store is sending out mixed messages and is not pursuing its image objectives.

MERCHANDISE MIX AND BUYERS' BEHAVIOR

Merchandise mix development, as shown in Exhibit 14.3, has three key buyer behavior-related factors that need to be examined. These three factors are buyer flexibility, buyer motivation, and buyer objectives (Samli 1989).

Buyer Flexibility

Buying at the retail level is an art as much as a science. The buyer is the person who pursues the fine art and science of buying the merchandise for the store. It is critical that a buyer have enough flexibility in terms of choosing the vendors, quality, and styles of merchandise. If this flexibility can be combined with careful inventory planning, then both the art and science of retail buying are likely to be optimized. The artistic part of buying enters into the picture because good merchandise has many aesthetic features, such as color, style, appeal, appearance, and fashion. Not only should the buyer have good taste, but this taste must be shared by the store's core customers. In addition, if there is more than one buyer involved, there should not be wide differences among their tastes. This is necessary for the store to develop and maintain the desired image.

On the other hand, there are many scientific aspects of retail buying that need to be known by the buyer. These scientific aspects are reflected in terms of certain merchandise planning tools such as stock lists, markups, markdowns, expense control factors, contribution returns, stock turnover analyses, return on merchandise investment and capital turnover, gross margin return on inventory (GMROI) (Sweeney 1973; McGinnis, Gable, and Madden 1984; Samli 1989), weighting technique, and open-to-buy computations, among others. Some of these tools are discussed in this chapter.

Buyer Motivation

Since buyers are artists of sorts, their motivation may create a positive stimulation for better performance. Exhibit 14.4 illustrates seven motivation factors for buyers. The retail manager must make sure that all of these factors are intact and are not counteracting each other. It is possible that there are more or fewer factors in play on the basis of the retail establishment in question. Whereas there may be fewer factors in action regarding the behavior of Wal-Mart buyers, there may be more factors in action in the behavior of a buyer who is working for Neiman-Marcus. However, if the buyer is properly motivated, the results of his or her efforts will certainly reflect on the store's overall performance. If, for instance, the retail establishment is suffering from a questionable image in the marketplace and the buyer is very much aware of it, the buyer's motivation is likely to be dampened. Similarly, if the buyer is not paid adequately, he or she may be more concerned with trying to make ends meet than with his or her performance. Having a boss who is not accessible or having almost no interaction with other buyers can be devastating.

As can be seen, each and every factor in Exhibit 14.4 plays a critical role in a buyer's psyche. It is critical that the buyer be well trained, well treated, well paid, and kept well informed. Without proper motivation, the buyer is not likely to perform to expectations or beyond.

Buyer Objectives

Buyers are professionals who need to be motivated but who also must have certain professional objectives that are consistent with the store's objectives and, furthermore, are consistent with their motivation. Buyers must realize that their personal objectives play a pivotal role in the well-being of the retail establishment.

The buyer's objectives, self-image, and identification with the store could bring his or her performance to a higher level, with similar effective performance by the store. If the buyer has clear-cut professional objectives that are consistent with the store's objectives, then the buyer's professionalism will work in the direction of a mutually satisfactory performance by the buyer and the store. Exhibit 14.5 reinforces these points. Naturally, the best results are those that are mutual and positive. It is clear that the retail establishment must make a special attempt to play an important role in the buyer's professional development and maturation process. If the buyer goes through periodic short courses and special programs, he or she can become a better professional. Much research is needed to determine the factors that influence this professionalization process.

One of the key concerns is the professional skills that the buyer must possess. Among these skills are (1) communication skills; (2) negotiation skills; (3) understanding the importance of alternatives; (4) prioritizing the store's needs, alternatives, merchandise sources, and categories; (5) knowing the impact of trends, styles, and fashions; and (6) merchandise knowledge. These are all extremely important training areas, but their discussion is not within the scope of this chapter. The reader must be able to develop his or her programs for a given store or a research situation according to the particularities of the conditions at hand.

MERCHANDISE MIX PLANNING

As has been reiterated throughout this chapter, successful merchandise mix development is dependent on effective planning, buying, and control. Preplanning is the first step in the planning process. Effective buying has already been discussed. This section presents a discussion of detailed merchandise planning and its parameters. Merchandise planning must get down to the nuts and bolts of quantities, mixtures, and styles of merchandise to be purchased and carried within certain periods of time within the carefully prepared constraints of a budget.

Merchandise mix is one of the most important weapons of retail competitive advantage leading to differential congruence. Exhibit 14.6 puts this notion into proper perspective. This exhibit illustrates the relationship between store objectives and merchandise mix. Regardless of how large and important the retailer is or how small it is, the relationships shown in Exhibit 14.6 hold. The hierarchical order shown in this exhibit indicates that merchandise mix development and management, to a very important extent, is the tool for retail objectives to be implemented.

In order to manage the merchandise mix well, the retailer must know and use the tools of merchandise planning. If the effectiveness of these tools is not understood and they are not implemented with rigor, the retail establishment will not be able to fulfill its goals.

Typically, general merchandise plans cover six-month periods. Such plans enable the retailer to physically see relationships and associations among various products and other variables (Golden and Zimmerman 1980). Merchandise plans are best formulated by using six steps (Berman and Evans 1995): (1) selection of control units, (2) sales forecasts, (3) inventory-level planning, (4) reduction planning, (5) planning purchases, and (6) planning profit margins. These are briefly discussed in the following section.

Control units are identified by using departmentwide classifications such as jewelry and sporting goods in a discount department store. In addition to departmentwide classifications, though within-department classifications can also be used. For instance, in the jewelry department certain lines such as fashion jewelry, gold jewelry, diamonds, and other precious and semiprecious stones may be featured. The utilization of control units leads to three lists that retailers must know: basic stock lists, model stock lists, and never-out lists. These three lists provide critical guidance for the retailer in merchandise mix management.

Basic stock lists include key merchandise that have stable sales patterns. Since these patterns are predictable and since these items provide lesser risk in terms of salability, these lists are specific and carefully detailed. Model stock lists are more often constructed primarily for certain shopping goods and fashion merchandise. These product lines fluctuate readily and cannot be included in detail on basic stock lists. In general, they represent relatively less predictable and less stable product lines and, hence, they are not as detailed as basic stock lists. Rather, they are a skeleton of certain sizes, prices, quality, and color groups. Never-out lists deal with products that the store must carry all the time. These products are either the core of the store's product line, or the store is identified, at least partially, with having these products. Thus, they play a role in the store's overall image (Hartley 1975; Samli 1989). Since customers expect the store to have these products, if it is out of them it is likely to create a credibility gap and, hence, to hurt its image. These lists are critical in selecting control units. Similarly, strategic business units and profit center analyses can be applied to this area (see Chapter 9).

As opposed to specific departments in department stores, in small retail establishments standard merchandise classifications may be used as control units. Every retail establishment has its own merchandise classification. However, it is critical that commonly accepted merchandise classifications also be considered. The retail establishment should not rely solely on its own internal merchandise classification. All retail establishments, small or large, should seek information from the outside. For example, there are different merchandise classifications and trade association data. As discussed in Chapter 17, various computerized information systems provide important data that can be used in different aspects of retailing, including merchandise mix planning. Based on these lists, the retailer can establish stock keeping units (SKU) which indicate groups of merchandise arranged for inventory maintaining and controlling.

Sales forecasts involve determining market potentials and expected changes in these potentials. There are many different forecasting techniques, within which we emphasize a general orientation. The retailer must follow three sets of information. First, external factors, such as changing personal income in the trading area or changing population of the trading area, may be utilized. Second, internal factors, such as total sales dollars or sales units and their variations, must be carefully traced. Third, the seasonality factor must be considered. This last factor is much more critical in some retail lines, such as apparel, than in others, such as groceries. If we combine these three variables, the following is constructed:

$$S = f(X, Y, Z)$$

Where

S = Sales volume
X = External factors
Y = Internal factors
Z = Seasonal factors

It is clear that the store's sales volume is a function of various external factors, certain internal factors, and seasonal variations (Samli 1989). It is critical to determine the relative role each of these factors plays on sales. Each store may have different impacts from certain variables. It is necessary for retail establishments to analyze their own sales and determine how their sales interact with these variables in order to predict the future (in other words, to forecast).

Every retailer should estimate sales trends by analyzing past sales patterns and subjectively evaluating expected changes. Exhibit 14.7 illustrates such a situation. Only a few critical product lines are analyzed. Estimates are based on an annual 8-percent growth for a six-month period (4-percent growth). The average sales figures are further adjusted to internal changes. For instance, as slacks and sweaters experience a decrease in sales, the forecasted growth is adjusted downward. The exhibit illustrates a dollar-control orientation to merchandise planning. The whole process could also take place on the basis of unit control. Other product lines, again on a dollar-control basis, are adjusted upward.

Inventory level planning is an essential component of merchandise planning. The retail store must have adequate stocks so that it will not lose sales. Similarly, if the store is overstocked, unnecessary investment in inventories can take away much of the store's profits. Every retailer must develop a system to plan timely purchases in adequate quantities. Such an accomplishment can keep the retailer ahead of the competition. The earlier discussion of EDI and bar-code procedures in this chapter can aid in the development of such a system.

Planning the inventory is primarily based on three key concepts: (1) average monthly stock, (2) average monthly sales, and (3) planned monthly sales. While the first indicates the portion of the total inventory that is expected to be on hand, the second is based on actual sales figures and the third is calculated from forecasts. Thus,

$$PI = PMS + BS$$
$$BS = AMS - AMS$$

Therefore

$$PI = PMS + (AMS_1 - AMS_a)$$

Where

PI = Planned inventories

PMS = Planned monthly sales

BS = Basic stock

AMS_1 = Average monthly stock

AMS_a = Average monthly sales

All retailers must achieve a certain level of sophistication so that they develop effective inventory plans. Such a level of sophistication calls for carefully developed analyses of the average monthly stock and average monthly sales. In addition, it is critical that all retailers develop reasonable forecasts from which planned monthly sales can be derived. There is rich literature on retailing and small business, in which a variety of such techniques are discussed. However, as seen in Exhibit 14.7, most small retailers use very pragmatic approaches to developing monthly sales estimates. Much research is needed to determine the particular practices of retail establishments and the most functional approaches to this topic.

Reduction Planning

Reduction planning refers primarily to markdowns, which are discussed in Chapter 15. Suffice it to say that, for many retailers, using reductions is not simply a pricing activity. Nor is it strictly a merchandising activity. It is indeed a promotional activity. Some reduction in retailing is always critical. Many retailers, therefore, do not use reductions to adjust inventories or generate quick cash, but as part of the total planned promotional activity.

Another type of reduction is planned regarding inventories. As retailers develop logistics and information sophistication, they will reduce the level of their inventories without losing sales. As discussed earlier in this chapter, EDI and bar-coding have such an impact (Margolies 1995). In such cases, the retail establishment plans such reductions not for promotional purposes, but for financial efficiency.

A third type of reduction, unfortunately, is imposed on the retailer. Shoplifting is a form of reduction that needs to be included in the merchandise planning process. It has been estimated that shoplifting accounts for almost 30 percent of stock shortages (Rothman 1980). Subsequently, there have been attempts to reduce this rate by increasing security in retail establishments and by using subliminal messages along with piped-in music that is played in the store.

Planning Purchases

In order to plan purchases, it is necessary to put the three considerations just discussed together. First sales are planned, then inventories are planned, and, finally, reductions are planned. Thus, planned sales are calculated as follows:

$$PP = AMS_1 + PMS + PMR$$

Where

PP = Planned purchases
AMS_1 = Average monthly stock
PMS = Planned monthly sales
PMR = Planned monthly reductions

Open-to-Buy (OTB) is one of the most critical concepts. OTB is the difference between planned purchases and actual purchase commitments made by a buyer during a month. It indicates a certain degree of flexibility on the part of the buyer. If all the customer's funds are committed to planned purchases, there is no OTB. In such cases, if there are some special opportunities for good buys or some last minute changes, they cannot be accommodated. Having some degree of flexibility by having some OTB, the buyer is likely to feel more involved in the well-being of the retail establishment. Such a feeling can be a special motivation to perform well.

Finally, as plans for purchase are developed, it is critical to make plans for reordering merchandise. Though at the beginning of this chapter a brief discussion was presented on the vendor's replenishment of inventories by computerized information systems, it is critical to consider the economic constraints of reordering, since most retailers still do it themselves. Manufacturers like for retailers to order in large quantities. This way the manufacturer enjoys economies of scale (savings based on large volume production) and the retailer gets quantity discounts and also enjoys the savings from elimination of the reordering process. On the other end of the spectrum, by ordering in small quantities the retailer eliminates (or at least reduces) the excessive costs of carrying large inventories. By the same token, it could also be costly for the retailer to run out of merchandise and lose sales. These economic constraints are brought forth and their negative impact is minimized by utilizing economic order quantity (EOQ), which can be illustrated as follows (Berman and Evans 1995):

$$EOQ = \frac{2DS}{PC}$$

Where

EOQ = Economic order quantity in units

D = Annual demand in units

S = Costs to place an order

P = Percentage of annual carrying cost to unit cost

C = Unit cost of an item

Such a formula can help optimize the buying efforts by minimizing the costs of overstocking and the losses from understocking. With modern information systems, EOQ can be calculated and revised continually.

CONTROLLING THE MERCHANDISE MIX

Much of our discussion regarding merchandise mix planning can also be used for control purposes. Each time a financial criterion such as planned monthly reductions or a qualitative criterion such as never-out lists are discussed for planning purposes, criteria for controls are also established (Samli 1989). Because the planning criteria set forth the key parameters for the merchandise mix, they also guide the control activity by facilitating comparisons between the planned and the actual. The five-step merchandise mix planning process discussed earlier provides financial or quantitative control criteria. On the other hand, basic stock lists, model stock lists, and never-out lists provide qualitative or unit control criteria. Though Exhibit 14.7 is based on dollar control, it can be set on a unit-control basis as well.

If, for instance, the retail establishment has been cultivating an image of being on the cutting edge in fashions and research indicates that the market views the store as a place that carries good quality and classical lines, then the retail establishment will have to be adjusted on this basis. Similarly, certain purchase reductions for its other lines will also be planned. Finally, the store buyers will have to change vendors to make such adjustments. As they get acquainted with new vendors, they may have to change their interaction patterns with vendors. For instance, the vendors that are handling very expensive fashion merchandise may be a bit more "snobbish" in their behavior. The retail buyer may treat them somewhat differently than the vendors of more long-lasting, classical lines, who may be treated by retail buyers more as peers.

BRANDS

All products need to be identified and distinguished. Brands give products distinction and identity. All products have a name in retailing. This name (i.e., brand) plays a varying role from very critical to almost neutral. The implication is that retailers do not use brands at the same level of intensity. In order to explore different possibilities in using brands as a strategic tool, it is necessary to understand the types of brands and their possible use. Marketing literature distinguishes three types of brands critical for retailing: national brands, private brands, and generic brands.

From the perspective of a retail decision maker, national brands are manufacturers' brands. These brands are known throughout the country and carry a national and uniform identity. Levis, Uncle Ben's, or Bayer Aspirin are examples. All these products can be located in different corners of the country. Many of them are also recognized and distributed worldwide. National brands have a significant power of their own. Not only can they carry themselves, but they often make a contribution to the store's promotional appeal as well.

For the average retailer, the profit margin for national brands is lower than that for private brands. Furthermore, there are usually certain strings attached in promoting or carrying national brands in a retail store. The retailer may be required to allow so much shelf space, use specific displays or point-of-purchase promotions, arrange gondolas, and meet other similar conditions. However, because of the fact that national brands have much market power and carry themselves in the marketplace, they are attractive and important for the retailer to carry in the store.

Private brands are basically retailers' or wholesalers' brands. The use of private brands in retailing can be a critical portion of strategic efforts in the direction of establishing differential congruence. There are many reasons why retailers consider developing their own private brands. Among these, the following are critical:

1. The retailer may already have a large captive audience. When Sears entered the insurance market with Allstate lines, it was enjoying the recognition and loyalty of large markets.

2. It is possible to make significant product innovations. Again, Sears's Allstate tires may be just slightly below the top line but may be considered a very good value for the money. It may make a significant improvement to the quality.

3. Private brand lines can be cost efficient. The retailer may have an efficient distribution and delivery system, or perhaps the retailer can promote the product only to a limited scale, at lower cost.

4. There may be obvious gaps in the market between the best and the worst. The retailer may come up with a compromise private brand. Publix grocery stores' own vitamin line is a typical example.

5. There may be a special need for the private brand to promote the store. Victoria's Dream is an illustration.

In addition to the impact of private brands in promoting the store, private brands can yield more profit for the store. They typically are about 15 percent cheaper than national brands.

The third alternative is generic brands. This is particularly critical in the pharmaceutical industry. As opposed to private or national brands, generic brands are priced, again, about 15 percent below the private brands. Similarly, though not strictly generic, there are situations where brand simply does not play a critical role. When tourists in Waikiki, Hawaii, pass by ABC discount convenience stores, they are hardly interested in the brand. The brand of the t-shirts or ready-made sushi is not critical at all. Quite often, convenience products are not pulled by their brand name. Location and the characteristics of the retail store play a more critical role.

In recent years, some retail establishments, instead of using different brand names, are using only their own names. Stores such as Gap and Victoria's Secret are combining the store's name and the product's name. They find it easier to project an image of quality by the store itself than by having different brand appeals. Here, in establishing a competitive edge and a resultant differential congruence, the retail store may be using a product pull or a store image pull as alternatives.

Of course, using generic brands implies all the emphasis of the store image, because if the product is generic, it has no brand. During the stagflation of the early 1980s, many no-brand products appeared. They simply had plain wrapping and a white label stating that the product was "soup" or "peanut butter." In times of economic hardship, such products are likely to return to retail stores.

STORE IMAGE PULL VERSUS PRODUCT PULL

In general terms, product mix typically makes a critical contribution to overall store image. However, in many cases the product image described particularly by the brand name can make the store more competitive. On the other end of the spectrum, the store can make the product. It is important to understand which is which and the specific impact of each. Store image and product image are two different competitive tools, and they may be used together to create synergism.

For example, ABC stores are part of a large chain of convenience stores catering almost exclusively to tourists in Honolulu, Hawaii. Assume they decided to attract more customers and perhaps upgrade their image and, hence, they decided to carry a sporty line by Calvin Klein. Since they are discount stores, they are likely to sell the product somewhat below the manufacturer's suggested price. As another example, assume Neiman-Marcus decides to strengthen its men's underwear lines. This means carrying a large line of Fruit-of-the-Loom men's underwear. In both cases, the store image and product image match is less than desirable. The ABC stores cannot possibly enhance their image by simply adding one line to their merchandise mix. In fact, in this case, it may be bad for Calvin Klein, since the company is "trading down" its name and one of its product lines.

Similarly, the Neiman-Marcus name and the image it projects carry much more of an "elite" appeal than does the Fruit-of-the-Loom brand. Exhibit 14.8 illustrates the store image versus the product image dichotomy and their relationship. As can be seen, the ideal situation is having a very strong store image pull reinforced with a very strong product image pull. This situation will create a certain type of synergism that is most desirable. On the opposite end of the spectrum, a store does not have much of an image pull. When this is combined with the lack of product image pull, then the result is disaster (lower-right-hand corner of Exhibit

14.8). In such a case, neither the store nor the product has any pull; people may buy products from the store, but they are hardly familiar with the store nor do they know much about the product. As long as enough traffic goes in and out of the store, it is likely to survive. Many small gift shops or other tourist traps in coastal cities or major beach or recreation areas belong in this category. However, the retail establishment in such cases has no way of impacting its destiny by proactive marketing. Exhibit 14.8 implies that Neiman-Marcus and the Calvin Klein line may have found an area of agreement and joined forces. The two may be complementing each other and, hence, both the Calvin Klein and Neiman-Marcus competitive edges may be raised to a higher plateau.

In many situations, store image pull may not be very strong. In such cases, products with substantial pull may be quite appropriate. A small middle-class department store chain may announce, for instance, that it exclusively carries the Estee Lauder line. This is the lower-left-hand quadrant in Exhibit 14.8.

The upper-right-hand quadrant of Exhibit 14.8 indicates the situation where the store has a strong image. In such cases, the store can use products with low product image pull and can push them. It is also important to note that the store may develop its own private brands which may be quite desirable. A specialty store, for instance, that has a very strong store image pull can have many convenience products treated as if they are specialty goods. From a manufacturer's perspective, having its products carried by a number of specialty stores with strong store images can be quite desirable. In such situations, trying to reinforce the store image is a more practical retail strategy than looking for new product lines with strong images. Much of the time a store such as Neiman-Marcus carries quite nondescript products with little or no identity. However, the store's loyal customers rely on the store's name and reputation rather than the product's brand image.

As can be seen, brand name and brand image play a critical role in retailing. The retailer must understand the relative importance of brand images on its customers. In order for a product to project an image that will strengthen the retailer's competitive edge, that particular product needs to be included in the consumers' "awareness" set as opposed to being a part of their "unawareness" set (Narayana and Markin 1975; Samli et al. 1978; Samli 1989).

AWARENESS VERSUS UNAWARENESS

The relationship between consumer behavior and product performance could be most effectively explained by classifying all existing brands into awareness and unawareness sets (Samli 1989). The awareness set represents those brands that the store's customers know and might be inclined to purchase. The unawareness set, on the other hand, indicates those products that are not known to the customer.

On the basis of these definitions, the retailer would naturally prefer that all components of the merchandise mix be included in the awareness set of the store's target-market customers. But being included in the awareness set does not indicate an automatic purchase or strong preference. In other words, the brands that are included in the awareness set do not have the same appeal to customers. On the basis of this premise, we divide the awareness set into three subsets: evoked set, inert set, and inept set (Exhibit 14.9). Evoked set includes a group of select brands which customers consider in their purchase choice. Inert set consists of those brands for which the consumer has neither positive nor negative evaluation. The consumer here is basically neutral. Finally, the inept set includes those brands that are rejected by the store customers because of unpleasant experiences they have had with these products or negative feedback they received about these products from others (Samli 1989).

Studies have shown that customers of a store almost automatically categorize the store's merchandise mix into these three groups (Narayana and Markin 1975). Thus, customers of the store accept a few products (brands), are indifferent to a few, and reject a few. In addition, they are either uninformed about or deliberately ignoring a few (unawareness set). Such an orientation to the store's products can enable the retailer to analyze the brand power of the merchandise mix. If, for instance, the inept set is growing, it means that the store is not buying and carrying proper merchandise. Similarly, if the unawareness set is large and growing, it may mean that the store is not promoting its products and is not informing its customers.

As part of merchandise mix control activity, the retailer can keep track of the performance of its brands. Some products, in time, may move from an evoked set to inert or inept sets. Similarly, some products may move from awareness to unawareness sets or vice versa. Retailers must periodically consider the performance of their brands so that they can develop a highly desirable merchandise mix.

INTERNATIONAL CORNER

During the past three decades or so, international trade has been growing in large proportions. Because of the reduction in import–export barriers, American retailers now have a much larger selection to choose from in developing their merchandise mix. During the past thirty years or so, many less developed countries improved their products. Because of lower labor costs and the utilization of more recent technologies, many textiles, small electronics, and other products are available to the American public through American (and some foreign) retailers. It is critical that American retailers have access to foreign imports and can make them available to their customers. One of the most critical aspects of this activity is related to international sourcing. It is possible for American retailers to use international products systematically and as part of their total offering on a prolonged basis. This means the retailer as an individual or as a group of stores must be involved in international sourcing activity. Such international sourcing can be built into the merchandise planning activity.

International sourcing for a retailer requires a careful examination of about seven key areas of inquiry. These are as follows:

1. Would the items sell in the specific market of the store?
2. Are there quality improvements over other alternatives?
3. Are there significant price differentials that will make it worthwhile for the store to abandon some of its brands in favor of imports?
4. Is this a one-time deal or could there be a long-term arrangement for such an international sourcing activity?
5. Is the country of origin favored by our customers?
6. Can the product be delivered on time and in desirable quantities?
7. Does the important product line fit into the retailer's overall product mix and the image it is projecting?

Two of these seven need special explanation. First, country of origin is a critical concept in terms of consumers' acceptance or rejection of the product. If the product is made in Japan and the consumer has had good experiences with other Japanese products, the particular product in question will be highly desirable. Second, the attractiveness of available foreign products is very important. If this product is not available on a regular basis, then would it hurt the store's overall appeal to whet its customers' appetite by offering a one-time good deal? It stands to reason that having a mutually beneficial international sourcing contract is a worthwhile pursuit for the retailer.

SUMMARY

This chapter deals with a critical topic, merchandise mix management. This means proper planning, effective buying, and careful control. The chapter posits that buying is the other lifeblood of retailing. Merchandise management basically has four key objectives: (1) providing a highly desirable merchandise mix, (2) adjusting the mix to changing consumer needs, (3) preplanning merchandise mix, and (4) developing an effective buying plan. Five specific merchandise policies are examined in the chapter: (1) deep and narrow assortment, (2) deep and wide assortment, (3) shallow and narrow assortment, (4) shallow and wide assortment, and (5) consistent and flexible assortment.

In the preplanning process, some of the advances in information systems, such as EDI and bar-coding, are used for better planning and vendor-fulfilled inventory replenishment. Efficient customer response, the merchandise planning process, and merchandise mix adjustment can all benefit from modern information systems.

Store buyers play an important role in the merchandise mix development process. Buyers' motivation must be understood. Seven factors are identified in the chapter as buyer motivators: (1) adequate training, (2) high morale, (3) reasonable remuneration, (4) interaction with management, (5) positive feedback, (6) playing a part in the results, and (7) good information.

In planning the merchandise mix, a five-step process is presented: (1) selection of control units, (2) sales forecasts, (3) inventory control, (4) reduction planning, and (5) planning purchases. Two types of merchandise controls, financial (or dollar) and unit, are identified.

In the merchandise mix management and control areas, the role of brands must be well understood. The retailer can use product or brand image as a key force to establish a competitive advantage, or it may use the store image for the same purpose. The ideal situation is to use both simultaneously.

Finally, the retailer must know if the customers are aware or unaware of its products. If customers are aware, do they like, are they neutral to, or do they dislike the products (evoked, inert, and inept)? The retailer ideally would like to see all of its brands be included in the evoked set.

Exhibits

Exhibit 14.1
Key Consumer Trends

Consumer Preferences	Retailing Consequences
Personal appearance and self-consciousness	Retailers are providing more grooming and apparel lines and services.
More casual	Retailers must carry more casual products in apparel lines, lounging furniture, etc.
Health care	Retailers are carrying more sports and exercise-related products and equipment. They also carry more health foods and food supplements.
Leisure orientation	More emphasis on leisure-related products, such as videos, CDs, and computer games.
Time consciousness	Retailers are forced to carry more efficient products, such as power tools, and more powerful computers.
More home improvement	More retailers are providing home improvement supplies along with advice for repair and decoration.

Source: Adapted and revised from Samli (1989).

Exhibit 14.2
Merchandise Preplanning

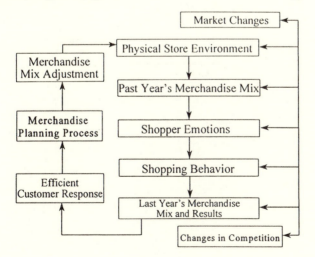

Exhibit 14.3
Blending Merchandise Mix Features with Store Buyers' Behavior

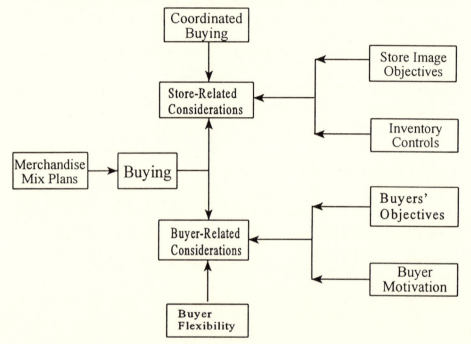

Exhibit 14.4
Critical Factors in Buyer Motivation

Factor	Description	Impact
Adequate Training	Providing buyers with necessary skills, such as communication and negotiation.	Optimizing buying process by establishing important relationships.
High Morale	Making sure that buyers have high morale by balancing work life and private life. Positive work conditions are critical.	Encouraging a proactive and positive approach to buying.
Reasonable Remuneration	A reasonable income with bonuses and additional incentives. Knowing that the company is supporting the buyer.	Providing a "worry-free" atmosphere to encourage more concentration on the work in hand.
Interaction with Management	Good working relationships with immediate supervisor and with other buyers. Good communication with store management.	Creating good communication.
Positive Feedback	The manager's, other buyers', and salespeople's careful approach to making changes or providing praise.	Giving stimulus to work harder and to do a better job.
Playing a Part in the Results	Working with department manager to give input into the development of the department's merchandise mix.	Higher level of involvement in both buying and selling.
Good Information	Information for buyers as to the department's market performance. Movement of the merchandise purchased.	More scientific information for better buying.

Source: Adapted and revised from Samli (1989).

Exhibit 14.5
Buyer's Relationship to the Store

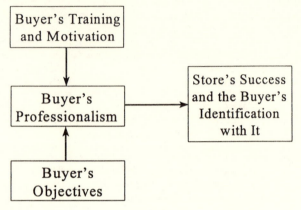

Exhibit 14.6
Implementation of Retail Objectives and the Role of Merchandise Mix

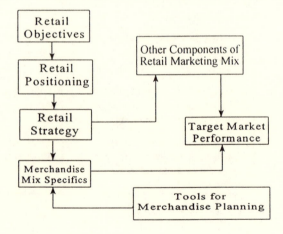

Exhibit 14.7
An Example of Merchandise Planning for a Clothing Store

Key Selected Product Lines	Five Years' Average Sales Quarterly	Average Increase or Decrease (%)	Expected Growth in the Local Economy	Final Numbers Based on Additional Subjective Adjustments
Suits	60,000	3.0	62,400	61,500
Shoes	10,000	7.0	10,400	10,550
Slacks	20,000	-4.0	20,800	20,000
Sports Shirts	35,000	8.0	36,400	32,800
Sweaters	8,000	-2.0	8,300	8,160
Sports Coats	50,000	5.0	52,000	52,500

Note: Estimates are based on 8-percent growth projections in the firm's trading area. Adjustments are made on the basis of the firm's own experiences.

Exhibit 14.8
Interaction between Product Image and Store Image

Product Image Pull

	High	Low
High	Ideal conditions, store image and product image are reinforcing each other.	Store image is playing the key role.
Low	Product image is playing the critical role in promoting the store.	Facing disaster. This situation needs to be avoided.

Store Image Pull

Exhibit 14.9
Alternatives in Brand Performance

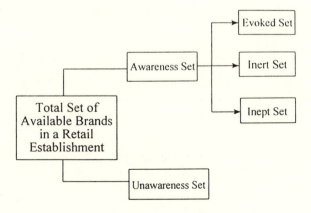

References

Babin, Barry J., and William R. Darden. 1995. "Consumer Self-Regulation in a Retail Environment." *Journal of Retailing* (Spring): 47–70.

Berman, Barry, and Joel R. Evans. 1995. *Retail Management*. Englewood Cliffs, N.J.: Prentice Hall.

Darlymple, Douglas J., and Donald L. Thompson. 1969. *Retailing: An Economic View*. New York: Free Press.

Departmental and Specialty Store Merchandising and Operating Results. Annual. New York: National Retail Merchants Association.

Gist, Ronald R. 1968. *Retailing: Concepts and Decision Making*. New York: John Wiley and Sons.

Golden, Lawrence, and Donald A. Zimmerman. 1980. *Effective Retailing*. Skokie, Ill.: Rand McNally.

Hartley, Robert F. 1975. *Retailing: Challenge and Opportunity*. Boston: Houghton Mifflin.

Kotler, Philip. 1994. *Marketing Management: Analysis, Planning and Control*. 5th ed. Englewood Cliffs, N.J.: Prentice Hall.

Levine, Joshua. 1995. "Wilted Flowers." *Forbes*, 10 April, 94.

Lusch, Robert F. 1982. *Management of Retail Enterprises*. Boston: Kent.

Margolies, Jeffrey M. 1995. "Best Practices in Retailing: The Grocery Industry and ECR." *Chain Store Age Executive with Shopping Center Age* (November): 92–94.

Markin, Rom J., Jr. 1971. *Retailing Management*. New York: Macmillan.

Mason, J. Barry, Morris L. Mayer, and Judy Wilkinson. 1993. *Modern Retailing: Theory and Practice*. Plains, Tex.: Business Publications.

May, Elenor G. 1974–1975. "Practical Applications of Recent Retail Image Research." *Journal of Retailing* (Winter): 15–20.

McCune, Jenny C. 1994. "In the Shadow of Wal-Mart." *Management Review* (December): 10–16.

McGinnis, Michael A., Myron Gable, and R. Burt Madden. 1984. "Improving the Profitability of Retail Merchandising Decisions-Revisited." *Journal of the Academy of Marketing Science* (Spring): 49–57.

Narayana, Chem L., and Rom J. Markin, Jr. 1975. "Consumer Behavior and Product Performance: An Alternative Conceptualization." *Journal of Marketing* (October).

Rothman, Marion Burk. 1980. "EAS for AII." *Stores* (June): 31.

Samli, A. Coskun. 1989. *Retail Marketing Strategies*. Westport, Conn.: Quorum Books.

Samli, A. Coskun, Glen Riecken, and Carolyn W. Salmon. 1978. "Narayana–Markin Consumer Behavior and Product Performance Model: A New Dimension." In *Developments in Marketing Science*. Miami: Academy of Marketing Science.

Staple Stock Replenishment. 1970. Dayton, Ohio: National Cash Register.

Staples, William A., and Robert Suerdlow. 1978. "Planning and Budgeting for Effective Retail Merchandise Management." *Journal of Small Business* (January): 1–6.

Sweeney, Daniel J. 1973. "Improving the Profitability of Retailing Merchandising Decisions." *Journal of Marketing* (January): 60–68.

Wilson, Marianne. 1994. "The Magic of Brand Identity." *Chain Store Age Executive with Shopping Center Age* (February): 66.

Wingate, John W., Elmer O. Schaller, and F. Leonard Miller. 1976. *Retail Merchandise Management.* Englewood Cliffs, N.J.: Prentice Hall.

"WSRG Seeks Unbiased View from IBM Consulting Group." 1995. *Chain Store Age Executive with Shopping Center Age* (September): 14C–16C.

Chapter 15

Pricing Strategies for Retailers

Retail pricing should be studied at two separate levels. Even though pricing at the retail level is an important area of consideration to begin with, the role pricing plays in retail marketing strategy is particularly critical. Retailers often shy away from detailed pricing decisions. Instead, they adopt a simplistic orientation to establishing prices. Perhaps the most critical consideration in this context is that pricing is quite often not utilized as a critical tool in developing an overall retail marketing strategy. Much of the time prices are used in a neutral sense. They are established on the basis of a cost-plus or manufacturer's suggestion. Even though the retailer may not be using pricing as an active element of the overall strategy, it still plays a de facto active role. This is due to the overall price consciousness of the market and the prevailing keen competition. Consumers often patronize stores on the basis of price levels that these stores project (Cox and Cox 1990).

Basically, there are internal and external factors influencing a retailer's pricing decisions. If the price is to be an active strategic element, then the retailer must know these internal and external factors. It is not clear which set of factors is more important in the store's pricing decisions.

FACTORS INFLUENCING PRICES INTERNALLY

There are three groups of internal factors: (1) price objectives, (2) strategic alternatives, and (3) goal-related pricing decisions (Samli 1989).

Price Objectives

Even though pricing is a powerful tool for the retail establishment to fulfill its objectives, much of the time this tool is not used properly by retailers. The use of pricing, at least partially, is determined by the firm's pricing objectives. The retail establishment can use price to achieve at least five different objectives: (1) a specified sales volume, (2) a certain amount of profit, (3) a specific return on investment, (4) an improved cash flow, and (5) projecting a carefully planned image.

Unfortunately, most retailers do not understand pricing and, as a result, they prefer to use some mechanical orientation toward establishing their prices. They do not see pricing as part of their overall marketing strategy. Instead, they prefer to assign pricing a neutral role by following, typically, the manufacturer's suggested price or by adding a certain markup to the cost of the product. Whether the retailer recognizes it, pricing plays an extremely important role in the retailer's success or failure, and should be an active tool in the retailer's marketing strategy (Dickinson 1993).

EXTERNAL RETAILING FACTORS

It is critical for a retailer to understand certain factors prevailing in the marketplace that influence pricing decisions. Among these are demand, price elasticity, the nature and level of competition, and price-perceived quality (Samli 1989).

Demand

Demand for a retail store is the number of customers who are willing and able to patronize that store and buy the products it is selling. This is the potential, but if this potential is not actualizing in terms of sales, the retail store is not likely to survive. However, where there is potential, there is the possibility of developing effective retail marketing strategies. To a substantial extent, the retailer's pricing strategy plays a very critical role. If all other mixes are effective and kept constant and the retail store utilizes an effective pricing mix, then it will sell more. The effective pricing mix, however, needs to be explored carefully.

As has been discussed throughout this book, markets are not homogeneous, and the retail establishment simply does not have only one perfectly identifiable target market. Thus, in considering its total demand, the retail store must take a segmentation approach in its pricing mix. In this overall effort, price must complement and not compete with other communications from the firm to these target markets (Dickinson 1993). The demand for the firm is the sum total of the estimated demands of the segments that the store is considering within the constraints of its total market. This demand can be depicted as follows:

$$Q_t = nqp$$

Where

Q = total market potential

n = number of customers

q = quantity purchased by an average customer

p = price of an average unit(s) (Kotler 1994)

However, here Q_t equals $Q_t = Q_1 + Q_2 + Q_3 \ldots Q_n$, which depicts the purchases in each market segment. By examining the formula, it is easy to see that

$$Q_t = n_1 q_1 p_1 + n_2 q_2 p_2 + n_3 q_3 p_3 \ldots n_Q q_Q p_Q$$

Price levels in different segments are likely to vary. Thus, the retail establishment, as it appeals to different segments with different products, uses different price levels. More critically, if the store is appealing to somewhat different segments with the same groups of products, then it will carry variations of the product mix so that it can provide adequate price mixes for different market segments. It must be reiterated that the retail store cannot have split images, such as being an upscale store for the well off and a bargain place for lower-income customers. Trying to appeal a number of market segments cannot be an exercise of extremes.

If, for instance, Neiman-Marcus, an upscale department store, establishes its target customers as high-income households and appeals to them with certain high prices in conventional household items, it may also have somewhat high prices for fashion items. While it is keeping an image of being an upscale store, it may have slightly different price levels for these segments based on factors other than high-income households, but overall prices will be on the higher side. A category killer such as Wal-Mart, on the other hand, will have overall prices on the lower side, but it will also look at different segments, as discussed earlier, and have somewhat different price levels for these different segments.

Price Elasticity

Price elasticity is not usually understood or practiced by the retailer. Similarly, it is rarely advocated by marketing academics as an important pricing tool. This general problem stems from the fact that elasticity is a difficult concept to measure or to calculate (Bolton 1989).

Price elasticity, as a concept, indicates the consumer's reaction to price changes. It can be defined as the percentage change in the quantity demanded that is attributable to a 1-percent change in price. If the quantity demanded is greater than 1 percent, then the demand is elastic; if the quantity demanded is smaller than 1 percent, then the demand is inelastic.

From a retailing perspective, elasticity is an important indicator of the store's competitive advantage or its monopoly power. If the store raises its prices and this situation yields a less-than-proportionate decrease in quantities sold, then the store has a relatively inelastic demand. In other words, it has a substantial degree of monopoly power. This is particularly true for certain upscale stores that enjoy especially powerful and positive images. Though they cannot completely ignore prices, they do not have to be engaged in all-out price competition. They can do well by using nonprice competition. Certainly, in this case, a local second-time-around apparel store cannot behave as if it is Saks Fifth Avenue. In essence, it is dangerous for any store to be engaged in nonprice competition without measuring the demand elasticity it is experiencing. Since measuring elasticity per se is rather difficult, the retail establishment can approximate its demand elasticity by using certain criteria.

Measurement of elasticity typically calls for experiments (Berman and Evans 1995; Samli 1989) such as the utilization of complicated econometrics analyses, and approximating the demand elasticity by a number of easy-to-assess variables. There are at least six variables identified: (1) competition, (2) ease of want satisfaction, (3) importance of the product, (4) urgency of need, (5) economic conditions, and (6) impact of total price.

Competition

Competition, directly as well as indirectly, plays a critical role in the retail establishment's price elasticity and, hence, its pricing decisions. Regardless of its name and its market strength, the retail establishment must pay attention to competition. Competition comes in two different forms, actual and potential. The retailer, first and foremost, has to price to compete with the existing competition. However, the retailer must also use preemptive pricing by making it less attractive for future competition to enter.

If the retail establishment is considered similar to other establishments, then it is obvious that if its prices are raised, its customers will go to these competing stores. Thus, its demand is price elastic. It is necessary for retailers to conduct regular comparative pricing research.

By doing so, they manage to keep themselves within the limits of price ranges that competitors are charging.

With regard to potential competition, the retailer should always be on the lookout for the entry of prospective competitors. If conditions are suitable for prospective competitors to enter and if the retail store is charging exorbitant prices because of its monopoly position, it is reasonable to assume that it is attracting competition. Thus, the retail establishment has the option of making much money in the short run and facing stiff competition in the long run, or lowering its prices and reducing its profits in the short run so that it will be difficult for competitors to enter the market in the long run. This is perhaps one of the reasons why 7-11 stores did not make it and were sold to local chains in different regions. They were capitalizing on their convenient locations and charging very high prices. They relied on the assumption that competition would not get keener, and their demand was relatively inelastic.

Ease of Want Satisfaction

Most of the products sold in a hardware store or in a grocery store are such that buying multiple units has no specific value. Consumers would not buy two or three garden hoses because they are on sale or multiple containers of salt, for example. There is no need for such purchases, since one container of salt or one garden hose is enough. It is easy to satisfy consumers' wants regarding these products. Therefore, their demand is not elastic. A significant decrease in price would not create a more-than-proportionate increase in quantity demanded. Many products are in this category; price reductions are not likely to increase amounts purchased by individual consumers.

Importance of Products

In many towns or cities there are two or three key upscale specialty stores. They set fashions and appeal primarily to local "innovators," who are the first to accept the new fashions (Mills 1985; Samli 1989). The orientation of local customers to these stores and/or to their products is that they have no substitutes. In such cases, demand for these products and for the stores is inelastic. Of course, these stores have to be reasonable and not price themselves out of the market. If they go beyond the reasonable point by raising their prices too high, their price inelasticity diminishes and the store loses its competitive advantage. In the meantime, however, the dependency on insulin for a diabetic person makes this product very important and, hence, its demand is relatively inelastic.

Urgency of Need

For whatever reason, if consumers need a product urgently, they are willing to pay the price. This situation creates a relative inelasticity in the demand. If there is a party in progress and the host or hostess realizes that they have less-than-adequate supplies or deficient variety, then one of them is likely to go to the nearest convenience store and buy whatever is lacking. In such cases, the price is not a factor, but the urgency of the need is. The host or the hostess will not question paying 50-percent more for the party supplies that they need at that particular time. The same principle applies to the convenience stores in hotels or airports. People buying things in these establishments do have a strong need, or at least a strong desire, for these products. Price in such cases, again, will not make a major difference. It is clear that if consumers feel strongly about buying a product or a service because of their perception of the urgency of their need for this product or the service, then the demand can be considered relatively inelastic.

Economic Conditions

Under adverse economic conditions, demand behaves as if it has a kink. If there is a recession in progress, demand will be somewhat elastic upward. If retailers increase their prices, they will experience a more-than-proportionate decrease in their volume. This is so because consumers become more careful with their money in recessions.

Demand, however, considered on the basis of downward influences, is relatively inelastic. If, for instance, a person during a recessionary period needs to buy a suit, he is likely to look for a suit that is priced low. However, this does not mean that if during that period the prices are reduced to half that person will buy two suits. Thus, the demand is relatively elastic if the prices are revised and is relatively inelastic if the prices are lowered.

Impact of Total Price

The price level can play a very important role. If, for instance, the prices of a store in general or the prices of its key product groups go up, its customers (despite their previous loyalty to that store or those product groups) may start looking for substitutes. Hence, at a certain price level demand becomes relatively price elastic. Ensure, a popular food supplement among older consumers, kept on raising its prices. Suddenly, some half a dozen or more powerful competitors appeared on the market. Thus, at a certain price level, Ensure's demand became relatively elastic.

The last two conditions used to approximate demand elasticity indicate the existence of certain price levels. The retailer must consider price levels as one of the strategic options. This point is discussed later on in this chapter.

Exhibit 15.1 illustrates how these six factors for approximating demand elasticities must be used in terms of whether prices should remain low or be raised. As can be seen, if the starting point is below the market, all of the factors in the first half of the exhibit indicate that the prices can be raised. If, however, they are above the market to begin with, then it may not be wise to raise them further. At the other end of the spectrum, the bottom half of the exhibit indicates that, given a certain feature of the six factors, it may not be wise at all to raise the prices, even if the starting point is below the market. If, however, they are at the market level to begin with, they may be raised.

Price-Perceived Quality

In American markets, perhaps more than anywhere in the world, there is a perceived connection between the price and the quality. This indicates that consumers do not always see the price as a sacrifice. Experiences of consumers in Houston, Texas, may be cited as examples. Stores such as Randall's Flagship, Rice Epicurean Market, and Fiesta Mart have put more emphasis on quality, service, variety, and atmosphere than the price per se ("Price Competition Threatens Houston's Upscale Grocers" 1995). The customers of these establishments expect super service and quality. Hence, they put more emphasis on quality than price. However, this situation also indicates that in their minds they associate quality with somewhat higher prices. A similar tendency to associate price and quality appears when consumers do not have any other information beside the price. It is critical to determine if this relationship between the price and quality is applicable to retail stores as well as certain products.

Price-perceived quality, according to Samli (1989), is effective within the constraints of price thresholds. He advocates that consumers do not think of simply one price but a range they will be willing to pay for the product or service in question. They exhibit varying degrees of responsiveness to price changes and price levels. According to the Weber–Fechner law, if some lower price thresholds are established below the actual low prices, consumers may perceive a low value and may think that the product is an undesirable purchase (Uhl 1979). In such cases, consumers will opt for higher prices if the perceived value and the overall evaluation of the retail store are consistent. In other words, if the consumer needs to buy a certain convenience good, for example, canned corn, in a convenience store such as a supermarket, the consumer is not likely to attach much value to it, especially if the product is priced even less than what the consumer had in mind as the price he or she was willing to pay. However, another convenience product line, such as men's underwear, can be privately branded and sold at Saks Fifth Avenue. In this case the convenience good develops a special value which is price- and store-perceived quality. Thus, if price-perceived quality is reinforced by the retail store's reputation, then higher price thresholds are likely to be established above the actual relatively high prices. The consumers may perceive a high value and may think of the product as a very desirable item to purchase. Certain specialty stores carrying a variety of specialty goods, such as expensive jewelry or appliances, may gain price-perceived value through price-perceived quality and store-perceived quality combined. Increased perceived value should increase the desirability of such products in the eyes of consumers.

DEVELOPING RETAIL PRICING STRATEGIES

Exhibit 15.2 illustrates a four-step orientation to establishing price strategies for retailers. These steps are related to (1) establishing retail objectives, (2) establishing pricing goals, (3) identifying pricing alternatives, and (4) connecting pricing alternatives in a store's pricing goals.

A firm has certain objectives. Of course, making money can be considered the first and most common objective; however, in the marketplace, making money is the *reward* which comes after fulfilling other objectives. The objectives of a retailer will be along the lines of goals that it will try to attain, both in the short run and the long run. These objectives provide a direction for pricing as well as overall strategic management of the retail establishment. Objectives can be related to sales, market share, profit, target market satisfaction, or positioning (Berman and Evans 1995).

If sales volume is a major objective and the retail establishment wants to increase its sales volume, then its prices are likely to be lower (assuming high price elasticity). If the market share is added onto the sales volume, then additional considerations regarding the prices (along with other elements of the four retail mixes) must be taken into account. Just what would it take to increase the store's market share by 5 or 10 percent?

Profit or expectations regarding return on investment also play a direct or indirect role in a store's prices. In the short run, to create cash flow, there may be a number of loss leaders. This is a direct impact. However, at the same time, some of the items may be marketed higher to generate greater profit. In the long run, overall price level may be increased so that a higher return on investment can be achieved. This is more of an indirect impact.

Target-market satisfaction can be related to any and all of these factors and more. If target markets are identified and served well, the store will benefit in the long run. Certainly, such an orientation has an impact on the store's prices.

Pricing Goals

As stated earlier, retail objectives have a significant impact on pricing goals. If the retail objectives are opposite to pricing goals, it will be difficult to manage the store effectively. Pricing goals need to be established to decide whether the store will use price aggressively, as a strategic tool, or passively, and not as a weapon to create competitive advantage for the retailer. Finally, pricing can be neutral by being neither passive or aggressive. In this case, price is established almost independently of competition (Dickinson 1993). Within these pricing constraints, there may be at least four pricing goals: (1) achieving a certain sales volume, (2) receiving a certain specified amount of profit in dollar terms, (3) establishing expectations regarding return on investment, and (4) generating early cash flow. In all of these and possibly many other alternatives, it is critical to determine how and in what way price is going to play a role. Of course, in almost all of these cases, price can be passive, aggressive, or neutral.

Exhibit 15.3 illustrates these goals and related pricing practices. There are a number of pricing practices in each of the goal alternatives. Each is briefly described. More detailed discussion of these is not within the scope of this book, but most basic retailing books cover these. It is critical, however, to realize that these goals are connected to pricing strategies (Exhibit 15.2).

Pricing Strategy Alternatives

Earlier in this book some of the key strategic options for retail stores were identified. Though pricing has its own strategic alternatives, it must be kept in mind that without proper pricing, the retail store cannot possibly implement its overall strategy. For instance, assume that the retail store is exercising a segmentation strategy. Its prices must reflect the strategic preference that it is trying to implement. If, for example, Wal-Mart caters to the lower middle class, it is using aggressive pricing (Exhibit 15.3). For its particular market, Wal-Mart may assume that price-perceived quality is not quite relevant. However, Bloomingdale's and Neiman-Marcus will position themselves in upper-upper or lower-upper market segments. They will use a passive pricing goal and practice it by skimming and blind item pricing. They will have to assume that price-perceived quality is very pertinent in their specific segments.

Connecting Goals and Strategies

Category killers such as Toys 'R Us or Wal-Mart use a cost-driven strategy which is based on basic economic principles. If the retail prices are lower with given relatively elastic demand, more units are sold. If "more units are sold" implies driving costs down, then prices can be lowered even further so that sales go up even more. Such cost-driven strategy uses aggressive pricing and keeps prices below the market.

Thus, pricing strategies are related to market level. Another group of pricing strategies is related to price leadership. Pricing strategies that are related to market level imply being above, at, or below the market level. Most big names in retailing, such as Neiman-Marcus, Bloomingdale's, Saks Fifth Avenue, and the like, at least partially practice above-the-market pricing. In these cases, the store's image is so highly regarded and accepted that their customers feel they are receiving something more than just the merchandise. They are not simply buying a necktie, they are buying the Neiman-Marcus image. They are buying status and belongingness. In such cases, within reason, the store is enjoying a high degree of customer loyalty, which translates into inelastic demand. Bloomingdale's, for instance, over the years has tried to appeal to a small group composed of those who enjoy big spending in a discriminating world of fashion and who want an ego trip in the process (Cohen and Jones 1978).

The middle-class general merchandise stores such as Sears, Montgomery Ward, and Tholheimers typically keep prices either passive or neutral. They opt for meeting the competition in their pricing decisions. Their position is often exercised by pointing out that they offer strong price–value relationships as opposed to very high brand–price relationships, trying to capitalize on price-perceived quality.

In trying to enhance their strong price–value relationships, many department stores advertise price-product-sale combinations. Though they may have somewhat different orientation for unadvertised products, they signal their price–value relationships for the whole store through their advertised price-product-sale combinations (Simester 1995). Both Montgomery Ward and Sears are middle-of-the-road retailers. Though they try to differentiate against each other, they primarily position themselves below very high-priced, prestigious name brands and upscale stores (Samli 1989; Cohen and Jones 1978).

It is obvious that aggressive pricing in conjunction with below-the-market strategy is used by discount stores and category killers. Wal-Mart, Toys 'R Us, or K-Mart, as well as many discounters, are category killers. The emphasis is on price competition, with few or no frills regarding customer services and other types of service and promotional activity. They do not promote their own labels or brands. Instead, they emphasize the classical supermarket principle of cash and carry (Britten 1978, 1982; Samli 1989).

Exhibit 15.4 illustrates an analysis of price-level strategies as they relate to different retail mix variables. Eleven variables are considered in the exhibit. They are grouped into four major categories: (1) merchandise, (2) service, (3) store atmospherics, and (4) general strategy.

Whereas pricing below the market is applicable to deep and wide best-selling assortments, lines that are still deep and wide but not necessarily only the best selling, are used by general merchandisers, particularly department stores that aim at meeting market prices. Finally, narrow and deep assortments are used by upscale specialty stores that price above the market. The other merchandise-related items in Exhibit 15.4 are self-explanatory.

In the service area, pricing below the market calls for no frills and almost no service. On the other end of the spectrum, pricing above the market implies that customers expect a variety of high-quality service.

Pricing below the market implies a bad location and a very modest internal layout. Again, on the other end of the spectrum, very elaborate and attractive atmospherics are expected.

While discount mass merchandisers are aiming prices below the market, department store type mass merchandisers aim at meeting market prices. Pricing above the market indicates segmenting or niche marketing to exclusive, above-average and relatively small consumer groups.

If the retailer has some degree of leadership in the marketplace, then the store can exercise the option of having variable markups. If the retail store pursues a general merchandising strategy, it tries to appeal to multiple segments differently. This implies a rather flexible pricing policy along with varying merchandising mixes. For example, supermarket retailers, in order to cut their prices further, have been trying to penetrate nonfood items, particularly in the health and beauty categories (Tilton 1992). Price flexibility implies flexible and varying markups. Flexible markups mean that the store has numerous special sales during which all of its markups are adjusted. This concept, primarily in Third World countries, implies haggling. Varying markup, on the other hand, means using different markups for different products as well as different product lines, as mentioned earlier in reference to grocery retailing. The basic principle here is to employ low markup for fast-moving merchandise and high markup for slow-moving merchandise. Though slow-moving products may be subjected to high markups, quite often these may come down during a special event, such as an annual after-Christmas sale. Since variable markup practices enable the firm to appeal to different markets more effectively, this practice actually gives the retail establishment some degree of market leadership position (Samli 1989).

If, on the other hand, the retail establishment is primarily selling convenience as in the case of 7-11 stores, Gate Stores in North Florida, and the like, then it may use a single markup policy uniformly for all of its products. Such stores bank on consumers' preference of convenience over prices in the purchase of small items.

TWO STRATEGIC TOOLS

Some retailing scholars have classified pricing practices as cost-driven pricing and demand-driven pricing (Berman and Evans 1995;

Dickinson 1993; Alpert 1971). However, many retailers find lowering costs rather difficult. Wal-Mart, for instance, did not want to increase gross margin per square foot; instead it increased sales at the same and sometimes even lowered gross margin ("The Profit Wedge" 1995). However, many retailers try to deemphasize cost-oriented pricing as the key force behind their marketing. During the past decade or so, almost all retailers have experienced a near doubling of costs. Only half of this is due to inflation; the other half represents a real increase in spending on a dollar-per-square-foot basis. This spending increase has been purposeful and is intended to increase the level of the retailer's competitive advantage ("The Profit Wedge" 1995). Because of very keen retailing competition and very changeable retailing markets and consumer behaviors, being excessively cost-price oriented becomes unrealistic. It can be a bit too costly and may not achieve the competitive edge the retailer is seeking. In some cases, it may even be the wrong focal point for competition. This is why purposeful spending to increase sales per square foot also has been a key alternative in the general orientation of pricing.

From a strategic perspective, it is most critical to think in terms of prices being raised or lowered. These two options relate to two important retailing tools that are used in the implementation of the pricing strategy, markups or markdowns. Of these two, it can be stated that markups are more demand and market oriented, and markdowns are more internal-cost oriented (Samli 1989). The reason for this is that price levels, almost invariably, face more consumer and competitive retaliation. Markdowns are more tactical and are used primarily to move slow-moving merchandise. Almost all textbooks include discussions dealing with the arithmetic of markups and markdowns (Berman and Evans 1995). However, it is posited here that understanding the strategic picture and how markups and markdowns fit into this picture is more critical. Therefore, the emphasis of our discussion is to conceptually explain these two phenomena.

Pricing and Product Categories

In Chapter 2 a discussion is presented relating to turnover and margins. Of course, in classical marketing, turnovers and margins are related to the conventional categorization of consumer goods, convenience, shopping, and specialty. It is generally known and accepted that convenience goods are priced by using low markups and counting on high turnover rates. Shopping goods have larger markups and lower turnover rates than convenience goods. Finally, specialty goods imply high markups and slow turnover rates. Of course, within each category, there are still faster and slower moving lines with relatively higher or lower markups.

The retailer must first know which products, which brands, and which groups of products are moving fast. Though some people advocate that slow-moving products should be advertised more heavily, this author believes that fast-moving products should be promoted more heavily. Contrary to the common way of thinking, their prices should not be raised, and more promotional support must be given to them rather than to those that are moving slowly. Well-advertised and low-priced fast-moving merchandise bring in the traffic so that slow-moving, more expensive products can be sold.

Markups

The margin between the cost and the retail price is a very critical consideration in terms of overall sales volume and profitability of the store. An effective markup policy provides the basis for successful pricing strategy. It is obvious from our discussion that the markup practices of the retailer must be based on external factors such as consumer demand, market conditions, and competition. However, general practice is such that many retailers look upon markups as an internal consideration and typically are quite arbitrary in establishing them.

Exhibit 15.5 illustrates that there are, in essence, three external factors that need to be considered: first, the total market potential; second, demand elasticity; and third, competitors' expected reaction. How big is the market and what will its long-range reaction be? Is the demand elastic so that raising the price could be dangerous? And finally, what would be the competitors' reaction? Would they retaliate by not raising their prices? Would it mean a loss rather than a gain for our store? Without having appropriate answers to these questions, raising prices by raising markups can be rather dangerous.

Exhibit 15.5 begins with a critical question: Is price critical in purchase decisions? A yes answer to this question implies that the demand is price elastic, and if the retailer does not realize this a raise in price will cause a significant decrease in the quantity. The situation may mean that the product has many substitutes or the economic conditions are adverse and people are more sensitive about prices and particularly price increases. Even though the demand is not highly price elastic, still a question must be raised regarding whether customers will reduce their purchase volume. Here the concern for a delayed reaction is particularly critical.

Though the price increase may not show any immediate repercussions, it may have a significant impact later on as the store's customers realize that there are other outlets for the same product that are charging less. At this point, the demand-elasticity factor can really be evaluated. If all the evidence in the market indicates a very elastic demand, the retail store must slowly go back to the original price. Of course, the proposed new price may bring the price of this product to the level of other retailers' prices. Here the question would be, "Just how good is this product in terms of a loss leader, or is it an important strategic business unit?" It is critical to decide if competitors would retaliate by perhaps cutting their prices and promoting this as a bargain. In the final analysis, the retailer must monitor the results of such price changes.

Markdowns

As stated earlier, unlike markups, markdowns are likely to be more internally oriented. Internal reasons may necessitate their use so that the retailer's internal merchandising problems can be solved. However, if they are used (or abused) extensively, they may cause serious problems for the store's image as it is perceived by its customers.

Markdowns are very commonplace in retailing. Almost all merchandise, if not sold within the desired period of time, may be marked down. Some merchandise may not sell at its original price and therefore have to be marked down. Exhibit 15.6 illustrates a logical flow process leading to markdowns. Obviously, markdowns are used for unsold items. First and foremost it is critical to explore why the merchandise is not moving fast or is not moving at all. From this perspective, markdowns or the need for them can be a retailing control factor (see Chapter 17). As can be seen, Exhibit 15.6 presents six reasons for the merchandise not selling. Though some scholars think that retailers use markdowns for mainly three reasons; (1) to remedy buying errors, (2) to compensate for changes in customer needs, and (3) to retaliate against competitors' actions (Rosenbloom 1981), there are other reasons as well. Many retailers have regular or occasional promotional events, such as anniversary sales, inventory reduction sales (after Christmas), end-of-season clearance sales, or pre-season sales, during which time markdowns become the focal point of the total exercise.

From this discussion, it is clear to see that markdowns can help to (1) move merchandise that is not moving fast enough, (2) attract more and new customers by offering special sales, (3) build customer loyalty among the group of customers who are attracted to special sales, (4) sell other merchandise that is not marked down, and (5) stimulate excitement about the store. As can be seen, markdowns should be an ongoing activity. As seen in Exhibit 15.6, perhaps the most important activity in markdown decisions is distinguishing the unsold items from those that are selling well and then being able to determine why these items or lines are not selling. Naturally, such scrutiny may point out some serious problems in buying or merchandising the products.

The options listed in Exhibit 15.6 must be related to the reasons why the products are not selling. If, for instance, customers totally dislike the product line, it may need to be discarded. In using markdowns, it is critical to decide how much of a price reduction must be made and for how long a period. There have been studies to establish the scope of markdown policy (Kingberg, Rao, and Shakun 1974). Since each individual consumer has a range of acceptable prices for a given product, it is critical to work within this range. Below it the individual may think that the product is inferior and above it the individual may think that it is very expensive (Gabor and Granger 1966; Monroe and Della Bitta 1978; Samli 1989). Either intuitively or by conducting research, the retailer must be able to approximate this range.

In both the case of markups and markdowns, Exhibits 15.5 and 15.6, respectively, indicate monitoring the results very closely. It must be understood that both markdowns and markups are managerial tools that must be used carefully and effectively. Determining the immediate impact of the markdown or markup actions has an implication for better use in the future.

Remedial Pricing under Critical Economic Conditions

If the sales volume is reduced and unused capacities are increasing, the retailer is in a devastatingly dangerous position. Unfortunately, the retailer may try to remedy the situation by raising its prices. This is what happened during the stagflation of the early 1980s. Unfortunately, the causes for the decline in sales volume were external, and raising prices made it even worse. In such cases the retailer must overcome the adversities of the market by expanding the business. This means the retailer does not reduce the promotional activity, does not lay off salespeople, and above all does not raise prices. By increasing the sales volume, it is possible to compensate for the loss of profit in each unit sold. Of course, in such hard times the retailer must consider modifying its merchandise mix. During stagflations or recessions, consumers' needs change and they become more frugal. In such times, cheaper or more economical products and different energy-efficient or cost-efficient product lines can be appropriate.

INTERNATIONAL CORNER

The U.S. retail market differs from its counterparts in other countries because of the intensity of competition and aggressively selective consumers ("Profound Societal Shifts Form Cadre of Powerful Value Retailers" 1995). This background has led some American retailers to operate successfully in overseas markets. Wal-Mart, K-Mart, Sears,

Kroger, and Dayton Hudson all have numerous overseas stores. However, because of price differentials, retailers from other countries are entering the U.S. markets from the lower end of the market. Payless ShoeSource displays a large variety of shoes made in China and priced economically. Also, in many department and discount stores there are many product lines that are produced in countries where labor costs are lower and, hence, the finished product can be priced substantially below American counterparts, such as shoes made in India and textiles produced in Hong Kong or Singapore. In such cases, the retailer must know the sources and coordinate their inflow with their marketing activities at home. This may mean special promotional activities featuring these products or making sure that they are on the store's never-out lists.

SUMMARY

This chapter emphasizes the role of pricing as a tool to implement an overall retail marketing strategy. However, pricing in itself has its own strategies as well.

After discussions on how to approximate demand elasticity for pricing, the chapter distinguishes retail objectives from pricing goals, and examines pricing strategies and implementation of retail pricing goals and strategies as they relate to each other. Pricing goals are identified as passive, aggressive, and neutral. Within this context, retail pricing strategies are discussed as pricing below the market, pricing at the market, and pricing above the market.

Finally, two critical pricing tools, markups and markdowns, are discussed. This discussion relates them to the overall pricing decision process and examines how they may play a critical role in the retail store's efforts to compete in the marketplace.

Exhibits

Exhibit 15.1
Conditions Impacting Price Levels

Condition	Below Market	Market	Above Market
High degree of competition	+	+	-
Wants are not satisfied easily	+	-	-
Product is not very important	+	+	-
Needs are not very urgent	+	+	-
Economic conditions are favorable	+	-	-
Total prices are too high	+	-	-
Competition is not so keen	-	+	+
Wants are satisfied easily	-	+	-
Product is very important	-	+	+
Needs are very urgent	-	+	+
Economic conditions are adverse	-	+	-
Total prices are quite reasonable	-	+	-

Source: Adapted and revised from Samli (1989).

Key: – implies prices should not be raised; + implies prices can, and perhaps should, be raised.

Exhibit 15.2
Retail Pricing Strategies

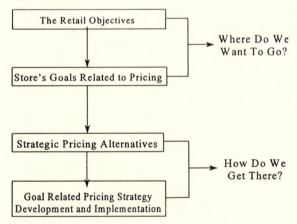

Exhibit 15.3
Pricing Practices Based on Goals

Pricing Goal	Practices	Meaning
Keeping prices passive	Differential pricing	Grouping merchandise into price categories
	Blind item pricing	Keeping a product unknown and unnoticed, and pricing it slightly higher
	Skimming	Charging high prices
	Copying competitors	Pricing the way competitors are pricing
Aggressive pricing	Experience-curve pricing	Market leader aggressive by lowering prices
	Meeting all prices	Not knowingly underpriced by competitors
	Price under competition	Being recognized as a low price store
	Knock-off pricing	Slightly different merchandise but much lower prices
Neutral pricing	Direct profitability	Maximizing the profit contribution of each item
	Cost plus - a fixed margin	Applying 40 percent to all products
	Cost plus- a variable margin	Pricing slow moving items with higher margins and fast moving items with lower margins

Source: Developed from Dickinson (1993).

Exhibit 15.4
Pricing at Different Market Levels

	STRATEGIC ALTERNATIVES		
Retail Mix Variables	**Pricing below the market**	**Pricing at the Market**	**Pricing above the market**
Merchandise:			
Product assortment	Concentration on best-selling product lines but deep and wide assortment	Deep and wide assortment	Narrow and deep assortment
Merchandise lines carried	Private labels, some name brands, closeouts	Strictly upscale name brands	Exclusively private brands, best name brands
Merchandise differentiation	Undifferentiated merchandise, mass-market appeal, almost exclusively price competition	Differentiated merchandise	Highly differentiated merchandise based on high-image apparel
Role of fashion in assortment	Fashion follower conservative	Concentration on accepted best-sellers	Fashion leader
Service:			
Personal service	Self-service, almost no sales people, limited information by store personnel, no special displays	Moderate assistance by salespeople	High level of assistance, extensive information, liberal exchange, large variety of adjustments, etc.

Special services	Cash and carry	Only at extra charge to customers	Included in price
Store Atmospherics:			
Location	Poor, inconvenient site	Close to competitors	Close to customers
Layout	Inexpensive fixtures, little or no carpeting, no paneling, merchandise racks	Moderate atmosphere, neutral or somewhat attractive	Very elaborate and attractive decor, many creative displays
Image	Store is known for its bargains and low prices	Store is known for its price quality combinations, a middle-class place	Store is known for its name and its exclusiveness
External appearance	Modest and unassuming	Reasonably nice	Very flashy
General Strategy:			
Key strategy emphasis	Mass merchandiser	Some mass merchandising; some differentiation	Segmenter and nicher

Source: Adapted and revised from Berman and Evans (1995) and Samli (1989).

343

Exhibit 15.5
A Decision Flowchart to Increase Markups

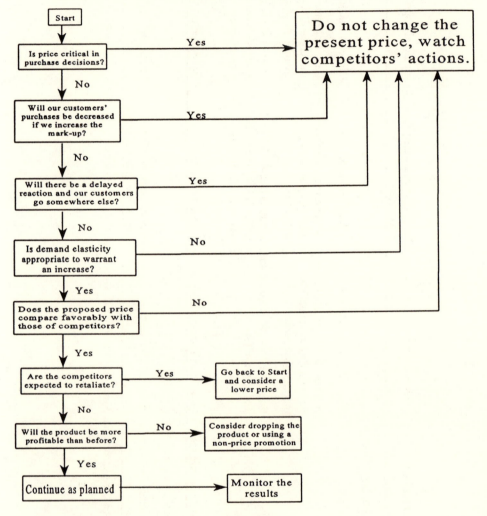

Source: Adapted and revised from Samli (1989).

Exhibit 15.6
A Decision Flowchart for Markdowns

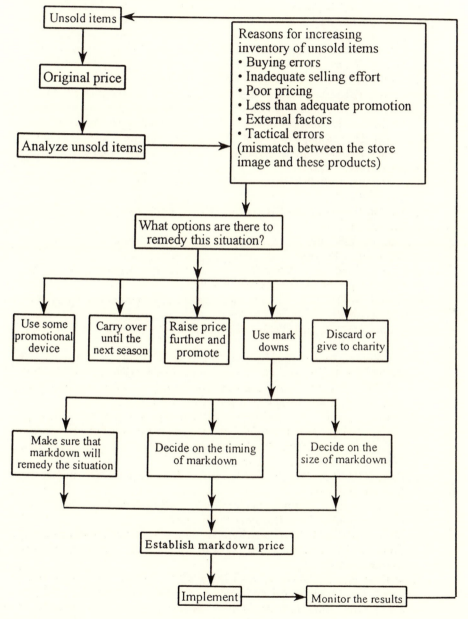

References

Alpert, Mark I. 1971. *Pricing Decision*. Glenview, Ill.: Scott, Foresman.

Berman, Barry, and Joel R. Evans. 1995. *Retail Management*. Englewood Cliffs, N.J.: Prentice Hall.

Bolton, Ruth N. 1989. "The Robustness of Retail-Level Price Elasticity Estimates." *Journal of Retailing* (Summer): 193–219.

Britten, Arthur B. 1978. "Off-Price Strategy." *Stores* (June): 46.

———. 1982. "Off-Price." *Stores* (March): 9–14.

Cohen, Arthur, and Ana Laid Jones. 1978. "Brand Marketing in the New Retail Environment." *Harvard Business Review* (September–October): 140–146.

Cox, Anthony D., and Dena Cox. 1990. "Competing on Price: The Role of Retail Price Advertisements in Shaping Store-Price Image." *Journal of Retailing* (Winter): 428–445.

Dickinson, Roger A. 1993. "Pricing at Retail." *Pricing Strategy and Practice* 1 (1): 24–35.

"44th Annual Report of the Grocery Industry." 1977. *Progressive Grocer* 56 (April): 23.

Gabor, Andre, and Clive Granger. 1966. "Price as an Indicator of Quality." *Economica* (February): 43–70.

Haberler, Gottfried. 1977. "The Problems of Stagflation." *AEI Studies of Contemporary Economic Problems*, 255–272.

Hawkins, Edward R. 1957. "Methods of Estimating Demand." *Journal of Marketing* (April).

Kent, B. Monroe. 1993. *Pricing: Making Profitable Decisions*. 2d ed. New York: McGraw-Hill.

Kingberg, Yoram, Ambar Rao, and Melvin Shakun. 1974. "A Mathematical Model for Price Promotions." *Management Science* (February): 948–959.

Kotler, Philip. 1994. *Marketing Management: Analysis, Planning and Control*. 5th ed.. Englewood Cliffs, N.J.: Prentice Hall.

Lunstrom, William J. 1986. "Supermarket Patronage in a Highly Priced Cognitive Market: Does Environment Influence Decision Factors." In *Retailing: Theory and Practice for the 21st Century*, ed. R. L. King. Miami: Academy of Marketing Science.

Lynn, R. A. 1967. *Price Policies and Marketing Management*. Homewood, Ill.: Richard D. Irwin.

Mason, J. Barry, and Morris L. Mayer. 1987. *Modern Retailing: Theory and Practice*. Plains, Tex.: Business Publications.

Mills, Michael K. 1985. "Strategic Retail Fashion Marketing Positioning: A Comparative Analysis." *Journal of the Academy of Marketing Science* (Summer): 212–225.

Monroe, Kent B., and Albert J. Della Bitta. 1978. "Models for Pricing Decision." *Journal of Marketing Research* (August): 413–428.

"Price Competition Threatens Houston's Upscale Grocers." 1995. *Chain Store Age Executive* (March): 49–50.

"The Profit Wedge: Key to Successful Retailing." 1995. *Chain Store Age Executive* (January): 46–59.

"Profound Societal Shifts Form Cadre of Powerful Value Retailers." 1995. *Chain Store Age Executive* (December): 11–13.

Ramon, Murry. 1980. "Survival at Your Fingertips." *Sales and Marketing Management* (June): 33–64.

Rosenbloom, Bert. 1981. *Retail Marketing.* New York: Random House.

Samli, A. Coskun. 1989. *Retail Marketing Strategies.* Westport, Conn.: Quorum Books.

Shama, Avraham. 1978. "Management and Consumers in an Era of Stagflation." *Journal of Marketing* (July): 43–52.

———. 1980. *Marketing in a Slow Growth Economy.* New York: Praeger.

Simester, Duncan. 1995. "Signalling Price Image Using Advertised Prices." *Marketing Science* (Spring): 166–188.

Tilton, Richard W. 1992. "Maintaining Competitive Edge." *Progressive Grocer* (May): 80.

Uhl, Joseph U. 1979. "Consumer Perception of Retail Food Price Changes." In *Pricing,* ed. Kent B. Monroe. New York: McGraw-Hill.

Weiss, E. B. 1975. "New Marketing Tactics Battle the Shortage of Liquid Capital." *Advertising Age* (September): 38–39.

Chapter 16

Retail Information Management Systems and the Emerging Information Technology

Throughout this book an attempt has been made to identify information needs of retailers and how that information is likely to be used in different aspects of their decision process. It has also been stated that retailing is perhaps the most dynamic sector in the American economy. The average life span of retail establishments was once estimated to be about five years. There is every reason to believe that this situation is likely to get worse. In addition, earlier studies have indicated that more than 30 percent of new retail establishments fail in the first six-month period (Samli 1993). Thus, survival in retailing, particularly in small-scale retailing, is a prime concern, but it is not and cannot be the only concern. Many retail establishments may survive at the periphery without making much money and without expanding. They simply survive marginally on a day-to-day basis. Thus, the retail establishment must first survive, but it must also grow and prosper beyond this marginal point of survival.

Today's retailer operates in an environment of turbulence (Samli 1993). This adverse environment makes survival and profitability goals very difficult to achieve without even thinking of growth. In general, retail failure percentages are getting higher. The emerging technological revolution, evolving socioeconomic trends in society, and newly forming or dramatically changing lifestyles are accelerating the unfriendliness factor in the retailer's immediate environment (Samli 1989; Berman and Evans 1995).

Since the retail establishment must survive, grow, and hopefully prosper, it is important to explore how these three goals can be met. In one sense, thus far, we have articulated how retail marketing strategies can be developed. These strategies enable the retailer to use its scarce resources in the best way to satisfy (indeed delight) its customers. In this whole process there are functional areas and planning areas where key decisions need to be made by a number of people in a retail environment. Successful strategy development and implementation is invariably based on an effective decision-making process. Such a process is composed of identifying goals, determining alternative ways of fulfilling these goals, deciding on the expected outcome of each alternative, evaluating the alternatives, and, finally, making a decision. Certainly, this decision-making process is equally necessary for both small and large retailers.

It is clear at this point that this decision process cannot take place and be successful unless there is adequate and appropriate information. Adequacy of information is related to quantity. After all, there are many retail decisions at different levels of management that call for a large number of information bits. If there is not an adequate information base, many of these decisions will be made arbitrarily, creating an unnecessary risk factor.

Appropriateness of information is related to quality. The available information must be such that it will facilitate certain decision areas. If the availability of appropriate information is unsatisfactory, then the retailer may be suffering from a data overload but, in essence, an information underload (Samli 1996). Hence, retail information must be carefully managed so that retail decisions can be facilitated.

The need for retailers to manage their information and how this should be accomplished are the topics of this chapter. It describes a concept called retail information management systems. The presence of such a system is essential in all phases and aspects of retailing. In order to understand RIMS, first of all we must recognize the information technology revolution in retailing.

TODAY'S EMERGING
INFORMATION TECHNOLOGIES

The following are some examples of information technologies:

- Rose's Stores opened a centralized return center. It will reduce the company's freight and handling costs by consolidating shipments of returns to vendors. Scanning Solutions, a facilities management company, is operating the facility. By simplifying store returns of merchandise through a sophisticated computer information flow system through scanning, the store's back rooms are kept clear and ready for other purposes (Fox 1993).

- Stride Rite Corp., the children's footwear giant that makes Keds and Sperry Topsiders, has used computerized order-taking technology to simplify shopping operations, improve its relationships with its customers, and improve the quality of data it collects from other retailers. The company has been using the electronic data internet with its trading partners (Gillin 1992).

- Women's Specialty Retailing Group (WSRG), a nationwide operator of some 1,350 women's specialty apparel stores, received help from IBM to develop a new information system. The system follows process merchandising planning. The participating stores are expected to use mainframes, midrange equipment, and personal computer local-area networks (LANs) to develop and use databases to share information to improve merchandising-related processes ("WSRG Seeks Unbiased View from IBM Consulting Group" 1995).

- Sheetz, a 165-convenience store chain in Altoona, Pennsylvania, has placed PC-based point-of-sale (POS) systems in some of its stores to develop scanning and item-level sales reporting.

- Saks Fifth Avenue implemented a quick response (QR) system based on information from POS terminals to facilitate replenishment and executive information systems ("Saks Beats the Odds Succeeds in QR Despite Hurdles" 1993).

- Virginia Specialty Stores, a 108-store chain catering to the apparel needs of large-size women, developed a Customer Profile System (CPS). It has increased the effectiveness of the company's promotional activities.

- While it was unique a while ago, database marketing has become a mainstream retail strategy. More retailers today than ever before understand that customer databases can be developed, organized, and used. This creates greater customer loyalty through more individualized customization based on targeted promotions using databases of consumers ("Database Marketing Goes Mainstream, Says Survey" 1995).

These examples indicate retail establishments' need, more than ever before, for an information system and the need to manage that system well. With the emerging technologies, it is obvious that not only are retail information management systems needed, but without the proper use of modern computer technologies, such RIMS cannot be managed adequately.

Using Information Technologies

From the examples given and existing literature, it is clear that very large retailers and major retail chains have been using revolutionary information technologies to their advantage. Some scholars claim that proper utilization of these technologies is making big retailers more powerful and, hence, is squeezing small retailers out of existence.

The following list presents a simple description of some of the emerging technologies and their possible impact on retailing ("Information Technology" 1995; *K-Mart Retail News Update* 1994; "Technology to Transform Retail" 1993):

- Neural networks, which utilize an artificial neuron to accept multiple inputs, make it possible for computers to actually "learn" through past experiences and thus identify appropriate actions when similar sets of circumstances or variables emerge in the future. They also route large-area networks by connecting them and developing a bridge. Thus, neural networks go beyond one store or one area and encompass large numbers of stores in multiple areas.

- Advanced expert systems allow a dialogue-driven program to be created so users can "consult" with experts in various fields through information previously entered into the computer system. They facilitate decision making by giving knowledgeable and sophisticated support.

- Advanced simulations are made possible through the use of high-power computers coupled with high-resolution graphics and digital-quality sound. These can graphically simulate different situations in two and even three dimensions. Three-dimensional simulations are what are now being referred to as "virtual reality."

- Digital imaging turns pictures, charts, graphics, and words into a digital form that can be read and manipulated through computers once they are scanned into the system.

- Digital interactive television will turn a television set into a delivery system for both products and services. Consumers will use a graphic interface to select what they want to view as well as to execute the purchase transaction. Direct broadcast satellites (DBS) will provide digital transmissions; this new generation of televisions will not only receive and display images, but will also process, store, create, and transmit information.

- Multimedia computers allow data, sound, graphics, and video to be integrated. These are being used to create interactive applications, such as informational kiosks and employee training systems. These can be particularly useful for retailers who need information in specific areas and in particular forms.

- Parallel processing refers to the ability to coordinate a large number of processors to simultaneously solve complex problems or manipulate large amounts of data.

- Object-oriented technologies are programming techniques and tools which build reusable components and pretested, graphic-based software codes. These speed development and customization of systems to specific user needs.

- Distributed computing actually refers to the distribution of application code and data across both the enterprise and multi-enterprise computer networks. These networks could be both wide-area networks (WANs) or local-area networks.

- Groupware and work-group computing are software applications which support the new organizational model for a company where an activity is carried out or a problem is solved by a team working across the computer network.

- Electronic data interchange networks share information on purchase patterns and purchase orders and are expected to expand into community-of-interest networks.

- Ethernet is a set of local-area network standards that allows networking information from different sources. This is a very significant source of information for retailers.

- Local-area networks link computers and peripheral devices in a limited area to share information and programs. These are particularly useful for regional chains that need to keep their member stores informed.

- Wide-area networks allow signals to be transmitted from a limited-area network to other LANs in distant locations. National chains may have special advantage in connecting their LANs.

- Decision support systems provide the ability of standardizing and processing a variety of data to facilitate decision making. These may be shared by LANs or by WANs to benefit individual units.

It becomes clear that these emerging technologies in a most general sense expand the retailer's capabilities to (1) improve the in-store performance by giving greater service, interaction, and excitement to shoppers in the store; (2) improve the methods and channels for delivering products and services to consumers; (3) improve the retailers' understanding of problems and enhance their capabilities to make better decisions; and (4) facilitate better communication and coordination within the store, within the retail complex, and within the supply chain ("Emerging Technology and Retailing" 1993).

The far-reaching impact of information technology cannot be totally explained by this list and the subsequent four points. It is, however, clear that emerging technologies can and will provide better information to retailers than what they are receiving today. Two key points need special attention: First, all retailers are not research oriented and, hence, even though they can have access to information, they are not inclined to use it (Samli 1996); second, most small retailers do not have access to information generated by emerging information technologies.

Traditionally, with the exception of some major chains and large department stores, retailers are not known for their research efforts. There are a number of reasons for this dilemma: (1) lack of appreciation of the need for research, (2) lack of know-how to undertake research, (3) deficient resources to engage in research, (4) intense involvement in day-to-day activities and, hence, lack of time to be involved in research, (5) inability to develop and implement research-driven decisions, and (6) misguided consideration that research is a luxury activity only for "fat cats." The techniques are also not quite developed for the retailer's use, and thus data collection and analyses are very complicated, particularly for the retailer (Lesser and Stearns 1986). On top of it all, the complexity of information technology makes research for retailers seem a very frightening undertaking, particularly for small retailers. However, because of the vulnerability created by internal deficiencies such as management skills or finances and because of excessive competition externally and adversities of the market, retailers must learn to make decisions based on information and, hence, they must develop an information system for their own use. Such a system will provide the necessary information base for routine, day-to-day decisions, certain tactical decisions, and, of course, strategic decisions as well. Without an information system behind their decisions, retailers will have an extremely difficult time making good decisions to enter the market, to survive, and to prosper.

Information Sources for Retailers

In essence, retail information is generated in two separate spheres: internal and external. Both of these information sources and information generated in both of these spheres are extremely critical. Quite often the retailer may pay attention to one or the other but, unfortunately, not always to both.

Retailers must have information systems that are simple and sensitive, particularly to changes in the local markets. This need for simplicity and sensitivity becomes greater for smaller retail establishments. It is clear that small retailers need a simple and functional RIMS, and along with simplicity goes cost. Small retailers cannot afford very costly RIMS. They simply do not have the means. This is a situation that gives large retailers an advantage over their small counterparts.

Internal sources of information are readily accessible, and internal information, therefore, is quite available and, particularly for small retailers, quite valuable. First, the sources provide a vital set of facts that are within the reach of the firm's decision makers. Second, the information can be easily gathered and manipulated for the needs of decision makers. Finally, this is the least costly way of gathering information to be used in the decision-making process (O'Brien 1970).

Internal Information

Typical internal information is related to sales, costs, and finances. Sales of different brands, products, and product groups indicate what the retailer should do in terms of promotion and sales increases. Costs of different products, transactions, and operations can indicate potential areas for cost cutting. Finances relating to bank accounts, interest, and credit may indicate how the money can be used for better results. Of course, individuals' performance and human resource utilization are particularly critical among internal data. Better utilization of internal talent can improve the store's overall performance in great proportions.

External Information

External information connects the retail establishment to the outside world. The larger the retail establishment, the more critical it is to be connected to the outside world. This connection is particularly important when the retail establishment has a large share of the market and competitive conditions or the economy is changing. If, for instance, the local economy is booming but the particular retail establishment's market share is declining (or remaining the same), the firm should be alarmed. There may be numerous reasons for this situation, but these reasons are not going to be explored unless the cause of the firm's unsatisfactory performance is identified.

Sources of external information are varied. Some sources and the information they disseminate are rather simple, but such simplicity does not mean the information is not important. The Department of Commerce may provide information about local population patterns, local income changes, and the local employment picture. If used properly, all of these can have great value for the retailer. However, some other sources and their information are rather complex. Information coming from LANs or WANs dealing with inventory controls, product reordering, or sales trends is complicated, costly, and more difficult to process. Electronic data interchange, for instance, is one of these outside sources connecting a whole network to facilitate business transactions. It has been suggested that EDI, instead of simply handling communication between retailers and their vendors, will handle communication linkages with many other interested parties, such as banks, government agencies, customers, and the like. Through such networks, information will be shared across the enterprise as well as the value chain.

Exhibit 16.1 illustrates one such network, without distinguishing internal and external sources but describing each information source and the type of information it is likely to impart. It must be reiterated that this is an information network of a group of interested parties and could not even have been imagined some ten years ago. It is quite likely that twenty-first-century retail establishments will compete in information gathering and using, in addition to conventional ways ("Emerging Technology and Retailing" 1993).

There have been many suggestions to expand retail external information sources and the types of information. Scholars have suggested that carefully developed external information systems based on shopping behavior must be constructed. They have further suggested that such an information base is essential to develop a desirable store image and manipulate it to position the store in a most desirable manner (Lesser and Stearns 1986; Pessemier 1980). With today's technological advances, developing information networks with such features is more plausible than ever before.

One additional dimension of Exhibit 16.1 is that a balanced RIMS of the type presented has a major international component, indicating product availability, electronic catalogs, and vendor product information throughout the world.

RIMS and Retail Decisions

RIMS is, in essence, a management information system (MIS) for retail establishments. Its vast and varied database can be used not only for the highest levels of decisions relating to planning, controls, risk, and opportunity assessment, but also for most routine and planned decisions at the lower levels of the retail establishment. Silverman's, for instance, a men's clothing-store chain, uses databases to help gift shoppers, track customer satisfaction, and target marketing efforts and, hence, has been revising its marketing strategies accordingly (Silverman 1995). Mrs. Fields, Inc., on the other hand, manages 650 cookie stores with the help of an innovative management information system called retail operations intelligence (ROI). The whole company is managed by a flat structure. ROI enables store managers to maintain daily contact with the company's top administrative staff. It automates information dissemination on various aspects of business, ranging from sales analysis to production planning, and allows store managers to concentrate on selling cookies (Schember 1990).

Exhibit 16.2 points out these two extremes. One may say that Silverman's decisions that are based on its RIMS are at the highest level of the triangle, whereas Mrs. Fields' decisions may be considered simple, routine, and dealing primarily with transactions.

The triangle in Exhibit 16.2 indicates that at the top only a few people or even just one person is making the most far-reaching decisions for the retail establishment. At the bottom, numerous people are making more routine decisions. Naturally, the characteristics and the format of RIMS would vary from one company to another. The critical point is that it must accommodate all of the decision levels indicated in Exhibit 16.2 and it must be the most suitable to the needs of the firm, regardless of how large or small it is and how complex or simple it may be.

Top-level, nonroutine, and more strategic decisions are based more on external information. For instance, understanding the changes in the local or national economy, knowing the changes in competition, and assessing the firm's market share are critical aspects in some strategic decisions.

Database Management

Exhibit 16.1 illustrates that a tremendous amount of information can be obtained by the retailer. This information can be put in the form of a database that needs to be managed carefully. In retailing, just as in any business or any decision-making situation, good decisions are based on good information which is derived from raw facts that are known as data (Rob and Coronel 1995; Samli 1996). Data are managed efficiently when they are stored in a database and information is extracted from this database when needed for the decision-making process. Exhibit 16.2 addresses this point. Nonprogrammed or nonroutine and far-reaching decisions are made on the basis of top management's policy and strategic planning by using primarily external data converted into information for decision making. In the lower level of the decision pyramid, most of the decisions are programmed, meaning that they are not strategic but primarily operational. In all cases, a database is necessary. Throughout this chapter, we have specified how retail information can and should be managed. However, it is extremely important to understand how these databases are generated and made available to retailers through modern computer technology.

With the technological advances in computers and database networking, it is possible for retailers to generate their own databases or to hook up with other databases for better management. It must be reiterated that RIMS are not only for large retailers who have vast resources to generate and use an information system, but for all retailers. Indeed, most small retailers need proper use of information for survival more than large firms do. In the 1980s, only a handful of cutting-edge corporations, such as Wal-Mart Stores, Inc. and Federal Express Corp., used networks to support novel business approaches. Today, getting wired to speed up internal processes and reach out to others electronically is not a luxury but an imperative. The modern retailer needs this networking for survival. Though there are many cost-saving aspects of networking, in retailing the key benefits are related to generating data and subsequently information for better decision making. For instance, Del Monte Corp. has been getting daily inventory reports electronically from grocers. If and when stocks fall to or below certain minimum levels, the Del Monte network immediately issues a restocking order. This way individual retailers can lower traditional inventories in favor of such a quick-response system.

It is obvious that the retail establishment needs a database, part of which is based on internal data and part on the external network. In Exhibits 16.1 and 16.3, the data that can be obtained through networks are identified. There are many other bits of information that need to be obtained through networks. If the company is part of a chain of retailers, it may be utilizing a set of local-area networks. Here, certain information is found regarding fast-moving merchandise, the impact of different prices on sales, acceptance of new models, or optimal merchandise mixes. Similar interaction among the units of the chain not only would enhance the performance of individual units, but would also help optimize the overall performance of the chain. Electronic data interchange, which is a series of standards that allows computer-to-computer exchange of information, is possibly one of the major alternatives to be used for this network activity. In fact, Exhibit 16.1 is the outcome of a futuristic version of EDI. For Merry Go Round Enterprises, Inc., information regarding 44 million pieces of apparel per year, to be distributed among 1,500 retail stores, is extremely important. The management system is based on the bar code and EDI-related data inflow. It facilitates sorting, preparing, distributing, and controlling the merchandise inventory (Gould 1993).

Electronic Data Interchange

EDI is perhaps the most widely used and advanced process among businesses when there is an already established network system. EDI is a process which deals with direct computer-to-computer information communication between organizations. This communication takes place within the constraints of a standard format, and permits the user to perform certain business functions. For retailers, it can provide the following advantages:

1. EDI can enhance or facilitate just-in-time (JIT) delivery and a quick-response system.
2. EDI can help improve economies of scale.
3. EDI can help enhance sales-force productivity by singling out the best sales performances and other related practices.
4. EDI can make it more efficient for buyers in retailing to perform their duties and be more creative and productive.
5. EDI can reduce inventory costs and can change the composition of inventories.
6. EDI can and should be used in employee training so that the overall performance of the retail establishment will be increased.

In addition to the EDI type of exchange, retailers may work with peers in other cities who are not direct competitors. Such networking activity can provide an invaluable managerial information base. For instance, through such networking the hottest selling products may be identified. Retail establishments may find out what promotional activity is most effective. In addition, they may determine the best advertising schedules, work schedules, inventory replacement periods, prices, and so forth. Such networking activity can be accomplished by WANs that connect the retailer to LANs.

Development and Implementation

Development and implementation of RIMS takes two clearly separate paths simultaneously. First, there is information flow, and second, personnel connections. Information flow is the technical aspect of RIMS. The system is developed and operationalized on the basis of data gathering, analysis, processing, and retrieving. The personnel side of the system is related to the training of the people who are responsible for generating the necessary information for the retailer's needs (Gibson et al. 1973; McLeod 1987; Samli 1996). These two paths or components must be developed and balanced adequately so that RIMS can be converted from simply an idea to a full-fledged functioning system facilitating the management of the retail establishment.

Constructing RIMS

Since RIMS must be suitable for the needs of the retail establishment in question, there cannot be just one ideal RIMS format. However, a facsimile of a RIMS model is presented in Exhibit 16.3. The model is composed of four key components: (1) data gathering, (2) data processing and data bank development, (3) a management information base, and (4) feedback and connection to the network (Dalton 1976; Dearden and Anthony 1976).

As stated earlier, the model presented has internal and external information modules. There may also be certain random information which is a coproduct of both internal and external information. For instance, the grocery chain may find out that it is doing very well with nonfood items. Because it is doing better than industry averages, it may allocate more room for these product lines in its stores. The search for additional information needs to be emphasized also. Once the output of RIMS is utilized by the store management, there may be indications that additional information is needed. As a result, the system can be regeared for this additional information.

The middle part of the model presents data bank development and revision. Such a data bank, in addition to being up to date, must have the following features: (1) flexibility, (2) ease of implementation of the information generated, (3) retrievability, (4) efficiency in terms of not wasting data and generating pertinent information, (5) adequacy in terms of providing information that is deemed necessary by the decision makers, and, finally, (6) having the necessary format as specified by the decision makers (Samli 1996).

The output of the proposed data bank should facilitate all of the decisions made at different levels of the retail organization, as illustrated in Exhibit 16.2. Here there needs to be enough flexibility so that management can quickly receive additional information if so desired. Finally, feedback is used to redirect the whole system. Here, needs relating to additional information are expressed. One critical point must be reiterated: At the point of feedback, the store's RIMS is connected in some manner to either a limited-area network, a wide-area network, or even both.

INTERNATIONAL CORNER

This chapter is particularly important for multinational retail chains. First, international retailers find themselves competing with local traditional retailers in different parts of the world. Without appropriate market information, they cannot possibly win such a competition. International retailers lack a tradition of having been in these markets and having served there, but modern information systems can easily make up for this lack in tradition and experience. Thus, international retailers are quite dependent on WANs and more. It is critical to keep track of the performance of each unit in different parts of the world. This aspect of international retailing is also very dependent on proper RIMS that are carefully developed for this purpose.

As discussed earlier in the chapter (Exhibit 16.1), a comprehensive RIMS would have a series of international information inputs. Such information inputs enable the retailer to explore the advantages of international sourcing, initiate just-in-time systems, or even generate a quick response system. It is reasonable to assume that international modules that are included in RIMS can particularly help large retailers that have extensive outreach worldwide. To the extent that these retailers can acquire good quality merchandise at affordable prices, consumers are likely to benefit.

SUMMARY

This chapter deals with the revolution that is being experienced in retail information technology and it explores just how this revolution can benefit retail decision makers. In order to explore this very critical area, first some of the most important emerging information technologies are discussed. Many of these technologies are related to networks where participants can exchange information among themselves or use the network to solve problems.

The retail establishment must develop a RIMS to take advantage of this revolution. RIMS is an MIS designed for a retailer. Retail information management systems are composed of four parts: data gathering, data processing, a management information base, and feedback.

Exhibits

Exhibit 16.1
Internal and External Sources of Information for RIMS

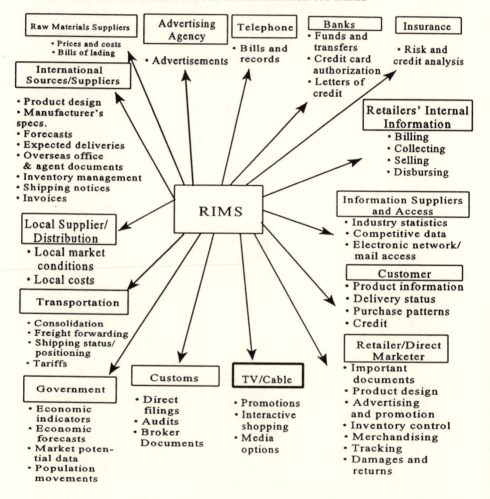

Source: Adapted and revised from "Emerging Technology and Retailing" (1993).

Exhibit 16.2
Retail Management Based on Information

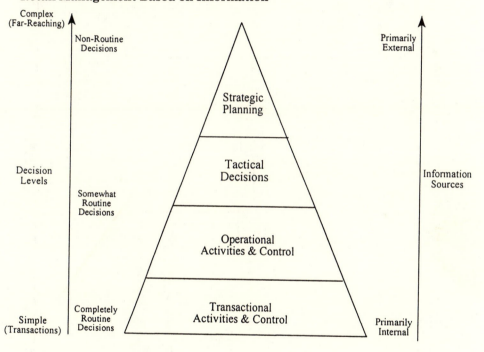

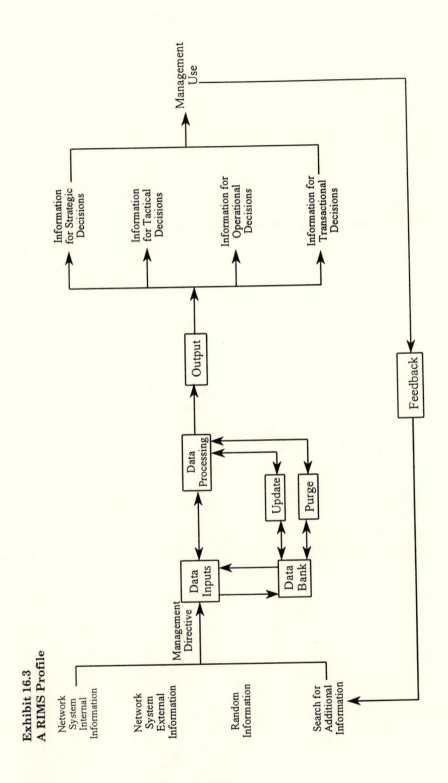

Exhibit 16.3
A RIMS Profile

Management Use

Information for Strategic Decisions

Information for Tactical Decisions

Information for Operational Decisions

Information for Transactional Decisions

Output

Data Processing

Update

Purge

Data Inputs

Data Bank

Management Directive

Feedback

Network System Internal Information

Network System External Information

Random Information

Search for Additional Information

References

Alderson, Wroe, and Stanley Shapiro, eds. 1963. *Marketing and the Computer.* Englewood Cliffs, N.J.: Prentice Hall.

Bates, Albert. 1977. "Ahead—The Retrenchment Era." *Journal of Retailing* 53 (Fall): 29–45.

Berman, Barry, and Joel R. Evans. 1995. *Retail Management.* Englewood Cliffs, N.J.: Prentice Hall.

Cox, Donald F., and Robert E. Good. 1967. "How to Build a Marketing Information System." *Harvard Business Review* 45 (May): 145–171.

"C-Stores Play Catch-Up." 1995. *Chain Store Age Executive* (January).

Dalton, Alan. 1976. "How Management Information Systems Work." *Supervisory Management* (January).

"Database Marketing Goes Mainstream, Says Survey." 1995. *Chain Store Age Executive* (January): 82–84.

Dearden, Johnny, and Robert Anthony. 1976. *Management Control Systems.* Homewood, Ill.: Richard D. Irwin.

Eldin, Hamed K., and May Croft. 1974. *Management Information Systems: Management Science Approach.* New York: Petrocelli.

"Emerging Technology and Retailing." 1993. *Chain Store Age Executive* (December): 58–64.

Fox, Bruce. 1993. "Scanning Streamlines Returns." *Chain Store Age Executive* (August): 49–50.

Gibson, Lawrence D., Charles S. Mayer, Christopher E. Nugent, and Thomas E. Vollman. 1973. "An Evolutionary Approach to Marketing Information Systems." *Journal of Marketing* 37 (April): 2–6.

Gillin, Paul. 1992. "Shoe Retailer Makes Strides with EDI." *Computerworld* 1 (June): 2.

Gould, Les. 1993. "Multiple Sort Systems Move 44 Million Items Out on Time." *Modern Materials Handling* (November): 48–50.

"Information Technology." 1995. *Business Week*, 26 June, 85–119.

K-Mart Retail News Update. 1994.

Lesser, Jack A., and James M. Stearns. 1986. "The Development of Retailing Information Systems Based on Shopping Behavior Theory." In *Advances in Marketing Science*, ed. Naresh Malhotra. Miami: Academy of Marketing Science.

Mason, J. Barry, and Morris L. Mayer. 1980. "Retail Merchandise Information System for the 1980s." *Journal of Retailing* (Spring): 56–76.

McLeod, Raymond, Jr. 1987. *Management Information Systems.* Chicago: Science Research Associates.

O'Brien, James J. 1970. *Management Information Systems.* New York: Van Nostrand.

Pessemier, Edgar A. 1980. "Store Image and Positioning." *Journal of Retailing* (Spring): 94–106.

Porter, M. E., and V. E. Miller. 1985. "How Information Gives You Competitive Advantage." *Harvard Business Review* (July–August): 149–160.

Rob, Peter, and Carlos Coronel. 1995. *Database Systems*. Danvers, Mass.: Boyd and Frazier.

"Saks Beats the Odds Succeeds in QR Despite Hurdles." 1993. *Chain Store Age Executive* (August): 54–61.

Samli, A. Coskun. 1980. "Retailing Information Management Systems: An Introduction to RIMS." In *Proceedings of ESOMAR Seminar on Information Systems in Action*. Amsterdam: ESOMAR.

———. 1993. *Counterturbulence Marketing*. Westport, Conn.: Quorum Books.

———. 1996. *Information Driven Marketing Decisions*. Westport, Conn.: Quorum Books.

Schafer, Edward A. 1972. "Management Control Over the Computer Activity." *Data Management* 10 (September): 45–55.

Schaffir, Kurt, and H. George Trentin. 1973. *Marketing Information Systems*. New York: AMACOM.

Schember, Jack. 1990. "Mrs. Fields' Secret Weapon." *Personnel Journal* (September): 56–58.

Silverman, Stephen M. 1995. "Retail Retold: Technology Takes the Old-World Concept of One-to-One Relationship Selling and Makes it New." *Inc* (Summer): 23–25.

Stuart, Paul. 1995. "For WSS, Program is the Answer." *Chain Store Age Executive* (August).

"Technology to Tranform Retail." 1993. *Chain Store Age Executive* (December): 58–60.

"WSRG Seeks Unbiased View from IBM Consulting Group." 1995. *Chain Store Age* (September): 14C–16C.

Zmud, R. W., and M. R. Lind. 1986. "The Use of Formal Mechanics for Linking the Information Systems Function with End-Users." In *Managers, Micros and Main Frames: Integrating Systems for End-Users*, ed. M. Jarke. New York: John Wiley and Sons.

Chapter 17

Strategic Control for Retailers

Strategic control can be defined as "the critical evaluation of plans, activities and results, thereby providing information for future action" (Schreyogg and Steinmann 1987, 91). A retail establishment as a merchandise control system must critically evaluate if it has what the customers want at the price and the time they want it, and if it is optimizing its sales by minimizing stock-outs and slow-moving merchandise. Above all, it must communicate with its markets properly. All of this activity relates to the retailers' future performance and the necessary improvement in that performance.

Since there is such a wide range of retail establishments and types of retailing firms, control systems vary significantly from one type of retailing to another. If you are the manager of a restaurant and see a frown on the face of one of your good customers, you may see $100 thousand written on that customer's face about to leave the restaurant. Twice a month that customer has a six-person business dinner. Thus, he is worth $100 thousand to you in the coming ten years (Peters 1987). Noticing the frown is part of a simple control mechanism. On the other end of the spectrum, a large consumer-goods company had to develop an integrated sales and marketing automation system to prioritize business functions to be utilized for performance evaluation and control (Goldenberg 1995). Getting a new customer is estimated to be five times more costly than keeping regular customers happy. Thus, keeping customers happy is good business. The retailer must be able to tell early on if the customers are happy (or better yet, delighted) and are coming back. Thus, there must be a control mechanism that will enable the retailer to evaluate performance and improve it if necessary.

This chapter has a two functions. First, it explores total control systems in retailing. Second, it examines some of the key areas of control, especially in the context of inventory control, accounting control, budget control, sales transactions control, and image control. Throughout the chapter, the emphasis is on the strategic aspect of control. As has been defined, the critical evaluation and information that the control function provides must be used for future action as quickly as possible.

THE CONTROL MECHANISM

As the retailer tries to bring actual results and goals (or desired results) closer together, it must quickly learn just how well it is doing and apply it to retail functioning. In other words, effective control leads to learning and proactive adjustment.

The Learning Organization

Regardless of their size and status, all retailers must have a control mechanism and learn from it. They must all be learning organizations. A basic definition of organizational learning means the development of new knowledge to alter behavior. Behavior change is the key to organizational improvement (Samli 1996). If the retailer cannot generate new information and learn from it, then it is not adequately involved in organizational learning (Aipi 1970). But learning in this case is not enough; the retailer must allow its behavior to be influenced by the newly acquired knowledge. Only in this way will its future performance be improved and its ability to cope with the increasing adversities of the market be enhanced (Slater and Narver 1994).

Exhibit 17.1 illustrates the control mechanism and how retail learning is applied to retail marketing in a proactive manner. It shows how actual results are brought closer together with goals through proactive behavior triggered by the control mechanism and learning (Lazer 1971).

Consider, for instance, an upscale grocery store in Florida. Just before the tennis season, it put together a special display of tennis balls. The display was located in a prominent place in the store and was very attractive. However, the sales were very slow. The store manager did not realize that, in that area where tennis is very popular, people bought their tennis balls at a much cheaper price than what the store offered. The learning process, along with the control mechanism, should have indicated that the price information was bad and that the balls must either sell much faster or be given away for some promotional activity (tennis for underprivileged kids, etc.).

Exhibit 17.1 illustrates that the planning process for desired results is based on the assessed market opportunities and company capabilities. Once the retail functions are planned and implemented, it is critical for the retailer to develop certain early indicators. For instance, realizing early on that a new department is not attracting attention, an inside-the-store coupon system is not stimulating business, or special markdowns are not moving merchandise allows quick corrective action to be taken.

Consider, for instance, the following early indicators (Samli 1993).

- The manager of X restaurant comes to work every morning (mid-morning) and finds a line of people waiting to go in. One morning, as he comes to work as usual, he finds nobody waiting to go into the restaurant.
- The manager of Y retail establishment typically sees customers come in, browse, and most often buy a number of items in the store. Lately the number of browsers has not changed, but the sales are down.
- The Z bank recently realized that many of its elderly customers (the majority of its customers) have been changing banks, leaving Z and going to competitors without giving a reason.

In all these cases, there are early indicators. If the causes of these were to be detected early, the control mechanism can be activated for corrective action. Of course, these early indicators and feedback leading to control provide a significant basis for learning. Learning what works and what does not work and why they work or do not work is critical for the performance and well-being of the retail establishment.

MARKETING AUDITS

A marketing audit is a systematic, critical, and impartial review and appraisal of the total marketing operations of the retail establishment. The review of these activities leads to reevaluating the desired results, the operational practices, and the organization employed to implement the policies to achieve the desired results (Kelly and Lazer 1961). Marketing audits, therefore, can be used both for diagnosing problems and prognosticating solutions. It is, therefore, a very critical managerial tool. It takes a snapshot of the organization where it stands and how it is performing at that point in time. Marketing audits can be external or internal.

The External Audit

There are many variables in the marketplace that can play a critical role in the retail establishment. It is critical for the retail manager to identify and prioritize these variables. It is not possible for a retail establishment to keep track of all of the possible external variables or indicators. However, clearly, it is critical for that retail establishment to examine its overall retail marketing environment.

A four-step procedure has been recommended: (1) List all the factors and variables that are particularly important for the retail establishment; (2) raise specific questions regarding this list; (3) establish ideal conditions for these questions; and (4) analyze the current status against the ideal in terms of time, money, and human resources (Wilson 1979). This four-step process provides the foundation of a periodic market audit for a retailer if diagnostic and prognostic planning, control, and corrective action are to be undertaken.

Exhibit 17.2 illustrates an effort to construct a market audit. As seen in the exhibit, such an effort covers at least four areas: (1) economy, (2) market, (3) customers, and (4) competition.

Economy

The key question areas regarding the economy are the following: Is the trading area growing? What are the demographic changes? How is the political climate? How are the economic conditions? In the column called "Direction of Developments," Exhibit 17.2 answers these questions. It would be almost impossible to establish ideal conditions for each exploration area. On the basis of the developments and the critical importance to the retail establishment, the "Critical Role" column is developed. The highest numbers indicate what must be explored immediately and perhaps must be incorporated into the marketing plans.

Market

In Exhibit 17.2, the market-related exploration areas deal with the changing size of the market, the key trends indicating growth or the lack thereof, the status of some of the key factors influencing the market, and, above all, the firm's share of the market. Of course, there may be many other areas that need to be questioned. Each retailing situation has its own facts. The retailer must understand those and explore them accordingly.

Customers

The retail establishment should always be on the lookout for the changes that are taking place in its target markets. A changing demographic profile of the area may mean new shopping patterns. The manager of a beach club located in an upscale beach community, for instance, might realize that the profile of the area population is changing. Many younger families with young children are moving in. They have less money and need to spend quality time with their kids. By reducing the membership fees slightly and by making the facilities more child friendly, the manager increases the membership and the business volume of the club.

Competition

The retailer must always be aware of its competition. If, for instance, supermarket X claims to be the place with the lowest prices, then it must be constantly comparing its prices with those of competitors. If the claim of being the lowest-price place is not factual, it can cause damage to the supermarket by creating a credibility gap.

Exhibit 17.2 is not an exhaustive list. There may be other and, indeed, even more important considerations that need to be included in the market audit.

The Internal Audit

In addition to the market audit, an internal audit exploring the firm's specific practices needs to be developed. Though the internal–external dichotomy is somewhat artificial in that they overlap and are critical together and simultaneously, the distinction here is important. While big retail chains, by definition, are forced to follow external market and economy-related changes, small retailers find themselves paying more attention to internal factors. This is primarily because a large retailer's well-being is closely related to its market share, whereas a small retailer's well-being depends primarily on its sales regardless of the economy. While the economy is going through a recession, the small retailer may be thriving. It does not take much for a small retailer to make a profit. But it takes significant economic factors in the marketplace for Sears or K-Mart to perform well.

Exhibit 17.3 illustrates some of the key areas that an internal audit would focus on. In the second column, the types of questions that would be raised are presented in dealing with these focus areas. Again, just as in Exhibit 17.2, this is not an exhaustive exhibit. Depending on the type of retailing and the issues that particular retailer is facing, there could be many other issues included in the "Focus Area" column. For some retailers, particularly those that may not have the experience, it has been quite beneficial to outsource internal audit activity (Schultz 1995). Whether it is done by insiders or outsiders, the fact remains that all the focus areas in Exhibit 17.3 must be explored. While internal audits are one of the best ways to learn the retail business from the inside, they can also sharpen or expand the store's core competencies, such as internationalization, improvement of service quality, and the like. All the focus areas of the internal audit have a financial and a nonfinancial aspect.

Financial Control

Financial control in retailing has always been with us in some form. Traditionally, merchandise groups have analyzed the profit contributions of various products. Early on it was impossible to keep track of the hundreds and thousands of different products in terms of their sales volume, inventory, turnover rates, and profit contributions. Instead, a number of homogeneous and logical merchandise groups have been used for control purposes. In recent years, however, the revolution in information systems (see Chapter 16) has made it possible for products to be analyzed individually so that their contribution to the profit picture can be assessed more realistically and accurately.

Financial criteria, either by themselves or in conjunction with almost all of the other retail functions, have very far-reaching implications. Among others, these include (1) forecasting of receipts and disbursements, (2) collection of cash and/or receivables, (3) control of disbursements, (4) control and analysis of cost information, (5) cash-flow controls, (6) inventory controls, (7) profit-margin adjustments, (8) price setting, and (9) profit contribution of products (Lusch 1982; Dickinson 1981). Though all nine areas are important, most are discussed in basic textbooks. Special references dealing with these concepts are cited at the end of this chapter. Items 6, 7 and 8 have been discussed in their respective chapters.

These nine financial considerations may change, not only from one type of retail activity to another, but also in time. In fact, new financial models are being developed to achieve financial audit, control, and corrective action.

Inventory Controls

Since a major aspect of their competitive advantage is in the inventory area, retailers are placing more and more emphasis on inventory management. However, retailers may be counting inventory for the wrong reasons. They clearly understand the impact of the inventory on their bottom line. Thus, they are appreciative of inventory-control activity in terms of its financial implications. However, only a few retailers have reported inventory-control activity for merchandising purposes such as updating stocks. In addition, none reported using inventory control for marketing purposes, such as making better decisions ("Inventory Management" 1995). It is maintained here that inventory controls are essential for better marketing strategies and practices.

Large multi-unit retailers, in particular, have many hindrances to maintaining inventory data integrity. There are at least five such hindrances that are reported by retailers:

1. *Selling Errors*—This may include misplacement of documents, citing or recording wrong prices, or not properly managing returns or replacements.

2. *Receiving Errors*—Different products that look alike may be grouped in a single category or single section, causing overstatement or understatement of merchandise in different departments.

3. *Merchandise Stocking Errors*—Somewhat similar to receiving errors, merchandise stocking could be wrong and, therefore, some merchandise may be lost in the process.

4. *Database Errors*—As long as data processing and computer systems are not up to date, all retailers face the problem of developing masterfile errors. Varying numbers of UPCs (universal product classifications) or SKUs create much opportunity for error.

5. *Physical Inventory Counting Errors*—Educating store associates to take physical inventory is widely talked about but seldom achieved. Lack of training easily increases the error factor.

More and more retailers are trying to eliminate these hindrances to maintaining data integrity regarding inventories. In this book, it has been posited more than once that inventory controls, just as with other tools that retailers have at their disposal, must be used for marketing decisions so that the competitive advantage of the retail establishment can be enhanced.

More specifically, finance-related inventory controls are emerging and becoming widely used. Three such concepts are briefly discussed here: (1) gross margin return on inventory (GMROI), (2) dollar contribution return on inventory (DCROI), and (3) gross margin return on merchandise investments (GMROMI).

Gross Margin Return on Inventory

Since various products have different turnover ratios and varying gross margins, the retail decision maker may choose to refine the store's turnover rates with gross margins (Dickinson 1981). GMROI facilitates this activity:

$$\text{GMROI} = \frac{Gross\ margin\ dollars}{total\ sales} \times \frac{total\ sales}{average\ dollar\ inventory\ (at\ cost)}$$

GMROI figures are very useful in determining and comparing profit contributions of different merchandise groups or departments.

Dollar Contribution Return on Inventory

If more refined analysis is desired, gross margin figures can be interpreted as a contribution to overhead figures. This means subtracting certain relevant costs from overhead. Thus, DCROI is calculated as follows:

$$\text{DCROI} = \frac{\textit{dollar contribution returns}}{\textit{average dollars in inventory (at cost)}}$$

Obviously, DCROI as opposed to GMROI indicates more specific and better-defined returns for a given inventory. If the returns attributable to product line A are three times as great as product line B, then the management may decide to provide more room for A in the total inventory, perhaps at the expense of B.

Gross Margin Return on Merchandise Investments

This technique is more refined than DCROI or GMROI. It is a relatively newer technique that allows the retail manager to further evaluate the profitability of various merchandise. It purports that the extent of supplier financing received by the retailer should be calculated separately:

$$\text{GMROMI} = \frac{\textit{gross profit}}{\textit{inventory and accounts receivable less accounts payable}}$$

GMROMI can be broken into two components:

$$\frac{\textit{gross profit}}{\textit{inventory and accounts receivable}} \times \frac{\textit{inventory and accounts receivable}}{\textit{inventory and accounts receivable less accounts payable}}$$

In this case, GMROMI states that the principal financial objective in managing the retail merchandise investments should be the gross-margin return on the retailer's own merchandise assets. This concept reinforces the need to focus on gross-margin management, inventory, and accounts receivable management as well as management of accounts payable. In this sense, GMROMI closely approximates the working capital investment of the retailer and, as such, it provides a very functional framework for managing finances of retail operations (Lusch and Serpkenci 1983).

Thus far, our discussion of financial controls indicates that the topic is far reaching, with many ramifications. Though they are very important, financial controls are based on financial effects. Therefore, typically, they are not the real cause of problems. With the exception of certain rare situations, the retailer's financial difficulties cannot be corrected with a financial solution. A sound retail marketing strategy is more likely to resolve rather than contribute to the firm's financial problems. Thus, it is necessary to explore nonfinancial variables.

Exhibit 17.4 presents three groups of nonfinancial performance indicators. The first group is composed of those factors that indicate customer satisfaction. The factors and their implications are clearly listed in the exhibit. The second group of criteria is related to customer dissatisfaction. Though only three such factors are cited in the exhibit, there can be many more. The third area is merchandise movements, which indicate what is happening to the store and to its merchandise mix. It is critical to realize that slow-moving merchandise must be moved and fast-moving merchandise must be moved even faster. Perhaps the most critical message of Exhibit 17.4 is that there can be many indicators, and particularly early indicators, that can be utilized by the retailer for control purposes. These indicators must activate some type of corrective action as quickly as possible.

The fourth area in Exhibit 17.4 stands by itself. It reflects the ongoing theme of this book: differential congruence. Many of the items listed in Exhibit 17.4 may directly or indirectly indicate the status of the store's differential congruence. Being able to match the store image and its customers' self-image means that the store is different and that the difference is its strength because it is well liked. Differential congruence, as has been maintained throughout this book, enhances customers' loyalty to the store and is beneficial to both parties. Operationalization of the congruence factor may vary from store to store.

There are a few other control criteria which fall into both the financial and nonfinancial categories. Inventory turns, for instance, is one such control factor. It can be used in absolute terms: "It is expected that the inventory turn rate for Department A is 4." It could also be used in relative terms: "Why is the inventory turn rate of Department B twice as high as for Department C?" Or it may be used for historical comparisons: "Why is it that the inventory turn rate of Department X is the lowest in ten years?"

Another control factor in this category that is used rather widely is sales per square foot, which can be used in the same way as inventory turn rate: in absolute terms, in relative terms, or for historical analysis. In originally developing a store's layout, the sales-per-square-foot criterion can be used in determining how much space should be allotted to various departments, product categories, and so on. Similarly, the store's overall performance as well as the performance of different departments or sections can be evaluated by such a control factor.

Finally, and most obviously, most retailers use gross-margin preference and gross-margin dollars for control purposes. Again, these can be used in absolute terms, in relative terms, or for historical perspective.

CONTINUOUS CONTROL FUNCTION

When a marketing system such as a retail store or a retail chain is being audited, the first consideration is its basic organization. This entails a general review of the retailing structure, which will point out how responsibilities are delegated and evaluated on the basis of how the job should be done. After all responsibilities are carefully assessed, each job is checked for its respective role in the store's overall efficiency and effectiveness (Naylor and Wood 1978).

The second consideration in this total system audit process is information. Chapter 16 deals with this particular topic. It is critical to reiterate that the system, for its own survival and success, must provide timely, accurate, necessary, and usable information for the decision-making process. The information must be generated by a formal system or organizational unit, and has to be tailored to the specific needs of each and every retailer (Samli 1996).

The third consideration in this general audit process is planning. This activity also needs to be formalized, with general activities of budgeting and scheduling indicating the details of what is to be performed when and for how much. This planning element must provide the basis for proper evaluation and adjustments of retail functions during the specified periods of time (Naylor and Wood 1978).

With these general audit considerations along with specific aspects of retail audits, it becomes clear that this whole process of control has to be continuous. This concept of continuous control is depicted in Exhibit 17.5. The key elements of Exhibit 17.5 are measurement criteria, revised standards, and revised objectives and goals. The exhibit demonstrates that the continuous control function is dependent on feedback which, in turn, depends on the key elements of the exhibit.

Measurement Criteria

Measurement criteria must be defined so that the performance of the retail establishment can be properly measured. Even if they are adequately defined at one point in time, measurement criteria are likely to change with the passage of time. Measurement must be timely, effective, efficient, and practical. It must be timely in that it must reflect the most recent trends and criteria. It must also be effective and must measure what it is supposed to measure. It must be able to do the job in the most direct and least costly manner. Finally, the measurement concept should be practical in the sense that it should not call for many special skills the firm does not have or be too difficult to apply.

It must be reiterated that the measurement issue is not exclusively quantitative, but could (and perhaps should) be qualitative and attitudinal. Thus, the general measurement of certain qualities of the store against a set of standard qualities becomes possible. This general measurement may have a number of subcomponents, each of which may be measured separately and against a general standard value. Each subcomponent may be set on a scale from bad to good, low to high, effective to ineffective, or satisfactory to unsatisfactory. If, for instance, there are ten subcomponents and only six are producing satisfactory results, the store needs to make a decision if this is satisfactory, or if those that are not producing satisfactory results are critical problems.

Each retail store must develop and judge its criteria according to its own objectives and goals.

Revised Standards

Standards basically include the most desirable quality and quantity, indicating the optimal situation for a retail establishment. Because of the dynamic nature of the retail environment, standards need to be continually revised and adjusted. There are two types of standards that particularly need to be adjusted in retailing: operating standards and appraisal standards. Operating standards basically deal with the lower level of an organization and are primarily quantitative (see Chapter 16). Appraisal standards, on the other hand, are more pertinent for top management and are relatively more qualitative (Lazer 1971).

Standards can be expressed in the form of inputs as well as outputs. Input data may be special point-of-sale displays, special promotions, and the like, whereas outputs may include number of orders placed, sales per square foot in each department, total sales volume, and many other subjective feedback indicators, many of which are shown in Exhibit 17.4.

The critical consideration is revising the standards. As the firm functions and survives, it is critical that the standards established to evaluate its performance be changed. As economic conditions and competition change, not only are the four retail mixes (merchandise mix, promotion mix, pricing mix, and human resources mix) likely to change, but new standards will be established to reflect these changes.

Revised Objectives and Goals

In Chapter 9, a distinction is made between strategic business units and profit centers. As economic conditions and competition change, it is quite natural to assume that SBUs and PCs may change their respective roles. A customer service (for example, delivery service) may move from being an SBU to being a PC. Many similar changes may be (indeed should be) expected. Similarly, there may be new SBUs or PCs emerging as some of the older ones disappear. In all of these cases, it is critical that the retailer recognize these changes and revise its objectives and goals accordingly.

INTERNATIONAL CORNER

There are some very large multi-unit international retailers. Among these are McDonald's (food chain); Benetton, the Body Shop, and Ikea (specialty retailers); and C&A Breninkmeyer, Pinault-Printemps, and Rallye (diversified retailers). As these and many other companies become more established in global markets, they will have more and more refined control mechanisms. However, the standards that may be established to evaluate performance may have to be varied from country to country or even from region to region. The example of Toys 'R Us must be considered here. In addition to leveraging its global buying power, the company is always seeking local vendors. It also works very closely with local vendors to create new products that can be marketed multinationally. At the same time, the company had to modify its store layout for some locations. While, for instance, in the United States the average store size is 40 thousand square feet, in Europe and Japan it is around 13 thousand square feet. In addition, differing labor and trading laws influence the company. In many European markets, Toys 'R Us cannot keep stores open on Sundays or are forced to close early on Saturdays. The company has overcome local hostility by including many locally sourced products in its merchandise mixes.

Many retailers are not quite as successful in international markets as they are in their respective domestic markets. Hence, their objectives and goals significantly vary from one market to another. Similarly, the retailer may have to use different criteria in each market to measure existing economic opportunities. Four such criteria are suggested for international market evaluation by retailers: (1) market size and growth, (2) political and economic stability, (3) economic openness and accessibility, and (4) the state of infrastructure, particularly relating to communications. All these criteria may have very different positions in various world markets and, hence, the retailer will have to adjust its management and control mechanisms accordingly ("Globalization of Retail Industry: A Strategic Imperative" 1996).

SUMMARY

The retailer must be able to bring about desired results. In a constantly changing and adverse environment this, above all, calls for corporate learning. The retailer not only must be planning the desired results (or objectives and goals) but must develop early indicators of performance effectiveness as feedback to activate the control mechanism. The retailer, in order to maintain a control function, utilizes internal and external audits which typically reveal early indicators that the retailer employs.

Because of the dynamic nature of the retailing environment, the retailer finds it necessary to revise the objectives and goals and the standards with which the whole evaluation process is performed. Because of the complexity of this total process, some retailers are inclined to outsource the total audit and control activity. It must be emphasized that this is an ongoing process and must take place continuously so that the retailer can survive and prosper.

Exhibits

Exhibit 17.1
The Control Mechanism and Retail Learning

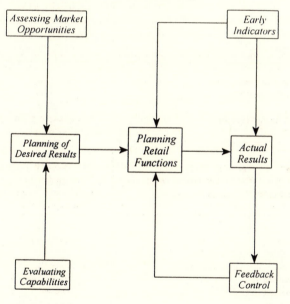

Exhibit 17.2
Market Audit for Retailers

Areas of Exploration	Direction of Developments	Critical Role*
Economy		
Trading area	Shrinking	10
Demographics	Changing	5
Political environment	Positive	1
Economic conditions	Favorable	1
Market		
Size of the market expressed in units	Growing	7
Size of the market expressed in $	Growing	7
Growth trends	Positive	8
Key factors influencing the market	Needs Exploration	9
Market share	Declining	10
Customers		
What is happening to our primary target market?	Growing	5
What is happening to our secondary target market?	Growing Faster	5
What are the changes in their shopping patterns?	Needs Careful Analysis	8
How is our differential congruence?	Changing Direction	9
Competition		
Major competitors	About the Same	4
What are the changes in their strengths		
What are the changes in their weaknesses	Need to be explored	5
Competitors' marketing	About the Same	5
Their market coverage and share	Growing	7
Key marketing practices	Changing	7

*10 = very critical; 1 = not very important.

Exhibit 17.3
Focus of Internal Audit

Focus Area	Questions for Redirection
• Improve company focus	Where should the resources be placed?
• Gain access to international opportunities	What types of international sourcing?
• Accelerate the benefits of reengineering	What are the key areas of reengineering? Do we need it?
• Reallocation of the firm's resources	How do we utilize our capital, physical and human resources better?
• Cost reduction	Where are critical points of cost cutting?
• Sales increase	What product lines, what brands, which departments, what specific practices lead to increase in sales?
• Improve the quality of service	How is our service quality? Do we have a system of listening to our customers?
• Merchandise mix adjustment	Are we up to date regarding product lines?
• Promotion mix adjustment	What change in the promotion mix are needed?
• Human resource management	How is our personnel? Do we need additional motivation, training, etc.?
• Pricing mix adjustment	Are our prices competitive? Do they project the image that has been planned?

Exhibit 17.4
Nonfinancial Indicators of Performance

	Implications
Customer Satisfaction Criteria	
Repeat Sales	Customers like the product and the store.
Customer Turnover	The store is attracting only new customers.
Customer Attitude	Customers indicate more liking for the store.
Frequency of Customer Visits	Customers like shopping here.
Sales to Target Market	Most sales are to the store's primary market.
Customer Dissatisfaction	
Customer Complaints	Clear dissatisfaction with some aspect of the store.
Merchandise Returns	Obvious dissatisfaction with the merchandise.
Stock-Outs	Not having the wanted merchandise.
Merchandise Movements	
Fast-Moving Merchandise	Satisfaction with the merchandise.
Slow-Moving Merchandise	Dissatisfaction with the merchandise.
Need for Special Displays	Need additional support to move the merchandise.
The Congruence Factor	
The Match between the Store Image and Customers' Self-Image	Customers are happy with the store and identify themselves with it.

Exhibit 17.5
A Continuous Control Mechanism for Retailers

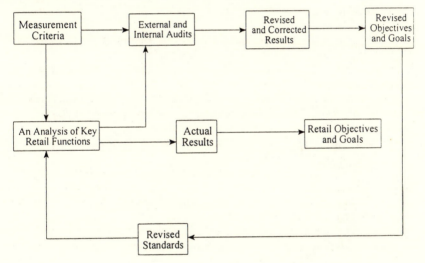

References

Aipi, Bo. 1970. *Planning and Control through Marketing Research*. London: Hutchinson.

Berman, Barry, and Joel Evans. 1995. *Retail Management*. Englewood Cliffs, N.J.: Prentice Hall.

Davis, Kenneth. 1981. *Marketing Management*. 4th ed. New York: John Wiley and Sons.

Dickinson, Roger A. 1981. *Retail Management*. Austin, Tex.: Austin Press.

"Globalization of Retail Industry: A Strategic Imperative." 1996. *Chain Store Age Executive* 69 (December): 6–22.

Goldenberg, Barton. 1995. "Defining User-Friendly Requirements for Your Sales and Marketing Automation System." *Sales & Marketing Management* (April): 16–20.

Hartley, Robert F. 1975. *Retailing: Challenge and Opportunity*. Boston: Houghton Mifflin.

"Inventory Management: The Focus Increases." 1995. *Chain Store Age Executive* (December): 1–6.

Kelly, Eugene, and William Lazer. 1961. "The Retailing Mix: Planning and Management." *Journal of Retailing* (Spring).

Kotler, Philip. 1994. *Marketing Management: Analysis, Planning and Control*. 5th ed. Englewood Cliffs, N.J.: Prentice Hall.

Kusche, Robert H., and Michael B. Russell. 1970. "The Marketing Audit: New Dynamics in Loan Assessment." *Journal of Commercial Bank Lending* (March): 53–58.

Lazer, William. 1971. *Marketing Management: A Systems Perspective*. New York: John Wiley and Sons.

Lusch, Robert F. 1982. *Management of Retail Enterprises*. Boston: Kent.

Lusch, Robert F., and Ray Serpkenci. 1983. "The New Model Offers Retailers a Realistic Estimate of Gross Margin Return from Merchandise Lines." *Marketing News* (February): 6.

Mahaian, Vigaz, Stuart I. Bretschneider, and John W. Bradford. 1980. "Feedback Approaches to Modeling Shifts in Market Response." *Journal of Marketing* (Winter): 69–74.

Monroe, Kent. 1979. *Pricing: Making Profitable Decisions*. New York: McGraw-Hill.

Naylor, John, and Alan Wood. 1978. *Practical Marketing Audits: A Guide to Increased Profitability*. London: Associated Business Programmes.

Peters, Tom. 1987. *Thriving on Chaos*. New York: Alfred A. Knopf.

Samli, A. Coskun. 1993. *Counterturbulence Marketing*. Westport, Conn.: Quorum Books.

———. 1996. *Information Driven Marketing Decisions*. Westport, Conn.: Quorum Books.

Schreyogg, G., and H. Steinmann. 1987. "Strategic Control: A New Perspective." *Academy of Management Review* (January): 91–103.

Schultz, David P. 1995. "Retailers Look Outside for Internal Audit Function." *Stores* (October): 67–68.

Slater, Stanley, and John C. Narver. 1994. *Market Oriented Isn't Enough: Build a Learning Organization.* Cambridge, Mass.: Marketing Science Institute.

Stores. 1980. (February): 42.

Wilson, K. M. S. 1979. *Management Controls and Marketing Planning.* London: Redwood Burn.

Wilson, Marianne. 1995. "The New World of Hills." *Chain Store Age Executive* (May): 202–203.

Index

ABOUT THE AUTHOR

A COSKUN SAMLI is Research Professor of Marketing and International Business at the University of North Florda, Jacksonville. Author or coauthor of more than 200 scholarly articles, eight books, and 30 monographs, he has been invited as a distinguished scholar to deliver papers to more than a dozen universities. He has lectured in countries around the world, is active in the Fulbright Commission, serves on the review boards of seven major journals, and is a Senior Fellow in the Academy of Marketing Science. Among his more recent books are three published by Quorum: *Counterturbulence Marketing: A Proactive Strategy for Volatile Economic Times* (1993), *International Consumer Behavior: Its Impact on Marketing Strategy* (1995), and *Information-Driven Marketing Decisions: Development of Strategic Information Systems* (1996).

ISBN 1-56720-186-5

90000>

EAN

9 781567 201864

HARDCOVER BAR CODE